AF905380

COMPUTER GRAPHICS

Edited by **Nobuhiko Mukai**

Computer Graphics
Edited by Nobuhiko Mukai

Published by InTech
Janeza Trdine 9, 51000 Rijeka, Croatia

Copyright © 2012 InTech
All chapters are distributed under the Creative Commons Attribution 3.0 license, which allows users to download, copy and build upon published articles even for commercial purposes, as long as the author and publisher are properly credited, which ensures maximum dissemination and a wider impact of our publications. After this work has been published by InTech, authors have the right to republish it, in whole or part, in any publication of which they are the author, and to make other personal use of the work. Any republication, referencing or personal use of the work must explicitly identify the original source.

As for readers, this license allows users to download, copy and build upon published chapters even for commercial purposes, as long as the author and publisher are properly credited, which ensures maximum dissemination and a wider impact of our publications.

Notice
Statements and opinions expressed in the chapters are these of the individual contributors and not necessarily those of the editors or publisher. No responsibility is accepted for the accuracy of information contained in the published chapters. The publisher assumes no responsibility for any damage or injury to persons or property arising out of the use of any materials, instructions, methods or ideas contained in the book.

Publishing Process Manager Dragana Manestar

Technical Editor Teodora Smiljanic

Cover Designer InTech Design Team

Additional hard copies can be obtained from orders@intechopen.com

Computer Graphics, Edited by Nobuhiko Mukai
p. cm.
ISBN 978-953-51-0455-1

We are IntechOpen, the first native scientific publisher of Open Access books

3,350+
Open access books available

108,000+
International authors and editors

114M+
Downloads

151
Countries delivered to

Our authors are among the
Top 1%
most cited scientists

12.2%
Contributors from top 500 universities

WEB OF SCIENCE™

Selection of our books indexed in the Book Citation Index in Web of Science™ Core Collection (BKCI)

Interested in publishing with us?
Contact book.department@intechopen.com

Numbers displayed above are based on latest data collected.
For more information visit www.intechopen.com

For EU product safety concerns:
IN TECH d.o.o., Prolaz Marije Krucifikse Kozulić 3, 51000 Rijeka, Croatia,
info@intechopen.com or visit our website at intechopen.com.

Meet the editor

Dr Nobuhiko Mukai received his B.E. and M.E. degrees in mechanical engineering from Osaka University in 1983 and 1985, respectively. He then joined Mitsubishi Electric Corp. and worked in the Information Technology R&D Center. In 1995, he entered Cornell University and received his M.E. degree in computer science in 1997. In 2000, he entered Osaka University and received his Ph.D degree in systems and human science in 2001. He then joined Musashi Institute of Technology as an associate professor in 2002 and has become a professor in 2007. He is currently with the department of computer science at Tokyo City University. His research interests include computer graphics, image processing, virtual reality and medical applications. He is a member of ACM, IPSJ, IEICE, VRSJ, ITE, IIEEJ, and SAS.

Contents

Preface

It is said that computer graphics has begun when Dr. Sutherland invented sketch pad system in 1963. Computer graphics has been developed with the help of computer power, and therefore the history of computer graphics is strongly connected to the history of computers. The first general-purpose electronic computer was ENIAC (Electronic Numerical Integrator and Computer), developed at the University of Pennsylvania in 1946. In past computer was expensive, large and slow; now it has become inexpensive, small and fast so many people are using computers all over the world. With the development of computers, computer graphics technology has also developed. During 1960s, the main topics of computer graphics were how to draw lines and surfaces, as well as how to remove the hidden lines and surfaces. In 1970s, modeling techniques of smoothed curve was one of the main themes, in addition to rendering surfaces with color gradation. After 1980s, standard libraries of computer graphics have been established at ISO (International Organization for Standardization). In addition, de facto standard has become open from several companies, and many useful tools of computer graphics have been developed.

As mentioned above, computer graphics has been developed with the development of computer, with modeling and rendering as the two main technologies. If one of them has not improved, we would not be able to create very beautiful and realistic images with computer graphics. In addition, a generation of real images is based on physical simulation. People can create real images by performing physical simulation with natural law. The most difficult task is how to generate the appropriate model that obeys the natural law of the target, and also how to render the object that is generated with the appropriate model.

This book covers the most advanced technologies for modeling and rendering of computer graphics. For modeling technology, there are some articles in various fields such as mathematical and surface based modeling. On the other hand, there are varieties of articles for rendering technologies with simulations such as fluid and lighting tone. In addition, this book includes some visualization techniques and applications for motion blur, virtual agents and historical textiles. I hope his book will provide useful insights for many researchers in computer graphics.

Nobuhiko Mukai
Computer Science, Knowledge Engineering, Tokyo City University,
Japan

1

Approach to Representation of Type-2 Fuzzy Sets Using Computational Methods of Computer Graphics

Long Thanh Ngo and Long The Pham
Department of Information Systems, Faculty of Information Technology, Le Quy Don, Technical University, Vietnam

1. Introduction

The type-2 fuzzy sets was introduced by L. Zadeh as an extension of ordinary fuzzy sets. So the concept of type-2 fuzzy sets is also extended from type-1 fuzzy sets. If A is a type-1 fuzzy set and membership grade of $x \in X$ in A is $\mu_A(x)$, which is a crisp number in [0, 1]. A type-2 fuzzy set in X is $\tilde{A}$, and the membership grade of $x \in X$ in $\tilde{A}$ is $\mu_{\tilde{A}}(x)$, which is a type-1 fuzzy set in [0, 1]. The elements of the domain of $\mu_{\tilde{A}}(x)$ are called *primary memberships* of x in $\tilde{A}$ and the memberships of the primary memberships in $\mu_{\tilde{A}}(x)$ are called *secondary memberships* of x in $\tilde{A}$.

Recently, there are many researches and applications related to type-2 fuzzy sets because of the advancing in uncertainty management. Karnik et al (2001A) proposed practical algorithms of operations on type-2 fuzzy sets as union, intersection, complement. Karnik et al (2001B) proposed the method of type-reduction of type-2 fuzzy sets based on centroid defuzzification. Mendel et al (2002) have developed new representation of type-2 fuzzy sets based on embedded type-2 fuzzy sets. This representation easily have designing of type-2 fuzzy logic system is easy to use and understand. Mendel (2004), Liu (2008) proposed some practical algorithms in implementing and storing data to speed-up the computing rate of type-2 fuzzy logic systems. Coupland et al (2007), Coupland et al (2008A), Coupland et al (2008B) proposed representation type-1 and interval type-2 fuzzy sets and fuzzy logic system by using computational geometry, the fast approach to geometric defuzzification of type-2 fuzzy sets, the approach is better in computing than analytic approaches. TIN is a method of representation of curved surface in 3D space for many applications in computer graphics and simulation. Many approaches Shewchuck (2002), Ruppert (1997), Chew (1989) are use to generate TIN from set of points based Delaunay algorithms.

The chapter deals with the new representation of type-2 fuzzy sets using TIN. The membership grades of type-2 fuzzy sets in 3D surfaces that are discretized into triangular faces with planar equations. Size of triangle is difference depending on slope of the surface. Authors proposed practical algorithms to implement operations on type-2 fuzzy sets by designing computational geometry algorithms on TIN. The result is shown and corroborated for robustness of the approach, rendering type-2 fuzzy sets in 3-D environment using OpenSceneGraph SDK.

The chapter is organized as follows: II presents TIN and geometric computation; III introduces type-2 fuzzy sets; IV presents approximate representation of type-2 fuzzy sets; V is operations of TIN and geometric operations of type-2 fuzzy sets; VI is conclusion and future works.

2. TIN and geometric computation

2.1 Delaunay triangulation

A *topographic surface* v is the image of a real bivariate function f defined over a domain D in the Euclidean plane, as

$$v = \{(x, u, f(x, u)) | (x, u) \in D\} \tag{1}$$

A polyhedral model is the image of a piecewise-linear function f that is described on a partition of D into polygonal regions $\{D_1, ..., D_k\}$ and the image of f over each region $D_i (i = 1, ..., k)$ is a linear patch. If all D_is $(i = 1, .., k)$ are triangles then the polyhedral model is called a *Triangulated Irregular Network* (TIN). Hence, v may be represented approximately by a TIN, as

$$v \cong \sum_{i=1}^{k} \{(x, u, f_i(x, u)) | (x, u) \in T_i\}, \bigcup_{i=1}^{k} T_i \equiv D \tag{2}$$

where f_is $(i = 1, ..., k)$ are planar equations.

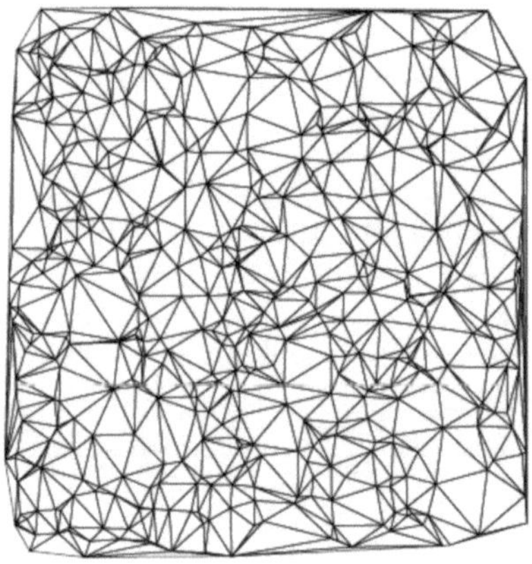

Fig. 1. A Delaunay Triangulation

The *Delaunay triangulation* of a set V of points in IR^2 is a subdivision of the convex hull of V into triangles that their vertices are at points of V, and such that triangles are as much equiangular as possible. More formally, a triangulation τ of V is a Delaunay triangulation if and only if, for any triangle t of τ, the circumcircle of t does not contain any point of V in its interior. This property is called the *empty circle property* of the Delaunay triangulation. Let u and v be two vertices of V. The edge uv is in D if and only if there exists an empty circle that passes through u and v. An edge satisfying this property is said to be *Delaunay*. Figure 1 Chew (1989) illustrates a Delaunay Triangulation.

An alternative characterization of the Delaunay triangulation is given based on the *max − min angle property*. Let τ be a triangulation of V. An edge e of τ is said to be *locally optimal* if and only if, given the quadrilateral Q formed by the two triangles of τ adjacent to e, either Q is not convex, or replacing e with the opposite diagonal of Q (*edge flip*) does not increase the minimum of the six internal angles of the resulting triangulation of Q. τ is a Delaunay triangulation if and only if every edge of τ is locally optimal. The repeated application of edge flips to non-optimal edges of an arbitrary triangulation finally leads to a Delaunay triangulation.

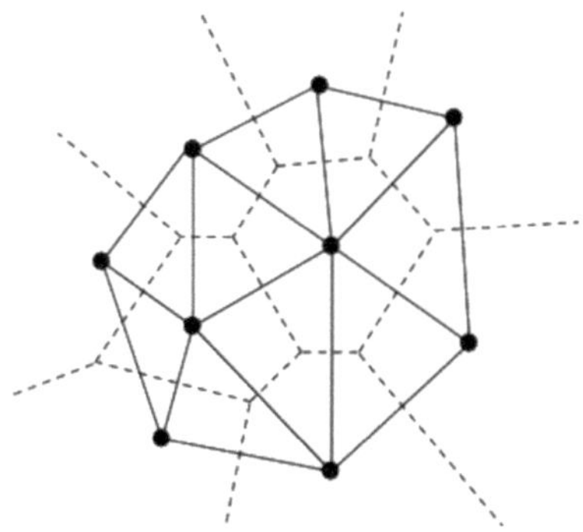

Fig. 2. The Delaunay triangulation (solid lines) and the Voronoi diagram (dash lines) from a point set.

The geometric dual of the Delaunay triangulations is the *Voronoi diagram*, which describes the proximity relationship among the point of the given set V. The *Voronoi* diagram of a set V of points is a subdivision of the plane into convex polygonal regions, where each region is associated with a point P_i of V. The region associated with P_i is called *Voronoi region* of P_i, and consists of the locus of points of the plane which lie closer to P_i than any other point in V. Two points P_i and P_j are said to be *Voronoi neighbours* when the corresponding Voronoi regions are adjacent. Figure 2 shows the Delaunay triangulation and the Voronoi diagram from a point set.

The usual input for two-dimensional mesh generation is not merely a set of vertices. Most theoretical treatments of meshing take as their input a planar straight line graph (PSLG). A PSLG is a set of vertices and segments that satisfies two constraints. First, for each segment contained in a PSLG, the PSLG must also contain the two vertices that serve as endpoints for that segment. Second, segments are permitted to intersect only at their endpoints. A set of segments that does not satisfy this condition can be converted into a set of segments that does. Run a segment intersection algorithm, then divide each segment into smaller segments at the points where it intersects other segments.

The *constrained Delaunay triangulation* (CDT) of a PSLG X is similar to the Delaunay triangulation, but every input segment appears as an edge of the triangulation. An edge or triangle is said to be *constrained Delaunay* if it satisfies the following two conditions. First, its vertices are *visible* to each other. Here, visibility is deemed to be obstructed if a segment of X lies between two vertices. Second, there exists a circle that passes through the vertices of the edge or triangle in question, and the circle contains no vertices of X that are visible from the interior of the edge or triangle.

The flip algorithm begins with an arbitrary triangulation, and searches for an edge that is not *locally Delaunay*. All edges on the boundary of the triangulation are considered to be locally Delaunay. For any edge e not on the boundary, the condition of being locally Delaunay is similar to the condition of being Delaunay, but only the two triangles that contain e are considered. For instance, Figure 4 demonstrates two different ways to triangulate a subset of

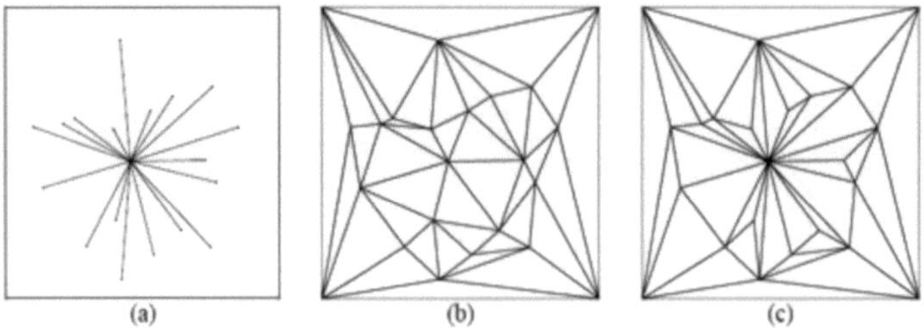

Fig. 3. (a) A planar straight line graph. (b) Delaunay triangulation of the vertices of the PSLG. (c)Constrained Delaunay triangulation of the PSLG.

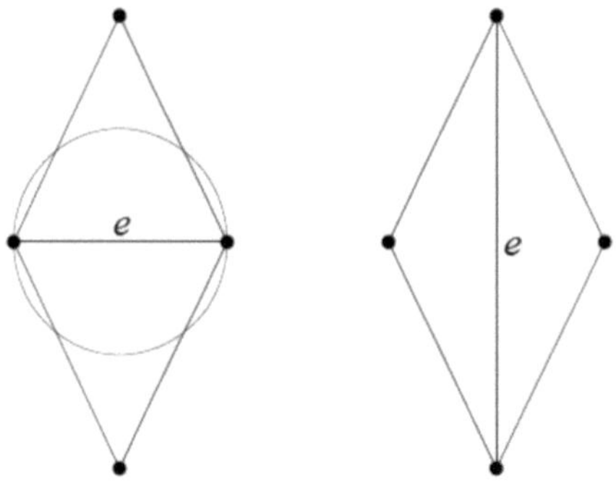

Fig. 4. Two triangulations of a vertex set. At left, *e* is locally Delaunay; at right, *e* is not.

four vertices. In the triangulation at left, the edge *e* is locally Delaunay, because the depicted containing circle of *e* does not contain either of the vertices opposite *e* in the two triangles that contain *e*. In the triangulation at right, *e* is not locally Delaunay, because the two vertices opposite *e* preclude the possibility that *e* has an empty containing circle. Observe that if the triangles at left are part of a larger triangulation, *e* might not be Delaunay, because vertices may lie in the containing circle, although they lie in neither triangle. However, such vertices have no bearing on whether or not *e* is locally Delaunay.

Whenever the flip algorithm identifies an edge that is not locally Delaunay, the edge is flipped. To flip an edge is to delete it, thereby combining the two containing triangles into a single containing quadrilateral, and then to insert the crossing edge of the quadrilateral. Hence, an edge flip could convert the triangulation at left in Figure 4 into the triangulation at right, or vice versa.

2.2 Half edge data structure and basic operations

A common way to represent a polygon mesh is a shared list of vertices and a list of faces storing pointers for its vertices. The half-edge data structure is a slightly more sophisticated boundary representations which allows all of the queries listed above to be performed in constant time. In addition, even though we are including adjacency information in the faces, vertices and edges, their size remains fixed as well as reasonably compact.

The half-edge data structure is called that because instead of storing the edges of the mesh, storing half-edges. As the name implies, a half-edge is a half of an edge and is constructed by splitting an edge down its length. Half-edges are directed and the two edges of a pair have opposite directions. Data structure of each vertex v in TIN contains a clockwise ordered list of half edges gone out from v. Each half edge $h = (eV, lF)$ contains end vertex (eV) and index of right face (lF). Suppose that a TIN has m faces and n vertices, it needs to have n lists of $3m$ half edges and memory is $n * (3 * m) * (2 * 4)$ bytes. Figure 5 shows data structure of vertex v with 6 half-edges indexed from 0 to 5, the ith half-edge contains the vertex v_i and the right face f_i of the edge.

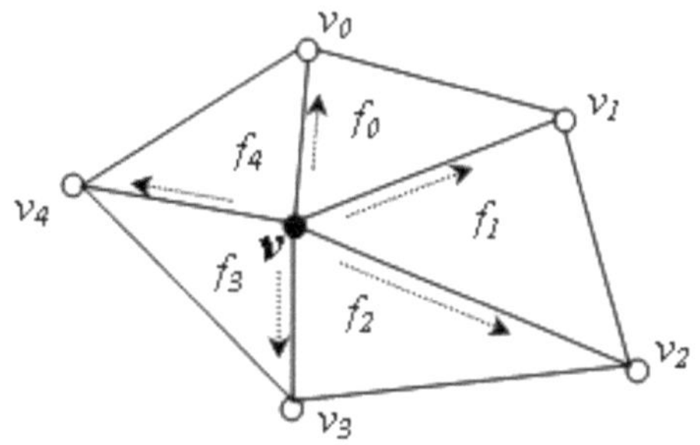

Fig. 5. List of half-edges of a vertex.

Some operations are built based on half-edges such as edge collapse operation, flip operation, insertion or deletion operation... The following is description of half-edge based algorithms.

Algorithm 2.1 (Insertion Operation). *Insert a new half edge h into the list of vertex v.*

Input: *The list of half edge of vertex v and new vertex eP.*

Output:*The new list of half edge of vertex v.*

1. *Identity i in the list of half edges of v so that the ray* (v, eP) *is between two rays* (v, v_i) *and* (v, v_{i+1}).
2. *Move* $k - i$ *half edges from position i to* $i + 1$ *in the list.*
3. *Insert the half edge h into position i.*

Figure 6 depicts an example of *edge collapse* operation after deleting the edge (v_0, v_1) from V. The first step of edge collapse is to identity indices i_0, i_1 of half edges h_0, h_1 in the lists of half edges of v_0, v_1, respectively. Then moving half edges (v_1, v_4), (v_1, v_5) of vertex v_1 into the list of v_0 at i_0, rejecting half edges $h_0, (v_3, v_1), (v_6, v_1)$, setting the endpoint of half edges $(v_4, v_1), (v_5, v_1)$ to be v_0. The following is the algorithm for edge collapse:

Algorithm 2.2 (Edge Collapse). *Remove the edge* (v_0, v_1) *and vertex* v_1 *from TIN.*

Input: *TIN T, edge* (v_0, v_1), *vertex* v_1.

Output: *TIN* T' *is the collapsed TIN.*

1. *Identity* i_0, i_1 *of half edges* h_0, h_1 *in lists of* v_0, v_1, *respectively.*
2. *Copy half edges of* v_1 *from position* $i + 2$ *to* $i - 2$ *(if exist) in the list to the list of half edges of* v_0 *at* i_0. *Then set endpoint of respective inverse half edges is* v_0.
3. *Delete half edges from position* $i - 1$ *to* $i + 1$ *of* v_1 *and their inverse half edges.*
4. *Delete vertex* v_1 *and its related data.*

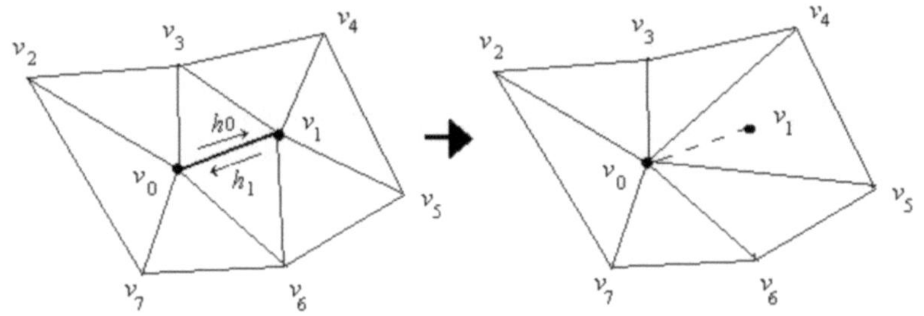

Fig. 6. Edge collapse.

Flip operation mentioned above is shown in Figure 7. The algorithm is applied to the edge which does not satisfy the empty circle property of Delaunay triangulation. The following is algorithm for flip operation:

Algorithm 2.3 (Flip Operation). *Flipping edge* (v_0, v_1) *become edge* (v_2, v_3).

Input: *TIN T, edge* (v_0, v_1).

Output: *TIN* T' *is the flipped TIN.*

1. *Replace edge* (v_0, v_1) *become edge* (v_2, v_3) *in TIN.*
2. *Move half edges* h_0, h_1 *of vertices* v_0, v_1 *to vertices* v_2, v_3 *and their endpoints are* v_3, v_2, *respectively.*
3. *Change right face of half edges* (v_0, v_3), (v_1, v_2).

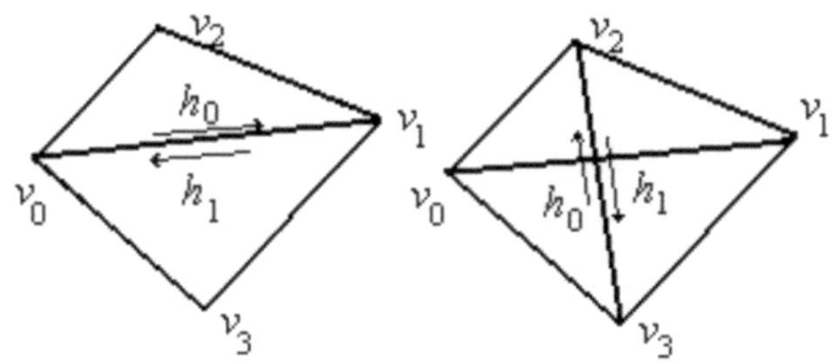

Fig. 7. Flip Operation.

3. Type-2 fuzzy sets

3.1 Fuzzy sets

Fuzzy set concept was proposed by L. Zadeh Zadeh (1975) in 1965. A fuzzy set A of a universe of discourse X is characterized by a *membership function* $\mu_A : U \rightarrow [0,1]$ which associates with each element y of X a real number in the interval [0, 1], with value of $\mu_A(x)$ at x representing the "grade of membership" of x in A.

A fuzzy set F in U may be represented as a set of ordered pairs of a generic element x and its grade of membership function: $F = \{(x, \mu_F(x)) | x \in U\}$. When U is continuous, F is re-written as $F = \int_U \mu_F(x)/x$, in which the integral sign denotes the collection of all points

$x \in U$ with associated membership function $\mu_F(x)$. When U is discrete, F is re-written as $F = \sum_U \mu_F(x)/x$, in which the summation sign denotes the collection of all points $x \in U$ with associated membership function $\mu_F(x)$.

In the same crisp theoretic set, basic operations of fuzzy set are union, intersection and complement. These operations are defined in term of their membership functions. Let fuzzy sets A and B be described by their membership functions $\mu_A(x)$ and $\mu_B(x)$. One definition of *fuzzy union* leads to the membership function

$$\mu_{A\cup B}(x) = \mu_A(x) \vee \mu_B(x) \tag{3}$$

where $\vee$ is a t-conorm, for example, maximum.

and one definition of *fuzzy intersection* leads to the membership function

$$\mu_{A\cap B}(x) = \mu_A(x) \star \mu_B(x) \tag{4}$$

where $\star$ is a t-norm, for example minimum or product.

The membership function for *fuzzy complement* is

$$\mu_{\neg B}(x) = 1.0 - \mu_B(x) \tag{5}$$

Fuzzy Relations represent a *degree* of presence or absence of association, interaction, or interconnectedness between the element of two or more fuzzy sets. Let U and V be two universes of discourse. A fuzzy relation, $R(U,V)$ is a fuzzy set in the product space $U \times V$, i.e, it is a fuzzy subset of $U \times V$ and is characterized by membership function $\mu_R(x,y)$ where $x \in U$ and $y \in V$, i.e., $R(U,V) = \{((x,y), \mu_R(x,y))|(x,y) \in U \times V\}$.

Let R and S be two fuzzy relations in the same product space $U \times V$. The intersection and union of R and S, which are *compositions* of the two relations, are then defined as

$$\mu_{R\cap S}(x,y) = \mu_R(x,y) \star \mu_S(x,y) \tag{6}$$

$$\mu_{R\cup S}(x,y) = \mu_R(x,y) \bullet \mu_S(x,y) \tag{7}$$

where $\star$ is a any t-norm and $\bullet$ is a any t-conorm.

Sup-star composition of R and S:

$$\mu_{R\circ S}(x,z) = \sup_{y \in V}[\mu_R(x,y) \star \mu_S(y,z)] \tag{8}$$

3.2 Type-2 fuzzy sets

A type-2 fuzzy set in X is denoted $\tilde{A}$, and its membership grade of $x \in X$ is $\mu_{\tilde{A}}(x,u), u \in J_x \subseteq [0,1]$, which is a type-1 fuzzy set in [0, 1]. The elements of domain of $\mu_{\tilde{A}}(x,u)$ are called primary memberships of x in $\tilde{A}$ and memberships of primary memberships in $\mu_{\tilde{A}}(x,u)$ are called secondary memberships of x in $\tilde{A}$.

Definition 3.1. *A type $-$ 2 fuzzy set, denoted $\tilde{A}$, is characterized by a type-2 membership function $\mu_{\tilde{A}}(x,u)$ where $x \in X$ and $u \in J_x \subseteq [0,1]$, i.e.,*

$$\tilde{A} = \{((x,u), \mu_{\tilde{A}}(x,u))|\forall x \in X, \forall u \in J_x \subseteq [0,1]\} \tag{9}$$

or

$$\tilde{A} = \int_{x \in X} \int_{u \in J_x} \mu_{\tilde{A}}(x,u))/(x,u), J_x \subseteq [0,1] \tag{10}$$

in which $0 \leq \mu_{\tilde{A}}(x,u) \leq 1$.

At each value of x, say $x = x'$, the 2D plane whose axes are u and $\mu_{\tilde{A}}(x',u)$ is called a *vertical slice* of $\mu_{\tilde{A}}(x,u)$. A *secondary membership function* is a vertical slice of $\mu_{\tilde{A}}(x,u)$. It is $\mu_{\tilde{A}}(x = x',u)$ for $x \in X$ and $\forall u \in J_{x'} \subseteq [0,1]$, i.e.

$$\mu_{\tilde{A}}(x = x',u) \equiv \mu_{\tilde{A}}(x') = \int_{u \in J_{x'}} f_{x'}(u)/u, J_{x'} \subseteq [0,1] \tag{11}$$

in which $0 \leq f_{x'}(u) \leq 1$.

In manner of embedded fuzzy sets, a type-2 fuzzy sets Mendel et al (2002) is union of its type-2 embedded sets, i.e

$$\tilde{A} = \sum_{j=1}^{n} \tilde{A}_e^j \tag{12}$$

where $n \equiv \prod_{i=1}^{N} M_i$ and $\tilde{A}_e^j$ denoted the jth type-2 embedded set of $\tilde{A}$, i.e.,

$$\tilde{A}_e^j \equiv \{\left(u_i^j, f_{x_i}(u_i^j)\right), i = 1,2,...,N\} \tag{13}$$

where $u_i^j \in \{u_{ik}, k = 1,...,M_i\}$.

Let $\tilde{A}, \tilde{B}$ be type-2 fuzzy sets whose secondary membership grades are $f_x(u), g_x(w)$, respectively. Theoretic operations of type-2 fuzzy sets such as union, intersection and complement are described Karnik et al (2001A) as follows:

$$\mu_{\tilde{A} \cup \tilde{B}}(x) - \mu_{\tilde{A}}(x) \sqcup \mu_{\tilde{B}}(x) - \int_u \int_v (f_x(u) \star g_x(w))/(u \vee w) \tag{14}$$

$$\mu_{\tilde{A} \cap \tilde{B}}(x) = \mu_{\tilde{A}}(x) \sqcap \mu_{\tilde{B}}(x) = \int_u \int_v (f_x(u) \star g_x(w))/(u \star w) \tag{15}$$

$$\mu_{\tilde{A}}(x) = \mu_{\neg \tilde{A}}(x) = \int_u (f_x(u))/(1-u) \tag{16}$$

where $\vee, \star$ are t-cornorm, t-norm, respectively. Type-2 fuzzy sets are called an interval type-2 fuzzy sets if the secondary membership function $f_{x'}(u) = 1 \ \forall u \in J_x$ i.e. a type-2 fuzzy set are defined as follows:

Definition 3.2. *An interval type-2 fuzzy set $\tilde{A}$ is characterized by an interval type-2 membership function $\mu_{\tilde{A}}(x,u) = 1$ where $x \in X$ and $u \in J_x \subseteq [0,1]$, i.e.,*

$$\tilde{A} = \{((x,u),1) | \forall x \in X, \forall u \in J_x \subseteq [0,1]\} \tag{17}$$

Uncertainty of $\tilde{A}$, denoted FOU, is union of primary functions i.e. $FOU(\tilde{A}) = \bigcup_{x \in X} J_x$. Upper/lower bounds of membership function (UMF/LMF), denoted $\overline{\mu}_{\tilde{A}}(x)$ and $\underline{\mu}_{\tilde{A}}(x)$, of $\tilde{A}$ are two type-1 membership function and bounds of FOU.

4. Approximate representation of type-2 fuzzy sets

Extending the concept of interval type-2 sets of upper MF and lower MF, we define a membership grade of type-2 fuzzy sets by dividing them into subsets: upper (lower) surface and normal surface as follows:

Definition 4.1 (Upper surface). *$\tilde{A}_{US}$ is called a upper surface of type-2 fuzzy set $\tilde{A}$ and defined as follows:*

$$\tilde{A}_{US} = \int_{x \in X} \Big[\int_{u \in J_x^+} f_x(u)/u \Big] / x \tag{18}$$

in which $J_x^+ \subseteq [u_x^+, 1]$ and $u_x^+ = sup\{u | \mu_{\tilde{A}}(x,u) = 1\}$.

Definition 4.2 (Lower surface). *$\tilde{A}_{LS}$ is called lower surface of type-2 fuzzy set $\tilde{A}$ and defined as follows:*

$$\tilde{A}_{LS} = \int_{x \in X} \Big[\int_{u \in J_x^-} f_x(u)/u \Big] / x \tag{19}$$

in which $J_x^- \subseteq [0, u_x^-]$ and $u_x^- = inf\{u | \mu_{\tilde{A}}(x,u) = 1\}$.

Definition 4.3 (Normal surface). *$\tilde{A}_{NS}$ is called a normal surface of type-2 fuzzy set $\tilde{A}$ and defined as follows:*

$$\tilde{A}_{NS} = \int_{x \in X} \Big[\int_{u \in J_x^*} f_x(u)/u \Big] / x \tag{20}$$

in which $J_x^* = [u_x^-, u_x^+]$.

For this reason, a type-2 fuzzy set $\tilde{A}$ is union of above defined sub-sets, i.e. $\tilde{A} = \tilde{A}_{US} \cup \tilde{A}_{NS} \cup \tilde{A}_{LS}$. Figure 8 is an example of type-2 fuzzy set that is union of subsets: upper surface, normal surface and lower surface.

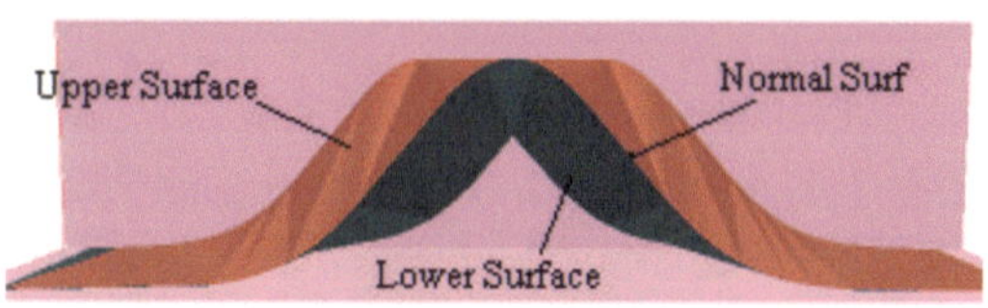

Fig. 8. Example of surfaces of type-2 fuzzy sets

A proximate representation of type-2 fuzzy sets is proposed by using a TIN that be able to approximately represent the 3-D membership function, is expressed as the following theorem.

Theorem 4.1 (Approximation Theorem). *Let $\tilde{A}$ be type-2 fuzzy set with membership grade $\mu_{\tilde{A}}(x,u)$ in continuous domain D. There exists a type-2 fuzzy set with membership grade is a TIN $T_{\tilde{A}}$, denoted $\tilde{A}_T$, so that $\tilde{A}_T$ is ϵ-approximation set of $\tilde{A}$, i.e,*

$$\|\mu_{\tilde{A}}(x,u) - \mu_{\tilde{A}_T}(x,u)\| < \epsilon, \ \forall (x,u) \in D. \tag{21}$$

Proof. If $\tilde{A}$ has membership grade consisting a set of patches of continuous linear surfaces (example of its membership grades are made by only using triangular and trapezoid membership grades), then TIN $\tilde{A_T}$ is created as follows:

1. Set V is the set of vertices of membership grades of $\tilde{A}$.
2. Set E is the set of edges of membership grades of $\tilde{A}$.
3. Call X = (V, E) is a planar straight line graph (PSLG). Make a TIN A_T is the constrained Delaunay triangulation from X. $\tilde{A_T}$ is a type-2 fuzzy set with membership function A_T.

Observe that A_T represents faithfully the membership grade of $\tilde{A}$.

If $\tilde{A}$ has membership grade consisting only one continuous non-linear surfaces. Let A^T is a TIN that represents $\tilde{A}$ in D. Suppose that $\exists(x_k, u_k) \in D$ so that $d_k = \|f_A(x_k, u_k) - f_{A_T}(x_k, u_k)\| \geq \epsilon$.

A^T is modified by inserting new vertex (x_k, u_k) as the following steps:

1. Find the triangle T_j of A^T, in which $(x_k, u_k) \in T_j$.
2. Partition the T_j into sub-triangles depending on the position of (x_k, u_k) on T_j.
   + If (x_k, u_k) lies on edge e_k of T_j, e_k is the adjacent edge of T_j and T_k. Partitioning T_j, T_k into four sub-triangles as Figure 9a.
   + If (x_k, u_k) is in T_j. Partitioning T_j into three sub-triangles as Figure 9b.
3. Verify new triangles that meet the constrained Delaunay triangulation. This operation may re-arrange triangles by using *flip* operation for two adjacent triangles.

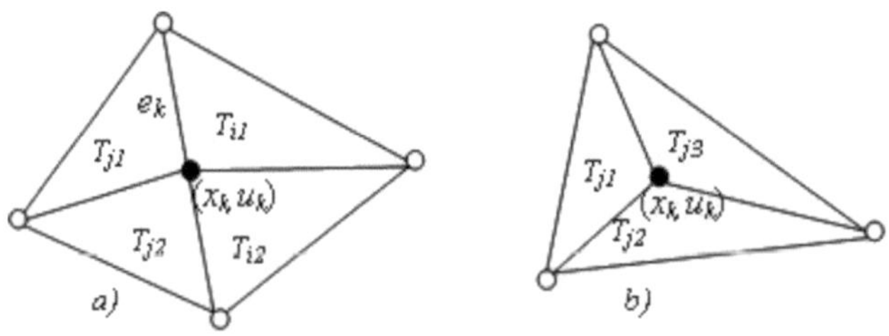

Fig. 9. Partitioning the t_j triangle.

The algorithm results in that T_j is divided into smaller sub-triangles. So we could find triangle T^* of TIN A^*_T, is modified TIN of A_T after N_k steps, so that T^* is small enough and contains (x_k, u_k). The continuity of the membership grade of $\tilde{A}$ shows that

$$d^*_k = \|f_A(x_k, u_k) - f_{A^*_T}(x_k, u_k)\| < \epsilon \tag{22}$$

We prove the theorem in the case that membership grade of $\tilde{A}$ is set of patches of continuous linear and non-linear surfaces. Suppose that its membership grade involves N patches of discrete continuous linear surfaces and M patches of discrete continuous linear surfaces, $S_1, S_2, ..., S_M$. N patches of continuous linear surfaces, that are represented by a TN S^*_T, is proven above section. According to above proof, each continuous non-linear surface A is represented approximately by a TIN A_T. So M continuous non-linear patches, $S_1, S_2, ..., S_M$ are represented by M TINs $S_{T1}, S_{T2}, ..., S_{TM}$. Because of the discreteness of M patches, M TINs representing patches are also discrete. For this reason, we could combine M TINs $S_{T1}, S_{T2}, ..., S_{TM}$ and S^*_T into only one TIN S_T. □

Definition 4.4. *A base-line of a TIN representing a type-2 fuzzy set is a polyline* $v_i(i = 1, .., N)$ *satisfying* $v_i.u = 0$ *and* $v_i v_{i+1}$ *is a edge of triangle of TIN.*

Figure 10 is the TIN that represent approximately of Gaussian type-2 fuzzy sets with $\epsilon = 0.1$. The primary MF is a Gaussian with fixed deviation and mean $m_k \in [m_1, m_2]$ and the secondary MF is a triangular MF. The dask-line is a base-line of TIN.

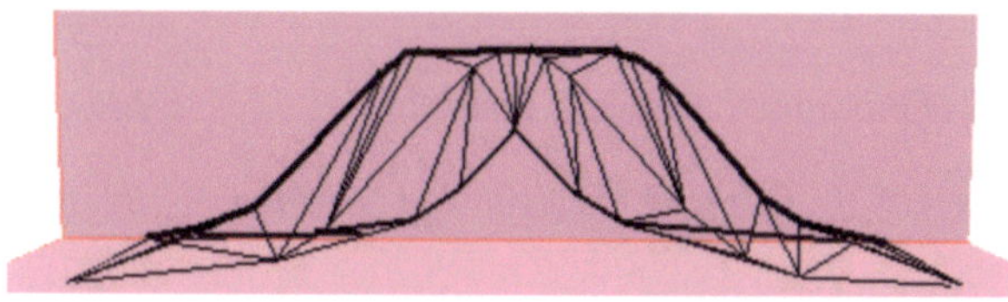

Fig. 10. Example of representation of a type-2 Gaussian fuzzy sets

5. Applications

5.1 Algorithms for operations on TIN

Data of TIN includes vertices, indices of faces and relations of them. Data of vertices is a list of 3D vectors with x, y and z components. Indices of faces are three indices of vertices of triangle. Relations between vertices and faces is used to speed up algorithms on TIN such as searching or computing algorithms.

The section introduces some algorithms operating on TIN such as: intersection of two TINs, minimum or maximum of two TINs. Algorithm on intersection is to create a poly-line that is intersection and break-line of TINs. Algorithm on maximum/minimum is to generate new TIN T_0 from two TINs T_1, T_2 satisfying $\forall(x,u)|\mu^{T_0}(x,u) = min(\mu^{T_1}(x,u), \mu^{T_2}(x,u))$ or $\mu^{T_0}(x,u) = max(\mu^{T_1}(x,u), \mu^{T_2}(x,u))$. The following is the detailed descriptions of algorithms.

Algorithm 5.1 (Intersection Algorithm). *Input:* T_1, T_2 *are two TINs representing two type-2 fuzzy sets.*

Outputs: Modified T_1, T_2 *are with some new vertices and edges on intersection poly-lines.*

1. *Computing* L_1, L_2 *are base-lines of* T_1, T_2*, respectively.*
2. *Find* $v_k^*(k = 1, .., M)$ *are the intersection points of* L_1, L_2.
3. *If* $M = 0$ *or set of intersection points is empty then return.*
4. *For each* $v_k^*(k = 1, ..., M)$
   $v^* \leftarrow v_k^*$. *Init queue* Q_k.
   While not find v^*
   (a) $v \leftarrow v^*$. *Insert* v *into queue* Q_k.
   (b) *Insert* v *into each of* T_1, T_2*, become* v_{T_1}, v_{T_2}.
   (c) *Find adjacent triangle* t_1^*, t_2^* *of* $v_{T_1} and v_{T_2}$*, respectively, so that* t_1^*, t_2^* *are intersected by a segment in* t_1^* *and* t_2^*.

(d) If existing new v^* point so that vv^* is a intersecting segment of t_1^* and t_2^* then

$v \leftarrow v^*$

Come back step a).

Else

Come back step 2).

Algorithm 5.2 (*maximum/minimum Algorithm*). *Input: T_1, T_2 are two TINs that represent two type-2 fuzzy sets.*

Output: T_0 is result TIN of minimum/maximum operation.

1. *Computing intersection of T_1, T_2 (using the algorithm of computing intersection).*
2. *Init queue Q.*
3. *for each triangle t of T_1 or T_2.*
   (a) *With maximum algorithm:*
   if t is triangle of $T_1(T_2)$ and be upper than $T_2(T_1)$ then push t into Q.
   (b) *With minimum algorithm:*
   if t is triangle of $T_1(T_2)$ and be lower than $T_2(T_1)$ then push t into Q.
   (c) *Generating TIN from triangles in Q.*

Fig. 11. Example of two fuzzy sets for operations

5.2 Join operation

Theoretic union operation is described the following using Zadeh's Extension Principle.

$$\mu_{\tilde{A}\cup\tilde{B}}(x) = \mu_{\tilde{A}}(x) \sqcup \mu_{\tilde{B}}(x) = \int_u \int_v (f_x(u) \star g_x(w))/(u \vee w) \tag{23}$$

where $\vee$ represents the max t-conorm and $\star$ represents a t-norm. If $\mu_{\tilde{A}}(x)$ and $\mu_{\tilde{B}}(x)$ have discrete domains, (23) is rewritten as follows:

$$\mu_{\tilde{A}\cup\tilde{B}}(x) = \mu_{\tilde{A}}(x) \sqcup \mu_{\tilde{B}}(x) = \sum_u \sum_v (f_x(u) \star g_x(w))/(u \vee w) \tag{24}$$

In (23) and (24), if more than one calculation of u and w gives the same point $u \vee w$, then in the union the one with the largest membership grade is kept. Suppose, for example, $u_1 \vee w_1 = \theta^*$ and $u_2 \vee w_2 = \theta^*$. Then within the computation of (23) and (24) we would have

$$f_x(u_1) \star g_x(w_1)/\theta^* + f_x(u_2) \star g_x(w_2)/\theta^* \tag{25}$$

where + denotes union. Combining these two terms for the common θ^* is a type-1 computation in which t-conorm can be used, e.g. the maximum.

Theoretic join operation is described as follows. For every pair of points $\{u, w\}$, such that $u \in F \subseteq [0,1]$ of $\tilde{A}$ and $w \in G \subseteq [0,1]$ of $\tilde{B}$, we find the maximum of v and w and the minimum of their memberships, so that $v \vee w$ is an element of $F \sqcup G$ and $f_x(v) \wedge g_x(w)$ is the corresponding membership grade. If more than one $\{u, w\}$ pair gives the same maximum (i.e., the same element in $F \sqcup G$), maximum of all the corresponding membership grades is used as the membership of this element.

If $\theta \in F \sqcup G$, the possible $\{u, w\}$ pairs that can give θ as the result of the maximum operation are $\{u, \theta\}$ where $u \in (-\infty, \theta]$ and $\{\theta, w\}$ where $w \in (-\infty, \theta]$. The process of finding the membership of θ in $\tilde{A} \sqcup \tilde{B}$ can be divided into three steps: (1) find the minimum between the memberships of all the pairs $\{u, \theta\}$ such that $u \in (-\infty, \theta]$ and then find their supremum; (2) do the same with all the pairs $\{\theta, w\}$ such that $w \in (-\infty, \theta]$; and, (3) find the maximum of the two supremum, i.e.,

$$h_{F \sqcup G}(\theta) = \phi_1(\theta) \vee \phi_2(\theta) \tag{26}$$

where

$$\phi_1(\theta) = \sup_{u \in (-\infty, \theta]} \{f_x(u) \wedge g_x(\theta)\} = g_x(\theta) \wedge \sup_{u \in (-\infty, \theta]} \{f_x(u)\} \tag{27}$$

and

$$\phi_2(\theta) = \sup_{w \in (-\infty, \theta]} \{f_x(\theta) \wedge g_x(w)\} = f_x(\theta) \wedge \sup_{w \in (-\infty, \theta]} \{g_x(w)\} \tag{28}$$

Based-on theoretic join and meet operation, we proposed TIN-based geometric algorithm for join operation. This algorithm uses two above mentioned algorithms involving intersection and min/max.

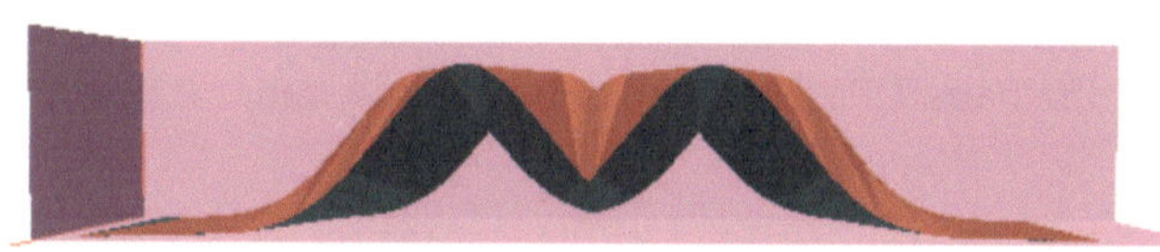

Fig. 12. Join operation

Algorithm 5.3 (*Join Operation*). *Input: $\tilde{A}$, $\tilde{B}$ are two type-2 fuzzy sets with TINs $T_{\tilde{A}}$, $T_{\tilde{B}}$.*

Output: $\tilde{C}$ is result of join operation.

1. *Find the upper surface by using the max-algorithm:*
   $T_{\tilde{C}_{US}} = max(T_{\tilde{A}_{US}}, T_{\tilde{B}_{US}})$
2. *Find the lower surface by using the max-algorithm:*
   $T_{\tilde{C}_{LS}} = max(T_{\tilde{A}_{LS}}, T_{\tilde{B}_{LS}})$
3. *Generate normal surface from $T_{\tilde{C}_{US}}$ and $T_{\tilde{C}_{US}}$ using Delaunay Triangulation.*

Figure 11 is two type-2 fuzzy sets that its primary MF is Gaussian MF and its secondary MF is triangular MF. Figure 12 is the result T2FS that are rendered in 3D environment.

Fig. 13. Meet operation

5.3 Meet operation

Recall theoretic meet operation is described as follows:

$$\mu_{\tilde{A}\cap\tilde{B}}(x) = \mu_{\tilde{A}}(x) \sqcap \mu_{\tilde{B}}(x) = \int_u \int_v (f_x(u) \star g_x(w))/(u \star w) \quad (29)$$

where $\star$ represents a t-norm. If $\mu_{\tilde{A}}(x)$ and $\mu_{\tilde{B}}(x)$ have discrete domains, (29) is rewritten as follows:

$$\mu_{\tilde{A}\cap\tilde{B}}(x) = \mu_{\tilde{A}}(x) \sqcap \mu_{\tilde{B}}(x) = \sum_u \sum_v (f_x(u) \star g_x(w))/(u \wedge w) \quad (30)$$

In a similar way, the point $u \star w$ with the largest membership grade is kept if more than one calculation of u and w gives the same one.

For every pair of points $\{u, w\}$, such that $u \in F \subseteq [0,1]$ of $\tilde{A}$ and $w \in G \subseteq [0,1]$ of $\tilde{B}$, we find the minimum or product of v and w and the minimum of their memberships, so that $v \star w$ is an element of $F \sqcap G$ and $f_x(v) \wedge g_x(w)$ is the corresponding membership grade.

If $\theta \in F \sqcap G$, the possible $\{u, w\}$ pairs that can give θ as the result of the maximum operation are $\{\theta, u\}$ where $u \in [\theta, \infty)$ and $\{w, \theta\}$ where $w \in [\theta, \infty)$. The process of finding the membership of θ in $\tilde{A} \sqcap \tilde{B}$ can be broken into three steps: (1) find the minimum between the memberships of all the pairs $\{u, \theta\}$ such that $u \in [\theta, \infty)$ and then find their supremum; (2) do the same with all the pairs $\{\theta, w\}$ such that $w \in [\theta, \infty)$; and, (3) find the maximum of the two supremum, i.e.,

$$h_{F_1 \sqcup F_2}(\theta) = \phi_1(\theta) \wedge \phi_2(\theta) \quad (31)$$

where

$$\phi_1(\theta) = \sup_{u\in[\theta,\infty)} \{f_x(u) \wedge g_x(\theta)\} = g_x(\theta) \wedge \sup_{u\in[\theta,\infty)} \{f_x(u)\} \quad (32)$$

and

$$\phi_2(\theta) = \sup_{w\in[\theta,\infty)} \{f_x(\theta) \wedge g_x()\} = f_x(\theta) \wedge \sup_{w\in[\theta,\infty)} \{g_x(w)\} \quad (33)$$

Algorithm 5.4 (*Meet Operation*). *Input: $\tilde{A}$, $\tilde{B}$ are two type-2 fuzzy sets with TINs $T_{\tilde{A}}$, $T_{\tilde{B}}$.*

Output: $\tilde{C}$ is result of meet operation.

1. *Find the upper surface by using the min-algorithm:*
   $T_{\tilde{C}_{US}} = max(T_{\tilde{A}_{US}}, T_{\tilde{B}_{US}})$
2. *Find the lower surface by using the min-algorithm:*
   $T_{\tilde{C}_{LS}} = max(T_{\tilde{A}_{LS}}, T_{\tilde{B}_{LS}})$
3. *Generate normal surface from $T_{\tilde{C}_{US}}$ and $T_{\tilde{C}_{US}}$ using Delaunay Triangulation.*

5.4 Negation operation

Algorithm 5.5 (*Negation Operation*)**.** *Input: $\tilde{A}$ is a type-2 fuzzy set. Output is result of negation operation.*

1. *For each vetex v_k of T_{US} or T_{LS} of $\tilde{B}$.*
   $v_k.y = 1.0 - v_k.y$
2. *Set $T'_{US} \leftarrow T_{LS}$, $T'_{LS} \leftarrow T_{US}$.*
3. *Set $\tilde{B} = \{T'_{US}, T_{NS}, T'_{LS}\}$.*

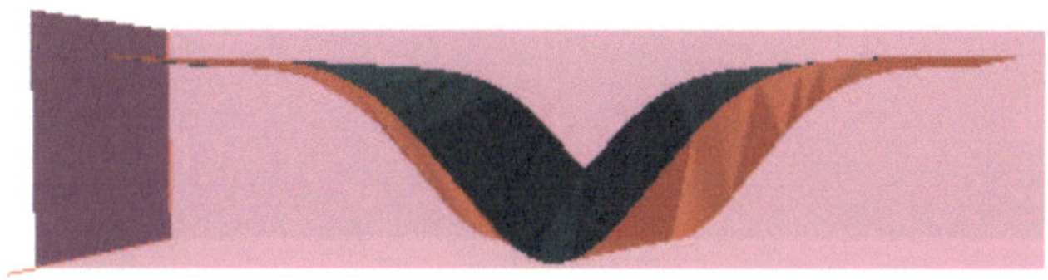

Fig. 14. Negation operation

5.5 Rendering and performance

The OpenSceneGraph (OSG) [http://www.openscenegraph.org] is an open source high performance 3D graphics toolkit, used by application developers in fields such as visual simulation, games, virtual reality, scientific visualization and modelling. Written entirely in Standard C++ and OpenGL it runs on all Windows platforms, OSX, GNU/Linux, IRIX, Solaris, HP-Ux, AIX and FreeBSD operating systems. The OpenSceneGraph is now well established as the world leading scene graph technology, used widely in the vis-sim, space, scientific, oil-gas, games and virtual reality industries.

We use the OSG for rendering of type-2 fuzzy sets. The approach is implemented for representation of general T2FS with various ε-approximation. Let $\tilde{A}$ is a general type-2 fuzzy set. The feature membership functions of $\tilde{A}$ are described as follows:

FOU is Gaussian function with upper MF and lower MF as follows:

Upper MF of FOU:

$$f_u(x) = \begin{cases} e^{-\frac{1}{2}(\frac{x-m_1}{\sigma})^2} \; if \; x<m_1 \\ 1 \; if \; m_1 \le x \le m_2 \\ e^{-\frac{1}{2}(\frac{x-m_2}{\sigma})^2} \; if \; x>m_2 \end{cases} \tag{34}$$

Lower MF of FOU:

$$f_l(x) = \begin{cases} e^{-\frac{1}{2}(\frac{x-m_2}{\sigma})^2} \; if \; x<\frac{m_1+m_2}{2} \\ e^{-\frac{1}{2}(\frac{x-m_1}{\sigma})^2} \; if \; otherwise \end{cases} \tag{35}$$

where $m_1 = 3.0$, $m_2 = 4.0$ and $\sigma = 0.5$.

The next feature of $\tilde{A}$ is set of points where $\mu_{\tilde{A}}(x,u) = 1.0$, involves points belong to the MF described as follows:

$$f_m(x) = e^{-\frac{1}{2}(\frac{x-(m_1+m_2)/2}{\sigma})^2} \tag{36}$$

ε	Extracted Point	Triangles	Time (miliseconds)	TIN
1 E-2	39	49	0.651	
5 E-3	51	65	0.899	
1 E-3	107	145	2.252	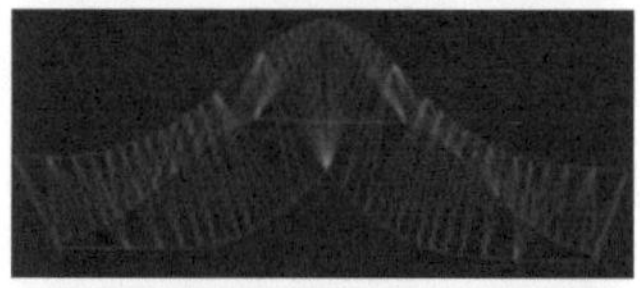
5 E-4	154	211	4.480	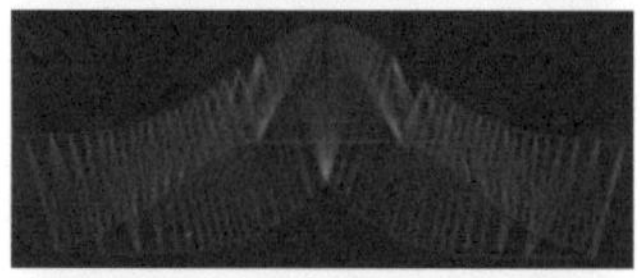
1 E-4	376	549	12.020	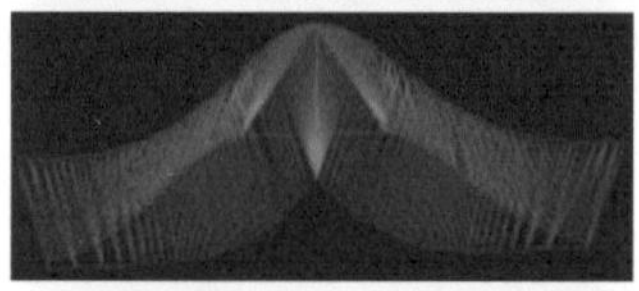
1 E-5	2460	4292	154.96	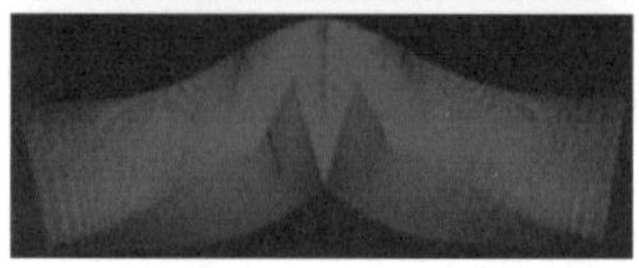

Table 1. Results of representation $\tilde{A}$

The new approach uses memory and computations less than previous approaches. If the TIN has N vertices, M faces then it takes N*12 bytes for vertices, M*6 bytes for faces and M*6 for relations between vertices and faces. For examples, triangular or trapezoid takes about 720 bytes with $N \cong M \cong 30$. Gaussian membership grades take about 200 vertices and 300 faces with accuracy $\epsilon = 0.01$, i.e 6000 bytes. Beside, the memory using for traditional approach takes about 100 000 bytes with step is 0.01 and x takes value in [0, 10].

We also tested the performance of algorithms with different membership grades. We implemented operations in 1000 times for each operation and summarized run-time (in milliseconds) in table 2.

Type-2 MF	Join	Meet	Negation
Triangular-Triangular	1	1	1
Gaussian - Triangular	474	290	1
Interval Gaussian	114	86	1

Table 2. The run-time of operations

6. Conclusion

The chapter introduces the new approach to represent a type-2 fuzzy sets using triangular irregular network. TIN has used to represent 3D surfaces by partitioning domain D into sub-triangle satisfying Delaunay criteria or constrained Delaunay criteria. This representation is used for membership functions of type-2 fuzzy sets that are 3D surfaces. We also proposed approach using half-edge to operate TIN in real-time application. Based-on this result, we have developed new computation to implement operations of type-2 fuzzy sets such as join, meet, negation. These operations is the base to develop computing for type-2 fuzzy logic systems.

The next goals is to continue improving geometry algorithms decrease computational time based on GPU. The second is to apply computing for developing type-2 fuzzy logic system using geometry algorithms.

7. Acknowledgment

This paper is sponsored by Vietnam National Foundation for Science and Technology Development (NAFOSTED), Grant No 102.012010.12, and RFit@LQDTU, Le Quy Don Technical University, Vietnam.

8. References

L.A. Zadeh (1975), The concept of linguistic variable and its application to approximate reasoning, *J.Information Science*, Vol. 8, 199 - 249.

M. Mizumoto, K. Tanaka (1976), Some properties of fuzzy sets of type-2, *J. Information and Control*, Vol. 31, 312 - 340.

N. Karnik, J.M. Mendel(2001-A), Operations on Type-2 Fuzzy Sets, *Fuzzy Sets and Systems*, Vol. 122, 327-348.

N. Karnik, J.M. Mendel(2001-B). Centroid of a type-2 fuzzy set, *Information Sciences*, Vol.132, 195-220.

N.N Karnik, J.M. Mendel, Q. Liang (1999), Type-2 Fuzzy Logic Systems, *IEEE Trans. on Fuzzy Systems*, Vol.7, No.6, 643-658.

Q. Liang, J.M. Mendel (2000), Interval Type-2 Fuzzy Logic Systems: Theory and Design, *IEEE Trans. on Fuzzy Systems*, Vol.8, No.5, 635-650.

J.M Mendel, R.B. John (2002), Type-2 Fuzzy Sets Made Simple, *IEEE Trans. Fuzzy Systems*, Vol. 10, no.2, 117-127.

J. M. Mendel (2004), On Computing the Centroid of a Symmetrical Interval Type-2 Fuzzy Set, *Proc. Conf. on Information Processing and Management of Uncertainty in Knowledge-Based Systems (IPMU)*, Perugia, Italy, 4-9.

S. Coupland, R. John (2007), Geometric Type-1 and Type-2 Fuzzy Logic Systems, *IEEE Trans. on Fuzzy Systems*, Vol. 15, No. 1, 3 - 15.

S. Coupland, R. John (2008), New geometric inference techniques for type-2 fuzzy sets, *International Journal of Approximate Reasoning*, Vol. 49(1), pp. 198-211.

S. Coupland, R. John (2008), A Fast Geometric Method for Defuzzification of Type-2 Fuzzy Sets, *IEEE Trans. on Fuzzy Systems*, Vol. 16, No.4, 929-941.

J. R. Shewchuck (2002), Delaunay Refinement Algorithms for Triangular Mesh Generation, *Computational Geometry: Theory and Applications*, Vol. 22(1-3),21-74.

J. Ruppert (1995), A Delaunay refinement algorithm for Quality 2-Dimensional Mesh Generation, *Journal of Algorithms*, Vol. 18(3), 548-585.

L. P. Chew (1989), Constrained Delaunay Triangulations, *Algorithmica* Vol. 4(1), 97-108.

J. M. Mendel, F. Liu, D. Zhai (2009), α-Plane Representation for Type-2 Fuzzy Sets: Theory and Applications, *IEEE Trans. on Fuzzy Systems*, 17(5), 1189-1207.

F. Liu (2008), An efficient centroid type-reduction strategy for general type-2 fuzzy logic system , *Information Sciences*, Vol. 178(9), 2224-2236.

L. T. Ngo, L. T. Pham, P. H. Nguyen, K.Hirota (2007), On approximate representation of type-2 fuzzy sets using triangulated irregular network, *Foundations of Fuzzy Logic and Soft Computing, Lecture Notes in Computer Science*, LNCS 4529, Springer, 584-593.

L. T. Ngo, L. T. Pham, P. H. Nguyen, K.Hirota (2009), Refinement geometric algorithms for type-2 fuzzy set operations, *Proceedings, IEEE-FUZZ 09,*, 866-871.

Janusz T. Starczewski (2009), Efficient triangular type-2 fuzzy logic systems, *International Journal of Approximate Reasoning*, Vol. 12, No.5, 799-811.

H. Hagras(2004), A Hierarchical Type-2 Fuzzy Logic Control Architecture for Autonomous Mobile Robots, *IEEE Trans. on Fuzzy Systems*, Vol. 12, No.4, 524-539.

H. Hagras(2007), Type-2 FLCs: A new Generation of Fuzzy Controllers, *IEEE Computational Intelligence Magazine*, Vol. 2, No. 1, 30-43.

C. Wagner, H. Hagras (2010), Toward General Type-2 Fuzzy Logic Systems Based on zSlices, *IEEE Trans. on Fuzzy Systems*, Vol. 18, No.4, pp. 637-660.

2

Self-Organizing Deformable Model: A Method for Projecting a 3D Object Mesh Model onto a Target Surface

Ken'ichi Morooka[1] and Hiroshi Nagahashi[2]
[1]*Graduate School of Information Science and Electrical Engineering, Kyushu University*
[2]*Imaging Science and Engineering Laboratory, Tokyo Institute of Technology*
Japan

1. Introduction

3D model fitting is one of the fundamental and powerful techniques in computer vision and computer graphics. The reason for using the fitting techniques includes establishing a relationship between an object of complex shape and a primitive object with a simple shape. Since object models often contain a huge number of points on the object surface, using the original models directly is computationally very expensive. On the other hand, the primitive models either have a compact data size or are represented by parametric functions. The relationship between the original and primitive models enables the complex shaped original models to be edited efficiently and easily through their corresponding primitives.

In addition, the fitting techniques provide the correspondence between multiple models by representing all models with a unified primitive model. This correspondence enables us not only to align the models but also to transfer the properties of one model, such as texture and motion data, to another model. Therefore, the fitting method is useful in a wide range of applications including Eigenspace-based object modeling (Allen et al., 2003; Blanz et al., 1998; Kurazume et al., 2007), texture mapping, 3D object morphing (Blanz et al., 1998) and computer animation (Noh et al., 2001; Sumner et al., 2004).

The fitting method has to meet certain requirements as described below. Appropriate primitive models are determined depending on the shape of target objects and/or the purpose of using the primitives. The choice of primitive models has an influence on some factors including the accuracy of recovering the object and the mapping distortion. Hence, the fitting method needs to deal with an arbitrary surface as a primitive. Some applications use the correspondence between given models. This correspondence can easily be found by fitting the models to a common primitive. Then, a fitting method is desired that allows users to specify the mapping between features of the models, such as mapping eyes to eyes and so on. Few existing methods, however, consider both these requirements simultaneously.

This paper presents a new method for fitting a deformable model to the points of a target object (Morooka et al., 2005; 2007). The deformable model is called a Self-organizing Deformable Model (SDM). The proposed fitting method is composed of two major steps.

First, we generate a rough model of the object by deforming the SDM based on competitive learning. Next, the accuracy of the model is improved by minimizing an energy function. The framework of the SDM allows users to move some vertices included in the SDM towards specific points on the target surface, and to collect the vertices in particular regions on the surface. This control of the SDM deformation process provides preferable models depending on the applications using them.

1.1 Previous and related works

Many researchers have concentrated on model fitting techniques. One fitting method uses a mapping function(Eck et al., 1995; Floater et al., 2003), which enables us to project the object mesh model onto a primitive object surface such as a planar or spherical one. There are several types of mapping functions including harmonic mapping and conformal ones. Most of the traditional methods that use a mapping function have been designed only for their specific primitives. Because of this limitation, the methods are harder to generalize. In (Tarini et al., 2004), although, a set of cubes is used as the primitive, the combination of several kinds of primitives would be more appropriate for the compact low-distortion mapping of complex shapes.

Deformable models have the potential for achieving such mapping by regarding the set of multiple primitives as the deformable model. This is because the deformable model can adapt to the new shape by deforming the original shape. The approaches using deformable models can be categorized into the deformation methods with or without a certain number of constraints. The constraints are the preservation of the volume and/or the shape features of the model. Constrained deformable models can generate a continuous global relationship between the initial and the deformed models. The relationship is used to create model animations, and transfer deformation from one model to another (Noh et al., 2001; Sumner et al., 2004). One technique for the constrained deformation is to modify the model by deforming its embedded space or the underlying skeleton of the model (Ju et al., 2005; Kavan et al., 2005; Sederberg et al., 1986). Recent approaches (Kun et al., 2004; Lipman et al., 2005; Zayer et al., 2005) introduce the Laplace or Poisson equations, and compute the vertex displacements which describe the difference between the initial and the deformed models. The deformable model without the constraints applies where the relationship between the initial and the deformed models is an arbitrary deformation. Such deformable models are useful for mapping between two models with different shapes. Therefore, we focus on the the unconstrained deformable models, and these types of the models are simply called deformable models.

In the method using deformable models(Duan et al., 1998; Gibson et al., 1997; Lachaud et al., 1999; McInerney et al., 2000), a mesh of a plane or sphere is often used as the initial deformable model, and then the mesh model is deformed by moving its vertices to fit the target object. Generally, fitting the deformable model to a target object is formulated as a minimization problem of an energy function, which measures the deviation of the model from the target. Since the model deformation uses both vertices of the model and numerous points on the target surface, the optimum deformation must be found in a large search space that includes many local minima. In obtaining such a deformation, certain initial conditions of the deformable model have a great influence on the computational cost and the fitting accuracy of the resulting model. However, the estimation of the initial model becomes more difficult when the shape of the object is complicated. It is not so easy for users to implement the preferable deformation. For example, an inadequate deformation may lead to certain problems such as the self-intersection of the model. Therefore, traditional methods that use deformable models need to find the optimal movement of vertices through trial-and-error.

Recent research (Kraevoy et al., 2004; Schreiner et al., 2004) has reported methods for finding the relationship between two models that preserves the correspondence of specific features. Although these methods obtain good mappings, they lead to high computational complexity and/or an increase in the data size of the output model compared with that of the original one.

The basis of the SDM deformation is the combination of competitive learning and an energy minimization method. In much the same way, some methods (Barhak et al., 2001; Ivrissimtzis et al., 2004; 2003; Liou et al., 2005; Yu, 1999) utilize a framework of competitive learning to recover the whole object surface. An exception to these methods is that of (Barhak et al., 2001), which focuses on a range image. The original purpose of competitive learning is to obtain a network that represents the distribution of given points. Therefore, direct use of competitive learning causes the accuracy of the resulting model to be inadequate for approximating the original object surface; that is, the model has a blurred surface of the original target object (Liou et al., 2005). Some methods (Ivrissimtzis et al., 2004; 2003; Yu, 1999) introduce a process of changing the number of vertices and their connectivity during the deformation. Contrastingly, in our proposed method, the SDM can recover a target surface while retaining the architecture of the SDM. This characteristic enables us to represent objects with a unified form, and to easily establish a correspondence between multiple models. Our method can, therefore, be used in various applications in computer vision and computer graphics.

2. Self-organizing deformable model

2.1 Notations

The SDM is a deformable mesh model represented by triangular patches. According to the notation adopted in (Lee et al., 1998), the SDM $\mathcal{M}$ can be regarded as a two-tuple:

$$\mathcal{M} = (\mathcal{V}, \mathcal{K}), \tag{1}$$

where $\mathcal{V}$ is the set of vertices of the SDM. The SDM contains N_v vertices, with each vertex $\boldsymbol{v}_i$ $(1 \leq i \leq N_v)$ of the SDM having 3D positional information. An abstract simplicical complex, $\mathcal{K}$, contains all the adjacency information for $\mathcal{M}$. In other words, $\mathcal{K}$ includes three different sets of simplices: a set of which includes uniquely identified vertices $\{i\} \in \mathcal{K}_v$, a set of edges $e = \{i, j\} \in \mathcal{K}_e$, and a set of faces $f = \{i, j, k\} \in \mathcal{K}_f$. Therefore, $\mathcal{K} = \mathcal{K}_v \cup \mathcal{K}_e \cup \mathcal{K}_f$. Our edge representation has a commutative property. For example, the edge e_3 as shown in Fig. 1 is composed of two vertices $\boldsymbol{v}_{i3}$ and $\boldsymbol{v}_{i4}$, and is described by $e_3 = \{i_3, i_4\} = \{i_4, i_3\}$. We represent each face of the SDM by a list of its three vertices arranged in a counterclockwise direction, e.g., the face f_2 shown in Fig. 1 is described by $f_2 = \{i_2, i_4, i_3\} = \{i_4, i_3, i_2\} = \{i_3, i_2, i_4\}$.

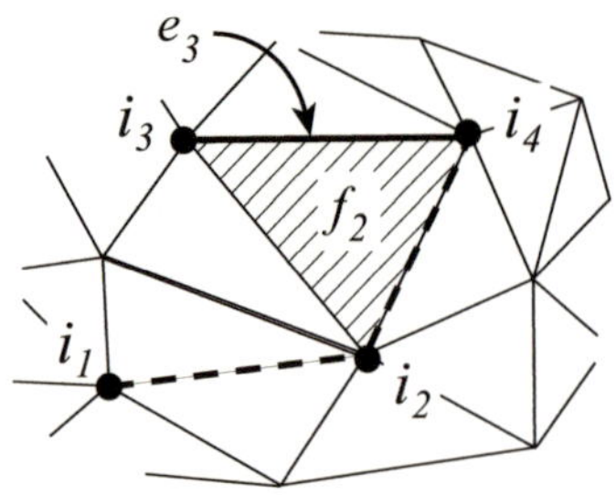

Fig. 1. Example of notations used in our SDM. Adapted from the article (Morooka et al., 2007). Copyright(c)2007 IEICE.

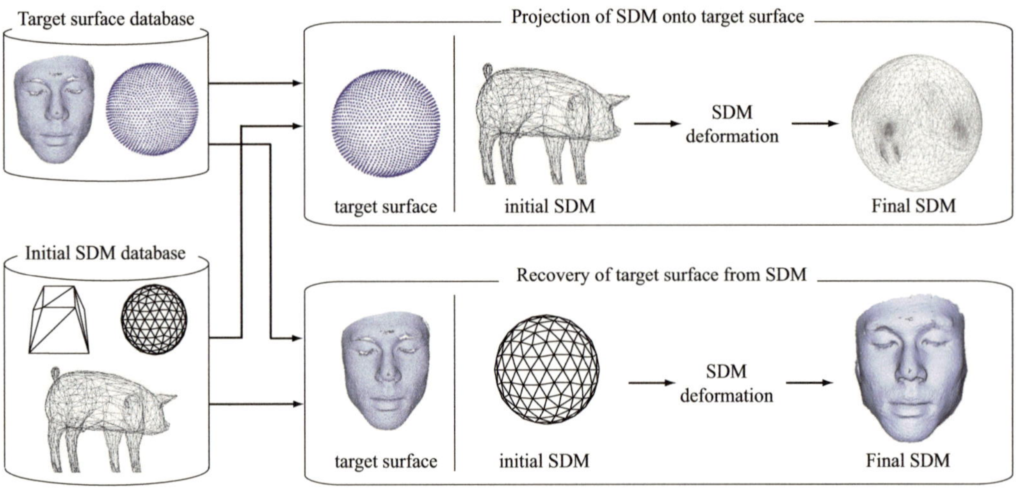

Fig. 2. Concept of Self-organizing Deformable Model. Adapted from the article (Morooka et al., 2007). Copyright(c)2007 IEICE.

Given two vertices $\boldsymbol{v}_{i1}$ and $\boldsymbol{v}_{i4}$ as shown in Fig. 1, a path from $\boldsymbol{v}_{i1}$ to $\boldsymbol{v}_{i4}$ is defined as a series of edges. Then, a topological distance $L(i_1, i_4)$ between the vertices is defined as the number of edges comprising the shortest path from $\boldsymbol{v}_{i1}$ to $\boldsymbol{v}_{i4}$. Another topological distance $L(i_4, i_1)$ from $\boldsymbol{v}_{i4}$ to $\boldsymbol{v}_{i1}$ is equal to $L(i_1, i_4)$. The shortest path from $\boldsymbol{v}_{i1}$ to $\boldsymbol{v}_{i4}$ is illustrated by dashed lines, and the topological distance $L(i_1, i_4)$ is 2. When the topological distance from a vertex $\boldsymbol{v}_i$ to an arbitrary vertex is r, the latter vertex is called the r-neighbors of $\boldsymbol{v}_i$ Given an arbitrary vertex $\boldsymbol{v}$, we regard as its neighbors the vertices for which the topological distance from each of the vertices to $\boldsymbol{v}$ is less than a threshold θ_r. Here, the maximum topological distance depends on the data size of the SDM, so we manually determine the value of the parameter θ_r according to the size of the SDM.

A target surface is represented by a set of points on the surface, called control points. We make the following three assumptions: 1) the surface orientation and surface normal at each control point are known; 2) the size of an initial SDM is sufficient to cover the target surface completely; and 3) the SDM and the target surface have the same topological type. This paper focuses on object surfaces of genus 0. From these assumptions, we can choose arbitrary shapes for both the SDM and target surface. As shown in Fig. 2, the initial SDM and the target surface can be selected from various kinds of models besides spheres, animals and human faces. A mesh model selected as an initial SDM can be projected onto various kinds of target surface as in other methods for surface parameterization. Furthermore, like general deformable models, the SDM can reconstruct surfaces of target objects.

2.2 Formulation of the SDM deformation

There are two purposes for deforming the SDM. Considering the SDM notation in Eq.(1), the first purpose is to project the SDM onto the target surface by changing the vertex positions in $\mathcal{V}$ while keeping the original topology for the vertices represented by $\mathcal{K}$. This projection is called topology-preserving mapping. With an initial SDM $\mathcal{M}^s$ and a final SDM $\mathcal{M}^d$, the topology-preserving mapping Φ is formulated as

$$\Phi : \mathcal{M}^s = (\mathcal{V}^s, \mathcal{K}) \longmapsto \mathcal{M}^d = (\mathcal{V}^d, \mathcal{K}) \qquad (2)$$

The second purpose of the SDM deformation is to approximate the target surface $\mathcal{S}$ by the final SDM $\mathcal{M}^d$. Competitive learning is used to represent the distribution of control points on the target surface. From a geometrical point of view, when applying competitive learning to the SDM deformation, the resulting SDM tessellates the target surface into the Voronoi regions, each of which includes almost the same number of control points on the target surface. The SDM cannot always recover the complex shape. For example, if we fit a spherical surface model as an initial SDM to the female model 'Igea' as shown in Fig. 4(c), and the fitting does not meet the second purpose, the final SDM is blurred and incomplete as shown in Fig. 7(c). Therefore, we formulate an error function for the approximated model to recover the target surface with good accuracy.

The second purpose is formulated by an error function for the approximated model. Various definitions of error functions are given in (Cignoni et al., 1998), and the error function in our method is defined as follows. Given a control point $\boldsymbol{p}$ on $\mathcal{S}$, we consider a line that starts at $\boldsymbol{p}$ and is perpendicular to the plane expanded by the face $f \in \mathcal{K}_f$. If the line intersects inside the face f, we let the intersection condition be true and calculate the distance between $\boldsymbol{p}$ and f. From the faces that satisfy the intersection condition, the face with the minimum distance is regarded as the corresponding face of $\boldsymbol{p}$. After finding all the correspondences between faces and control points, for each face f_m, its corresponding control points are collected into a set $\boldsymbol{\Omega}_m$. Here, we denote as $\boldsymbol{\Gamma}_i$ the set of faces $f_m \in \mathcal{K}_f$ that include the vertex $\boldsymbol{v}_i$. Then, the error function is defined as the distance $D(\mathcal{M}^d, \mathcal{S})$ between $\mathcal{M}^d$ and $\mathcal{S}$:

$$D(\mathcal{M}^d, \mathcal{S}) = \sum_{\{i\} \in \mathcal{K}_v} \sum_{f_m \in \boldsymbol{\Gamma}_i} \sum_{\boldsymbol{p}_u \in \boldsymbol{\Omega}_m} \frac{\{H(\boldsymbol{p}_u, f_m)\}^2}{3|\boldsymbol{\Gamma}_i||\boldsymbol{\Omega}_m|}, \qquad (3)$$

where $|\boldsymbol{\Gamma}_i|$ and $|\boldsymbol{\Omega}_m|$ represent the total number of elements in $\boldsymbol{\Gamma}_i$ and $\boldsymbol{\Omega}_m$. The function $H(\boldsymbol{p}, f)$ returns the Euclidean distance between a control point $\boldsymbol{p}$ and the perpendicular foot of $\boldsymbol{p}$ on a face f.

From Eqs.(2) and (3), the deformation of $\mathcal{M}^s$ is formulated as the optimization problem of finding $\mathcal{M}^d$ that satisfies the following conditions:

$$\mathcal{M}^d = \tilde{\Phi}(\mathcal{M}^s); \tag{4}$$

$$\tilde{\Phi} = \arg\min_{\Phi} D(\Phi(\mathcal{M}^s), \mathcal{S}). \tag{5}$$

3. SDM deformation

3.1 Overview

Generally, the topology-preserving projection function Φ in Eq.(2) is nonlinear, and a deformation from $\mathcal{M}^s$ to $\mathcal{M}^d$ is not always unique. The Self-Organizing Map (SOM)(Kohonen et al., 2001) is a well-known method for finding a topology-preserving mapping, and it enables us to obtain a network that represents the distribution of the given input data. The network consists of a set of units and a set of edges connecting two units. Each unit has a positional vector that provides the position of the unit in the input data space. Initially, the SOM algorithm selects an input data randomly, and computes its Euclidean distance to every unit in the network. Next, the unit with the minimum distance is selected as the winner of the input data. The positions of the winner unit and its neighbor units are slightly adjusted towards the input data. These processes are repeated until no units can be further modified.

During the learning process of the SOM, the network is deformed by moving units in the input data space. We introduce the SOM framework into the SDM deformation by regarding the relationship between the SDM and control points as being equivalent to that of the SOM and the input data. Then, the vertices of the SDM and their 3D positions correspond to the units of the SOM and their positional vectors in the input data. However, from a geometrical point of view, problems occur when the SOM algorithm is applied directly to the SDM deformation. The major problems and their solutions are described below.

3.2 SDM deformation based on SOM

3.2.1 Determination of winner vertex

In the SOM algorithm, when a control point is selected randomly, a winner vertex is determined from the Euclidean distances between the control point and the vertices of the SDM. However, this determination may select a vertex that is on the opposite side of the target surface as shown in Fig. 3(a), where the control point and the selected vertex are marked by '•' and '■'. In this case, the selected vertex and its neighbors are moved into the target surface. As a result, the final SDM is projected onto the limited area of the target surface as shown in Fig. 3(b). Such a phenomenon is called a collapsed SDM.

To avoid this problem, traditional deformable models based on competitive learning (Ivrissimtzis et al., 2004; 2003; Yu, 1999) change the number of vertices of the models and their connectivity during the deformation. On the other hand, the purpose of the SDM deformation is to recover the target surface while keeping the architecture of the SDM. Considering this requirement, we deal with the collapse problem by using a signed distance SD between a

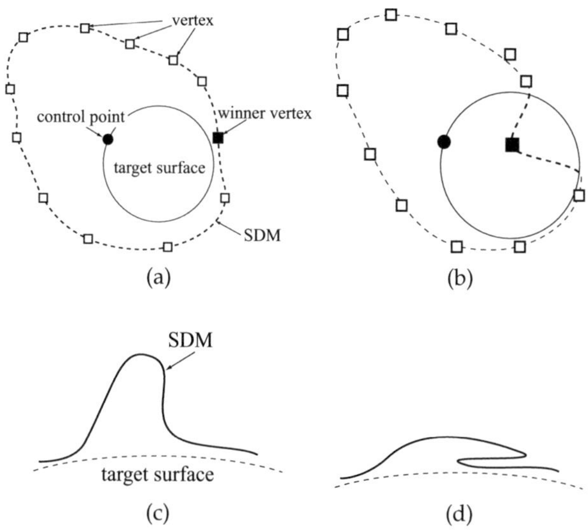

Fig. 3. Examples of a collapsed SDM caused by (a-b) moving certain vertices of the SDM into a target surface, and (c-d) folding over itself. Adapted from the article (Morooka et al., 2007). Copyright(c)2007 IEICE.

control point $\boldsymbol{p}$ and a vertex $\boldsymbol{v}$:

$$SD(\boldsymbol{v}, \boldsymbol{p}) = \boldsymbol{n_p} \cdot (\boldsymbol{v} - \boldsymbol{p}), \tag{6}$$

where $\boldsymbol{n_p}$ is a unit normal vector at $\boldsymbol{p}$. SD has positive values if $\boldsymbol{v}$ is outside the surface on which $\boldsymbol{p}$ exists. Otherwise, SD takes negative values for $\boldsymbol{v}$ inside the surface. The absolute value of SD denotes the Euclidean distance between $\boldsymbol{p}$ and $\boldsymbol{v}$. In our method, the winner vertex is selected so that the signed distance between the vertex and the control point is non-negative and the minimum of all vertices.

3.2.2 Update of vertices

After determining the winner vertex $\boldsymbol{v}_c$ of a control point $\boldsymbol{p}$, $\boldsymbol{v}_c$ and its neighbors are updated by moving towards $\boldsymbol{p}$. In practice, the update of these vertices $\boldsymbol{v}_i$ is formulated as

$$\boldsymbol{v}_i \leftarrow \boldsymbol{v}_i + \epsilon(t)\lambda(i|c)\Delta\boldsymbol{v}_i; \tag{7}$$

$$\Delta\boldsymbol{v}_i = \boldsymbol{p} - \boldsymbol{v}_i, \tag{8}$$

where t is a time parameter, and $\epsilon(t)$ $(0 < \epsilon < 1)$ is the learning rate that determines the magnitude by which the vertex is adapted towards the point. At the start of implementing the SOM algorithm, $\epsilon(t)$ is usually set to a large value to achieve the global adjustment of the SDM. During the learning process, the learning rate gradually decreases to zero according to the specified learning rate function. We define $\epsilon(t)$ as follows (Fritzke et al., 1997):

$$\epsilon(t) = \epsilon_s(\frac{\epsilon_d}{\epsilon_s})^{t/T} \tag{9}$$

Here, ϵ_s and ϵ_d are the initial and the final learning rates.

The neighborhood function $\lambda(i|c)$ in Eq.(7) denotes the adaptation rate of an arbitrary vertex $\boldsymbol{v}_i$ for a winner vertex $\boldsymbol{v}_c$. In our method, $\lambda(i|c)$ is a decreasing function of the topological distance $L(i,c)$ between two vertices $\boldsymbol{v}_i$ and $\boldsymbol{v}_c$:

$$\lambda(i|c) = \exp[-\frac{1}{2}\{\frac{L(i,c)}{\sigma(t)}\}^2] \tag{10}$$

The standard deviation $\sigma(t)$ of the neighborhood function in Eq.(10) is called the neighborhood radius. At the start of the learning process, the large neighborhood radius is used to map the winner vertex and its neighbors onto the same portion of the target surface. Similar to the learning rate, the neighborhood radius typically decreases with time t, and the deformation algorithm converges. Therefore, the neighborhood radius is formulated by

$$\sigma(t) = \sigma_s(\frac{\sigma_d}{\sigma_s})^{t/T}, \tag{11}$$

where σ_s and σ_d are the initial and final values.

T is the maximum time for selecting winner vertices. The adaptation of the winner vertex and its neighbors causes the vertices to move towards the target surface, and may sometimes generate a collapsed SDM. To solve this problem, our method updates the vertices as follows.

For each vertex in the SDM, we compute the signed distances between the vertex and all control points, and select the closest control point with a non-negative signed distance. If the signed distance between the selected control point and the vertex is more than a given threshold τ, the vertex is assigned to a 'free' label. Otherwise, the vertex is assigned to an 'anchor' label. Here, to determine the value of the threshold τ, we use the average distance L between the 1-ring neighbor points of the target surface, and the threshold is set to $\tau = 2 * L$.

A vertex with a 'free' label is moved closer to the target surface while keeping its relative position with respect to the winner vertex $\boldsymbol{v}_c$. This movement is formulated by Eq.(7) and the translation vector $\Delta\boldsymbol{v}$ of the vertex $\boldsymbol{v}$

$$\Delta\boldsymbol{v}_i = \boldsymbol{p} - \boldsymbol{v}_i + \alpha(\boldsymbol{v}_i - \tilde{\boldsymbol{v}}_c) \tag{12}$$

where $\tilde{\boldsymbol{v}}_c$ is its 3D position before updating. The constant parameter α has to be small enough to avoid the self-intersection of the SDM. We empirically set α to $\alpha = 0.3$.

On the other hand, a vertex with an 'anchor' label is considered to be on the target surface. The adaptation of a vertex with the 'anchor' label using Eq.(12) sometimes causes the vertex to move into the target surface, and generate a collapsed SDM. To solve this problem, we move the vertex with an 'anchor' label along the target surface during the deformation. The movement is achieved by using a geodesic path from the vertex $\boldsymbol{v}$ to a control point $\boldsymbol{p}$. The function $\Psi(\gamma|\,\boldsymbol{v},\boldsymbol{p})$ $(0 \leq \gamma \leq 1)$ is defined so that the function returns the 3D positional vector of the point on the geodesic path. In addition, $\Psi(0|\,\boldsymbol{v},\boldsymbol{p}) = \boldsymbol{v}$ if $\gamma = 0$, and $\Psi(1|\,\boldsymbol{v},\boldsymbol{p}) = \boldsymbol{p}$ if $\gamma = 1$. Using the geodesic path, we update the vertex $\boldsymbol{v}_i$ with an 'anchor' label according to the following equation:

$$\boldsymbol{v}_i \leftarrow \Psi(\epsilon(t)\lambda(i|c)|\,\boldsymbol{v}_i,\boldsymbol{p}). \tag{13}$$

The geodesic path is computed efficiently using given techniques (Surazhsky et al., 2005). Then, all geodesic paths between two arbitrary points on the target surface are calculated off-line, and stored in a database. In the on-line SDM deformation, we obtain the geodesic path from the vertex merely by finding its closest point.

3.2.3 SDM after finishing the deformation

As stated above, our method introduces certain techniques to avoid a collapsed SDM. Nevertheless, the final SDM may contain foldovers, thus replicating the major problem of the original SOM algorithm. One solution to this problem is to restart the learning process using a different learning rate, the value of which decreases gradually, or by using another neighborhood function with a larger neighborhood radius (Duda et al., 2000). We can also use these ideas to create the SDM without foldovers.

For each vertex $\boldsymbol{v}$, we select the faces satisfying the following: 1) the topological distance between $\boldsymbol{v}$ and at least one of the vertices of the face is less than a given threshold; and 2) the perpendicular lines from $\boldsymbol{v}$ intersect the face. We compute the distance between $\boldsymbol{v}$ and each perpendicular foot of $\boldsymbol{v}$ on the selected face. If the minimum distance is less than a threshold, the SDM is considered to include a foldover, and we update the parameters of the learning rate and the neighborhood function in Eqs.(9) and (11):

$$\begin{aligned} \epsilon_s \leftarrow h_1\epsilon_s; \quad \epsilon_d \leftarrow h_2\epsilon_d; \\ \sigma_s \leftarrow h_3\sigma_s; \quad \sigma_d \leftarrow h_4\sigma_d. \end{aligned} \tag{14}$$

We empirically set $h_1 = 0.1$, $h_2 = 0.1$, $h_3 = 0.1$, and $h_4 = 0.1$. Using Eq.(14), the value of the updated learning rate decreases more slowly than the original learning rate. This changing of the learning rate can avoid a local minimum, that is, foldovers. On the other hand, the updated neighborhood function deals with only the vertices and the 1 or 2-ring neighbor to reduce the computational cost.

In addition, when applying the SOM algorithm to the SDM deformation, the final SDM $\mathcal{M}^d$ has the characteristic that the Voronoi region of each vertex of the SDM includes almost the same number of control points. This means that $\mathcal{M}^d$ cannot always recover the object surface completely because $\mathcal{M}^d$ may not be satisfied by Eq.(5). We further deform the SDM by minimizing an energy function to improve the accuracy of the reconstructed target surface by the SDM.

The algorithm for the deformation chooses candidates for the next position of a vertex, and computes the energy function in the case of the vertex being moved to any of the candidates. We select as the next position of the vertex the candidate with the minimum valued energy function. Although the mesh deformation using the energy function is similar to the active balloon model, the energy function in our method is based on an external energy function, that represents the fitness of the SDM for the target surface. Using the error function in Eq.(3), the value of the energy function E for the vertex $\boldsymbol{v}_i$ is computed by

$$E(\boldsymbol{v}_i) = \sum_{f_m \in \boldsymbol{\Gamma}_i} \sum_{\boldsymbol{p}_u \in \boldsymbol{\Omega}_m} \{H(\boldsymbol{p}_u, f_m)\}^2. \tag{15}$$

3.3 Algorithm

1. Assign a 'free' label to all vertices.
2. Initialize the time parameter t to $t = 0$.
3. From the set of control points on the target surface, randomly choose a control point $\boldsymbol{p}^{(t)}$ at time t.
4. Determine the winner vertex $\boldsymbol{v}_c^{(t)}$ from

$$\boldsymbol{v}_c^{(t)} = \arg \min_{\{i\} \in \mathcal{K}_v} SD(\boldsymbol{v}_i, \boldsymbol{p}^{(t)}). \tag{16}$$

5. Adapt the positions of the winner vertex $\boldsymbol{v}_c^{(t)}$ and its neighbors according to their labels:

$$\boldsymbol{v}_i \leftarrow \begin{cases} \boldsymbol{v}_i + \epsilon(t)\lambda(i|c^{(t)})\Delta\boldsymbol{v}_i & : (\boldsymbol{v}_i \text{ with a 'free' label}) \\ \Psi(\epsilon(t)\lambda(i|c^{(t)})|\ \boldsymbol{v}_i, \boldsymbol{p}^{(t)}) & : (\boldsymbol{v}_i \text{ with an 'anchor' label}) \end{cases} \tag{17}$$

   where $c^{(t)}$ is the vertex label of $\boldsymbol{v}_c^{(t)}$. The learning rate $\epsilon(t)$, the neighborhood function $\lambda(i|c)$, and the translation vector $\Delta\boldsymbol{v}$ are obtained from Eqs.(9), (10), and (12).
6. Compute the signed distances between the moved vertices and their closest control points. If the distance is less than the threshold τ, the vertex is assigned to an 'anchor' label.
7. If no vertices are moved, or $t \geq T$, go to step 8. Otherwise, $t \leftarrow t + 1$ and go to step 3. Here, T is the maximum time for selecting winner vertices.
8. If the SDM includes foldovers, update the parameters according to Eq.(14), and go to step 2. Otherwise, go to step 9.
9. For each vertex $\boldsymbol{v}_i$:
   (a) By regarding the control point $\boldsymbol{p}$ included in $\boldsymbol{\Omega}_m$ as the corresponding point of $\boldsymbol{v}_i$, choose potential vectors $\tilde{\boldsymbol{v}}_u$ from $\tilde{\boldsymbol{v}}_u = \boldsymbol{v}_i + w(\boldsymbol{p} - \boldsymbol{v}_i)$ for updating the position of $\boldsymbol{v}_i$. The parameter w is a variable that gives the rate of moving $\boldsymbol{v}_i$ to $\boldsymbol{p}$.
   (b) Find the vector $\boldsymbol{v}_i^*$ satisfying

$$\boldsymbol{v}_i^* = \arg \min_{\tilde{\boldsymbol{v}}_u} E(\tilde{\boldsymbol{v}}_u), \tag{18}$$

   where $E(\boldsymbol{v}_i)$ is the energy function in Eq.(15). In addition, update $\boldsymbol{v}_i$ from $\boldsymbol{v}_i \leftarrow \boldsymbol{v}_i^*$.
10. Compute the distance between the SDM and the target surface using Eq.(3). If the distance is less than a given threshold θ_e, the process is terminated. Otherwise, go to step 8.

Generally, in the SOM algorithm, the maximum time T for selecting winner vertices is set to a large value to achieve good accuracy for the SOM. In addition, the parameter T acts as a criterion for adopting the energy-based deformation process. Therefore, a large value for the parameter T leads to a deformation process that requires much computational time, even though the SDM is hardly deformed during the process. To avoid this situation, we use another criterion: when no vertices are moved, the algorithm is terminated regardless of the learning time t.

3.4 Modification of the SDM deformation algorithm

With the above algorithm, object mesh models used as the SDM can automatically be fitted to the given target surfaces. In addition, users can more easily control the deformation of the SDM more easily than the general deformable models. This characteristic provides the opportunity to obtain more preferable models depending on the applications using the models. Given below are some of the ways of modifying the algorithm for the SDM deformation.

3.4.1 Selection of a control point

After a winner vertex has been determined from a given control point, both the winner vertex and its neighbors move towards the control point. If some control points are chosen more often than others, more SDM vertices tend to move toward these control points. This means that the choice of the control points influences the density of vertices of the SDM on the target surface. Since the control points are randomly chosen, the choice can be controlled by changing the selection probability of the control points. For example, if all control points are chosen with the same probability, the vertices of the resulting SDM are located on the target surface according to the distribution of the control points. As a further example, if the selection probability of the control points from a particular region of the target surface is higher than that of other regions, the vertices of the SDM tend to move toward that particular region.

Let us consider the reconstruction of an object with a complex shape. Then, the reconstruction accuracy of the resulting model can be improved by moving more vertices of the SDM towards the area with the complex shape. One way of achieving this movement is to determine the selection probability of the control points based on the curvatures at the points. In practice, the selection probability P_u of control point $\boldsymbol{p}_u$ is computed as

$$P_u = \frac{C_u}{Z} + \beta \tag{19}$$

where C_u is the curvature at control point $\boldsymbol{p}$, and Z is a normalization factor such that $\sum P_u = 1$. The positive parameter β ($\beta > 0$) is used to set the selection possibility of all vertices with a non-zero value. Using the probabilities, control points are chosen by a roulette wheel selection which is one of the selection methods in generic algorithm. In a roulette wheel selection, control points with high selection probabilities are more likely to be selected, but there is also a chance of selecting control points with small probabilities.

3.4.2 Determination of a winner vertex

The SDM framework can move an arbitrary vertex towards a special control point as described below. This movement is achieved by introducing the constraint that the vertex is always selected as the winner of the special point. To begin with, users specify feature control points $\tilde{\boldsymbol{p}}$ and their corresponding vertices $\tilde{\boldsymbol{v}}(\tilde{\boldsymbol{p}})$. In the SDM deformation algorithm, if the t-th selected control point $\boldsymbol{p}^{(t)}$ is one of the feature points, its corresponding vertex is automatically

SDM ↓ target surface		pig ↓ sphere	rabbit ↓ cylindrical surface	armadillo ↓ Cylinderman	lion ↓ Animal	sphere ↓ Igea
SDM	vertices	3,516	67,037	16,980	9,154	10,242
	patches	7,028	134,070	33,947	18,304	20,480
target surface	points	2,526	79,602	11,305	8,602	33,587
(η_0, η_1)		(11, 5)	(10, 0)	(5, 7)	(11, 6)	(10, 0)
processing time [sec.]		61	286	1,055	644	231

Table 1. SDMs and target surfaces used in our experiments, and computational time for deforming the SDMs. The results except for the projection of the sphere to Igea are adapted from the article (Morooka et al., 2007). Copyright(c)2007 IEICE.

determined as the winner vertex. The determination is formulated by rewriting Eq.(16) as

$$\boldsymbol{v}_c^{(t)} = \begin{cases} \tilde{\boldsymbol{v}}(\boldsymbol{p}^{(t)}) & : (\boldsymbol{p}^{(t)} \in \mathcal{F}) \\ \arg\min_{\{i\} \in \mathcal{K}_v} SD(\boldsymbol{v}_i, \boldsymbol{p}^{(t)}) & : \text{(otherwise)}, \end{cases} \tag{20}$$

where $\mathcal{F}$ is the set of the pairs $(\tilde{\boldsymbol{p}}, \tilde{\boldsymbol{v}}(\tilde{\boldsymbol{p}}))$ of the feature points $\tilde{\boldsymbol{p}}$ and their corresponding vertices $\tilde{\boldsymbol{v}}(\tilde{\boldsymbol{p}})$. Under this constraint, the SDM is deformed in such a way that the vertex moves constantly towards the control point.

(a)Cylinderman (b)Animal (c)Igea

Fig. 4. Examples of target surfaces. Fig.4(a) and (b) are adapted from the article (Morooka et al., 2007). Copyright(c)2007 IEICE.

4. Experimental results

To verify the applicability of our proposed method, we conducted several experiments that involved applying the SDM to various 3D object models. The well-known "rabbit", "Igea", and "armadillo" were included as models in our experiments. These models were downloaded from Cyberware and Stanford University websites. We set the parameters in the SDM deformation as follows:

$$\epsilon_s = 0.5, \quad \epsilon_d = 0.05, \quad \sigma_s = 3.0, \\ \sigma_d = 0.1, \quad w = 0.01, \quad \theta_e = 0.2. \tag{21}$$

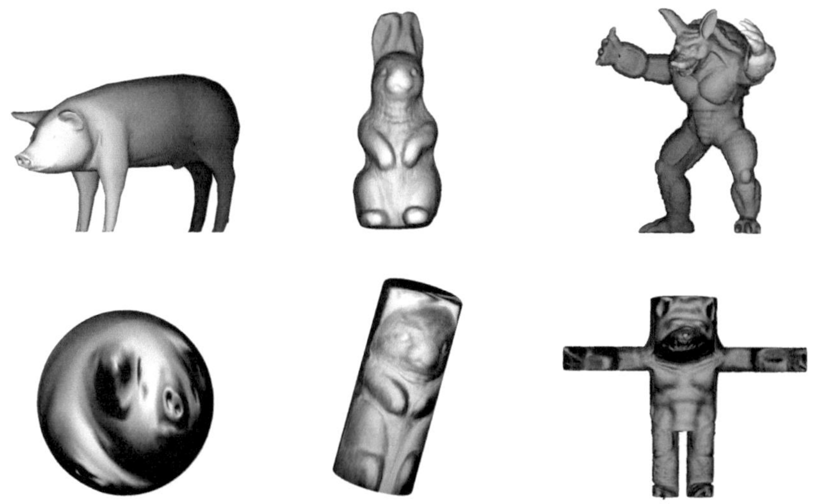

(a) pig - spherical surface (b) rabbit - cylindrical surface (c) armadillo - Cylinderman

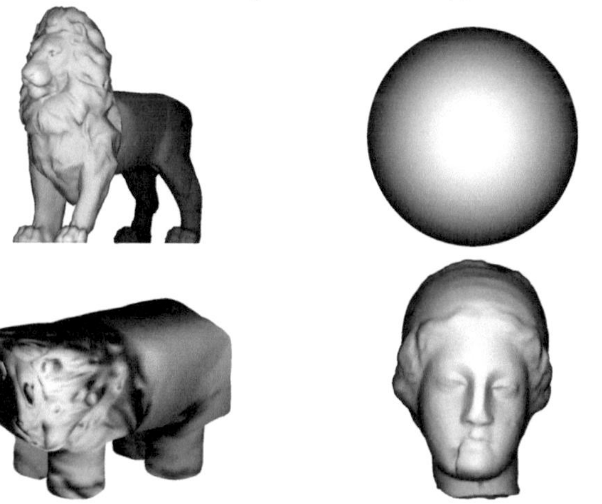

(d) lion - Animal (e) spherical surface - Igea

Fig. 5. Projection of SDMs onto various kinds of target surfaces; top : initial SDMs; bottom : SDMs projected onto target surfaces. Fig.5(a)-(d) are adapted from the article (Morooka et al., 2007). Copyright(c)2007 IEICE.

Given the target surface with N_v vertices, the maximum number T of selecting the control points is set to $\eta_0 N_v$. We denote as a parameter η_1 the repeat count of restarting the learning process. Finally, $(\eta_0 + \eta_1)N_v$ control points are selected in the SDM deformation. These parameters used in our experiments are shown in Table 1.

4.1 Fitting of SDMs to target surfaces

In the first experiment we project a mesh model onto another kind of target surface. The target surfaces used in our experiments are a spherical surface, a cylindrical surface, a roughly quadrupedal surface, and a simple humanoid surface. The latter two models, shown in Fig.

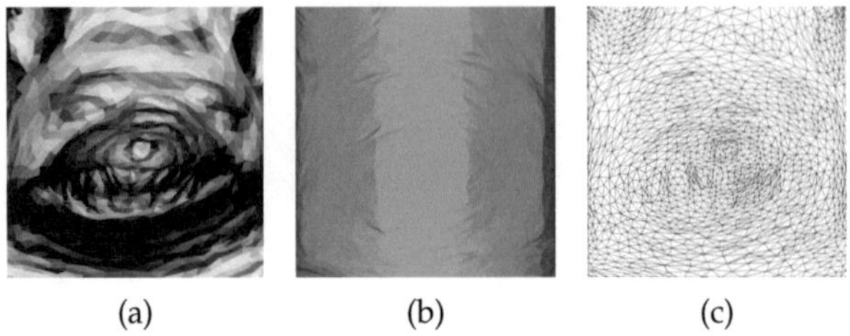

Fig. 6. Facial part of armadillo projected onto Cylinderman. Adapted from the article (Morooka et al., 2007). Copyright(c)2007 IEICE.

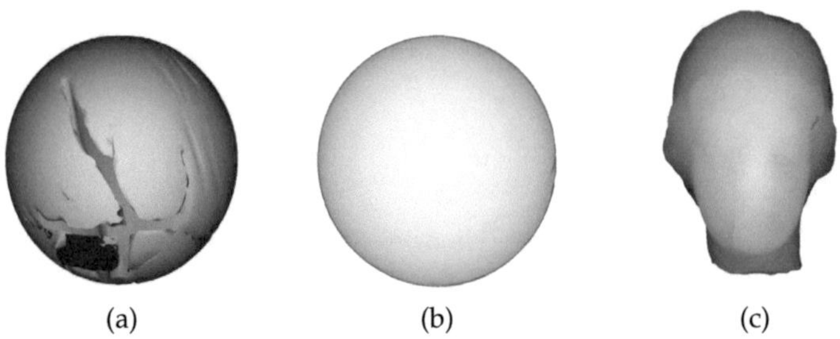

Fig. 7. The models obtained using the original SOM algorithm.

4, are called "Animal" and "Cylinderman". Since all the target surfaces are represented by parametric functions, the control points needed to represent each surface are calculated from the functions. Table 1 shows the number of vertices and faces of the initial SDMs, and the number of control points together with the computational time for each projection.

The top row in Fig. 5 shows the initial SDMs, while the bottom row displays the projected models. In each of these figures, the normal of the initial SDM is mapped onto the final SDM and its shape approximates the target surface. Amongst these experiments, the projection of the "armadillo" model onto the Cylinderman proved to be the most time-consuming because of the complex shapes. Fig. 6 shows the facial part of the projected armadillo in shading and wireframe representations. Fig. 6(a) displays an enlarged view of the model shown in Fig. 5(c), while the shading model shown in Fig. 6(b) is obtained using normals of the final SDM. The SDM can be projected onto the target surface smoothly without foldovers. It is clear from these results that our method can project mesh models onto various kinds of mapping surfaces in a unified framework compared with previous works that required mapping functions.

Next, we compare our proposed method to that which applies the original SOM algorithm to an SDM deformation. We refer to the latter method as the comparison method. The pig model used in the first experiment is projected onto a spherical surface using the comparison method. Fig. 7(a) is the shading model obtained from the comparison method. The model is projected onto a limited area of the target surface. Some unnatural edges are seen on the model surface. By contrast, Fig. 7(b) is the shading model given in Fig. 5(a). Since the SDM deformation introduces certain processes to avoid the collapse problem, the SDM can be projected onto the target surface while not containing any foldover areas. Next, we fit a spherical surface model as an SDM to the female model 'Igea' as shown in Fig. 4(c). The purpose of the SOM algorithm is to represent the distribution of the control points by the SOM. Therefore, in the comparison

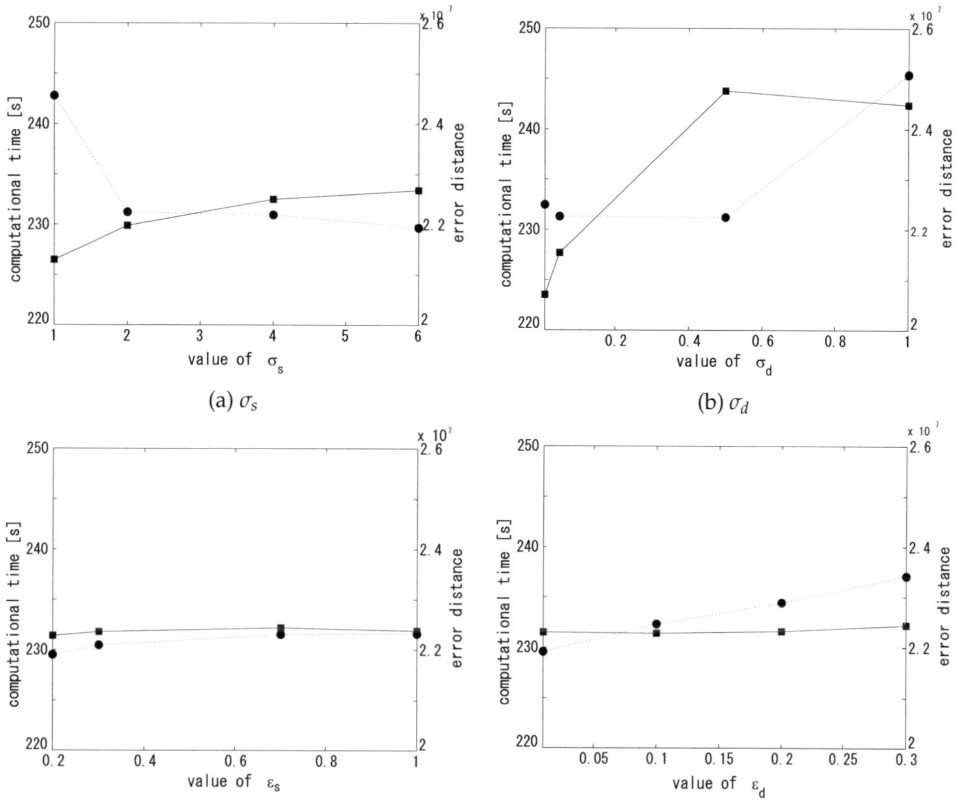

(c) ϵ_s (d) ϵ_d

Fig. 8. Comparison of the computational time and the error distance in Eq.(3) in the SDM deformation by changing the parameters: (a)σ_s, (b)σ_d, (c)ϵ_s and (d)ϵ_d.

method, the final SDM as shown in Fig. 7(c) is blurred and incomplete. Fig. 5(e) displays the model obtained using our proposed method. According to these figures, our method can approximate the original shape.

With reference to the parameters in the SDM deformation, we verified the sensitivity of our method to these parameters. This verification uses the example mapping from a spherical surface as the initial SDM to the Igea as the target surface in Fig. 5 (e). In this experiment, the four main parameters σ_s, σ_d, ϵ_s and ϵ_d are used, and their values in Eq.(21) are regarded as the original ones. Only one parameter is set to a value selected from the following sets:

$$\sigma_s = \{1.0, 2.0, 4.0, 6.0\}, \qquad \sigma_d = \{0.01, 0.05, 0.5, 1.0\},$$
$$\epsilon_s = \{0.2, 0.3, 0.7, 1.0\}, \qquad \epsilon_d = \{0.01, 0.1, 0.2, 0.3\}, \tag{22}$$

while the other parameters use the original values. The SDM deformation is performed by using the various parameter sets. Fig. 8 shows the computational time and the error distance between the final SDM and the target surface in Eq.(3) when changing each parameter. In this figure, the computational time and the error are represented by a straight line and a dotted one. The computational time and the error using the original values of the parameters are 231.4 [sec] and 2.2×10^{-7}. Noting these results, the accuracy of all the final SDMs is good regardless of the settings of the parameters. On the other hand, the computational time and the error tend to increase in the SDM deformation using the parameters so that the ratio σ_d/σ_s or ϵ_d/ϵ_s is large. The reason for this is that the parameters leads to the retention of a large adaptation rate or the large learning rate during the deformation process, and to a slow convergence of the SDM deformation.

In our experiments, we determined the parameters through some preliminary experimental work. The SDM deformation is based on the SOM algorithm, which contains the parameters such as the learning rate in Eq.(9) and the neighborhood radius in Eq.(11). However, there is no theoretical framework for the optimal selection of the parameters included in the SOM algorithm. For optimal selection, one way is to incorporate the Bayesian framework into the SOM algorithm (Bishop et al., 1998; Utsugi, 1996; 1997). This incorporation enables us to regard the SOM algorithm as an estimating algorithm for the Gaussian mixture model. Given the input data, self-organizing mapping is performed by estimating a probability distribution, generating the data by using the expectation-maximization algorithm. The optimal hyperparameters in the model can be estimated from the data. Our future work will include the extension of the SDM using the Bayesian framework.

As shown in Table 1, the deformations of the SDMs with complex shapes require more computational time than other SDM deformations. Since the model obtained by the SDM tends to include a foldover, the SDM deformation is restarted several times to remove the foldover from the SDM. Our future work includes the development of a method to reduce the computational time of the SDM deformation.

4.2 Control of deforming SDM

In Section 3.4, we noted some of the advantages of the SDM deformation. This experiment was conducted to verify the possibility of controlling the SDM deformation. To begin with, we acquired facial range data from 29 males using a range finder. The range data of each face was composed of about 85,000 points, and the points were used directly as control points. A model of each face was obtained by fitting a spherical SDM to the facial range data. Then, we set the single constraint that certain specific feature vertices of the SDM always moved towards their corresponding control points one by one. In practice, we manually chose 12 vertices in the SDM. These are illustrated in Fig. 9(a) as black points. We also selected 12 control points by hand from the facial range data as shown in Fig. 9(a). If one of these control points was chosen in step 3 of the SDM deformation algorithm, its corresponding vertex was automatically determined as the winner vertex.

Fig. 9(b)-(d) shows the process of deforming the sphere under the constraint, while Fig. 9(d) shows the final model. Fig. 9(e) shows another facial model generated by deforming the SDM without the constraint. Observation of these figures show that the final model recovers the shape of the face while the twelve feature vertices in the final model are located at their target points. The 29 face models are obtained under the above constraint. Since the models obtained contain the same number of vertices and the same topological information, we can easily find

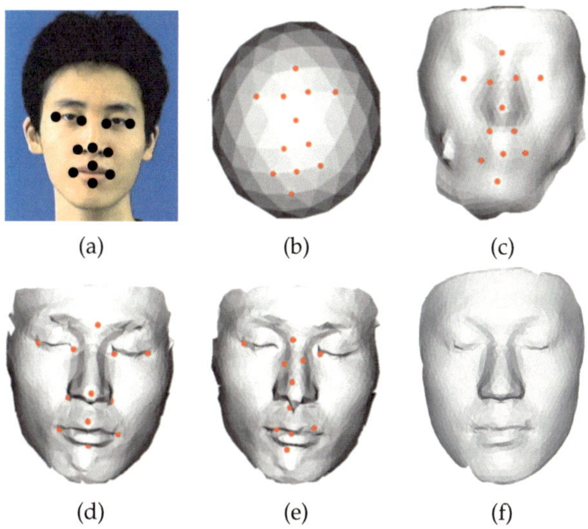

Fig. 9. Control of deforming SDM: (a) the target points of a male face on a photographic image; (b-d) the process of deforming the SDM under the constraint that some vertices of the SDM correspond to control points on the target surface; (e) the facial surface recovered from spherical mesh model without the constraint; (f) the average model of 29 faces. Adapted from the article (Morooka et al., 2007). Copyright(c)2007 IEICE.

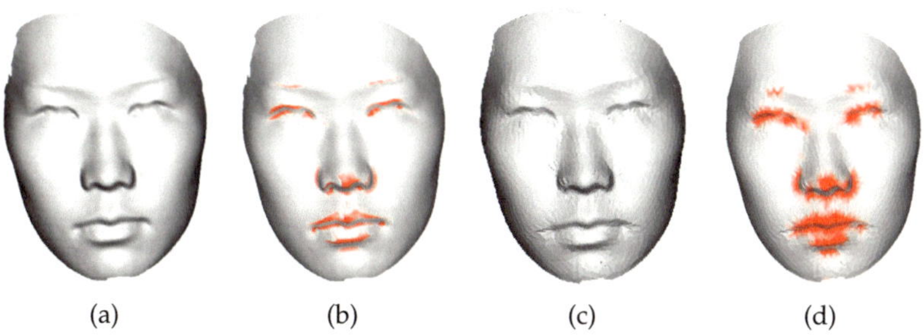

Fig. 10. Control of deforming SDM by changing the selection probability of control points.

a structural correspondence between any two facial models. This correspondence is useful to computer vision and computer graphics applications. As an example of an application, we generate the average model of male faces by computing the average position of each vertex with the same label. Fig. 9(f) shows the average facial mesh model.

Also the SDM deformation can be controlled by changing the selection possibility of the control points. In this experiment, a spherical surface and a female face as shown in Fig. 10(a) are used as the initial SDM and target surface, respectively. The target surface is resampled so that the control points are distributed uniformly. From Eq.(19), we determine the selection possibility of the control point. The determination uses the average curvature at the control point $\boldsymbol{p}$ as the curvature $C(\boldsymbol{p})$ in Eq.(19). The average curvature is computed by the method in (Hameiri et al., 2002). Fig. 10(b) shows the visualization of the high average curvature of the face. In particular, the eyes, nose, and mouth areas contain points with high curvatures.

After the SDM deformation, the final SDM is obtained as shown in Fig. 10(c). The distribution of the vertices is represented by the average distance A_i between each vertex $\boldsymbol{v}_i$ and its 1-ring neighbors. When many vertices are intensively collected in certain regions, the average distance between the vertices is small. On the other hand, the average distance is large when regions contain a small number of vertices. Using the average distance, the red color R_i of the vertex $\boldsymbol{v}_i$ is assigned by

$$R_i = \begin{cases} (A_i - A_{min})/(A_{max} - A_{min}) & : (A_i < \text{threshold}) \\ 0 & : (\text{otherwise}), \end{cases} \tag{23}$$

where A_{min} and A_{max} are, respectively, the minimum and maximum average distances between the vertices whose A_i is less than a given threshold. Fig. 10(c) shows the final SDM, while Fig. 10(d) shows the visualization of the distribution of the vertices in the final SDM. Comparing Figs.10(b)-(d), the SDM deformation can recover the target surface while locating many vertices in the regions with high curvatures by controlling the selection possibilities of the vertices.

5. Conclusion

This paper proposed a method for fitting mesh models to a given surface using the Self-organizing Deformable Model (SDM). The basic idea behind the SDM is the combination of competitive learning and energy minimization. Although the SDM and the target surface must have the same topological type, there are few other constraints when using the SDM. Our SDM can be applied to various target surfaces, whereas traditional methods using mapping functions only deal with a specific target surface. Furthermore, compared with deformable models based on energy minimization, our proposed method enables us to control the SDM deformation easily by changing the ways in which control points are chosen and a winner vertex is determined. The experimental results show that our SDM is a powerful tool for use in various fields in computer vision and computer graphics. For example, the SDM enables us to establish the correspondence between two mesh models by mapping them onto a common target surface. We are currently developing SDM-based applications.

6. Acknowledgment

This work was supported by a Grant-in-Aid for Scientific Research(C) (No. 23500244) of The Ministry of Education, Culture, Sports, Science, and Technology, Japan.

7. References

Allen, B.; Curless, B.; & Popović, Z. (2003). The space of human body shapes: reconstruction and parameterization from range scans, *Proc. SIGGRAPH '03*, pp.587–594, 2003.

Barhak, J.; & Fischer, A. (2001). Parameterization and reconstruction from 3D scattered points based on neural network and PDE techniques, *IEEE Transactions on Visualization and Computer Graphics*, vol.7, no.1, pp.1–16, 2001.

Bishop, C.M.; Svensén, M.; & Williams, C.K.I. (1998). GTM : the generative topographic mapping, *Neural Computation*, vol.10, no.1, pp.215–235, 1998.

Blanz, V.; Mehl, A.; Vetter, T.; & Seidel, H.P. (2004). A statistical method for robust 3d surface reconstruction from sparse data, *Proc. of the 3D Data Processing, Visualization, and Transmission*, pp.293–300, 2004.

Cignoni, P.; Rocchini, C.; & Scopigno, R. (1998). Metro: Measuring error on simplified surfaces, *Computer Graphics Forum*, vol.17, no.2, pp.167–174, 1998.

Duan, Y.; & Qin, H. (2004). A subdivision-based deformable model for surface reconstruction of unknown topology, *Graphcal Models*, 66(4), 181–202 (2004)

Duda, R.O.; Hart, P.E.; & Stork, D.G. (2000). *Pattern Classification (2nd Edition)*, Wiley-Interscience.

Eck, M.; DeRose, T.; Duchamp, T.; Hoppe, H.; Lounsbery, M.; & Stuetzle, W. (1995). Multiresolution analysis of arbitrary meshes, *Proc. SIGGRAPH '95*, vol. 29, pp. 173–182, 1995.

Floater, M.; & Hormann, K. (2003). Recent advances in surface parameterization, *Multiresolution in Geometric Modeling 2003*, pp. 259–284, 2003.

Fritzke, B. (1997). Some competitive learning methods, 1997.

Gibson, S.; & Mirtich, B. (1997). A survey of deformable modeling in computer graphics, *Technical Report TR97-19*, Mitsubishi Electric Research Lab. (1997)

Hameiri, E.; & Shimshoni, I. (2002). Estimating the Principal Curvatures and the Darboux Frame from Real 3D Range Data, *Proc. 3DPVT 2002*, pp. 258–267, 2002.

Ivrissimtzis, I.; Lee, Y.; Lee, S.; Jeong, W.K.; & Seidel, H.P. (2004). Neural mesh ensembles, *Proc. Int. Symp. on 3DPVT*, pp. 308–315, 2004.

Ivrissimtzis, I.P.; Jeong, W.K.; & Seidel, H.P. (2003). Using growing cell structures for surface reconstruction, *Shape Modeling International 2003*, pp. 78–88, 2003.

Ju, T.; Schaefer, S. & Warren, J. (2005). Mean value coordinates for closed triangular meshes, *ACM Trans. Graph.*, vol. 24, no. 3, pp. 561–566, 2005.

Kavan, L.; & Zara, J. (2005). Spherical blend skinning: a real-time deformation of articulated models, *Proc. the 2005 symposium on Interactive 3D graphics and games*, pp. 9–16, 2005.

Kohonen, T. (2001). *Self-Organizing Maps*, Springer-Verlag New York, Inc., Secaucus, NJ, USA, 2001.

Kraevoy, V.; & Sheffer, (2004). A. Cross-parameterization and compatible remeshing of 3D models, *Proc. SIGGRAPH '04*, pp. 861–869, 2004.

Kun, Y.; Zhou, K.; Xu, D.; Shi, X.; Bao, H.; Guo, B.; & Shum, H.Y. (2004). Mesh editing with Poisson-based gradient field manipulation, *Proc. SIGGRAPH '04*, pp. 644–651, 2004.

Kurazume, R.; Nakamura, K.; Okada, T.; Sato, Y.; Sugano, N.; Koyama, T.; Iwashita, Y.; & Hasegawa, T. (2007). 3D reconstruction of a femoral shape using a parametric model and two 2d fluoroscopic images, *Proc. ICRA'07*, pp. 3002–3008, 2007.

Lachaud, J.O.; & Montanvert, A. (1999). Deformable meshes with automated topology changes for coarse-to-fine 3d surface extraction, *Medical Image Analysis*, vol. 3, no. 2, pp. 187–207, 1999.

Lee, A.W.F.; Sweldens, W.; Schröder, P.; Cowsar, L.; & Dobkin, D. (1998). MAPS: Multiresolution adaptive parameterization of surfaces, *Proc. SIGGRAPH '98*, pp. 95–104, 1998.

Liou, C.Y.; & Kuo, Y.T. (2005). Conformal self-organizing map for a genus-zero manifold, *The Visual Computer*, vol. 21, no. 5, pp. 340–353 , 2005.

Lipman, Y.; Sorkine, O.; Alexa, M.; Cohen-Or, D.; Levin, D.; Rössl, C.; & Seidel, H.P. (2005). Laplacian framework for interactive mesh editing, *International Journal of Shape Modeling*, vol. 11, no. 1, pp. 43–62 , 2005.

McInerney, T.; & Terzopoulos, D. (2000). T-snakes: Topology adaptive snakes, *Medical Image Analysis*, vol. 4, no. 2, pp. 73–91, 2000.

Morooka, K.; & Nagahashi, H. (2005). Self-organizing Deformable Model : A New Method for Fitting Mesh Model to Given Object Surface, *Proc. of Int. Symp. Visual Computing*, pp. 151–158, 2005.

Morooka, K.; Matsui, S.; & Nagahashi, H. (2007). Self-organizing Deformable Model : A New Method for Projecting Mesh Model of 3D Object onto Target Surface, *IEICE Transactions on Information and Systems (Japanese Edition)*, vol. J90-D, no. 3, pp.908–917, 2007.

Noh, J.Y.; & Neumann, U. (2001). Expression cloning, *Proc. SIGGRAPH '01*, pp. 277–288, 2001.

Schreiner, J.; Asirvatham, A.; Praun, E.; & Hoppe, H. (2004). Inter-surface mapping, *Proc. SIGGRAPH '04*, pp. 870–877, 2004.

Sederberg, T. W.; & Parry, S. R. (1986). Free-form deformation of solid geometric models, *Proc. SIGGRAPH '86*, pp. 151–160, 1986.

Sumner, R.W.; & Popovic, J. (2004). Deformation transfer for triangle meshes. *Proc. SIGGRAPH '04*, pp. 399–405, 2004.

Surazhsky, V.; Surazhsky, T.; Kirsanov, D.; Gortler, S.; & Hoppe, H. (2005). Fast exact and approximate geodesics on meshes, *Proc. SIGGRAPH '05*, pp. 553–560, 2005.

Tarini, M.; Hormann, K.; Cignoni, P.; & Montani, C. (2004). Polycube-maps, *Proc. SIGGRAPH '04*, pp. 853–860, 2004.

Utsugi, U. (1996). Topology selection for self-organizing maps, *Network: Computation in Neural Systems*, vol. 7, no. 4, pp. 727–740, 1996.

Utsugi, U. (1997). Hyperparameter selection for self-organizing maps, *Neural Computation*, vol. 9, no. 3, pp. 623–635, 1997.

Yu, Y. (1999). Surface reconstruction from unorganized points using self-organizing neural networks, *Proc. IEEE Visualization '99*, pp. 61–64, 1999.

Zayer, R.; Rössl, C.; Karni, Z.; & Seidel, H.P. (2005). Harmonic guidance for surface deformation, *Comput. Graph. Forum*, pp. 601–609, 2005.

3

Bounding Volume Hierarchies for Collision Detection

Hamzah Asyrani Sulaiman[1] and Abdullah Bade[2]
[1]University Teknikal Malaysia Melaka, Durian Tunggal, Melaka,
[2]University Malaysia Sabah, Kota Kinabalu, Sabah,
Malaysia

1. Introduction

In virtual environment world, performing collision detection between various 3D objects requires sophisticated steps to be followed in order to properly visualize their effect. It is challenging due to the fact that multiple objects undergo various motion depending on the application's genre. It is however an essential challenge to be resolved since it's many use in the computer animation, simulation and robotic industry. Thus, object intersection between rigid bodies has become one of the most important areas in order to bring realism to simulation and animation.

Rigid bodies stand for geometric models that are fixed and assumed to remain static until there is some force being applied on it. In collision detection case, when two geometric models have collided, the system would notice that both objects couldn't change it dimensions and sizes. Any deformation to rigid bodies is neglected because of this behaviour and the collisions only affect location or movement of both objects. Since in the early era of 3D simulation and animation, problems prevailed in detecting object interference parts, and numerous attempts by researchers have been made to find the solution of the collision detection between rigid bodies. Baraff has made one of the earliest researches concerning detecting object interference between rigid bodies (Baraff, 1989).

Later in 1993, M.C. Lin conducted a research of detecting object interference between two rigid bodies. M.C. Lin defined that there are two types of contact between rigid bodies that could be identified. They are tangential collision and boundary collision (Lin, 1994). Tangential collision happens when there is intersection between two surfaces at 90 degrees at geometric contact point. It means that the collision happens either from 90 degrees from above, bottom, right or left surfaces of corresponding polygons. Meanwhile boundary collision occurred when there is one object wants to check for potential collision from inside the object boundary. For example, a circle has it owns boundary made of certain radius. If one point inside this radius has intersected with another circle, then boundary collision has occurred. (Lin, 1994)

Whilst, Redon explained that there are two common types of performing collision detection between rigid bodies namely discrete collision detection (DCD) and continuous collision detection (CDC) (Redon et al., 2002). DCD is performed by sampling the object motion towards the object that is going to be intersected and detect the object interpenetrations (Tu and Yu, 2009, Rocha and Maria Andre'ia Formico, 2008, Kockara, 2007, Bade et al., 2006, Klosowski et al., 1998, Baciu, 1998, Cohen et al., 1995, Garcia-Alonso et al., 1994, Cohen et al., 1994, Gilbert and Foo, 1990, Baraff, 1990). DCD is the approach that has been used by researchers to perform collision detection in term of speed. CDC, on the other hand, computes from the first time of contact when object collided. It is much slower in comparison to DCD method because CCD focuses on accuracy of collision detection.

In most 3D applications, DCD is the most useful compared to CCD. The differences between these two are on their manipulation of time and object movement. DCD is preferred because of its simplicity and fast collision detection compared to the CCD algorithm. DCD checks the intersection within a fix time instant while CCD algorithm uses the object trajectory. As checking for object trajectory requires future object location to be known in very small time frames, the CCD algorithm cannot be performed as fast as DCD algorithm. However, CCD is useful for accurate collision detection where high precision is needed. It also has a small false positive (collision miss) compared to the DCD algorithm. As an example, an application such as clothes, medical, hair or any deformable bodies' simulation requires collision of the object to be detected at high precision state where it involves accurate collision detection algorithm. Fast collision detection algorithm on the other hand is useful for computer games development where the response of potential colliding objects need to be known as fast as possible.

In DCD algorithm, hierarchical representation for object is commonly used (Tu and Yu, 2009, Larsson, 2009, Chang et al., 2008, Liu et al., 2007, Nguyen, 2006). By enveloping the object in virtual environment with hierarchical representation, the detection time could be reduced by performing collision checking for specific node in hierarchical tree. Bounding-Volume Hierarchies (BVH) is the most fashionable approach used by researchers to perform collision checking. It represents the object into hierarchical manners where each node contains single Bounding-Volume (BV) that enclosed set of triangles (Larsson and Akenine-Moller, 2008, Sobottka and Weber, 2005, Chang et al., 2008, Liu et al., 2007).

Figure 1 illustrates the different between CCD and DCD algorithm.

In order to perform fast DCD approach, BVH itself must be able to have very efficient node so the traversal algorithm for the BVH could traverse as fast as possible avoiding any unnecessary node that does not involve in collision. Thus, researchers has come out with solution by using heuristic, it could produces balance BVH tree where until specific level of BVH tree. Once the balance BVH tree had reached, the primitive-primitive testing inside leaf nodes will be tested against another BVH tree. However, it still suffers from limitation of performing fast response to the collision detection due to balance level that had been generated is not well-organized where some nodes contains unbalance set of triangles or size of BV.

2. Hierarchical approaches

Virtual environment is composed of many objects that could be static or in motion, where each objects may have thousands of primitives. Testing object interference between these primitives could become troublesome as the number of pair intersection tests that need to be performed is exploding (Bergen, 2004). Hence, spatial data structures is becoming one of the

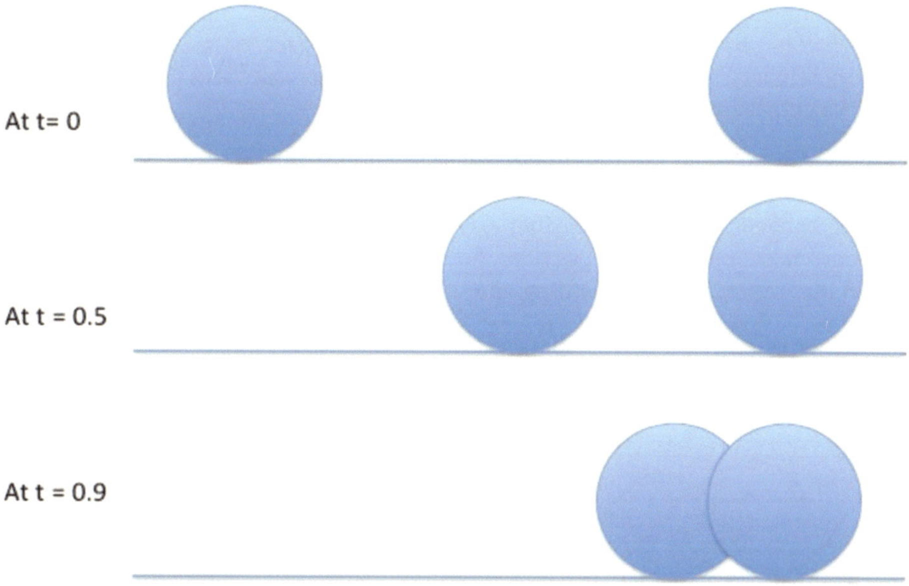

(a)

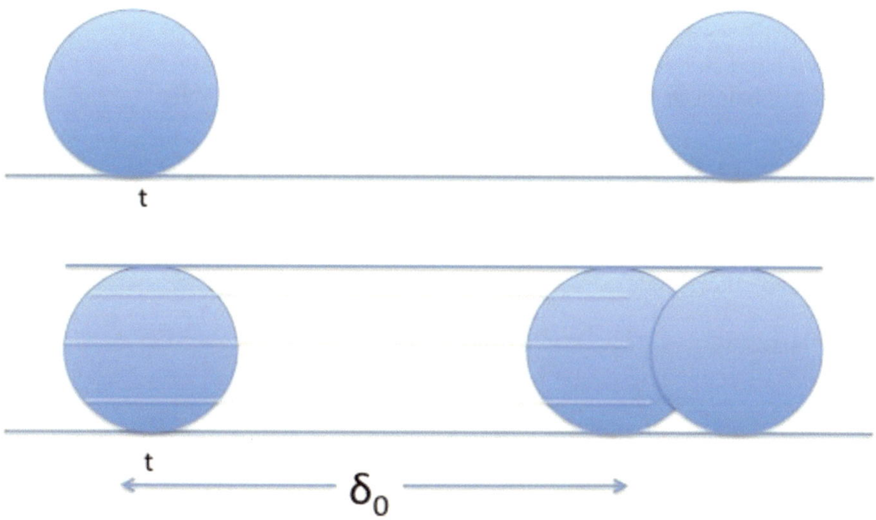

(b)

Fig. 1. (a) Discrete Collision Detection - During the detection, object might be sampling for example, every 0.1 seconds. While (b) Continuous Collision Detection - During the detection, every object movement is calculated in order to find the accurate time of contact.

efficient solution for accelerating collision detection checks in massive environments (Bergen, 2004). According to (Bergen, 2004) for n objects there are $\binom{n}{2}=\frac{1}{2}n(n-1)$ potentially collided pairs. There are two types of spatial data structures being used for collision detection: spatial division and BVH. Spatial partitioning divides the spaces of virtual environment and causes the environment to be divided into cells while BVH only divides each object that exists in virtual environment. However for spatial partitioning case, when it comes to large-scaled simulation, the tree depth increases and it will slow down the performance of the simulation.

Furthermore, since spatial partitioning divide the cell into smaller cells, it cannot cover the object very tightly as bounding-volume could. Thus, the accuracy of detecting object interference between environments that use spatial partitioning might decrease since it might report false positive intersection. Bounding-volume hierarchy provides a better solution to the researchers by providing simpler and tighter tree hierarchy. Figure 2 depicts the BVH tree.

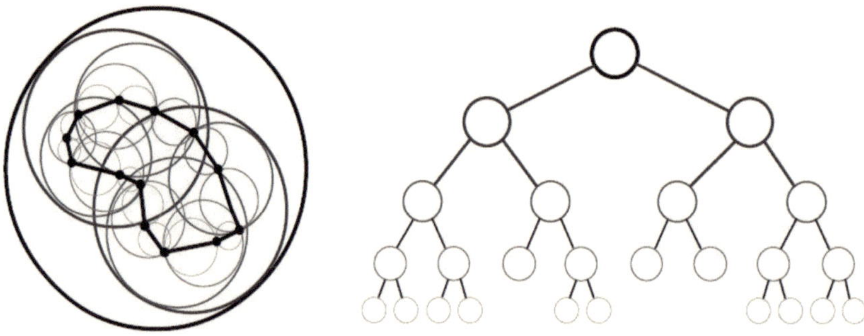

Fig. 2. The left hand side image shows a BVH with Sphere BV while on the right hand side image, shows unbalanced hierarchical form using binary type hierarchy

2.1 Hierarchy characteristics

Figure 3 describes in general of hierarchical tree characteristic. Haverkort suggested useful characteristics of hierarchy tree using bounding-volumes but also suitable for any kind of hierarchical (Haverkort, 2004).

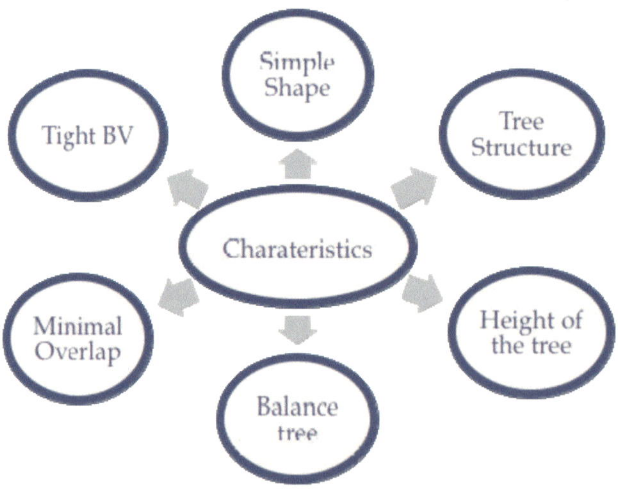

Fig. 3. Hierarchical Tree characteristics

As illustrated in Figure 3, the main important attribute is to find a suitable bounding-volume (BV) for the targeted application. If the application requires an accurate collision detection scheme especially for medical and fluid simulation, then tight BV is needed. For computer games development and fast response simulation, simple and low count surfaces BV is the most suitable. Examples of them include the Axis-Aligned Bounding-Box (AABB), Oriented Bounding-Box (OBB), and Sphere. This is due to the reason that when intersection occurs, it first checks for the intersection points between bounding volume without calculating the complex primitives in geometric models. Then, when there is an intersection between top-level bounding-volume (root of hierarchy), further checks between children nodes of hierarchy will be conducted down through the tree until the correct intersection is found. However, there is trade-off between simple and tight bounding-volume. Simple bounding-volume seems to perform faster intersection test while tight bounding-volume goes for the accuracy but slow intersection test.

The structure of the tree is also one of the important elements in tree building since it determines the speed of the tree traversal when collision needs to check part of the primitives bounded by the BV. For example, the binary-type tree is faster than quad-type tree in term of reaching the bottom of the tree. The binary-type tree only needs to check for two nodes that are either left or right node compared to the quad-type tree that needs to checks four nodes. But in term of the accuracy, sometimes it depends on the intersection itself as quad-type tree can spend less time than binary-type tree if the quad-tree managed to find the collision at earlier level of the tree hierarchy. The number of primitives reside in the nodes also depends on well-organized algorithm that is used to split up the upper node into several nodes (depends again on the type of the tree).

It also needs to be determine the height of the tree by own algorithm as the process can be lengthy and could also ultimately leads to infinite tree height (when set of triangle failed to split themselves and repeat the process all over again). Faster traversal can be achieved if the algorithm used to split up the tree is successful at dividing the nodes into certain level (less is good) and carried out primitives-primitives testing or one BV one triangle testing. One BV one-triangle testing is the primitive checking using the BV itself. Whereas the triangle testing could lead to a faster collision checking but could also bring false positive result if the BV is not a suitable one. Faster traversal from root to specific node can be achieved if the height of the hierarchy is small but it might not always be sufficient.

Creating a balance tree hierarchy for the object is an important task for collision detection in order to improve result speed. As the height of the tree is getting deeper and longer, the tree must be able to well balance on it as it affects the traversal processes. Giving an example of binary-tree traversal system when the left node is deeper than the other one (right node), it will slow down the process of collision checking at the particular nodes. Thus it is essential that the tree hierarchy is kept balanced out with respect to nodes, volume and density.

The design and the construction of the hierarchy tree must also have minimal overlap between its volumes. This is to make sure that the process of tree traversal does not check for the same intersection between nodes multiple times. The last characteristic is to use appropriate tight BV with an appropriate hierarchy tree type for our application. Tight BV is used for accurate collision checking between other objects that are also bounded by the tight BV. K-Dop, Elipsoid, and Convex Hull are the examples of the BV that can tightly bounded the object but mainly used for the accurate collision detection.

2.2 Bounding-volume

Generally in any simulation, computation is very high when detecting interference between two rigid bodies. For example, a car model with 10,000 polygons surface hit the building that has 40 polygons surface is waiting for signal that object has been intersected. Each polygon surface will be checked one by one to find which parts of the car and the building has come into intersection. Even though the computer may be able to calculate in milliseconds, but imagine if the simulation environment consists of multiple objects that each of them has tens of thousands polygon surfaces. So, one of the way to overcome this is by implementing the bounding-volume.

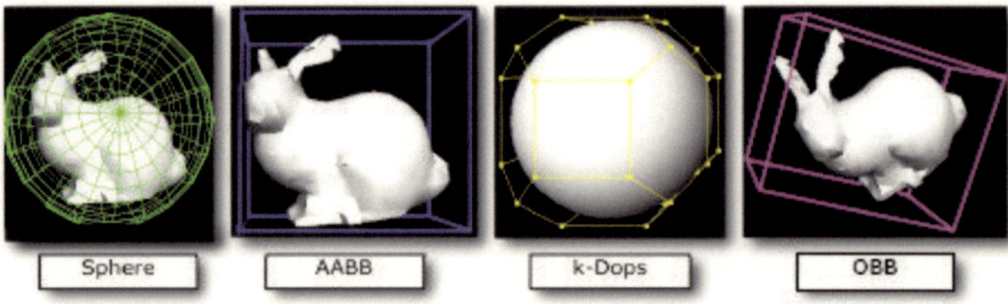

Fig. 4. Common Bounding Volume in previous researches (Suaib et al., 2008, Bade et al., 2006).

The purpose of using BV is to reduce the computational cost to detect object interference. If the object performs primitive-primitive testing without applying BV, it could consume longer time, as it needs to check each triangle with other object triangle set. However, time to check for each collision can be reduced through enveloping highly complex object with BV. Instead of using single BV, BVH could help performing collision detection better than a single BV. BVH provides a hierarchical representation that could split the single BV into certain level before performing primitive-primitive testing for accurate collision detection. It can also be used for fast collision detection method by stopping at certain level using stopping function or criteria and approximately response to the collision as object that has been collided. It depends heavily on what kind of application that been developed as some application prefers speed and others accuracy.

At present time, there are several famous bounding volumes such as spheres (Weller and Zachmann, 2009, Madera et al., 2009, Chang et al., 2009, Rocha and Maria Andre'ia Formico, 2008, Larsson et al., 2007, Spillmann et al., 2007, Benitez et al., 2005, Gareth and Carol, 2004, Bradshaw and O'Sullivan, 2002), Axis Aligned Bounding Box (AABB) (Tu and Yu, 2009, Zhang and Kim, 2007, Weller et al., 2006), Oriented Bounding Box (OBB) (Tu and Yu, 2009, Chang et al., 2009, Gottschalk et al., 1996), Discrete Oriented Polytope (k-DOP) [3], new type of bounding volume; Oriented Convex Polyhedra (Suaib et al., 2008, Bade et al., 2006), and hybrid combination bounding volume (Tu and Yu, 2009, Kockara, 2007). Most large scale 3D simulations used bounding box because it iss simple, require small space of storage, fast response of collision, and easy to implement (Lin and Manocha, 2004). Figure 4 illustrates most commonly used bounding volume.

2.3 Hierarchical tree building strategies

There are three different ways to construct a tree: top down, bottom up, or insertion method. Top down methods can be presented as a growing tree of two or more subsets while the bottom up grouped the subsets to form internal node until they becomes root node. Insertion methods can be implemented by inserting one object at one time into the tree. Each type has its own unique characteristic as shown Figure 5.

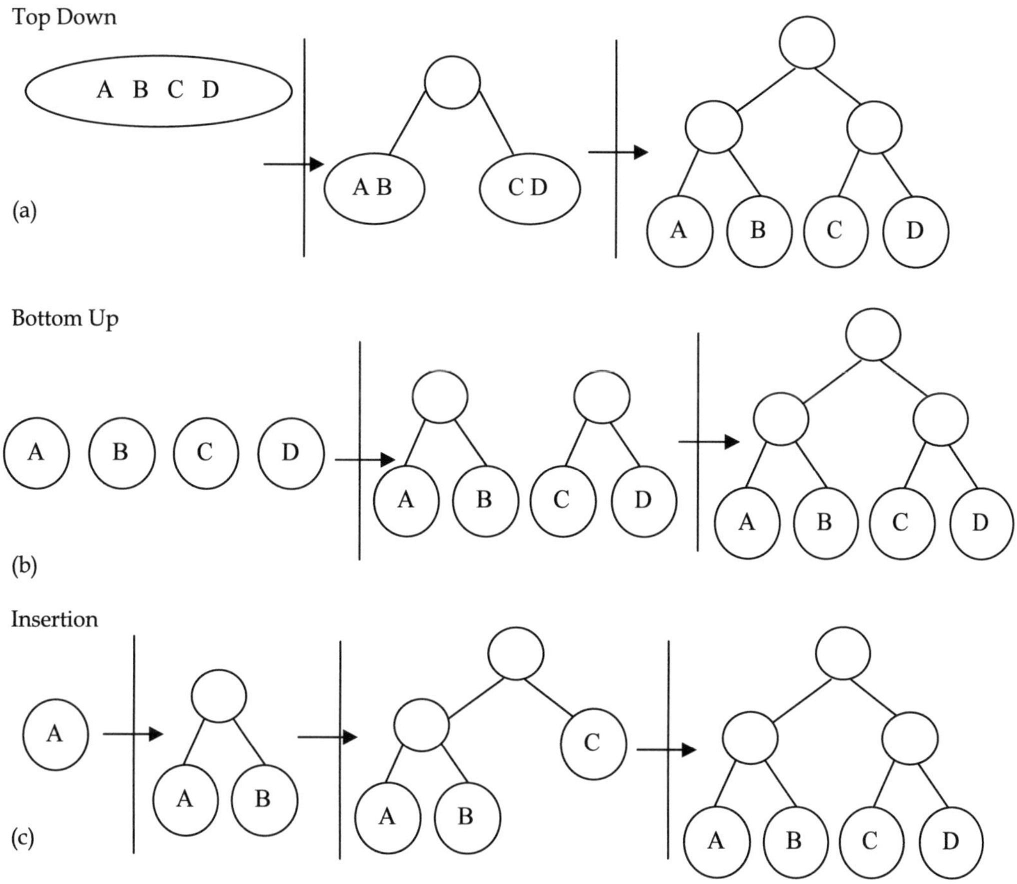

Fig. 5. Hierarchy tree based of four objects using (a) top-down, (b) bottom-up, and (c) insertion construction (Ericson, 2004).

Among the three, top-down approach is the most popular technique to be used to construct hierarchy tree. (Gottschalk, 2000, Gottschalk et al., 1996) proposed an OBB-tree while (Tu and Yu, 2009) constructed binary AABB BVH that use top-down hierarchy where each set of primitives is tightly bounded with bounding-volume. However, depending on the application type, they might not always produce the best result. From Figure 5, top-down approach seems to fully cover the objects with large bounding-volume for example sphere. Then, it is recursively partitioned into two separate parts that has smaller spheres, that is connected to the root of the hierarchy. These two separate parts will then keep partitioning until a particular stopping criteria is reached or only a single primitive is available. Top-down approach commonly use splitting algorithm in order to find the correct splitting of the tree.

In contrary, bottom up approach are more complicated to put into as it has slower construction time but it is efficient in producing the best tree (Omohundro, 1989). From Figure 5, each primitive will be bounded with the smallest bounding-volume. Then, these volumes will be grouped together to perform the upper nodes called leaf nodes. However, from this point, some merging criterion or clustering rule must be followed in order to merge two or more leaf nodes into parent nodes. Afterward, these nodes will be enclosed with a bounding-volume and replace the original set of nodes. This procedure will continue until a single bounding-volume is left that will become root of the hierarchy tree. Bottom-up approach regularly use merging algorithm when merging two or more leaf nodes into parent nodes.

The third hierarchy type is the insertion method or incremental method. Starting from an empty tree, single primitive will be inserted one by one at a time by finding the insertion location. It depends fully on the cost metric. Incremental insertion algorithm as presented (Goldsmith and Salmon, 1987) in Figure 6 was the first algorithm to construct incremental hierarchy tree. It used cost function to control the insertion or primitives into hierarchy tree. First the algorithm estimates the cost of inserting primitives at different places in the hierarchy, and then the algorithm automatically picks the lowest cost and the cheapest place to insert primitives into tree. There are three rules that need to be followed when a primitive needs to be inserted into as tree (Goldsmith and Salmon, 1987) :-

1. *p* can become the child of parent *o*
2. *p* can be combined with another *q* of a group *o* to establish new group called *o′* which automatically becomes child of *o*.
3. *p* can becomes child of parent *o′* of a group *o* recursively. Then, partially formed hierarchy is traversed until either case 1 or 2 is reached.

However, the problem of this method is that it can become worst as it depends on the insertion order of the nodes. Various insertion methods can be designed but it is challenging to find the best one. Apart from that, a well-balanced hierarchy tree can become a totally an unbalanced tree (worst case) if no proper insertion algorithm is used.

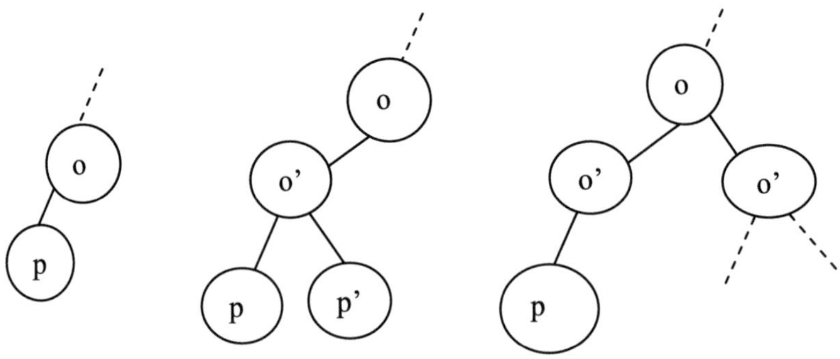

Fig. 6. Rule 1(left) group o has p as a child. Rule 2 (middle) merging two primitives to create new o′. Rule 3(right) recursively insert primitive into parent nodes (Goldsmith and Salmon, 1987).

2.4 Partitioning strategies and splitting algorithm

The simplest way to partition an object is to split the object equally with respect to local coordination axes of the object. The split can be done according to the median-cut algorithm style or several other strategies as follows(Ericson, 2004):-

- *Minimize the sum of the volumes (or surface areas) of the child volumes.* Minimizing the sum of value can effectively minimize the probability of intersection - tightness bounding volume must be used.
- *Minimize the maximum volume (surface area) of the child volumes.* Divides the child volume into equal size by making larger volume as small as possible.
- *Minimize the volume (surface area) of the intersection of the child volumes.* Complex to be implemented as it depends on the tightness of bounding volume.
- *Minimize the separation of the child volumes.* Where each child will be separated, it helps to decrease the probability of both children being traversed at the same time.
- *Divide primitives equally between the child volumes.* Divide the object into two equal parts as mentioned earlier.
- *Hybrid combination of multiple bounding-volumes*

(Müller et al., 1999) had explained the splitting criteria that have been used to partition a set of primitives into two subsets until certain stopping criteria are reached. In this optimized hierarchical method, each object will be divided into several pieces called subsets. By using a certain cost function, it can be ensured that the best possible splitting plane is used. However, the splitting procedure is applied only to the bounded object. This means that no BV will be decomposed into pieces.

Normally, root of the hierarchy is created by sorting each primitive using its centres. A cost function is then used to determine the best possible partitions that split the object volume into two parts or subsets. The splitting parts or subsets constitute the left and right side of the hierarchy. Then splitting algorithm continues to repeat the above process recursively until there is only one big BV enclosing the whole object.

2.4.1 Choosing the splitting point

There are some options available to determine splitting point along the axes (Ericson, 2004) (please see Figure 7):-

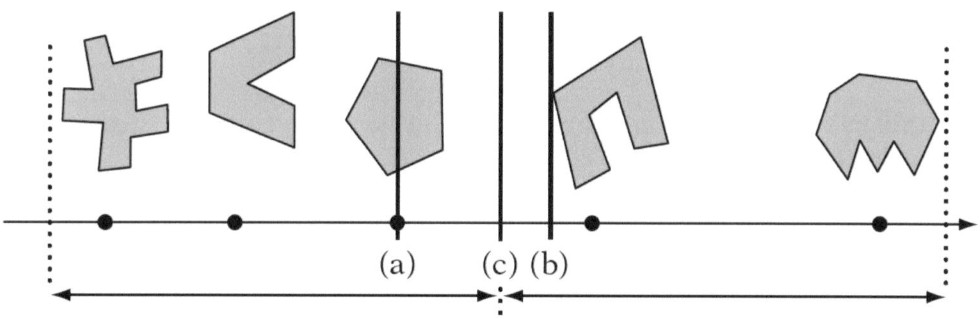

Fig. 7. An example of (a) Object median splitting (b) Object mean splitting (c) Spatial median splitting based on (Ericson, 2004)

- *Median of the centroid coordinates* (object median) - split at the object median (distributed parts) resulting a well-balanced tree.
- *Mean of centroid coordinates* (object mean) - (Klosowski et al., 1998) stated that better performance is obtained using object mean compared to object median. It was claimed that splitting at the object mean gives smaller volume trees.
- *Median of the bounding-volume projection extents* (spatial median) - splitting the volume into two equal parts.

Meanwhile, (Gottschalk et al., 1996) constructed OBB trees using top-down approach. The first procedure is to enclose all primitives by an oriented bounding box, and the recursive partition is made possible by using certain rules. Their subdivision rule proposed as applied to the object is to find the longest axes and the splitting point is determined through an orthogonal plane on one of its axes. Objects are partitioned according to the side of the splitting point but this does not involve the primitive. Figure 8 and 9 depicts the splitting example (Gottschalk et al., 1996).

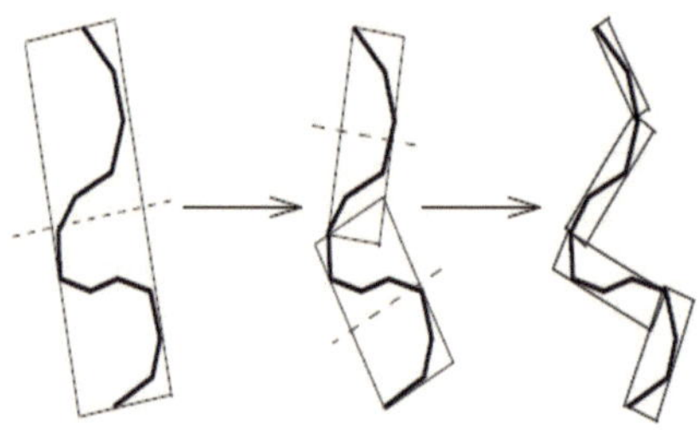

Fig. 8. Splitting along the farthest axis of object bounded with OBB using centre points (Gottschalk et al., 1996).

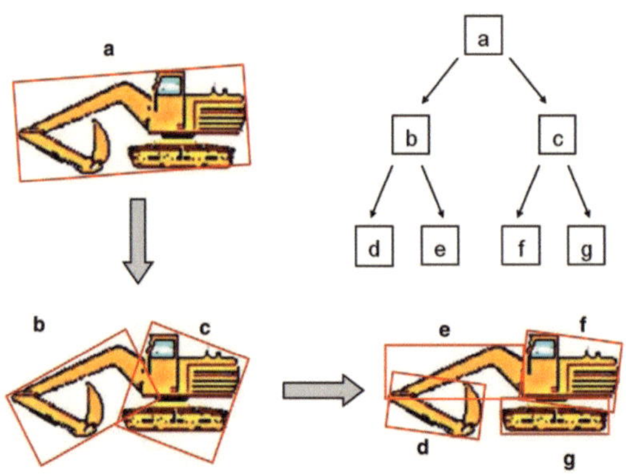

Fig. 9. OBB tree recursively divides the object into two parts using binary tree and top-down approach (Kamat and Martinez, 2007).

2.4.2 Merging algorithm

Merging algorithm has been described in (Erleben et al., 2005), and its implementation can be found from the Open Tissue website. The algorithm started by building graph of the data structure. Nodes in the graph correspond to the primitives and the edges on the other hand correspond to the nearest neighbour relations. Here, an edge in the graph indicates that two

BVH nodes are good candidates to be merged into group. A heuristic function is used to determine collisions and large primitive BVs into one single BV. A collision here means that any edge between two colliding nodes in the graph must be added into the graph. Figure 10 depicts the operation of grouped BVs.

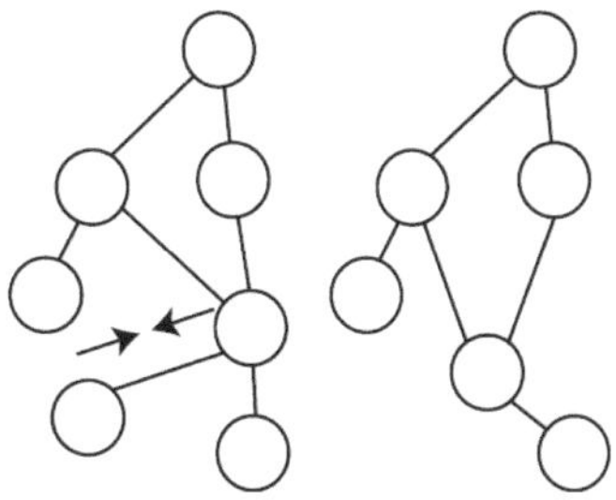

Fig. 10. Edge collapsed and merged into one single node.

3. Bounding volume hierarchies

BVH is simply a tree structure that represents geometric models with specific bounding volumes. It works like a tree that has a root (upper division), a group of leafs (middle division) and a leaf (last division). Each node has it bounding-volumes that cover the children nodes. The main idea of BVH is to build a tree that has a primary and secondary root where each of the secondary nodes is stored as leaf. BVH allows intersection to occur without searching for non-colliding pairs from the hierarchy tree. For example, given two objects with their BVH, when root of the hierarchies do not intersect, the calculation will not be done for both objects. However, when roots of both hierarchies intersect, it will check for intersection between roots of one of the hierarchy's tree with the children of the other hierarchy's tree. In this case, it recursively checks again whether there is intersection between both objects at middle level until the correct intersection is found. Figure 1 previously shows how object is partitioned into several parts. While Figure 11 depicts the basic algorithms for detecting collision between two hierarchies (Kamat and Martinez, 2007, Nguyen, 2006)

```
Beginning at the root nodes of two given trees
1.      Check for intersection between two parent nodes
2.      If there is no intersection between two parents
3.              Then stop and report "no collision"
4.      Else check all children of one node against all
        Children of the other node
5.      If there is intersection between any children
6.              Then If at leaf nodes
7.                      Then report "possible collision"
8.              Else go to Step 4
9.      Else skip and report "no collision"
```

Fig. 11. BVH traversal algorithm proposed by (Nguyen, 2006) for collision detection between two BVH

3.1 BVH construction

The construction of BVH is started by selecting type of the tree. There are multiple types of BVH construction available. One of the most popular tree constructions is binary tree, which has following nodes definition:-

a. **Nodes** - A node may contain specific value or a condition that represents a separate data structure or a tree of its own. In BVH, it contains bounding-volume with their tree ID. Each node may become parent, child or leaf nodes (in computer science tree grow downward where the root is at the top of the tree). The node that produces child nodes is called parent node, superior node or ancestor node. The length starting from root node down to the leaf node determines the height of the tree. The depth of the tree is the length of the path to its root.
b. **Root Nodes** - The topmost node in binary tree is called root node. Actually, root node does not have any parents. It is the starting node where all the operations of the tree will begin normally. Root Node is connected to each child nodes downward by using branch or subtree connector. Branch of subtree connector is one of the important elements that are connecting each node with their parent nodes.
c. **Leaf Nodes** - The bottommost node in binary tree is called the leaf nodes. It does not have any child nodes and mostly contain the last value or conditions. In BVH, it may contain few triangles or maybe one triangle.
d. **Internal Nodes** - The functional node where it has both parent nodes and child nodes. It is not leaf nodes as it still has child nodes and linked by parent node.
e. **Subtree** - A portion of a tree data structure that can be viewed as a complete tree in itself. It represents some other parts of the tree that can be manipulated by user in programming.

Binary approach in top down fashion is selected, as it is the most preferred approach by researchers. It can traverse faster and is very efficient compared to other version of BVH tree. There are few common operations involved in construction and implementation of binary tree for BVH construction. Among others are enumerating all the items, searching for an item which is bounding-volume, removing a whole section of a tree for non-intersected area when performing collision detection (called pruning), traverse down from the root to leaf nodes or leaf nodes to the root, and report any intersected area between two intersected BVH that possible to collide. The construction of BVH is then implemented using C++ language by loading 3D object into the environment. Then, the object vertices is calculated and stored into a temporary location, as it is required for the BVH tree construction.

Next step is to choose a suitable BV for the BVH tree. The purpose of using BV is to reduce the computation cost of detecting object interference. If the object performs primitive-primitive testing without BV, it could consume time, as it needs to check each object triangle with other object triangle set. However, the time to check for each collision can be reduced through enveloping highly complex object with BV. Instead of using single BV, BVH is used to achieve improved collision detection. BVH provides a hierarchical representation that could split the single BV into certain level before performing primitive-primitive testing. It can also be used for fast collision detection method by stopping at certain level using stopping function or criteria and approximately response to the collision as the object has been collided.

At present, there are several well-known BVs such as spheres (Liu et al., 2007), Axis Aligned Bounding Box (AABB) (Zhang and Kim, 2007, Weller et al., 2006, Tu and Yu, 2009), Oriented Bounding Box (OBB) (Chang et al., 2009, Gottschalk et al., 1996, Tu and Yu, 2009), Discrete Oriented Polytope (k-DOP) (Klosowski et al., 1998), Oriented Convex Polyhedra (Bade et al., 2006), and hybrid combination BV (Kockara, 2007).

3.2 BVH cost function

This section will describe the overview of hierarchical method that is used in the proposed urban simulation. BVH is proven to be the most efficient method for collision detection (Sulaiman et al., 2009, Chang et al., 2008, Bergen, 2004, Bergen, 1999). Thus, in this research, the hierarchical cost function that has been used by previous researchers will be used. Basic cost function was first formulated by (Weghorst et al., 1984) for hierarchical method in ray tracing and later was applied by (Gottschalk et al., 1996) and enhanced by (Klosowski et al., 1998). The calculation of execution time is formulated as follows:

$$T = N_v \times C_v + N_p \times C_p + N_u \times C_u + C_o \quad (1)$$

Where

T: total execution time for detecting interference
N_v: number of BV pairs overlap tests
C_v: time require for testing a pair of bounding-volumes
N_p: numbers of primitive pairs overlap tests
C_p: time require for testing a pair of primitives for interference
N_u: numbers of nodes that need to be updated
C_u: cost of updating each node
C_o: Cost of one-time processing

From the formula 1, N_v shows the number of the BV that is currently overlapped when the objects has come into contact while N_p shows number of the primitive itself when overlapped. Given of example of two rigid bodies that enclosed with their BVHs. When both objects come into contact, the system will calculated how much BV between these two rigid bodies has been overlapped and we also measure its C_v. Next, the system also will store the information of the number of primitive inside the BVs that need to perform intersection test in order to determine the exact number of primitives that currently overlapping and with the C_p to measure time require to test each primitive-primitive testing. Meanwhile, N_u takes into account the numbers of nodes that need to be updated once the intersection has occurred (where each node has a BV and few primitives inside). C_u is the time taken to update each node while C_o is for any additional time taken for transformation update or coordinate update of each objects.

The formula shows that the most important factors that determine the performance of collision detection between rigid bodies are the tightness of bounding-volumes and the simplicity of bounding-volumes. When we have lower number of overlap tests (lower N_v and N_p) per intersection between two rigid bodies for example, the object must be bounded with tight bounding-volumes and will eventually decrease the potential of object interference hence increase performance. However when we enclosed the objects with simple bounding-volumes (lower C_v and C_p), it is resulting significant increment of the intersection tests between bounding-volumes. Minimizing one value will cause another value to increase. This is the challenge in all collision detection to find which one is the most important.

4. References

Baciu, G. Recode: An Image-based Collision Detection Algorithm. *In:* WONG, W. & SUN, H., eds., 1998. 125-125.

Bade, A., Suaib, N., A, M. Z. & M, T. S. T. 2006. Oriented convex polyhedra for collision detection in 3D computer animation. *Proceedings of the 4th international conference on Computer graphics and interactive techniques in Australasia and Southeast Asia.* Kuala Lumpur, Malaysia: ACM.

Baraff, D. 1989. Analytical methods for dynamic simulation of non-penetrating rigid bodies. *Proceedings of the 16th annual conference on Computer graphics and interactive techniques.* ACM.

Baraff, D. 1990. Curved surfaces and coherence for non-penetrating rigid body simulation. *SIGGRAPH Comput. Graph.,* 24, 19-28.

Benitez, A., Ramirez, M. D. C. & Vallejo, D. 2005. Collision Detection Using Sphere-Tree Construction. *Proceedings of the 15th International Conference on Electronics, Communications and Computers.* IEEE Computer Society.

Bergen, G. V. D. 1999. A fast and robust GJK implementation for collision detection of convex objects. *J. Graph. Tools,* 4, 7-25.

Bergen, G. V. D. 2004. *Collision Detection in Interactive 3D Environments,* United States of America, Elsevier, Inc.

Bradshaw, G. & O'Sullivan, C. 2002. Sphere-tree construction using dynamic medial axis approximation. *Proceedings of the 2002 ACM SIGGRAPH/Eurographics symposium on Computer animation.* San Antonio, Texas: ACM.

Chang, J.-W., Wang, W. & Kim, M.-S. 2008. Efficient Collision Detection Using a Dual Bounding Volume Hierarchy *Geometric Modeling and Processing.* Berlin Heidelberg.

Chang, J.-W., Wang, W. & Kim, M.-S. 2009. Efficient collision detection using a dual OBB-sphere bounding volume hierarchy. *Computer-Aided Design,* In Press, Corrected Proof.

Cohen, J. D., Lin, M. C., Manocha, D. & Ponamgi, M. 1995. I-Collide: an interactive and exact collision detection system for large-scale environments. *Proceedings of the 1995 symposium on Interactive 3D graphics.* Monterey, California, United States: ACM.

Cohen, J. D., Manocha, D., Lin, M. C. & K.Ponamgi, M. 1994. Interactive and Exact Collision Detection for Large-Scale Environments. *Technical Report TR94-005.*

Ericson, C. 2004. *Real-Time Collision Detection (The Morgan Kaufmann Series in Interactive 3-D Technology) (The Morgan Kaufmann Series in Interactive 3D Technology),* Morgan Kaufmann Publishers Inc.

Erleben, K., Sporring, J., Henriksen, K. & Dohlman, K. 2005. *Physics-based Animation (Graphics Series),* Charles River Media, Inc.

Garcia-Alonso, A., Nicol, Serrano, S. & Flaquer, J. 1994. Solving the Collision Detection Problem. *IEEE Comput. Graph. Appl.,* 14, 36-43.

Gareth, B. & Carol, O. S. 2004. Adaptive medial-axis approximation for sphere-tree construction. *ACM Trans. Graph.,* 23, 1-26.

Gilbert, E. G. & Foo, C. P. 1990. Computing the distance between general convex objects in three-dimensional space. *Robotics and Automation, IEEE Transactions on,* 6, 53-61.

Goldsmith, J. & Salmon, J. 1987. Automatic Creation of Object Hierarchies for Ray Tracing. *IEEE Comput. Graph. Appl.,* 7, 14-20.

Gottschalk, S., Lin, M. C. & Manocha, D. 1996. OBBTree: a hierarchical structure for rapid interference detection. *Proceedings of the 23rd annual conference on Computer graphics and interactive techniques.* ACM.

Gottschalk, S. A. 2000. *Collision queries using oriented bounding boxes.* The University of North Carolina at Chapel Hill.

Haverkort, H. J. 2004. *Results on Geometric Networks and Data Structures.* PhD, Technische Universiteit Eindhoven.

Kamat, V. R. & Martinez, J. C. 2007. Interactive collision detection in three-dimensional visualizations of simulated construction operations. *Engineering with Computers,* 23, 79-91.

Klosowski, J. T., Held, M., Mitchell, J. S. B., Sowizral, H. & Zikan, K. 1998. Efficient Collision Detection Using Bounding Volume Hierarchies of k-DOPs. *IEEE Transactions on Visualization and Computer Graphics,* 4, 21-36.

Kockara, S. H., T.; Iqbal, K.; Bayrak, C.; Rowe, Richard; 2007. Collision Detection - A Survey. *IEEE International Conference on Systems, Man and Cybernetics, 2007. ISIC.*

Larsson, T. 2009. *Adaptive Bounding-Volume Hierarchies for Efficient Collision Queries.* PhD, Malardalen University.

Larsson, T. & Akenine-Moller, T. 2008. Bounding Volume Hierarchies of Slab Cut Balls. Malardalen University.

Larsson, T., Akenine-Möller, T. & Lengyel, E. 2007. On Faster Sphere-Box Overlap Testing. *Journal of Graphics Tools,* 12, 3-8.

Lin, M. C. 1994. EFFICIENT COLLISION DETECTION FOR ANIMATION AND ROBOTICS. University of California at Berkeley.

Lin, M. C. & Manocha, D. 2004. Collision and Proximity Queries. *In Handbook of Discrete and Computational Geometry, 2nd Ed.* Boca Raton, FL: CRC Press LLC.

Liu, L., Wang, Z.-Q. & Xia, S.-H. A Volumetric Bounding Volume Hierarchy for Collision Detection. 10th IEEE International Conference on Computer-Aided Design and Computer Graphics, 2007 2007. 485-488.

Madera, F. A., Day, A. M. & Laycock, S. D. A Hybrid Bounding Volume Algorithm to Detect Collisions between Deformable Objects. Second International Conferences on Advances in Computer-Human Interactions, 2009. ACHI '09. , 2009. 136-141.

Müller, G., Schäfer, S. & Fellner, D. W. 1999. Automatic Creation of Object Hierarchies for Radiosity Clustering. *Proceedings of the 7th Pacific Conference on Computer Graphics and Applications.* IEEE Computer Society.

Nguyen, A. 2006. *IMPLICIT BOUNDING VOLUMES AND BOUNDING VOLUME HIERARCHIES.* Doctor of Philosophy, Stanford University.

Omohundro, S. 1989. Five Ball tree Construction Algorithm. *Technical Report TR-89-063.* International Computer Science Institute, Berkeley, CA.

Redon, S., Kheddar, A. & Coquillart, S. 2002. Fast Continuous Collision Detection between Rigid Bodies. *Computer Graphics Forum.*

Rocha, R. D. S. & Maria Andre'ia Formico, R. 2008. An evaluation of a collision handling system using sphere-trees for plausible rigid body animation. *Proceedings of the 2008 ACM symposium on Applied computing.* Fortaleza, Ceara, Brazil: ACM.

Sobottka, G. & Weber, A. Efficient Bounding Volume Hierarchies for Hair Simulation. Proc. Second Workshop Virtual Reality Interactions and Physical Simulations (VRIPHYS '05), 2005. 101-110.

Spillmann, J., Becker, M. & Teschner, M. 2007. Efficient updates of bounding sphere hierarchies for geometrically deformable models. *J. Vis. Comun. Image Represent.*, 18, 101-108.

Suaib, N. M., Bade, A. & Mohamad, D. Collision Detection Using Bounding-Volume for avatars in Virtual Environment applications. The 4th International Conference on Information & Communication Technology and Systems, August 2008 2008 Institut Teknologi Sepuluh Nopember (ITS), Surabaya, Indonesia. 486 - 491.

Sulaiman, H. A., Bade, A., Daman, D. & Suaib, N. M. 2009. Collision Detection using Bounding-Volume Hierarchies in Urban Simulation. *The 5th Postgraduate Annual Research Seminar.* Faculty of Computer Science & Information System, UTM.

Tu, C. & Yu, L. Research on Collision Detection Algorithm Based on AABB-OBB Bounding Volume. First International Workshop on Education Technology and Computer Science, 2009. ETCS '09. , 2009. 331-333.

Weghorst, H., Hooper, G. & Greenberg, D. P. 1984. Improved Computational Methods for Ray Tracing. *ACM Trans. Graph.*, 3, 52-69.

Weller, R. & Zachmann, G. 2009. Inner Sphere Trees. *In:* DIX, J. (ed.). Clausthal-Zellerfeld, Germany: Clausthal University of Technology.

Weller, R. E., Klein, J. & Zachmann, G. A Model for the Expected Running Time of Collision Detection using AABB Trees. *In:* HUBBOLD, R. & LIN, M., eds. Eurographics Symposium on Virtual Environments (EGVE), 8--10 May 2006 Lisbon, Portugal.

Zhang, X. & Kim, Y. J. 2007. Interactive Collision Detection for Deformable Models Using Streaming AABBs. *IEEE Transactions on Visualization and Computer Graphics*, 13, 318-329.

4

Modeling and Visualization of the Surface Resulting from the Milling Process

Tobias Surmann
Institute of Machining Technology, Technische Universität Dortmund
Germany

1. Introduction

In milling of arbitrary free formed surfaces many errors can occur which may lead to inacceptable surface quality because of dynamic effects. One of these dynamic effects are tool vibrations which consist of a static part i. e. a static tool deflection and of a dynamic part. A special case are self excited vibrations called chatter vibrations. These chatter vibrations can grow up to a very high amplitude and thus may lead to high tool wear or even tool breakage. In any case chatter leads to a high surface roughness.

Besides the prediction of whether a milling process is free of chatter or not, the resulting surface quality is of high importance. Though chatter free milling produces a smooth surface structure, the absolute contour error may be high because of high amplitudes of the tool vibration since chatter-free does not necessarily mean vibration-free (Surmann & Biermann, 2008). Every change of feed rate or a change of the feed direction may also lead to surface artifacts. Chatter produces a high roughness and so called chatter marks (Fig. 1) with a negative surface location error in the majority of cases (i. e. too much material is removed).

There has been done a lot of research in the field of chatter theory and milling simulation (Altintas, 2000; Schmitz & Smith, 2008) for non transient milling processes i. e. the tool engagement conditions do not change over time. In general milling processes for free formed surfaces, the engagement conditions change often and rapidly. For that reason, it is hard to control the process parameters in order to optimize the process and the surface quality over an entire NC-program.

A simulation of the dynamic milling process, which calculates the tool vibration trajectory along arbitrary NC-programs, can help to predict the surface quality by converting the trajectory into a geometric model of the workpiece. This model has to provide the possibility of rendering and of measuring the surface error. In this work, the surface model is represented by a discrete set of surface points which are created during a simulation run. In this way, the simulation is able to start at any position within an arbitrary NC-program and does not have to simulate all the way up to the position of interest.

For the prediction of process forces, which are the source of tool vibrations in the milling of free formed surfaces, a simulation technique is required, which provides the modeling of continuous chip shapes from arbitrary NC-paths with the option to feed back tool deflections into the geometric model. This is necessary for the modeling of self excited milling tool vibrations.

Fig. 1. Typical surface artifacts on milled surfaces. Top left: Marks resulting from changes of feed velocity. Top right: Chatter marks before and in corners. Botton left: Artifact resulting from change of feed direction. Bottom Right: High roughness because of chatter marks.

This article presents a simulation, which is capable of expressing the chip forms as continuous volume models with the ability of reproducing varying chip thicknesses resulting from tool vibrations. The cutting force calculation generates surface points, which are used to generate the surface model. By knowledge of the surface points and the tool vibration trajectory, a realistic surface model can be used to predict surface errors and chatter marks.

2. Modeling of the chip form

As chip form we define the form of the part of the material that is removed while the tool moves along one tooth feed. From this chip form the chip thickness distribution along the cutting edges can be calculated in order to compute the actual cutting force.

2.1 Set theoretical approach

Taking into account that the tool moves along an NC-program in steps of the tool feed f_z, the chip form C_n at the n-th tooth feed can be expressed as a set formula

$$C_n = W_0 \backslash \left(\bigcup_{i=1}^{n-2} T_i \right) \backslash T_{n-1} \cap T_n, \tag{1}$$

where W_0 is the stock material and T_i is the envelope of the rotating tool at the corresponding position of the i-th tooth feed. Hereby, the boolean operators $\cup, \cap$ and $\backslash$ denote the union, the intersection and the difference respectively of the point sets represented by the workpiece and the tool models. Since the cutting velocity is assumed to be much greater than the feed velocity, the equation delivers a perfect description of the removed material at the n-th cut.

The equation can be directly converted into a CSG (Constructive Solid Geometry) tree. At the same time the sets W_0 and T_i are represented by CSG subtrees themselves.

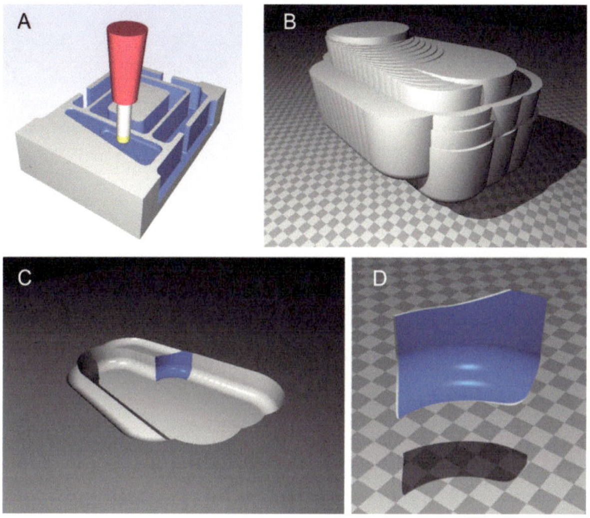

Fig. 2. A local workpiece model (C) at a tool position (A) can be modelled by subtracting the sweep volume (B) of the tool from a stock workpiece. The intersection between this local workpiece and the tool envelope results in the chip shape (D)

2.2 Minimizing the CSG tree

The reason why milling simulations, which are based on CSG, are said to be inefficient is that the size of the set union in the set equation may become very large and the further processing of the chip shape becomes very slow. However, instead of modeling the whole workpiece like Kawashima et al. (1991) did, it is sufficient for the construction of the chip form to model only the local region close to the milling tool at the position of the current cut n (Fig. 2). This is done by taking only those T_i into account, which intersect with the tool model entity T_n. In order to find these necessary T_i efficiently, an octree (Foley et al., 1994) space division data structure is applied to store the NC-program (i. e. the line segments of the given tool path from which the tool positions are taken). So it is possible to exclude most of the unneeded tool path segments with only a few simple intersection tests between box shaped subspaces of the octree and the bounding box of the milling tool model T_n.

3. Force computation

In order to compute the forces acting on the milling tool while removing the chip shape we divide each cutting edge into small linear segments of length b. We assume that each of these segments represents a small cutting wedge for which the mechanics of the oblique cut (Fig. 3) are supposed to be valid and the Kienzle-Equation

$$F_i = b \cdot k_i \cdot h^{1-m_i} \qquad \text{with} \quad i \in \{c, n, t\} \tag{2}$$

applies, where the k_i and m_i are the specific cutting force parameters which can be looked up in tables or have to be determined experimentally.

The force acting on a specific wedge results from its related uncut chip thickness h and the

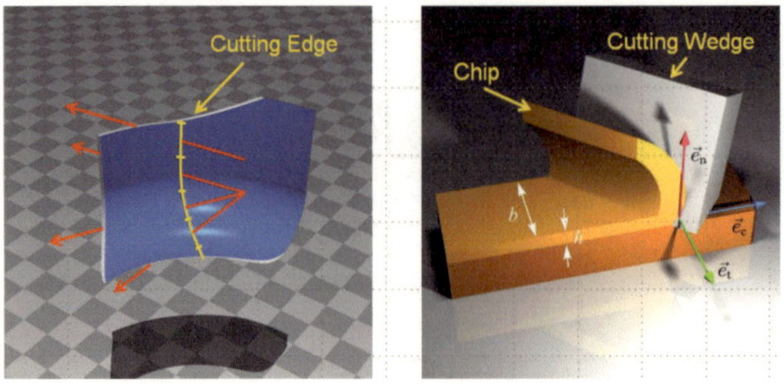

Fig. 3. By casting rays through the chip shape the chip thickness h can be evaluated (left). By the model of the oblique cut (right) the cutting forces can be calculated.

local coordinate system determining the cutting direction $\vec{e}_c$, the normal direction of the cut $\vec{e}_n$ and the tangential direction $\vec{e}_t$.

These vectors are dependent on the position $l, 0 \leq l \leq 1$ on the cutting edge and on the current angular position ϕ of the cutting edge on the tool envelope. Thus, the chip thickness h is a function of l and ϕ as well. The over all force $\vec{F}(l, \phi)$, acting on a cutting edge segment at position l, ϕ can be expressed as

$$\vec{F}(l,b,\phi) = F_c(b,h(l,\phi)) \cdot \vec{e}_c(l,\phi) + F_n(b,h(l,\phi)) \cdot \vec{e}_n(l,\phi) + F_t(b,h(l,\phi)) \cdot \vec{e}_t(l,\phi). \tag{3}$$

The chip thickness $h(l, \phi)$ can now be computed by intersecting a ray

$$\vec{x} = \vec{p}(l,\phi) + t \cdot \vec{e}_n(l,\phi) \tag{4}$$

with the CSG-model of the chip form. Hereby, $p(l, \phi)$ is a point on the cutting edge at the revolution angle ϕ and the position l on the paramtric curve representing the cutting edge. The distance between entry and exit point is the chip thickness h.

Let φ be the current angle of revolution of the tool, n the number of cutting edge segments and $\Delta\phi$ the pitch angle between the cutting edges. The Force acting on then j-th cutting edge is then

$$\vec{F}(j,\varphi) = \sum_{i=0}^{n-1} \vec{F}\left(\frac{i}{n}, b, j \cdot \Delta\phi + \varphi\right). \tag{5}$$

Now we have to sum up the forces over all z cutting edges in order to get the force acting on the entire tool at rotation angle φ

$$\vec{F}(\varphi) = \sum_{i=0}^{z-1} \vec{F}(i,\varphi). \tag{6}$$

In order to model the cutting forces along a tool path we model the chip forms in steps of the tooth feed f_z. Furthermore, each partial revolution along a tooth feed is devided into j angle steps $\Delta\varphi$ with

$$\Delta\varphi = \frac{2\pi}{zj}. \tag{7}$$

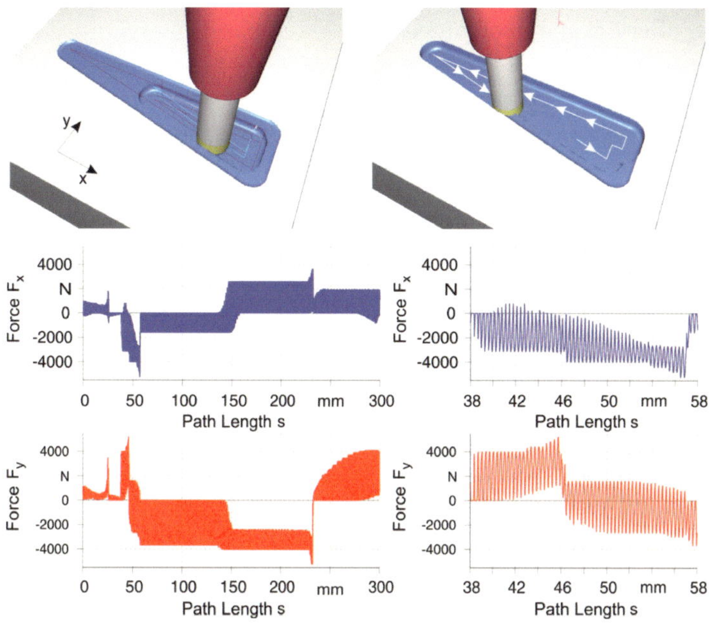

Fig. 4. Milling forces along a section of an NC-program.

From the spindle speed n we get a time step Δt of

$$\Delta t = \frac{j}{zn}. \tag{8}$$

At the beginning of a simulation run the current rotation angle φ and the time t is set to 0 and the first chip form is constructed. For this chip form the milling force $\vec{F}(\varphi)$ is computed and saved as $\vec{F}(t)$. As a next step as well φ as t are increased by $\Delta\varphi$ and Δt respectively and the milling force is computed again. After the force computation at the angle

$$\varphi = \frac{2\pi}{z} - \Delta\varphi \tag{9}$$

φ is reset to 0 again and the next chip form is modelled and processed in the same way. Fig. 4 shows the force progression along a section of a tool path producing a pocket.

4. Machine model

Since real machines cannot be assumed to be ideal stiff, they will respond to an acting force not only with a static deflection but also with a vibration. In order to model this response we use a set of harmonic oscillators for each coordinate direction. Each oscillator consists of three modal parameters: natural angular velocity ω_0, modal mass m and damping constant γ. With these values we can compute the response on applied impulses on the tool tip.

4.1 Response of a harmonic oscillator to an impulse

At first we deal with only one oscillator. We asume that the oscillator has at time t_0 the velocity v_0 and the displacement x_0. Further we assume that a force F_0 acts for a period of Δt. The new values x_1 and v_1 after Δt can be computed by

$$x_1 = A \cdot e^{(iw-\gamma)\Delta t} + B \cdot e^{(-iw-\gamma)\Delta t} \tag{10}$$

$$v_1 = A \cdot (-\gamma + i\omega) \cdot e^{(iw-\gamma)\Delta t} + B \cdot (-\gamma - i\omega) \cdot e^{(-iw-\gamma)\Delta t}. \tag{11}$$

Here, A and B are defined as

$$A = \frac{1}{2i\omega} \cdot \left(v_0 + \frac{\Delta t}{m} \cdot F_0 + (\gamma + i\omega) \cdot x_0 \right) \tag{12}$$

and

$$B = \frac{1}{2i\omega} \cdot \left(-v_0 - \frac{\Delta t}{m} \cdot F_0 + (-\gamma + i\omega) \cdot x_0 \right) \tag{13}$$

respectively. Generally, starting at a displacement x_j with the velocity v_j we can now compute the related values x_{j+1}, v_{j+1} of the next time step after application of a force F_j by a linear combination of the current values and the actual force

$$x_{j+1} = a \cdot x_j + b \cdot v_j + c \cdot F_j \tag{14}$$

$$v_{1+1} = d \cdot x_j + e \cdot v_j + f \cdot F_j. \tag{15}$$

The constants $a \ldots f$ can be precalculated from the above equations and are valid as long as the time step Δt does not change.

4.2 MDOF oscillator model

In order to model the response of a milling machine with respect to the tool tip we use a set of uncoupled oscillators for each coordinate direction. A force acting on the tool tip is then applied to each oscillator and the responses are superposed. Let m be the number of oscillators used for one direction and let $x_{k,j}$ and $v_{k,j}$ be the displacement and the velocity respectively of the k-th oscillator at time step j, then the overall response $\hat{x}_{j+1}$ of the machine tool at time step $j+1$ reads as

$$\hat{x}_{j+1} = \sum_{k=0}^{m-1} x_{k,j+1}. \tag{16}$$

The modal parameters modal mass, natural frequency and damping constant of the single oscillators have to be adjusted to the measured frequency responce functions (FRF) of the

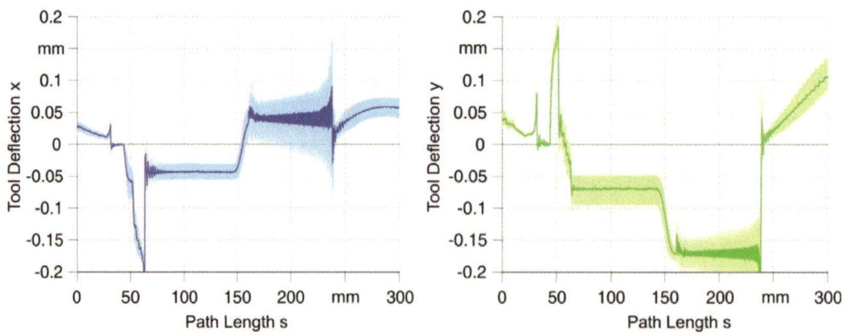

Fig. 5. Milling tool vibrations along a section of an NC-program (dark colors denote the displacement at the point in time of surface generation).

actual machine tool in x- and y-direction in advance. For this, an evolutionary algorithm is applied which optimizes the modal parameters in a way that the FRF of the superposed oscillators fit the measured FRF.

5. Modeling the regenerative effect

As seen in Fig. 4, the cutting forces are not constant and thus they excite vibrations of the milling tool. Vibrating tools produce a wavy surface which in return produces a modulation of the milling force. This feed back is called regenerative or self-excited vibrations. The geometric model of the chip form can be easily used for simulating this regenerative effect.

The equations 4 to 6 describe the force computation for one tooth feed in discrete rotation angle steps $\Delta\varphi$, where each angle φ is assigned a specific point in time t. Thus, instead of $\vec{F}(\varphi)$ we can write $\vec{F}(t)$. The two tool models T_{n-1} and T_n of Eq. 1 generate the surfaces of the last cut and the current surface which are responsible for the regenerative effect.

Let $\vec{x}(t)$ and $\vec{x}(t-T)$ be the tool displacements at time t and time $t-T$ respectively. We now move the tool models according to those two displacements just before the evaluation of the chip thickness along the cutting edges. After computation of the Force $F(t)$ and the computation of the resulting displacement $\vec{x}(t+\Delta t)$, the displacements are reset, the tool is rotated by $\Delta\varphi$ and the procedure is repeated with the current rotation angle and the displacements $\vec{x}(t+\Delta t)$ and $\vec{x}(t+\Delta t-T)$.

Fig. 5 shows the simulated tool vibration along the same tool path as Fig. 4.

6. Point-based workpiece model

In contrast to the work of Gao et al. (2006); Li & Shin (2006); Omar et al. (2007), where the surfaces are modelled as a high resolved continous triangulation, in this work a simpler way is presented which generates a point-based surface model which is capable of rendering the surface of complex parts generated by NC-milling processes.

In NC-milling of geometrically complex parts problems or errors resulting in artifacts on the surface cannot be recognized until the process is finished. Especially for the industrial application of a simulation system it is important that the simulation provides a surface model which is capable of displaying these surface errors. Thus, this section will deal with the geometric modeling and visualization of the resulting surface structure as a point-based surface model.

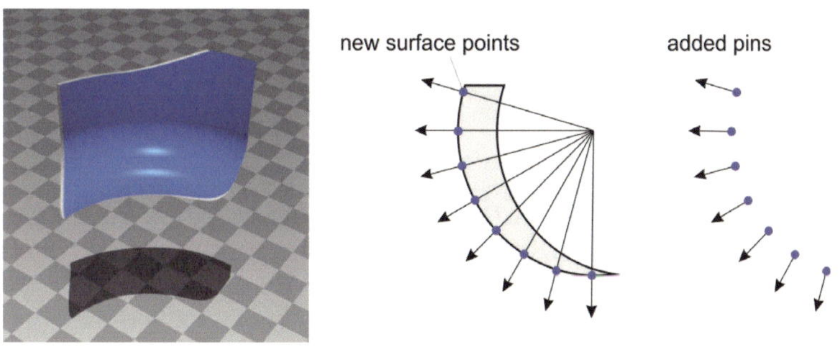

Fig. 6. The exit points of the rays used to compute the chip thicknesses are applied to form a surface model consisting of pins.

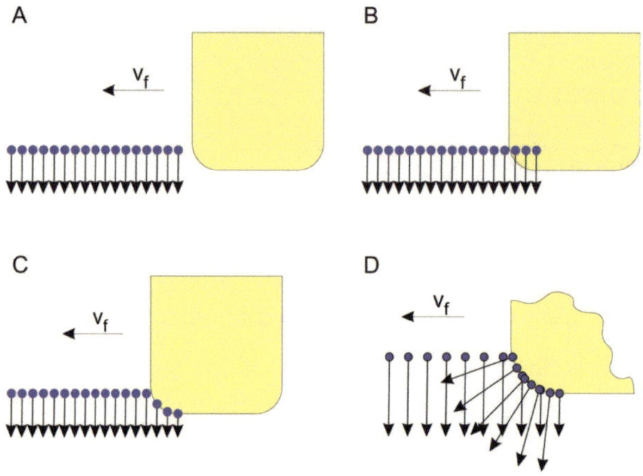

Fig. 7. The material removal from the pin model (A) is conducted by cutting the pins which intersect with the tool envelope (B) while the tool moves through the workpiece. The points are moved to the intersection points (C) and finally the new pins are added (D).

6.1 Adding points

Since the presented milling simulation system does not make use of a global workpiece model but of a locally modelled chip form it is capable of starting at any point within an NC-program. Thus, for visualization of the surface we need a model that produces the newly generated surface of a section of the tool path. Therefore, we make use of the fact that the backside of a chip form (Fig. 6) for a short time represents a small part of the surface, i. e. the newly generated surface of the current cut. When computing the chip thickness by casting rays through the chip form the exit points of the rays represent surface points. At each cut these points together with a normal vector of length d are added to a set of points representing the workpiece surface. The couple of point and normal vector is called *pin* because of its appearance. Each tooth feed produces a set of new pins (Fig. 6).

6.2 Removing material

We suppose there is already a set of pins (Fig. 7 A), through which the tool model, i. e. the envelope of the rotating tool, is moving. Points, which come to lie inside the tool (Fig. 7 B) are moved along their normal vector upon the tool envelope. The tie points stay the same, i. e. the pin becomes shortened (Fig. 7 C). Pins which entirely lie inside the tool envelope are deleted.

By successive cutting, removing and adding pins a model of the newly machined surface grows. Fig. 8 displays the result by a 3D-Example from the milling simulation system.

6.3 Estimation of the tool deflection before cutting

In the previous section we assumed the tool model to move exactly along the given tool path. This enables a visualization of the ideal suface but does not produce surface errors as the actual process does. For a material removal featuring surface errors we determine the tool displacement at each cut at the point in time where the remaining surface is produced. This displacement is applied to the tool additionally before conducting the cut of the pin model.

Again, we use the set of newly generated pins of a tooth feed which is displayed in Fig. 9 by means of the chip form of Fig. 2. Since most of the pins are surface points only for a short

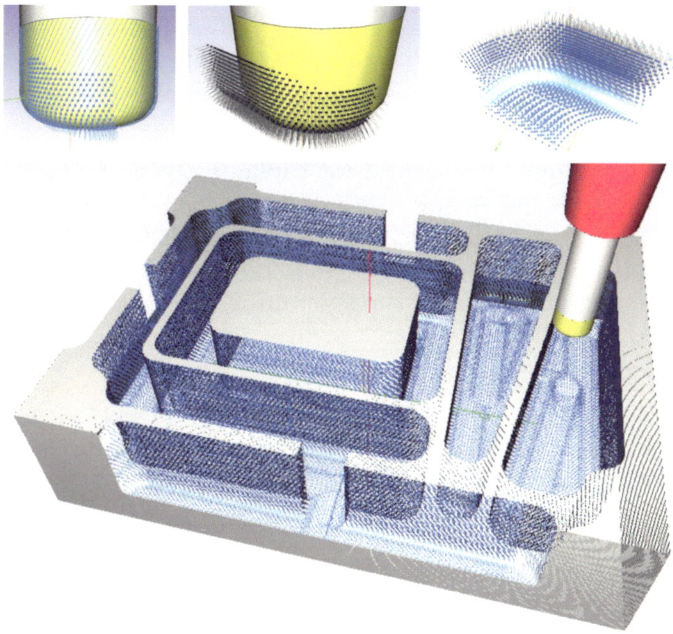

Fig. 8. Example of a pin model generated by an NC-program. Top row: points of the chip form (left) and generated surface part (middle and right)

period of time and will be removed again by the following cut, we have to find out those points which will contribute to the final surface. For these points P_i applies that their normal vectors $\vec{n}_i$ are perpendicular to the feed direction $\vec{v}_f$:

$$\vec{n}_i \cdot \vec{v}_f = 0 \Rightarrow P_i \text{ is finally surface point.} \tag{17}$$

Unfortunately, the tool rotaion is divided into discrete angular steps $\Delta\varphi$, so that the criterion has to be understated like

$$\frac{\vec{n}_i \cdot \vec{v}_f}{|\vec{n}_i| \cdot |\vec{v}_f|} \leq \cos(\Delta\varphi) \Rightarrow P_i \text{ is nearly surface point.} \tag{18}$$

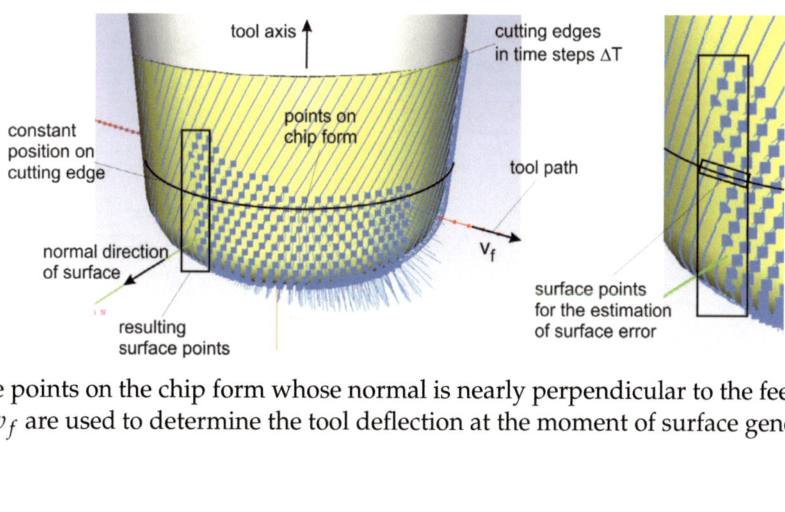

Fig. 9. The points on the chip form whose normal is nearly perpendicular to the feed direction v_f are used to determine the tool deflection at the moment of surface generation.

We can test each point for this criterion directly on its creation. In the positive case the point is added to a set S carrying all the points that form the remainig part of the surface (marked in Fig. 9). Additionally, each point $P_i \in S$ is assigned with the displacement $\vec{d}_i$ the tool had when the specific point was created.

In order to estimate the tool displacement for cutting the pins we use the average tool displacement $\vec{d}_{avg}$ of the points from a subset of S lying on a specific height. This height can be the middle of the total axial immersion (Fig. 9, right). Before cutting the pins the tool model is translated by $\vec{d}_{avg}$ from its ideal position. The result of many succeeding cuts is a point-based surface model including the surface errors resulting from dynamic effects.

7. Point based rendering

Processed surfaces like generated by digitizing often are available as point sets without any relationship between the points. A triangulation often is too time consuming or error-prone if the shape of the object is geometrically complex. Especially when the surface is

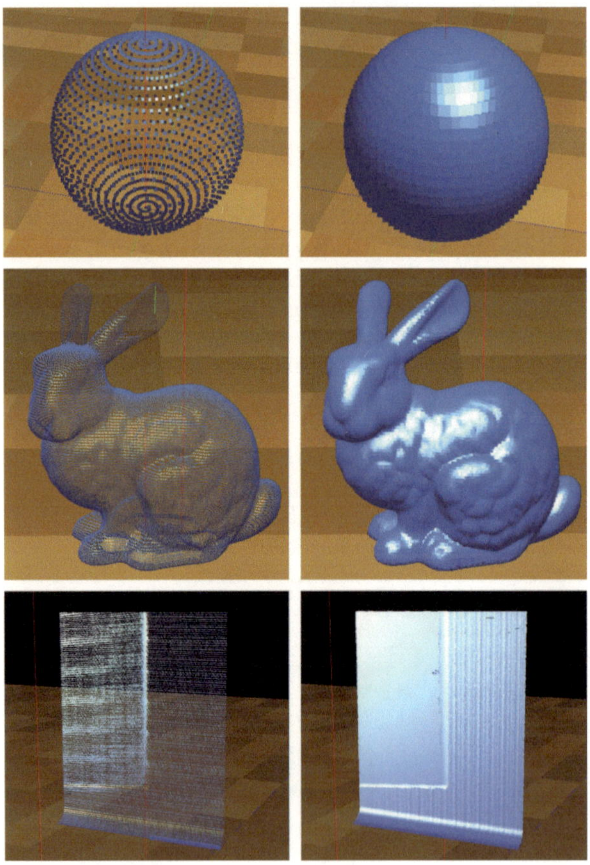

Fig. 10. Splat-rendered objects (Sphere, Stanford Bunny and milled surface containing chatter marks) with low splat size (left) and large splats to make the impression of a closed surface.

continually modified like in the milling simulation a very fast and efficient rendering method is demanded.

Taking a look at Fig. 8 reveals, that a pure rendering of the points together with a shading by usage of normal vectors already provides a good visulaization of the surface. The next sections deal with two direct point-based rendering techniques.

7.1 Splat rendering

In case the points carry normal vectors, like they do in the pin model, it is possible to make use of the graphics hardware and just render the points (Foley et al., 1994; Wright et al., 2010) on the screen. Hereby, the points are shaded by using their normal vectors and are rendered as big splats (Akenine-Möller & Haines, 2002). From a specific splat size the surface seems to be a closed surface (Fig. 10). Using this technique the points become two-dimensional not before putting them on the screen whereby the simplest method is to draw squares with the edge length of a. The splatsize $a(d)$ can additionally adapted to the distance d to the viewer with a certain constant k:

$$a(d) = \frac{k}{d}. \tag{19}$$

The constant k determines the splat size and has to be adjusted dependently on the density of the points, that the surface seems to be closed at all distances (Fig. 10).

This method is useful when there is no demand for very high visualization quality but for visualization eficiancy and speed. However, surface errors can be recognized directly while the simulation is still in progress.

7.2 Point based raytracing

For a photorealistic rendering of simulated surface models the ray tracing technique (Akenine-Möller & Haines, 2002; Foley et al., 1994; Shirley, 2005) is much more suitable. Of high importance for a ray tracing system is that the objects provide a possibility to compute intersections with a ray. Therefore, the next section is about an algorithm for the direct computation of intersections between a ray and a point-set based on the method presented by Linsen et al. (2007) and Goradia et al. (2010).

The points within a point-set surface can be considered as representatives for a closed surface. Together with a normal vector and other properties like color and material these

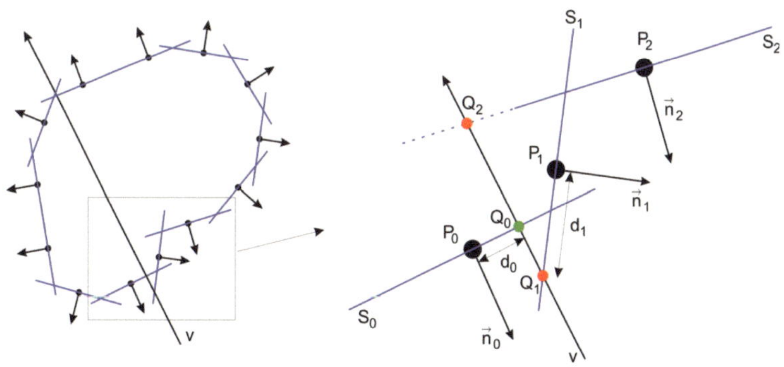

Fig. 11. Principle of ray intersection with surfels. The Point Q_0 has the minimal distance to its related surface point P_0 and thus is selected as the intersection result.

representatives are called *surfel* (surface element). These surfels are a circular disc with radius r and with the related point in the center. Additionally, it is alligned perpendicular to the related normal vector.

7.2.1 Intersection of ray and surfel

A surfel S describes a plane f by its point P and its normal vector $\vec{n}$ by

$$f: \qquad (\vec{x} - \vec{P}) \cdot \vec{n} = 0. \tag{20}$$

The intersection point Q with the view ray v starting at the camera position B with the viewing direction $\vec{v}$

$$v: \qquad \vec{x} = \vec{B} + t \cdot \vec{v} \tag{21}$$

results from inserting Eq. 21 into Eq. 20, and by computing the factor t

$$t = \frac{\vec{P} \cdot \vec{n} - \vec{B} \cdot \vec{n}}{\vec{v} \cdot \vec{n}}. \tag{22}$$

Using the factor t with Eq. 21 we get a point

$$\vec{Q} = \vec{B} + t \cdot \vec{v}. \tag{23}$$

This point is intersection point with the surfel if

$$d = |\vec{Q} - \vec{P}| \leq r \tag{24}$$

applies.

7.2.2 Multiple Intersections

A set of surfels representing a closed surface generally leads to intersections of a ray v with more than one surfel (Fig. 11). At first we ignore the surfels whose normals point into the same direction as the view ray v and thus

$$\vec{n}_i \cdot \vec{v} \geq 0 \tag{25}$$

applies. Thus, in Fig. 11 only Q_0 and Q_1 remain as possible intersections. A simple and effective method to decide which intersection to use is to take that point Q_i whose distance d_i from the related surfel center is minimal. In Fig. 11 this is point Q_0.

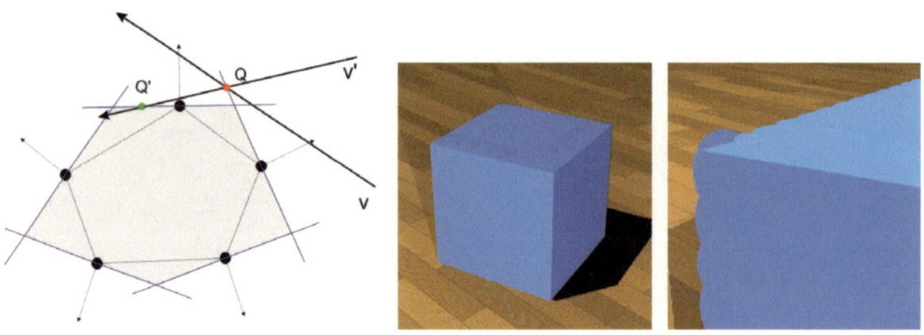

Fig. 12. Artifacts occur, if the object has sharp edges.

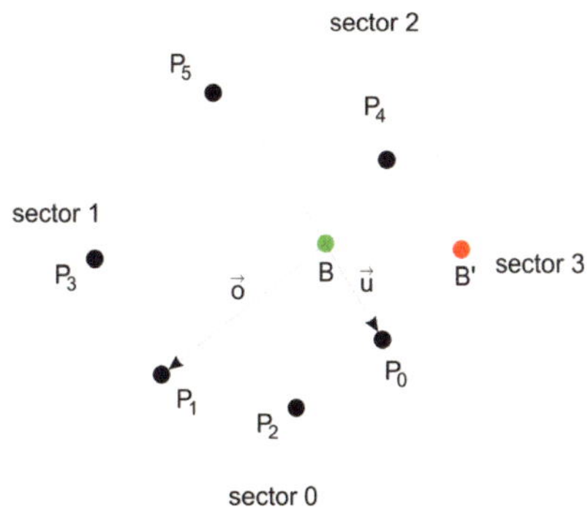

Fig. 13. First step in testing whether a point B is inside the convex cover of a 2D point set.

7.2.3 Point in convex cover

Fig. 12 shows on the left hand side a surface represented by a triangulation of the points. The presented intersection algorithm with the shown ray v would result in the point Q which definitly lies far outside the triangulation. The ray v' which also passes through Q would intersect the surfels in point Q'. This algorthm is obviously view dependent.

Therefore, the silouette of a point set surface with an inhomogenious density would have a frayed silhouette or undesired shadow castings especially when using large surfel radii (Fig. 12). To overcome this issue we improve the intersection algorithm in a way that only those rays can lead to an intersection, which intersect the convex cover of the point set.

Therefore, at first, we only take the projection of the points $P_0 \cdots P_n$ of the point set surface as well as the camera position B onto the view plane into account. At the beginning of the algorithm we compute the vectors $\vec{u} = \vec{P_0} - \vec{B}$ and $\vec{o} = \vec{P_1} - \vec{B}$.

The vectors $\vec{u}$ and $\vec{o}$ span together with the point B four sectors (Fig. 13). Now we test each

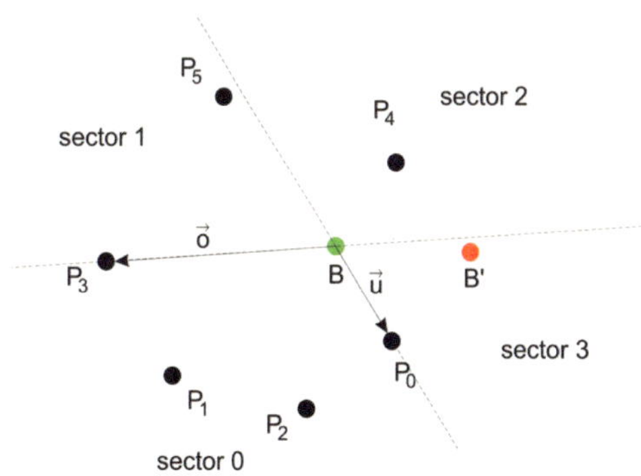

Fig. 14. Second step in testing whether a point B is inside the convex cover of a 2D point set.

point P_i, $i > 1$ in which sector it lies:

Sector 0 Nothing happens and we continue with tne next point.

Sector 1 Vector $\vec{o}$ is replaced by $\vec{P_i} - \vec{B}$ and the next point is tested.

Sector 3 Vector $\vec{u}$ is replaced by $\vec{P_i} - \vec{B}$ and the next point is tested.

Sector 2 The point B lies inside the convex cover and the algorithm terminates.

If all the points P_i have been tested and no point fell into sector 2, B does not lie inside the convex cover and the ray does not hit the point-set surface. In the example of Fig. 13 with point P_2 nothing would happen. After testing P_3 we have the situation shown in Fig. 14. P_4 lies in sector 2 when tested and terminates the algorithm. Thus, point B lies inside the convex cover.

Using B' for computing the vectors $\vec{u}$ and $\vec{o}$ no points P_i come to lie inside sector 2 and thus B' would be recognized as not lying in the convex cover.

By performing this test before computing the intersection with the surfels, the silhouette of point-set surfaces is rendered very sharp (Fig. 15).

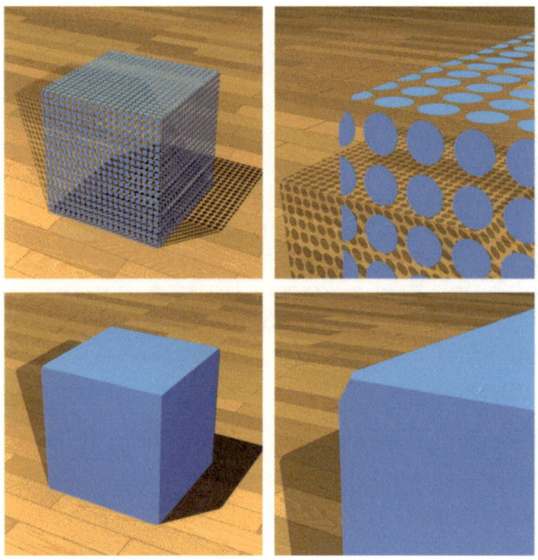

Fig. 15. Using the convex cover criterion, the edges appear sharp and without artifacts. However, corners may be cut because the silhouette of objects now appears as if it was triangulated.

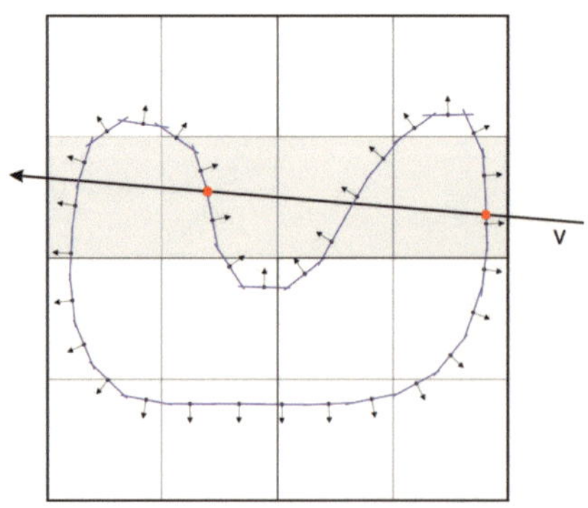

Fig. 16. By partitioning of the points into patches even intersections between a ray and concave objects can be computed.

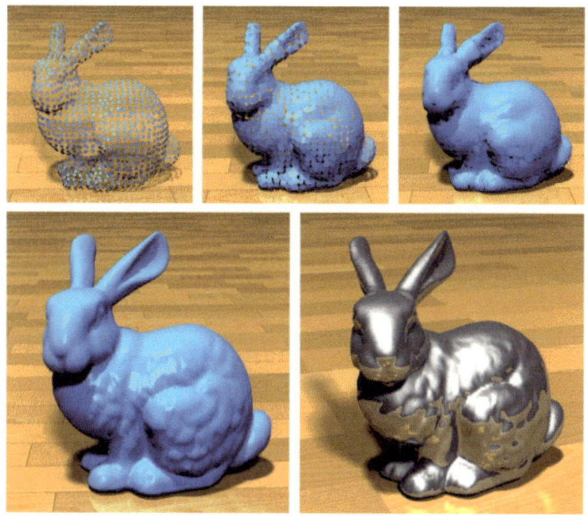

Fig. 17. Stanford Bunnies with a low resolution point-set and different surfel radii (top). High resolution Bunny with different materials (bottom) (source: Stanford University Computer Graphics Laboratory).

7.2.4 Partitioning into patches

In order to render concave objects the point-set surface has to be partitioned into small patches with a size similar to the smallest features of the object. (Fig. 16). Hereby it is possible to relate multiple intersections to different parts of the surface. For higher efficiency of the intersection algorithm the patches should be organized in a space partitioning datastructure like an octree.

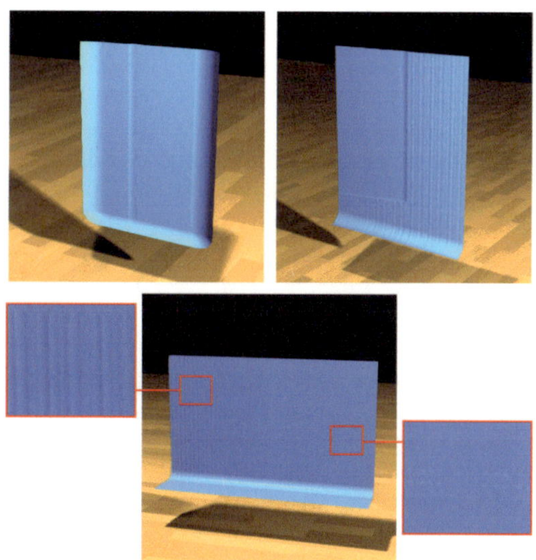

Fig. 18. Even milled surfaces can be rendered photorealistically. The surfaces on the top are related to the two bottom surfaces in Fig. 1. The bottom surface shows the result of a transient process with stable milling (right) and chatter (left).

Fig. 17 shows results for the Standford Bunny and Fig. 18 for some surfaces generated by the milling simulation, where surface structures are clearly visible (cf. Fig. 1).

8. Conclusion

By usage of concepts from the field of computer graphics and geometric modeling it is possible to simulate geometrically complex processes such as the milling process. We have shown that a CSG approach is applicable for usage in milling simulations. Together with an physics based oscillator model even regenerative chatter vibrations can be simulated.

The direct surfel-based raytracing has been improved in order to render objects with sharp edges. This enables the application of the direct surfel-based raytracing for technical surfaces such as milled workpieses.

9. Acknowledgement

This article features developments of the collaborative research center SFB/TR10 which is kindly supported by the German Research Foundation (DFG).

10. References

Akenine-Möller, T. & Haines, E. (2002). *real-Time Rendering*, AK Peters, Natick, Massachusetts.

Altintas, Y. (2000). *Manufacturing Automation: Metal Cutting Mechanics, Machine Tool Vibrations, and CNC Design*, Cambridge University Press.

Foley, J. D., v. Dam, A., Feiner, S. K. & Hughes, J. F. (1994). *Grundlagen der Computergraphik*, Vol. 1 of *1*, 1 edn, Addison-Wesley Publishing Company, Inc.

Gao, T., Zhang, W., Qiu, K. & Wan, M. (2006). Numerical simulation of machined surface topography and roughness in milling process, *Journal of Manufacturing Science and Engineering* 128(1): 96–103.

Goradia, R., Kashyap, S., Chaudhuri, P. & Chandran, S. (2010). Gpu-based ray tracing of splats, *18th Pacific Conference on Computer Graphics and Applications (PG)*, pp. 101–108.

Kawashima, Y., Itoh, K., Ishida, T., Nonaka, S. & Ejiri, K. (1991). A flexible quantitative method for nc machining verification using a space-division based solid model, *The Visual Computer* pp. 149–157.

Li, H. & Shin, Y. C. (2006). A comprehensive dynamic end milling simulation model, *Journal of Manufacturing Science and Engineering* 128(1): 86–95.

Linsen, L., Müller, K. & Rosenthal, P. (2007). Splat-based ray tracing of point clouds, *Journal of WSCG* 15: 51–58. rosenthallinsenvcgl.

Omar, O., El-Wardany, T., Ng, E. & Elbestawi, M. (2007). An improved cutting force and surface topography prediction model in end milling, *International Journal of Machine Tools and Manufacture* 47(7-8): 1263 – 1275.

Schmitz, T. L. & Smith, K. S. (2008). *Machining Dynamics*, Springer, New York. ISBN 978-0-387-09645-2.

Shirley, P. (2005). *Fundamentals of Computer Graphics*, 2 edn, Peters, Wellesley. ISBN-13: 978-1568812694.

Surmann, T. & Biermann, D. (2008). The effect of tool vibrations on the flank surface created by peripheral milling, *CIRP Annals - Manufacturing Technology* 57(1): 375 – 378.

Wright, R. S., Haemel, N., Sellers, G. & Lipchak, B. (2010). *OpenGL SuperBible: Comprehensive Tutorial and Reference*, 5 edn, Addison-Wesley Longman, Amsterdam. ISBN-13: 978-0321712615.

5

A Border-Stable Approach to NURBS Surface Rendering for Ray Tracing

Aleksands Sisojevs and Aleksandrs Glazs
Riga Technical University,
Latvia

1. Introduction

Ray tracing has become a popular method for generating high quality images. Most of the modern ray tracing based applications only deals with triangles as basic primitives. NURBS surface representation is common for most of 3D modelling tools because of its compactness and the useful geometric properties of NURBS surfaces. Using the direct ray tracing of NURBS surfaces, one can achieve better quality of rendered images [1]. There are many approaches to solving this problem.

In 1982 Kajiya [5] used ideas from algebraic geometry to obtain a numerical procedure for intersecting a ray with a bicubic surface patch. His method is robust, not requiring preliminary subdivisions to satisfy some a priori approximation. It proceeds more quickly for patches of lower degree. The algorithm is simply structured and does not require memory overhead. But unfortunately the algorithm has many disadvantages. It does not significantly utilize coherence. The algorithm computes all intersections of the given ray with a surface patch, even if just closest intersection need to be found. And finally the algorithm performs enormous amounts of floating point operations. Kajiya estimates that 6000 floating point operations may have to be performed in order to find all of the intersections between one ray and one bicubic patch. In the modern ray tracing applications global illumination algorithms are commonly used, and million of rays can be tested against one parametric patch. It makes the proposed algorithm unpractical [2].

T.Nishita, T.W.Sederberg, and M.Kakimoto [7] described methods crossing for problem solution in star - rational Bezier surface. This method was called Bezier clipping. This method can be classified as an algorithm partly based on division and partly as calculation method. After ray representation as crossing of two planes, ray - surface crossing problem can be projected from 4D space to 2D space. This method reduces the number of arithmetical operations which is necessary to perform de Casteljau subdivision with 50% in every subdivision iteration. Nishita highlighted that Bezier cutting idea can be successfully applied in cases when we need to resolve problem of cropped region estimation. At the same time Nishita noted that described method does not resolve some tasks, one of them being the frequent point search problem and the instability of the method in some surface special cases.

W. Martin et al. [6] proposed a method for reverse NURBS surface visualization in ray tracing. Using node vector processing for generating hierarchic structure of limited space, as a result tree depth declines in comparison with other subdivision methods. The idea is to use handling of node vector so that after NURBS surface transformation Bezier surface set is developed. This surface is wide enough and has narrow limiting box. Bezier surfaces do not use large volumes of memory and are used only for limiting box hierarchic structure construction. The advantage of this method is that achieved plane surface is a good starting condition for Newton's iterative method. NURBS surface calculation scheme that is proposed in the work is based on node vector handling. Unfortunately, algorithm of NURBS surface calculation works slower than Bezier surface calculation. Newton method requires to calculate surface point and two partial derivations for every iteration to get quadric convergence. It is better to divide the initial NURBS surface on Bezier surface during initial processing. This requires extra memory volume to save every surface separately, but it allows to speed-up the calculation significantly.

S.W. Wang, Z.C. Shih and R.C. Chang [11] proposed an algorithm that combines Bezier cutting algorithm and Newton iterative algorithm in order to create effective method for ray coherence application. The first intersection point of the running ray with the Bezier surface is calculated using Bezier iterative algorithm. All following intersection points in the same pixel row are calculated using Newton iterative algorithm. The last calculated intersection point is used as previous result for the following intersection point. The device for barrier detection is used to check-up whether the intersection point that is calculated using Newton iterative algorithm is the last point. When Newton's method is not achieving convergences, then Bezier cutting is used as a replacement for calculating the intersection point.

A. Efremov, V. Havran and H.P. Seidel [1] and [2] proposed the method for NURBS surface visualization in ray tracing using following method: object's every NURBS surface is transformed into equivalent rational set of Bezier surface and exactly this set is mapped. To solve rational Bezier surface problem Bezier cutting method, that is described in [7], is used. And, also [1] and [2] proposes some modifications that improve the activity and effectiveness of Bezier cutting method.

Schollmeyer and Froehlich [9] describe an approach for NURBS surface ray tracing, where surface trimming is used to set of monotonic Bézier curves. For finding of intersection point the bisection method is used. But in this case, the number of calculations increases too.

In particular and NURBS surface is extensively used in computer graphics and computer aided design. Unfortunately, most of the algorithms for intersecting rays with parametric surfaces are expensive or have problems in some special cases. Therefore, most of modern ray tracing applications tessellate parametric surfaces into triangles during the preprocessing step of image generation. Such approach significantly increases computation speed, but can compute wrong images (if tessellation was not good enough) and requires additional memory for storage of generated triangles. Therefore, the problem of finding fast and robust algorithms for ray tracing parametric surfaces is still opened research issue [2].

This paper presents an effective approach for finding ray – NURBS surface intersection points, which are used for high-quality visualization of NURBS surfaces.

2. Ray-Surface Intersection problem

The mathematical task of finding an intersection point between the ray and a parametric surface can be described as a nonlinear equations system [6]:

$$\begin{cases} S'_X(u,v) = C_X(t) \\ S'_Y(u,v) = C_Y(t) \\ S'_Z(u,v) = C_Z(t) \end{cases} \tag{1}$$

where: S'_X, S'_Y, S'_Z - are the surface equations,
$C_X(t), C_Y(t), C_Z(t)$ - are the ray equations.

A NURBS surface patch in Cartesian 3D space can be formulated as [3, 8]:

$$S'(u,v) = \frac{\sum_{i=0}^{n}\sum_{j=0}^{m} P'_{i,j} \cdot w_{i,j} \cdot N_{i,p}(u) \cdot N_{j,q}(v)}{\sum_{i=0}^{n}\sum_{j=0}^{m} w_{i,j} \cdot N_{i,p}(u) \cdot N_{j,q}(v)} \tag{2}$$

where: $P'_{i,j}$ - are the control points;
$w_{i,j}$ - are the weights;
$N_{i,p}(u), N_{j,q}(v)$ - are the B-spline polynomials;
$n+1, m+1$ - are the number of control points in each parametric direction;
p,q - are the B-spline polynomials degree;
u,v - are the parameters.

2.1 Projection to R^2

Typically calculation is performed in $\mathbf{R}^3$ for non-rational patches and in $\mathbf{R}^4$ for rational [7].

Transforming the computation from 3D space to 2D space is important technique to reduce the comparison cost of finding ray-surface intersection point. Woodward [12] (also alluded to by [6]) shows how the problem can be projected to $\mathbf{R}^2$. This means that the number of arithmetic operations to calculate a rational patch is reduced by 25%. This approach is used in [7] for rational Bezier patch subdivision. But this approach is good for other parametrical surface patch calculation by ray tracing too. In case of NURBS surfaces, the task of ray-surface intersection point search is transformed to the problem of non-linear equations system solving:

$$\begin{cases} S_X(u,v) - x_R = 0 \\ S_Y(u,v) - y_R = 0 \end{cases} \tag{3}$$

where: $S_X(u,v), S_Y(u,v)$ - are the surface equations on the projection plane,
x_R, y_R - is the ray projection.

The system (3) solving task is divided into two parts: preprocessing with root preliminary search and iterative root finding.

2.2 Preprocessing

Other color values in gradient texture interpolate evenly and are put on the surface. The next task is to read data from the color map. Hence, it is proposed to develop preliminary value map in order to find preliminary parameters a u and v value in each pixel. The map is composed of surface data that is coded in RGB channels. Red channel includes surface number. Mathematical relation can be described in following way:

$$R = Nr + 1 \tag{4}$$

where: R is value of red channel, which is changing in diapason [1; 255];
Nr is surface number, which is changing in diapason [0; 254].

In case if R=0, we can say that in this pixel ray does not intersect any point. Taking into account 24 bits image coding in RGB color system we can say that surface number is changing in diapason [0; 254];

Green and blue channels consist of congener gradient texture that is on peace surface. Let's say, that color value in every channel is a whole number in diapason [0; 225]. Color value corner surface points can be given in the way it is described in the first table.

Surface point	Color value
$S(u_{min}, v_{min})$	$(R \;\; 0 \;\; 0)$
$S(u_{max}, v_{min})$	$(R \;\; 255 \;\; 0)$
$S(u_{min}, v_{max})$	$(R \;\; 0 \;\; 255)$
$S(u_{max}, v_{max})$	$(R \;\; 255 \;\; 255)$

Table 1. Corner control points color value

Other color values in gradient texture interpolate evenly and are put on the surface. Green and blue channels consist of congener procedure in gradient texture that is put on peace surface. Color value depends on u and v parameters and this can be calculated in following way:

$$\begin{cases} G = Round\left[255 \cdot \dfrac{(u - u_{min})}{(u_{max} - u_{min})}\right] \\ B = Round\left[255 \cdot \dfrac{(v - v_{min})}{(v_{max} - v_{min})}\right] \end{cases} \tag{5}$$

The map is coded using the OpenGL graphics library. The example of preliminary values map is shown in Fig. 1.

The next task is to read data from the color map. Input data in this case is R, G and B color value in every separate pixel. In this case we can find the preliminary value of parameters in following way:

$$\begin{cases} u_0 = \dfrac{1}{255} \cdot (u_{max} - u_{min}) \cdot G + u_{min} \\ v_0 = \dfrac{1}{255} \cdot (v_{max} - v_{min}) \cdot B + v_{min} \end{cases} \tag{6}$$

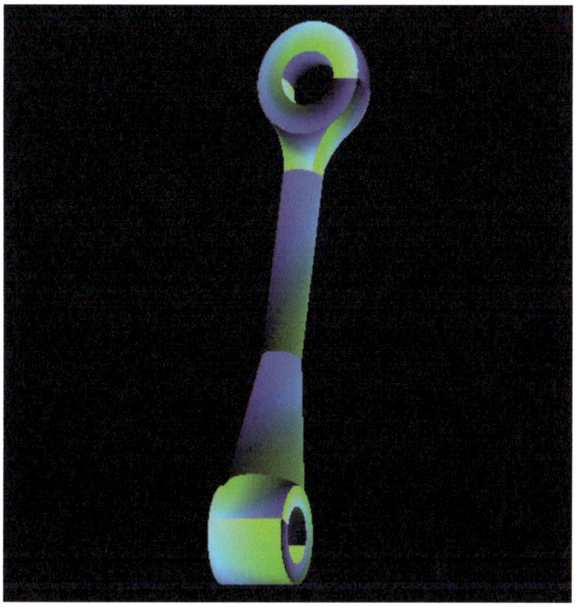

Fig. 1. The example of preliminary values map.

where: u_0, v_0 – are the parameters preliminary value in pixel;
$u_{\min}, u_{\max}$ – are the parameter u minimum and maximum;
$v_{\min}, v_{\max}$ – are the parameter v minimum and maximum;
G – is the color value in green channel;
B – is the color value in blue channel.

The patch number can be calculating from (4) as follows:

$$Nr = R - 1 \tag{7}$$

where: Nr is surface number, which is changing in diapason [0; 254];
R is value of red channel, which is changing in diapason [1; 255].

2.3 Intersection test

The Newton iteration [10] can be used for solving system (3) solving. In this case, an iteration step takes the form:

$$\begin{bmatrix} u_{i+1} \\ v_{i+1} \end{bmatrix} = \begin{bmatrix} u_i \\ v_i \end{bmatrix} - \left[J(u_i, v_i) \right]^{-1} \cdot \left[F(u_i, v_i) \right] \tag{8}$$

where matrix for inversion can be calculated as follows:

$$\left[J(u,v) \right] = \begin{bmatrix} \dfrac{\partial S_X}{\partial u} & \dfrac{\partial S_X}{\partial v} \\ \dfrac{\partial S_Y}{\partial u} & \dfrac{\partial S_Y}{\partial v} \end{bmatrix} \tag{9}$$

is Jacobian matrix and

$$\left[F(u,v)\right]=\begin{bmatrix}S_X - x_R\\ S_Y - y_R\end{bmatrix} \tag{10}$$

The equation (8) can be described as follows:

$$\begin{bmatrix}u_{i+1}\\ v_{i+1}\end{bmatrix}=\begin{bmatrix}u_i\\ v_i\end{bmatrix}+\begin{bmatrix}\Delta u\\ \Delta v\end{bmatrix} \tag{11}$$

The increment matrix can be described as follows:

$$\begin{bmatrix}\Delta u\\ \Delta v\end{bmatrix}=-\left[J(u_i,v_i)\right]^{-1}\cdot\left[F(u_i,v_i)\right] \tag{12}$$

2.4 Proposed approach

The NURBS patch surface equation on the projection plane can be described as follows:

$$\begin{cases} S_X(u,v)=\dfrac{x(u,v)}{w(u,v)}\\ S_Y(u,v)=\dfrac{y(u,v)}{w(u,v)}\end{cases} \tag{13}$$

where:

$$x(u,v)=\sum_{i=0}^{n}\sum_{j=0}^{m}P_{i,j}^{X}\cdot w_{i,j}\cdot N_{i,p}(u)\cdot N_{j,q}(v) \tag{14}$$

and

$$y(u,v)=\sum_{i=0}^{n}\sum_{j=0}^{m}P_{i,j}^{Y}\cdot w_{i,j}\cdot N_{i,p}(u)\cdot N_{j,q}(v) \tag{15}$$

and

$$w(u,v)=\sum_{i=0}^{n}\sum_{j=0}^{m}w_{i,j}\cdot N_{i,p}(u)\cdot N_{j,q}(v) \tag{16}$$

where: $P_{i,j}^{X}, P_{i,j}^{Y}$, – are the control points x and y coordinates on the projection plane.

In next parts of the paper for simplification equations $x(u,v)$, $y(u,v)$ and $w(u,v)$ is described as x, y and w. NURBS surface partial derivatives, which are elements of Jacobian's matrix, can be calculated as follows [8]:

$$\frac{\partial S_X}{\partial u}=S_X\cdot\left(\frac{\partial x}{\partial u}\cdot\frac{1}{x}-\frac{\partial w}{\partial u}\cdot\frac{1}{w}\right) \tag{17}$$

and

$$\frac{\partial S_X}{\partial v} = S_X \cdot \left(\frac{\partial x}{\partial v} \cdot \frac{1}{x} - \frac{\partial w}{\partial v} \cdot \frac{1}{w} \right) \tag{18}$$

For S_Y:

$$\frac{\partial S_Y}{\partial u} = S_Y \cdot \left(\frac{\partial y}{\partial u} \cdot \frac{1}{y} - \frac{\partial w}{\partial u} \cdot \frac{1}{w} \right) \tag{19}$$

and

$$\frac{\partial S_Y}{\partial v} = S_Y \cdot \left(\frac{\partial y}{\partial v} \cdot \frac{1}{y} - \frac{\partial w}{\partial v} \cdot \frac{1}{w} \right) \tag{20}$$

Using equations (17)-(20) after transformation, the increment matrix (12) takes the form:

$$\begin{bmatrix} \Delta u \\ \Delta v \end{bmatrix} = \frac{w}{M} \cdot \begin{bmatrix} M_U \\ M_V \end{bmatrix} \tag{21}$$

where:

$$M = \begin{vmatrix} x & \frac{\partial x}{\partial u} & \frac{\partial x}{\partial v} \\ y & \frac{\partial y}{\partial u} & \frac{\partial y}{\partial v} \\ w & \frac{\partial w}{\partial u} & \frac{\partial w}{\partial v} \end{vmatrix} \tag{22}$$

and

$$M_U = \begin{vmatrix} x & x_R & \frac{\partial x}{\partial v} \\ y & y_R & \frac{\partial y}{\partial v} \\ w & 1 & \frac{\partial w}{\partial v} \end{vmatrix} \tag{23}$$

and

$$M_V = \begin{vmatrix} x & \frac{\partial x}{\partial u} & x_R \\ y & \frac{\partial y}{\partial u} & y_R \\ w & \frac{\partial w}{\partial u} & 1 \end{vmatrix} \tag{24}$$

The equation (11) can be described is as follows:

$$\begin{bmatrix} u_{i+1} \\ v_{i+1} \end{bmatrix} = \begin{bmatrix} u_i \\ v_i \end{bmatrix} + \frac{w}{M} \cdot \begin{bmatrix} M_U \\ M_V \end{bmatrix} \tag{25}$$

How is can to see from (21) the increment matrix can describe the solving of next system of linear equations:

$$\begin{bmatrix} x & \frac{\partial x}{\partial u} & \frac{\partial x}{\partial v} \\ y & \frac{\partial y}{\partial u} & \frac{\partial y}{\partial v} \\ w & \frac{\partial w}{\partial u} & \frac{\partial w}{\partial v} \end{bmatrix} \cdot \begin{bmatrix} \Delta a^* \\ \Delta u^* \\ \Delta v^* \end{bmatrix} = \begin{bmatrix} x_R \\ y_R \\ 1 \end{bmatrix} \tag{26}$$

where: Δa^* – redundancy root.

In this case the increment matrix (21) is partial solving of system of linear equations by Cramer rule and can be found as follows:

$$\begin{bmatrix} \Delta u^* \\ \Delta v^* \end{bmatrix} = w \cdot \begin{bmatrix} \Delta u \\ \Delta v \end{bmatrix} \tag{27}$$

For practical implementation can be better the Gaussian elimination use. In this case the system of linear equations can be described as extended matrix:

$$\left[\begin{array}{ccc|c} x & \frac{\partial x}{\partial u} & \frac{\partial x}{\partial v} & x_R \\ y & \frac{\partial y}{\partial u} & \frac{\partial y}{\partial v} & y_R \\ w & \frac{\partial w}{\partial u} & \frac{\partial w}{\partial v} & 1 \end{array}\right] \tag{28}$$

In this case the restriction is big number of division operator using.

2.5 Border criteria

As known the NURBS surface parameters is defended in diapason, what can be described as follows:

$$u \in [u_{\min};\ u_{\max}]\ \&\ v \in [v_{\min};\ v_{\max}] \tag{29}$$

In the process of the iterative procedure there can be a situation, that new parameters values is outside of diapason from (23). This case is showed in Fig. 2.

In this case the correction of the result is necessary. This task is divided into two parts: parameter v correction using parameter u border and the next step is parameter u correction using parameter v border.

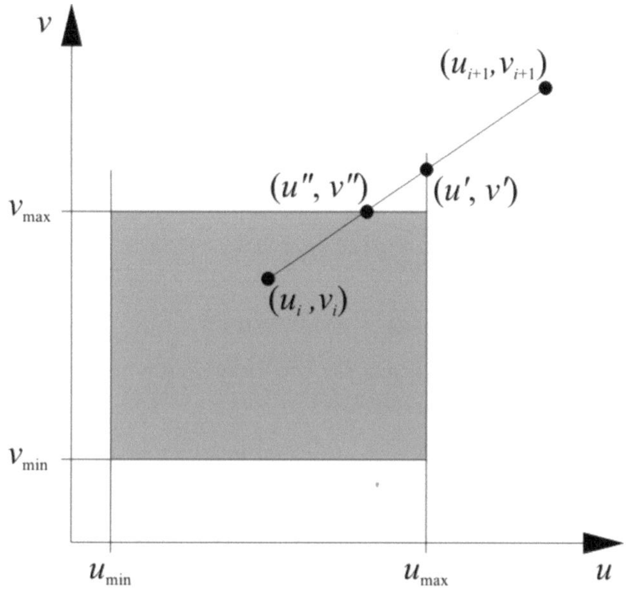

Fig. 2. Iteration step result outside parameters diapason.

First step can be described as follows: if equation $u_{i+1} \in [u_{min}; \;\; u_{max}]$ is correct then we can go to the second step. Otherwise the correction can be described as follows:

$$u' = \begin{cases} u_{min} & if \quad u_{i+1} < u_{min} \\ u_{max} & if \quad u_{i+1} >_{max} \end{cases} \tag{30}$$

And the next step:

$$v' = \frac{v_{i+1} - v_i}{u_{i+1} - u_i} \cdot u' + \frac{u_{i+1} \cdot v_i - u_i \cdot v_{i+1}}{u_{i+1} - u_i} \tag{31}$$

If equation $v' \in [v_{min}; \;\; v_{max}]$ is correct then the correction can be finished with the result of iteration step in point $(u';v')$. Otherwise, the second correction step is necessary.

Second step can be described by analogy with the first step. The parameter v correction can be described as follows:

$$v'' = \begin{cases} v_{min} & if \quad v' < v_{min} \\ v_{max} & if \quad v' > v_{max} \end{cases} \tag{32}$$

And the next step, parameter u correction, as follows:

$$u'' = \frac{u' - u_i}{v' - v_i} \cdot v'' + \frac{u_i \cdot v' - u' \cdot v_i}{v' - v_i} \tag{33}$$

After second correction step it is possible to guarantee, that $u'' \in [u_{min}; \;\; u_{max}]$ and $v'' \in [v_{min}; \;\; v_{max}]$, and the result of iteration step is the point $(u'';v'')$.

2.6 Termination criteria

In this work, five criteria are used to decide when to terminate the Newton iteration. This criterion is analogical to termination criteria in work [6] and [13].

The first condition is the success criterion: if we are closer to the root than some predetermined ε_1 then we report an intersection:

$$\left\| \left[F(u_i, v_i) \right] \right\|_2 < \varepsilon_1 \tag{34}$$

where $\|...\|_2$ - is norm of vector $[F]$ in 2D Euclidian space.

But in (25) is necessary to use next success criterion: if we are closer to the root values increment then some predetermined ε_2 and ε_3:

$$\begin{cases} |M_U| < \varepsilon_2 \\ |M_V| < \varepsilon_3 \end{cases} \tag{35}$$

It possible report an intersection point determination if is correct first or second termination criteria. Otherwise, we continue the iteration. The other three criteria are failure criteria, meaning that if they are met, we terminate the iteration and report a miss.

We do not allow the new (u_{i+1}, v_{i+1}) estimate to take us farther from the root then the previous one:

$$\left\| \left[F(u_{i+1}, v_{i+1}) \right] \right\|_2 > \left\| \left[F(u_i, v_i) \right] \right\|_2 \tag{36}$$

A maximum number of iteration steps has been performed, also indicating divergence:

$$i < i_{\max} \tag{37}$$

A final check is made to assure that the matrix $[M]$ is not singular. In the situation where $[M]$ is singular, either the surface is not regular or the ray is parallel to a silhouette ray at the point $S(u_i, v_i)$. In either situation, to determine singularity, we test:

$$\left| \det(M) \right| < \varepsilon_4 \tag{38}$$

3. Experimental results

In this work the proposed method, as well as the methods suggested by Martin et al. were implemented. In order to visualize a scene the 1 ray/pixel approach was used. The size of the obtained image is 512x512 pixels. 4 scenes were visualized during the experiment: the first scene - duck that what is taken from VRML programming language standard examples, the second scene visualized experimental object from the first scene, in total 27 VRML ducks, the third scene visualized experimental object - mobile phone and the fourth scene visualized practical object - modelled machine component.

All surfaces of experimental scenes were described with the help of NURBS surface. Achieved images were shown in Fig. 4-8.

As it is possible to see from these figures the proposed method gives an advantage on quality of the images (there's no distortion on the borders of patches). Image rendering time is shown in Table 2 and in Fig 3.

Objects	Proposed method, sec.	Martin et al. Method, sec.
"Duck"	5,578	6,437
"27 Ducks"	9,0	11,86
"Mobile phone"	4,297	5,422
"Machine component"	1,890	2,203

Table 2. Images rendering time in seconds

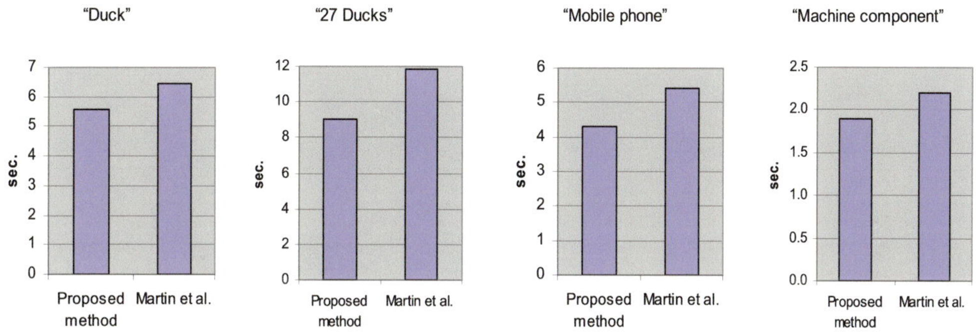

Fig. 3. Images rendering time

As seen from the table, the proposed method gives stable results in the fastest rendering time in our experiments (compared to method Martin et al.).

For comparison we shall consider the time of visualization in percentage, by taking earlier known method (Martin et al.) for 100%. The results are shown in Table 3.

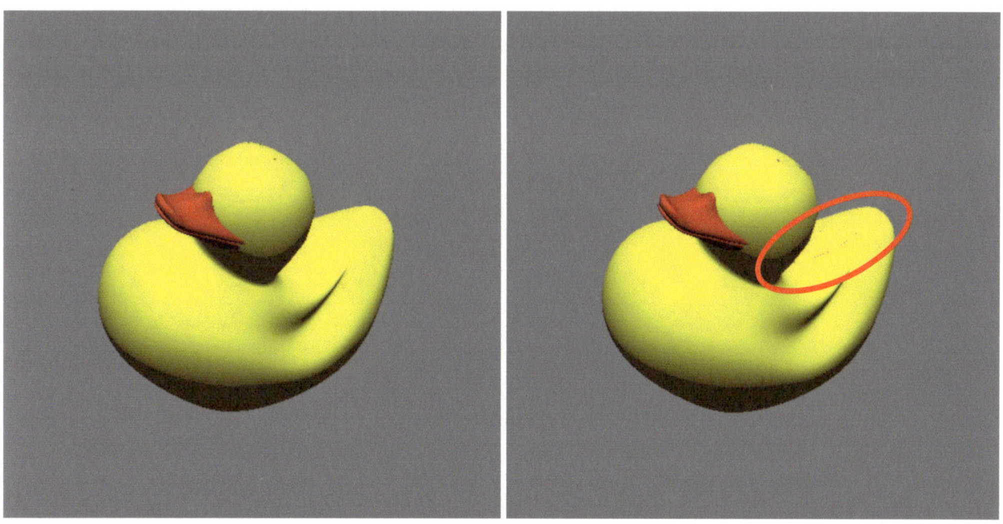

Fig. 4. The image of a scene "Duck" obtained using the proposed method (left) and the method Martin et al.(right).

Objects	Proposed method, %	Speed-up of rendering, %
"Duck"	86,66	13,34
"27 Ducks"	75,89	24,11
"Mobile phone"	79,251	20,749
"Machine component"	85,792	14,208

Table 3. Image rendering time in percentage (Martin et al. - 100%)

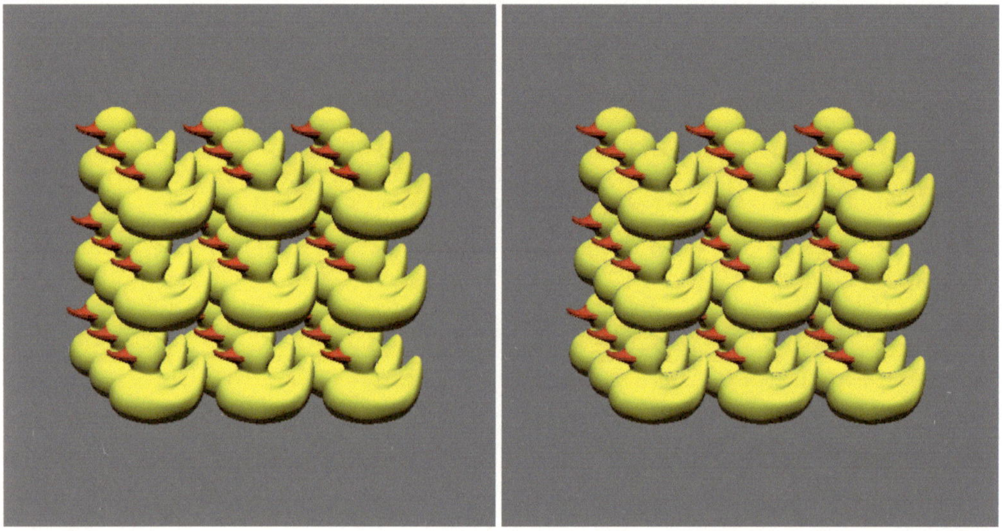

Fig. 5. The image of a scene "27 Ducks" obtained using the proposed method (left) and the method Martin et al.(right).

Fig. 6. The image of an object "Mobile phone" obtained using the proposed method (left) and the method Martin et al.(right).

As we can see from Table 3 data the proposed method gives stable visualization time reduction (compare with existing methods) in experiment. Table 3 proves that proposed method gives time reduction 13,3 - 24,1% in experiment in comparison with algorithm Martin et al.

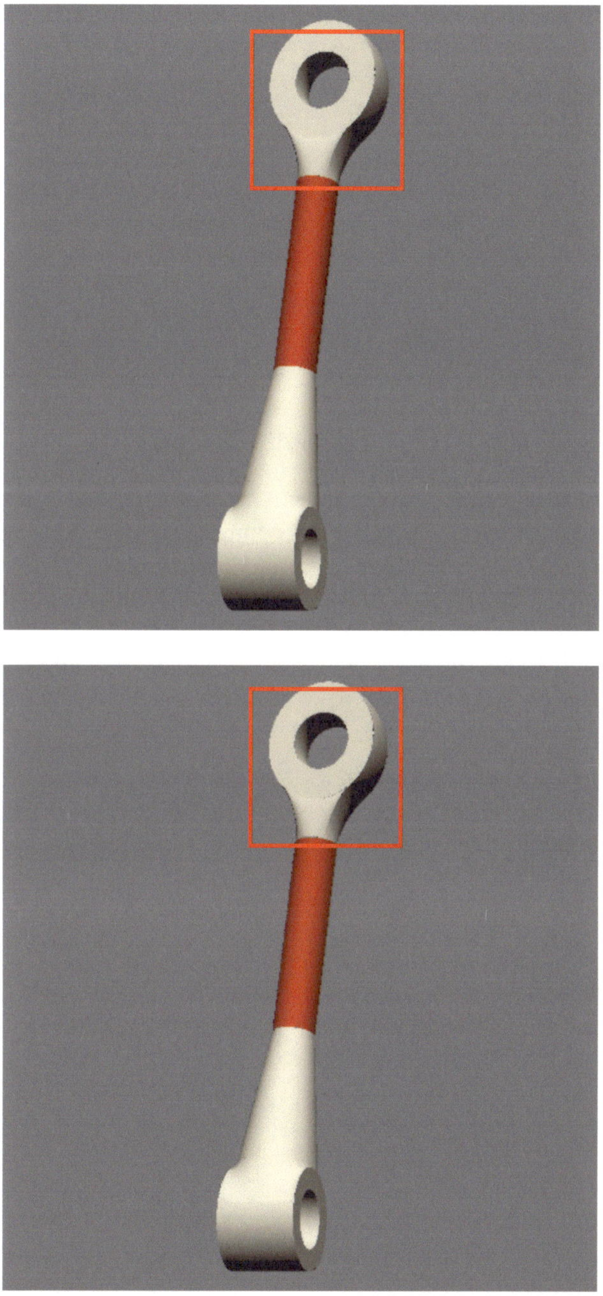

Fig. 7. The image of an object "Machine component" obtained using the proposed method (left) and the method Martin et al.(right).

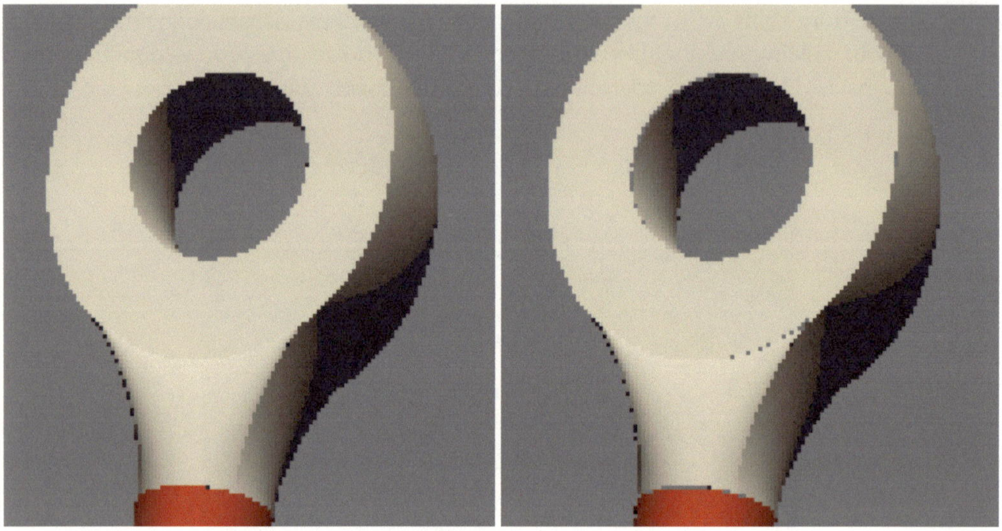

Fig. 8. The 4x enlarged fragment of image of an object "Machine component" obtained using the proposed method (left) and the method Martin et al.(right).

The next experiment that was conducted in order to check-up the described experiment is the comparison with existing CAD system. A comparison with Autodesk AutoCAD 2010 system was conducted. "Machine element" was chosen an object's example. To conduct object's visualization in CAD system Autodesk AutoCAD 2010 this object was made with NURBS surfaces in visualization programs and was imported to Autodesk AutoCAD 2010. To ensure correct comparison the object was colored in one color and equivalent lightening settings were adjusted. Fragments that were made larger in the visualization result, are shown in Fig. 9

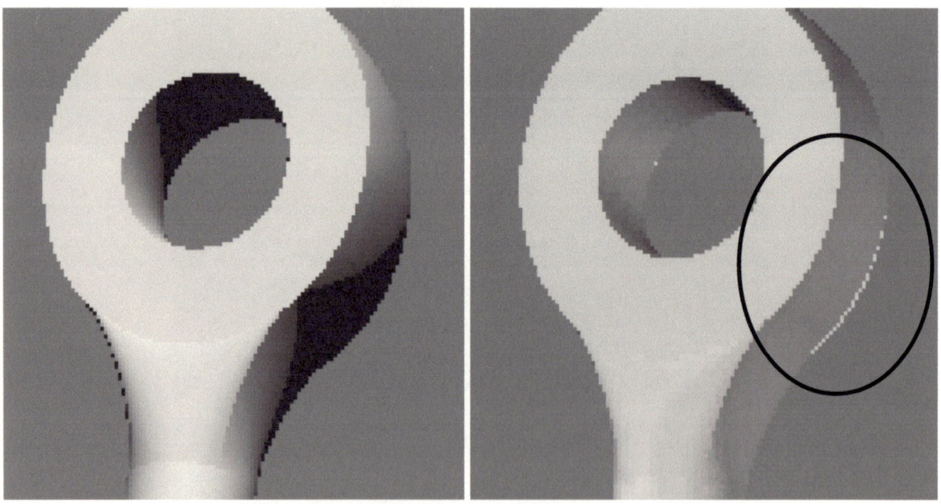

a) b)

Fig. 9. Objects "Machine element" visualization, using:
a) proposed method, b) Autodesk AutoCAD 2010

From Fig. 9 we can see that the proposed method gives better result regarding image quality, because the object has not any defects on surface borders. Image visualization times in the experiment are following: 1, 89 seconds using proposed method; 10, 24 seconds using Autodesk AutoCAD 2010 visualization. As we can see from given data, proposed method give visualization time reduction in experiment (the difference is 5, 4 times).

4. Conclusion

In this work an efficient approach to direct NURBS surface rendering for ray tracing is proposed. The proposed approach based on Newton method and Cramer rule combination. The proposed approach, as well as the methods suggested by Martin et al. was implemented.

The results (in Figures 4 - 8) shows, that:

- As seen from comparison of Fig.4 - Fig.8. the use of the proposed method results in better quality of the image than Martin et al. method. The proposed method has no distortions on the image, while method Martin et al. has some faults (like distortion on border of patches).
- The modified proposed method results in faster image rendering time. This method works on 14% - 24% faster than the method of Martin et al.

5. References

[1] Efremov, A.; Havran, V.& Seidel, H.-P. (2005). Robust and numerically stable Bézier clipping method for ray tracing NURBS surfaces, *Proceedings of the 21st spring conference on Computer graphics*, pp. 127-135, ISBN 1-59593-204-6, New York, USA

[2] Efremov A., 2005, Efficient *Ray Tracing of Trimmed NURBS Surfaces*, Master's thesis, Computer Graphics Group, Max-Planck-Institut für Informatik, Saarbrücken, Germany, 162 p.

[3] Hearn, D. & Baker, M.P. (2003) *Computer Graphics with OpenGL, 3rd Ed.* ISBN 978-0130153906, Prentice Hall, USA.

[4] Himmelblau, D., 1972. Applied Nonlinear Programming. McGraw-Hill Book Company, Boston, USA.

[5] Kajiya J.T., (1982) Ray Tracing Parametric Patches. *Proceedings of the 9th annual conference on Computer graphics and interactive techniques.* - Boston: SIGRAPH, 1982. - pp. 245 - 254.

[6] Martin, W. et al, 2000. *Practical Ray Tracing of Trimmed NURBS Surfaces.* Journal of Graphics Tools, Vol. 5, No. 1, pp. 27-52.

[7] Nishita, T. et al, 1990. Ray tracing trimmed rational surface patches. Journal ACM SIGGRAPH Computer Graphics, Vol. 24, No. 4, pp. 337–345.

[8] Rogers, D.F. and Adams, J.A., 1990. Mathematical Elements for Computer Graphic, 2nd Ed. McGraw-Hill Book Company, Boston, USA.

[9] Schollmeyer A., and Froehlich, B., 2009. *Direct Trimming of NURBS Surfaces on the GPU,* Jounal ACM Transactions on Graphics, Vol. 28, No. 3, Article 47.

[10] Taha H.A., 2003. Operations Research: an Introduction, 7th Ed. Prentice Hall, New Jersey, USA.

[11] Wang S.-W., Shih Z.-C., Chang R.-C. (2001). An Efficient and Stable Ray Tracing Algorithm for Parametric Surfaces, Journal of Information Science and Engineering, Nr.18. - pp. 541 - 561.

[12] Woodward C. 1989. Ray tracing parametric surfaces by subdivision in viewing plane. Theory and practice of geometric modeling, Springer-Verlag, New York, USA, pp. 273 – 287.

[13] Yang C.-G. 1987. On speeding up ray tracing of B-spline surfaces. Journal Computer Aided Design, Vol. 19, No. 3, pp. 122-130.

6

Design and Implementation of Interactive Flow Visualization Techniques

Tony McLoughlin and Robert S. Laramee
Swansea University
United Kingdom

1. Introduction

The demand for flow visualization software stems from the popular (and growing) use of Computational Fluid Dynamics (CFD) and the increasing complexity of simulation data. CFD is popular with manufacturers as it reduces cost and the time of production relative to the expense involved in creating a real physical model. Modifications to a physical model to test new prototypes may be non-trivial and expensive. CFD solvers enable a high degree of software-based testing and refinement before creating a real physical model.

The visualization of CFD data presents many different challenges. There is no single technique that is appropriate for the visualization of all CFD data. Some techniques are only suitable for certain scenarios and sometimes an engineer is only interesting in a sub-set of the data or specific features, such as vortices or separation surfaces. This means that an effective flow visualization application must offer a wide range of techniques to accommodate these requirements. The integration of a wide variety of techniques is non-trivial and care must be taken with the design and implementation of the software.

We describe our flow visualization software framework that offers a rich set of state-of-the-art features. It is the product of over three years of development. The paper provides more details about the design and implementation of the system than are normally provided by typical research papers due to page limit constraints. Our application also serves as a basis for the implementation and evaluation of new algorithms. The application is easily extendable and provides a clean interface for the addition of new modules. More developers can utilize the code base in the future. A group development project greatly varies from an individual effort. To make this viable, strict coding standards [Laramee (2010)] and documentation are maintained. This will help to minimize the effort a future developer needs to invest to understand the codebase and expand upon it.

Throughout this chapter we focus on the design and implementation of our system for flow visualization. We address how the systems design is used to address the challenges of visualization of CFD simulation data. We describe several key aspects of our design as well as the contributing factors that lead to these particular design decisions.

The rest of this chapter is organized as follows: Section 2 introduces the reader to the field of flow visualization and provides information for further reading. Section 3 describes the user requirements and goals for our application. Section 4 provides an overview of the application design. A description of the major systems is then provided with the key classes and relationships are discussed. The chapter is concluded in Section 5. Throughout the chapter, class hierarchies and collaboration graphs are provided for various important classes of the system.

2. Related work and background

The visualization of velocity fields presents many challenges. Not the least of which is the notion of how to provide an intuitive representation of a 3D vector projected on to a 2D image plane. Other challenges include:

- Occlusion in volumetric flow fields
- Visualizing time-dependent flow data
- Large, High-dimensional datasets – it is common place to see datasets on the Giga- and Tera-byte scale.
- Uncertainty. Due to the numerical nature of CFD and flow visualization, error is accumulated at every stage. This needs to be minimized in order to provide accurate visualization results.

This is by no means an exhaustive list but serves as a representation to give the reader a feel for the context of the system. Flow visualization algorithms can be classified into 4 sub-groups: direct, texture-based, geometric and feature-based. We now provide a description of each of these classes and highlight some of key techniques in each one.

Direct flow visualization

This category represents the most basic of visualization techniques. This range of techniques maps visualization primitives directly to the samples of the data. Examples of direct techniques are color-mapping of velocity magnitude or rendering arrow glyphs [Peng & Laramee (2009)].

Texture-based flow visualization

This category provides a dense representation of the underlying velocity field, providing full domain coverage. This range of techniques depicts the direction of the velocity field by filtering a (noise) texture according the local velocity information. This results in the texture being smeared along the direction of the velocity. Line Integral Convolution (LIC) by Cabral and Leedom [Cabral & Leedom (1993)] one seminal texture-based technique. Other texture-based variants include Image-space advection (ISA) by Laramee et al. [Laramee et al. (2003)] and IBFVS [van Wijk (2003)], both of which use image-based approaches to apply texture-based techniques to velocity fields on the surfaces of CFD meshes. It should be noted that due to the dense representation of the velocity field, texture-based techniques are more suited to 2D flow fields and flow fields restricted to surfaces. Three-dimensional variants do exist [Weiskopf et al. (2001)] but occlusion becomes a serious problem and reduces effectiveness. We refer the interested reader to [Laramee et al. (2004)] for a thorough overview of texture-based techniques.

Geometric flow visualization techniques

This category involves the computation of geometry that reflects the properties of the underlying velocity field. The geometry used is generally curves, surfaces and volumes. The geometric primitives are constructed using numeric integration and using interpolation to reconstruct the velocity field between samples.

Typically the geometry remains tangent to the velocity as in the case of streamlines and streamsurfaces [Hultquist (1992)] [McLoughlin et al. (2009)]. However non-tangential geometry also illustrate important features; streaklines and streaksurfaces [Krishnan et al. (2009)] are becoming increasingly popular. In fact this application framework was involved in the development of a novel streak surface algorithm [McLoughlin, Laramee & Zhang (2010)]. A thorough review of geometric techniques is beyond the scope of this paper and we refer the interested reader to a survey on the topic by McLoughlin et al. [McLoughlin, Laramee, Peikert, Post & Chen (2010)].

Feature-based flow visualization

Feature-based techniques are employed to present a simplified sub-set of the velocity field rather than visualizing it in its entirety. Feature-based techniques generally focus on extracting and/or tracking characteristics such as vortices, or representing a vector field using a minimal amount of information using topological extraction as introduced by Helmann and Hesselink [Helman & Hesselink (1989)]. Once again a thorough review of this literature is beyond the scope of the presented paper and we refer the interested to in-depth surveys on

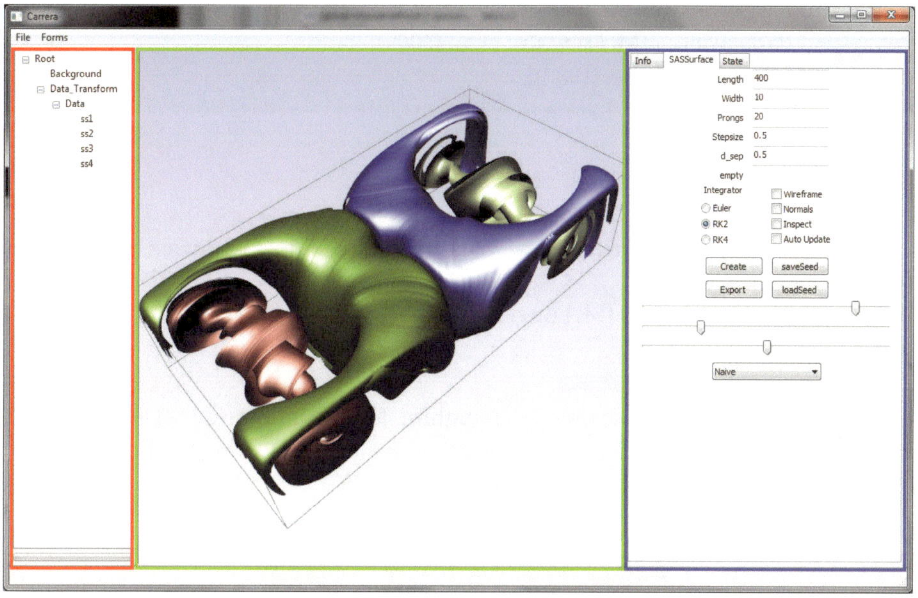

Fig. 1. A screenshot of the application showing the GUI providing controls for streamsurfaces computed on a simulation of Rayleigh-Bénard convection. The application window is split up into three distinct regions. 1. The **Application Tree** (highlighted by the red box) is used to manage the assets in the scene. 2. The **Rendering Window** (highlighted by the green box) displays the visualization results and allows the user to interactively modify the viewing position and orientation. 3. The **Asset Control Pane** (highlighted by the blue box) displays the current set of controls for the selected asset. The GUI is context sensitive for the benefit of the user and the asset control pane only displays the controls for a single tool at any given time. Should a different visualization tool be selected a new set of controls are displayed and the unrequired ones removed. This approach is adopted to provide a simple, uncluttered interface, allowing the user to focus only on the necessary parameters/controls.

feature-based flow visualization by Post et al. and Laramee et al. [Laramee et al. (2007); Post et al. (2003)].

3. System requirements and goals

Our application framework is used to implement existing advanced flow visualization techniques as well as being a platform for the development and testing of new algorithms. The framework is designed to be re-used by future developers researching flow visualization algorithms to increase efficiency and research output. Figure 1 shows a screenshot of the application in action.

Support for a wide-variety of visualization methods and tools

Our application is designed as a research platform. A variety of visualization methods have been implemented so that new algorithms can be directly compared with them. Therefore, the system is designed to be easily extensible. Some of the key flow visualization methods and features that are integrated into our application framework include the following:

1. Integral Curves (with illumination) [Mallo et al. (2005)]
2. Stream- and Pathsurfaces [McLoughlin et al. (2009)]
3. Isosurfaces [Lorensen & Cline (1987)]
4. Streaksurfaces [McLoughlin, Laramee & Zhang (2010)]
5. Slice probes
6. Line Integral Convolution (LIC) [Cabral & Leedom (1993)]
7. Critical Point Extraction
8. Parameter Sensitivity Visualization [McLoughlin, Edmunds, Laramee, Chen, Max, Yeh & Zhang (2011)]
9. Clustering of integral curves [McLoughlin, Jones & Laramee (2011)]
10. Vector field resampling
11. Image output to multiple formats
12. Integral curve similarity measures [McLoughlin, Jones & Laramee (2011)]
13. Computation of the Finite Time Lyapunov Exponent (FTLE) [Haller (2001)]

Fig. 2. Traversing left-to-right from top-to-bottom, examples of visualization techniques 1-9.

Interactivity

Users generally require flexibility over the final visualization and favor feedback as quickly as possible after modifying visualization parameters. Our system is designed to enable a high level of interaction for the user. Providing such a level of interaction allows for easier exploration of the data. The user can also tailor the resulting visualization to their specific needs. This level of interactivity is also of use to the developer. Some algorithms are inherently dependent upon threshold values and parameters. Providing the functionality for these to be modified at run-time allows the programmer to test varying values without having to modify and recompile the code. Once the final value has been found it is then possible to remove the user-option and hard code as a constant if required.

Support for large, high-dimensional, time-dependent simulations

The application is used to visualize the results of large simulations comprised of many time-steps. Not every time step has to present in main memory simultaneously. Our application uses a streaming approach to handle large data sets. A separate data management thread continually runs in the background. When a time-step has been used this manager is responsible for unloading the data for a given time-step and loading in the data for the next (offline) time-step. A separate thread in used to minimize the interruption that occurs from the blocking I/O calls. If a single threaded solution was used the system would compute the visualization as far as possible with the in-core data and then have to halt until the new data is loaded. Note that in many cases the visualization computation still out performs the data loading in a multi-threaded solution, however, the delay may be greatly reduced.

Simple API

The system is intended for future developers to utilize. In order to achieve this the system must be composed of an intuitive, modular design maintaining a high level of re-usability. Extensive documentation and coding conventions [Laramee (2010)] are maintained to allow new users to be able to minimize the overhead required to learn the system. The system is documented using the doxygen documentation system [van Heesch (197-2004)], the documentation can be found online at http://cs.swan.ac.uk/~cstony/documentation/.

4. System design and implementation

Figure 3 shows the design of our application. The major subsystems are shown along with the relationships of how they interact with one another.

The *Graphical User Interface* subsystem is responsible for presenting the user with modifiable parameters and firing events in response to the users actions. The user interface is designed to be minimalistic. It is context sensitive and only the relevant controls are displayed to the user at any time. The GUI was created using the wxWidgets library [wxWidgets GUI Library (n.d.)]. wxWidgets provides a cross-platform API with support for many common graphical widgets – greatly increasing the efficiency of GUI programming. The *3D Viewer* is responsible for all rendering. It supports the rendering of several primitive types such as lines, triangles and quads. The 3D viewer is implemented using OpenGL [Architecture Review Board (2000)] for its platform independence. The *Simulation Manager* stores the simulation data. It stores vector quantities such as velocity and scalar quantities such as pressure. The simulation manager is also responsible for ensuring the correct time-steps are loaded for the desired time. The *Visualization System* is used to compute the visualization results. This system is comprised of several subsystems. Each major system of the application is now described in more detail.

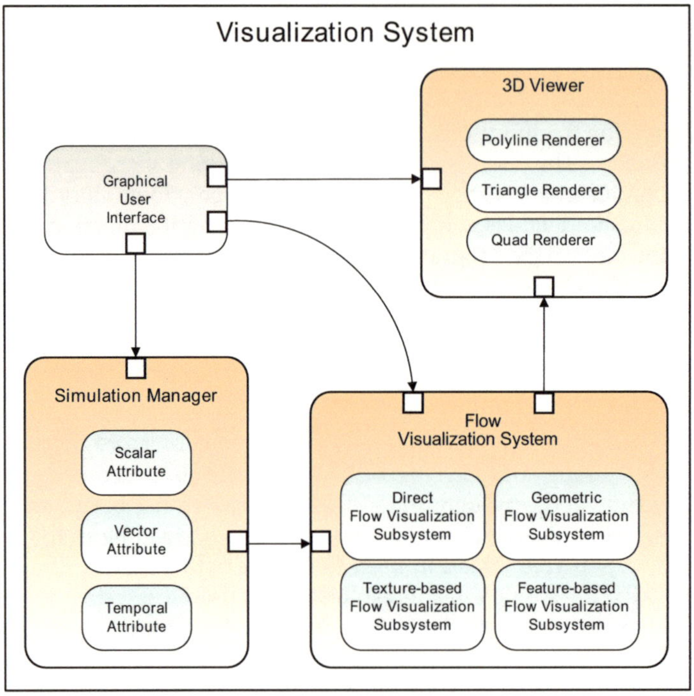

Fig. 3. An overview of our system design. This shows the major subsystems of the framework and which systems interact with one another.

4.1 Visualization system design

The visualization system is where the visualization algorithms are implemented. The application is designed to separate the visualization algorithm logic, the rendering logic, and the GUI. This allows part of the visualization system to be integrated into other applications – even if they use different rendering and GUI APIs. This system is comprised of four sub-systems.

4.1.1 Geometric flow visualization subsystem

Figure 4 illustrates the processing pipeline for the geometric flow visualization subsystem. Input and output data is shown using rectangles with rounded corners. Processes are shown in boxes.

The geometric-based visualization subsystem uses the simulation data as its main input. After the user has set a range of integration parameters and specified the seeding conditions the initial seeding positions are created. Numerical integration is then performed to construct the geometry by tracing vertices through the vector field. This is an iterative process with which an optional refinement stage may be undertaken depending on the visualization method. For example, when using streamsurfaces, extra vertices need to be inserted into the mesh to ensure sufficient sampling of the vector field. Afterwards the object geometry is output. The penultimate stage takes the user-defined parameters that direct the rendering result. Most of the implemented algorithms in our application reside within this sub-system.

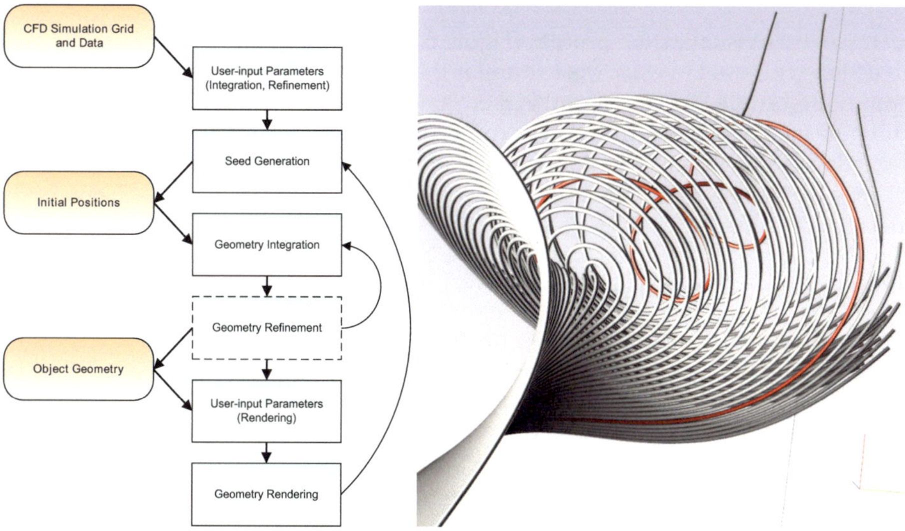

Fig. 4. (Left) The processing pipeline for the geometric flow visualization subsystem. (Right) A set of streamlines generated by the geometric flow visualization subsystem. The streamlines are rendered as tube structures to enhance depth perception and provide a more aesthetically appealing result. The visualization depicts interesting vortical behavior in a simulation of Arnold-Beltrami-Childress flow [Haller (2005)].

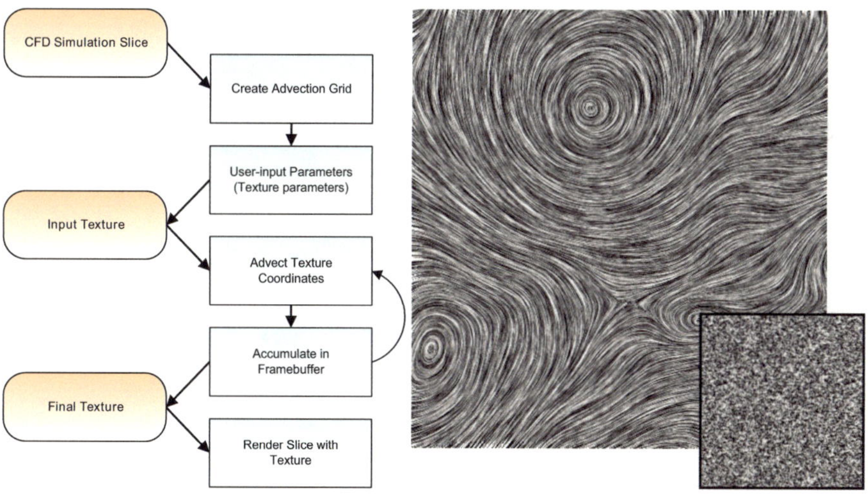

Fig. 5. (Left) The processing pipeline for the texture-based visualization subsystem. (Right) A Line Integral Convolution (LIC) visualization using the texture-based visualization system. This image was generated by 'smearing' the noise texture (inset) along the direction of the underlying vector field at each pixel. The visualization is of a simulation of Hurricane Isabel. The eye of the hurricane can be seen towards the top of the image.

4.1.2 Texture-based visualization subsystem

The texture-based visualization process (Figure 5) also takes in the simulation data as input. An advection grid (used to warp the texture) is then set up and user-parameters are specified. An input noise-texture (Figure 5 inset) is then 'smeared' along the underlying velocity field – depicting the tangent information. The texture advection is performed as an iterative process of integrating the noise texture coordinated through the vector field and accumulating the results after each integration. The resultant texture is then mapped onto a polygon to display the final visualization.

4.1.3 Direct flow visualization subsystem

The direct visualization sub-system presents the simplest algorithms. Typical techniques are direct color-coding and glyph plots. The left image of Figure 6 shows a basic glyph plot of a simulation of Hurricane Isabel. The right image includes a direct color-mapping of a saliency field showing local regions where a larger change in streamline geometry occurs.

4.1.4 Feature-based flow visualization subsystem

Feature-based algorithms may involve a lot of processing to analyze entire the simulation domain. There exists many types of feature that may be extracted (such as vortices), and each feature has a variety of algorithms to detect/extract them. In our application we implemented extraction of critical points (positions at which the velocity diminishes). The right image of Figure 6 shows a set of critical points extracted on a synthetic data set. A red highlight indicates a source or sink exists in the cell and a blue highlight indicates that a saddle point is present in the cell.

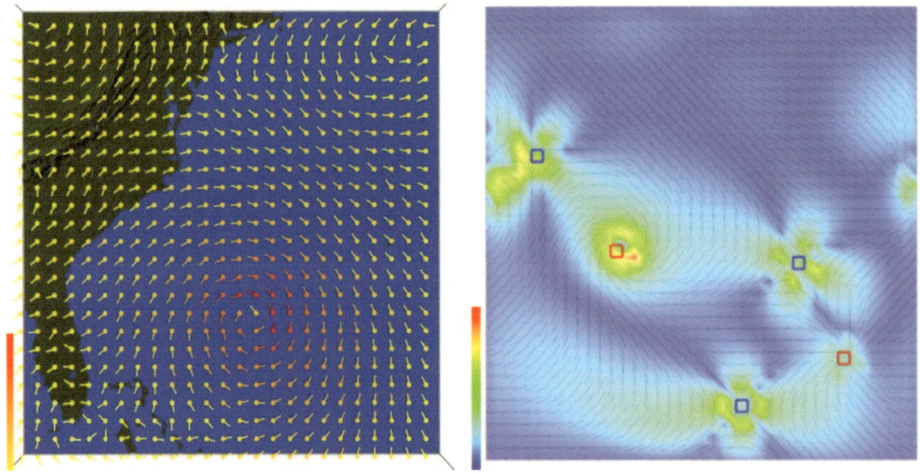

Fig. 6. Direct and feature-based visualizations. The left image shows a basic glyph plot of the velocity field of a simulation of Hurricane Isabel. The right image shows the critical points extracted on a synthetic data set. The cells that contain the critical points are highlighted. A red highlight indicates the critical point is a source or a sink and a blue highlight indicates a saddle point. This visualization also contains a direct color-mapping of a saliency field based on local changes in streamline geometry.

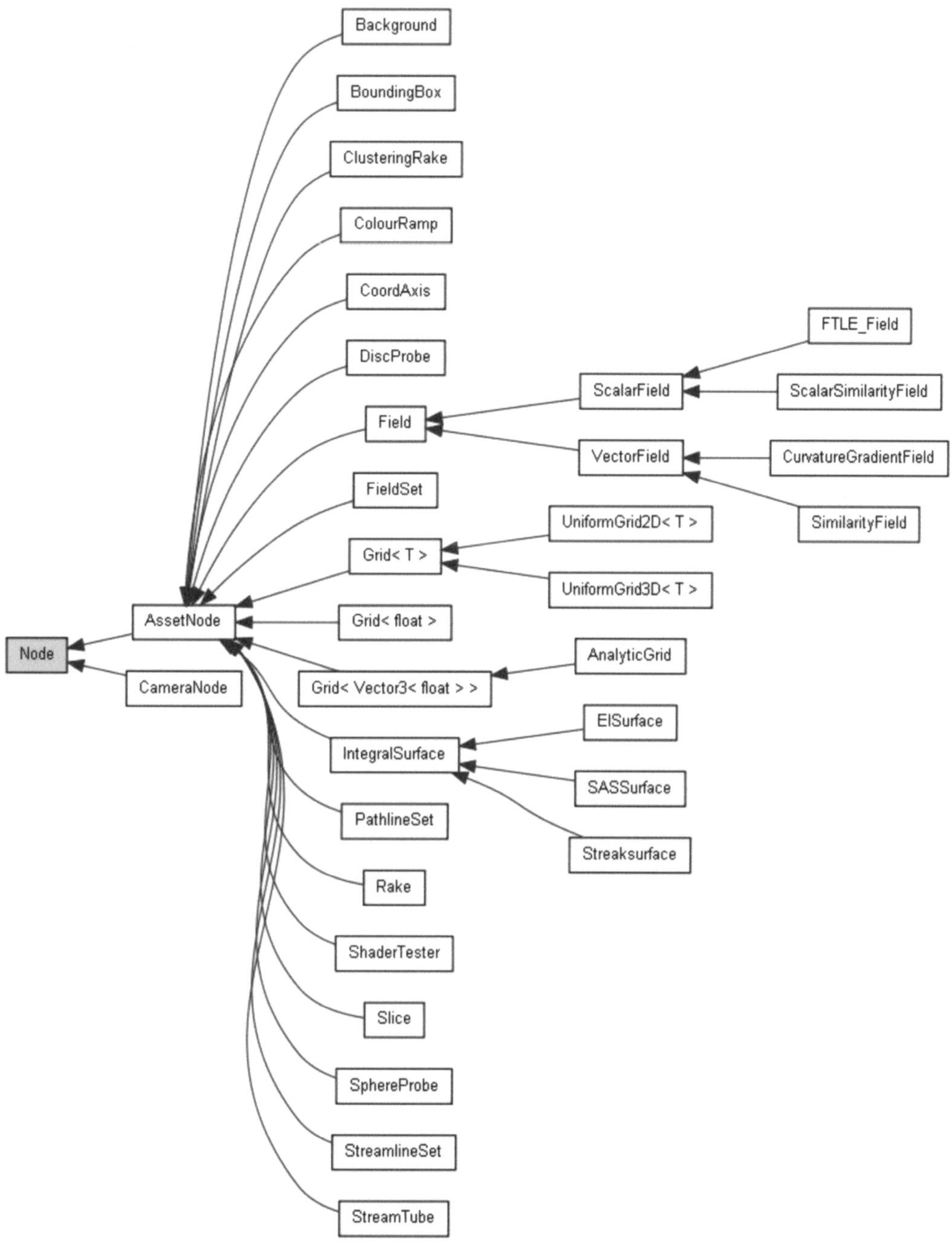

Fig. 7. Inheritance diagram for the node classes. The asset node is the interface from which all integrated visualization techniques inherit and implement.

4.2 Graphical user interface and asset management

The perfect visualization tool does not (yet) exist. Each piece of research that has been undertaken over the past several decades focuses on a specific problem. Thus, a general solution that is suitable for all visualization problems has not been discovered – and may never be found. To this end, visualization applications must support a variety of techniques in order to be useful. When referring to a visualization tool/technique in terms of our software, we refer to them as *assets*. Our asset management system is designed with the following requirements:

- A common interface for assets, simplifying the process of adding new assets in the future and ensuring the application is extendable.
- A common interface between assets and the application GUI. Again this simplifies expansion in the future and ensures a basic level functionality is guaranteed to be implemented. This also provides a consistent user interface for the user.
- Enforcing the re-use of existing code.
- The same method of adding assets for the visualization at run-time.

Fortunately the object-oriented programming paradigm and the C++ programming language provides us with a powerful set of tools to realize these requirements. The rest of this section discusses aspects of the GUI design and our framework for managing the visualization assets.

4.2.1 Application tree and scene graph

In order to provide a flexible system, that allows the user to interactively add and remove assets at run-time, we utilize a scene graph. A scene graph is a tree data structure in which all assets are represented by nodes within the tree. When a frame is rendered, a pre-order, depth-first traversal of the tree is carried out, starting from the root node. As each node is visited, it is sent to the rendering pipeline. Transformations applied to a node are passed onto it's children. We provide two node types: *Asset Nodes* and *Camera Nodes*. These are derived from a base node which provides a common interface and are not directly instantiable. The inheritance diagram for the node types is shown in Figure 7.

The tree structure used for the scene graph lends itself to be represented using a GUI tree control (see Figure 8). The tree control directly depicts all of the nodes in the scene graph and the tree hierarchy. The user manipulates the scene graph through the tree control. Assets can be added to the scene graph by selecting a node to which an asset is attached. Right-clicking upon an asset presents a context menu with an option to add a new node into the scene graph (see Figure 9). Following this option another context menu is presented with a variety of assets which the user is able to add. When an asset is selected to be added, it is inserted into the scene graph as a child node of the currently selected node (the node which was right-clicked). Removal of a node is achieved using a similar method – the right-click context menu gives the option of removing a node. When a node is removed from the scene graph all of its children are also removed. This ensures that there are no dangling pointers and acquired resources are freed. The *resource acquisition is initialization* (RAII) [Meyers (2005)] programming idiom is obeyed throughout the application to ensure exception safe code and resources are deallocated.

From a user perspective, this system allows a flexible method with which to interactively add and remove the visualization tools at run-time. The current tool set is always displayed to provide fast and easy access. From a developer perspective, this system provides a consistent

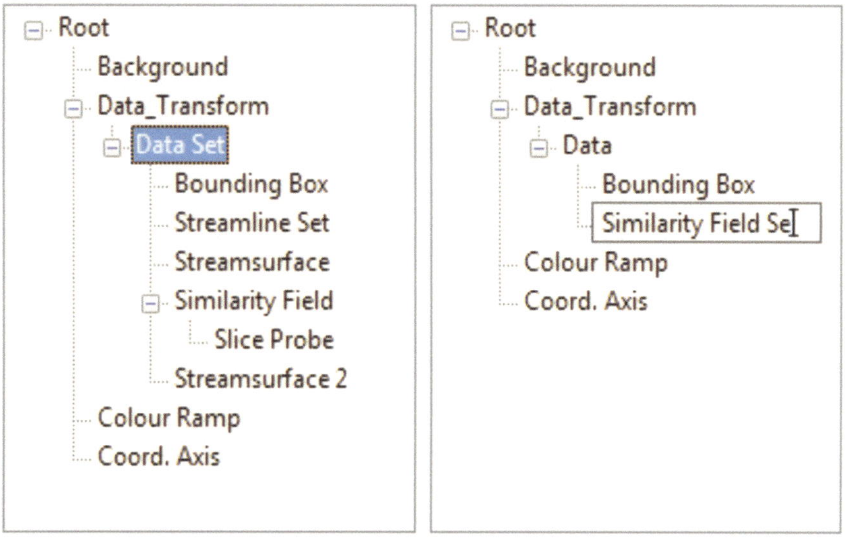

Fig. 8. Screenshots of the application tree during the run-time of different sessions. The application tree is a GUI tree control that represents the nodes in the scene graph. (Left) Several visualization assets, such as streamline sets and slice probes, are currently being employed. (Right) The user is editing the label of one of the assets.

interface. The logic for adding and removing a node is maintained in the scene graph, application tree, and node classes. It does not need implementing on a per-asset basis. When a new visualization technique is implemented, all that is required is that the developer inherits from the asset node class and provides the implementation for the pure virtual functions described by the abstract asset node class (described in more detail in Section 4.2.3). In addition to the asset node, we provide a class called *camera node* which is responsible for storing and configuring the projection and viewpoint information. We now discuss the camera node and the asset node classes in more detail.

4.2.2 Camera node

3D APIs such as OpenGL and DirectX have no concept of a camera. The viewpoint is always located at the position $(0.0, 0.0, 0.0)$ in eye-space coordinates (for a thorough discussion of coordinate spaces and the OpenGL pipeline we refer the reader to [Woo et al. (2007))]. However, the concept of a camera navigating through a 3D scene provides an intuitive description. We can give the appearance of a movable camera by moving the scene by the inverse of the desired camera transformation. For example, to simulate the effect that the camera is panning upwards, we simply move the entire scene downwards.

As outlined in Section 4.2.1, all child nodes inherit the transformations of their parent. The camera node is set as the root node in the scene graph. The inverse transformation matrix is re-computed when the camera is manipulated. All other nodes are added as a descendant of the camera node and are, therefore, transformed by it's transformation matrix. Thus, the camera parameters are the main factor for setting the viewpoint and orientation. This is in line with the camera analogy described at the beginning of this section.

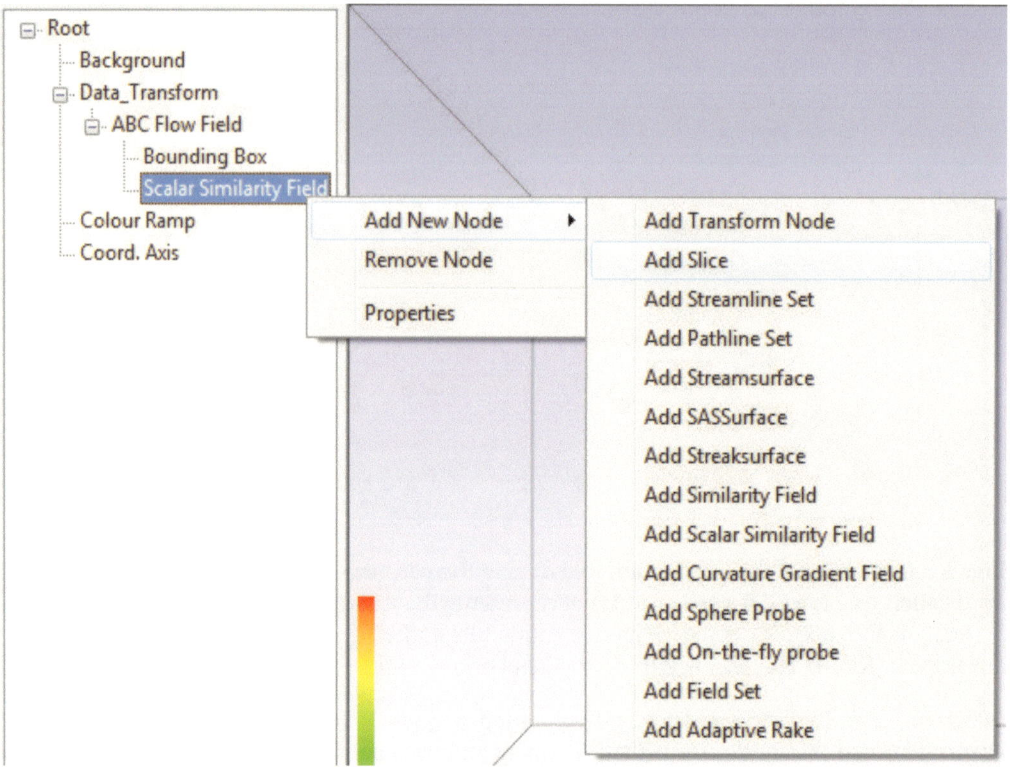

Fig. 9. The tree control is used to add new nodes into the scene graph. The user selects which node they want add an asset to. A context menu then presents the user with a list of assets. When an asset is selected it is added to the scene graph as a child node of the currently selected node.

This method can be extended to render to multiple viewports with different view points. This could be realized by maintaining a list of camera nodes, each maintaining their own set of view parameters (like using multiple cameras in real-life). For each view point, the relevant camera node can be inserted into the root node position. The scene graph is then traversed sending each node to the rendering pipeline. This allows the same scene graph to be used, the only change is the initial camera transform.

4.2.3 Asset node

Figure 10 shows the collaboration graph for the asset node class. This class is designed to provide a consistent interface for all visualization methods integrated into the application. It is an abstract class and therefore provides an interface that declares common functionality. The class provides three pure virtual function signatures:

- SendToRenderer()
- setDefaultMaterial()
- loadDefaultConfiguration()

The SendToRenderer() function issues a command to the class to send it's geometry to the 3D viewer. The setDefaultMaterial() function is an initialization function that sets

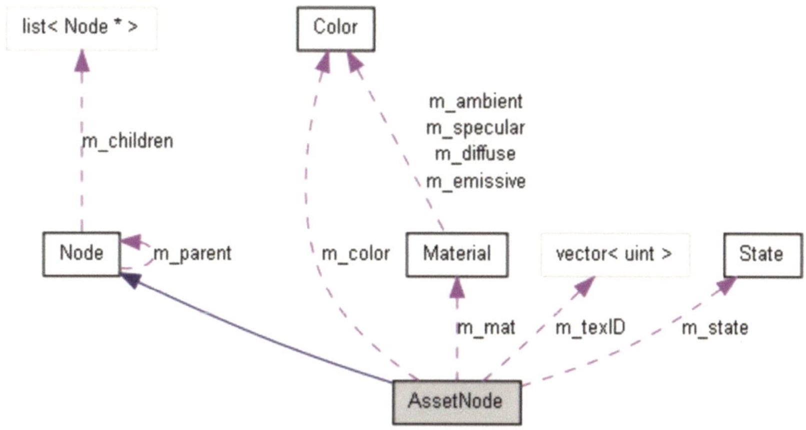

Fig. 10. Collaboration diagram for the asset node class. The boxes represent classes in our framework.

the initial/default material properties that are used by the OpenGL API. Finally the loadDefaultConfiguration() function loads the default set of parameters for the visualization method from file. The configuration files follow the INI file format [*INI File* (n.d.)]. This function is provided to ensure that all visualization methods are loaded with sensible default values (where necessary). By providing the configuration information in a file and not hard-coding it into the application brings several benefits. A change to default parameters does not result in any re-compilation bringing speed benefits during development. It also means that the end user can change the default settings without having to have or understand the source code. It also allows users on different machines to each have their own set of default parameters tailored to their requirements. It would be a simple task to allow per-user configuration files on a single machine, however we have not implemented this functionality as it is superfluous to our requirements as a research platform.

The asset node class also provides several member variables that are inherited:

- (unsigned int) m_vboID
- (unsigned int) m_indexID
- (vector⟨unsigned int⟩) m_texID
- (Material) m_mat
- (Color) m_color
- (State) m_state
- (bool) m_inited

OpenGL assigns numeric ID's to all buffers. Asset nodes provide variables to store a vertex buffer (m_vboID), an index buffer (m_indexID) and a list of textures (m_texID). More than one texture can be assigned to an asset node in order to facilitate multi-texturing. Materials are settings that affect how geometry reflects to the light within OpenGL. A material is separated into several components: *ambient*, *diffuse*, *specular* and *emissive*. The asset node provides all renderable objects with a material property. It also provides a color property, this is used in a similar fashion to material but it much more lightweight with less flexibility. OpenGL is a state machine, where the current state affects how any primitives passed to it are rendered. Whether lighting and/or texturing is enabled are examples of some of the states used by OpenGL [Architecture Review Board (2000)]. Every asset node has a state member variable which allows the node to stores various OpenGL state settings plus other non-OpenGL state parameters. The state class is described in more detail in Section 4.3.2.

4.2.4 Asset user-interaction and the asset control pane

User specified parameters for the various visualization assets are provided through the asset control pane. When an asset is selected in the application tree control (Section 4.2.1), the asset control pane is updated. The asset control pane shows only the controls for the currently selected asset. This helps reduce clutter in the GUI and provides an easier experience for the user. The asset control panel also populates the controls with the current values of the asset, therefore the GUI always represents the correct values for the selected asset. The asset panel can be seen in the blue box of Figure 1.

The use of C++ pure virtual functions ensures that the GUI panels for all visualization assets must implement functionality to update itself according to the current state of the active asset it is controlling. The GUI panels are now discussed in more detail.

4.2.5 Asset panels

Figure 11 shows an examples of the asset panel at runtime. The left panel shows the controls displayed when a streamsurface asset is selected by the user. The right image shows the asset panel when the user has selected a different visualization asset, in this case a streamline set. Note how the streamsurface panel has now been removed and it replaced with the streamline set panel. Other relevant controls for the selected tool (such as state parameters) are neatly set in separate tabs. This has two benefits. It keeps the visualization tool parameters and the OpenGL rendering parameters for the tool separate. We can also re-use the same GUI panel for state controls as the parameters are common across all visualization methods.

Asset panel controls are event-driven. When a control is modified an event is fired which is then handled by the visualization system. The event handler typically obtains an handle to the currently selected visualization asset and calls the correct function. The visualization system is then updated and feedback is presented to the user. Asset panels utilize multiple inheritance. While multiple inheritance has its shortcomings, i.e., the diamond problem, but can provide powerful solutions to problems if used with care. Figure 12 shows the inheritance diagram for a typical asset panel (in this case the streamsurface panel). Note that only a single level of inheritance is used. Throughout the design of this system, keeping the inheritance levels as low as possible was set out as a requirement. This ensures shall depth of inheritance trees (DIT) which makes the code easier to extend, test, and maintain. All asset panels inherit from two base classes. One of these classes is unique to all derived classes and the other one is common to all derived classes. The class *CommonPanel*, as its name implies, is inherited by all asset panels. It contains information such as the string that is displayed when the panel is shown in the asset control pane and enumeration of the panel type. It also provides the signature for a pure virtual function, $UpdatePanel()$. This function is used to populate the panels controls with the correct values (by querying the currently selected asset). The second class panels inherit from are unique auto-generated classes that are output from using a GUI building tool called wxFormBuilder. The auto-generated classes provide panel layout and controls. They also provide interface for the events that are fired from that panel. The asset

Fig. 11. Two examples of asset panels taken at runtime. The panel on the left shows the controls for streamsurfaces. When a streamsurface asset is selected in the application tree, this panel is inserted into the asset control pane. The right image shows the result of the user then selecting a streamline set asset. The streamsurface control panel is removed from the asset control pane and the streamline set control pane is inserted in its place. Only the relevant controls to the currently selected asset are displayed to the user. This leads to a less cluttered GUI and the user is not burdened with manually navigating the GUI to find the appropriate controls.

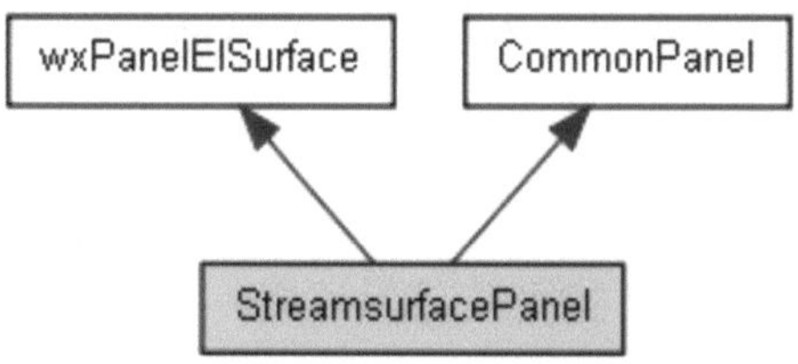

Fig. 12. Inheritance diagram for asset panel types. This example shows the streamsurface panel. Asset panels use multiple inheritance, they inherit from *CommonPanel* and another class that is auto-generated using a GUI builder. Using this method provides fast creation of GUI controls (using the form builder and generated class) and allows us to provide a common interface and behavior for all panels (using the common panel class).

panel then provides the implementation for the interface. In our system the auto-generated classes are prefixed with the letters "wx" to differentiate them from user created classes.

The asset panels are designed with both developers and users in mind. The updating panel in the asset control pane ensures that only the relevant controls are displayed. The controls are also located in the same place within the application. Therefore, the user does not have to search around for various options. Similar to the node structures (Section 4.2.1), the panels are organized in a manner that facilitates easier implementation that ensures a certain level of functionality. The use of a GUI builder greatly facilitates the developer increasing the productivity when creating GUI components.

4.3 3D viewer

This section details the 3D viewer system of our application. We discuss some key implementation details and outline how our application manages various rendering attributes such as materials and textures.

The 3D viewer system is implemented using the OpenGL API. The OpenGL API was chosen because it provides a high level interface for utilizing graphics hardware and it is platform independent. The 3D viewer is responsible for providing the feedback from the visualization software. Recall that OpenGL defines a state machine whose current rendering state affects how the primitives that are passed through the graphics pipeline are rendered. State-machines can make debugging difficult; unexpected behavior may arise simply from a state being changed that the developer is unaware of. Querying the current state may be difficult at times and almost always relies on dumping text to a console window or file. To try and alleviate this issue our system implements a wrapper around for OpenGL state machine. Our *OGL_Renderer* (OpenGL Renderer) class provides flags for the OpenGL states used within our system. Other states may be added as they are added and utilized by the system. We also provide accessor and mutator functions for retrieving and manipulating state values. Our wrapper provides several benefits:

- Breakpoints may be set to halt the program when a specific state value has been modified.
- Bounds checking may be performed as states as a sanity check, making sure no invalid values are set.
- When using an integrated development environment (IDE), the class can be queried easily and does not rely on the outputting of large volumes of text that the user has to manually search through.
- Some OpenGL code can be simplified making development easier and more efficient.
- Separating the graphics API code allows for other APIs to be used in the future if the requirement arises. This is very difficult if API specific code is embedded throughout the entire codebase.
- It aids the developer by being able to focus more on the visualization algorithms rather than the rendering component. Thus, promoting the system as a research platform.

Our system only requires a single rendering context (if multiple viewports are present, the same rendering context can be used). We utilize the Singleton design pattern [Gamma et al. (1994)] so that instantiation of the OGL_Renderer is restricted to a single instance. We note that a singleton has downsides as it is in essence a global variable. However, the OpenGL state machine is inherently global and the fact we only want a single rendering context makes a singleton suitable for our needs. In our case, a singleton provides a much cleaner solution than continually passing references around is much preferably than every object (that needs to) storing it's own reference to the renderer object. Access to the singleton is provided by using the following C++ public static function:

```
static OGL_Renderer& OGL_Renderer::Instance()
{
    static OGL_Renderer instance;
    return instance;
}
```

The first time that this function is called, an instance of the OGL_Renderer is created and the reference to it is returned. Future calls to this function do not create a new instance (due to the static variable) and a reference to the current instance is returned.

4.3.1 Rendering

OpenGL rendering code can be ugly and cumbersome if not carefully designed. The API uses C-style syntax which does not necessarily interleave itself well with C++ code in terms of code readability. Many calls are usually made to set the OpenGL state before sending the geometry data along the rendering pipeline. Here is an example of OpenGL code that renders a set of vertices that are already stored in a vertex buffer on the GPU.

```
...
glBindBuffer(GL_ARRAY_BUFFER, vertexBufferID);
glEnableClientState(GL_VERTEX_ARRAY);
glVertexPointer(3, GL_FLOAT, sizeof(Vector3<float>), NULL);

glBindBuffer(GL_ARRAY_BUFFER, normalBufferID);
glEnableClientState(GL_NORMAL_ARRAY);
glNormalPointer(GL_FLOAT, sizeof(Vector3<float>), NULL);

glBindBuffer(GL_ARRAY_BUFFER, textureBufferID);
glEnableClientState(GL_TEXTURE_COORD_ARRAY);
glTexCoordPointer(1, GL_FLOAT, sizeof(float), NULL);

glBindBuffer(GL_ELEMENT_ARRAY_BUFFER, indexId);

glDrawElements(GL_TRIANGLE_STRIP, numVerts,
               GL_UNSIGNED_INT, NULL);

glDisableClientState(GL_TEXTURE_COORD_ARRAY);
glDisableClientState(GL_NORMAL_ARRAY);
glDisableClientState(GL_VERTEX_ARRAY);

glBindBuffer(GL_ARRAY_BUFFER, NULL);
glBindBuffer(GL_ELEMENT_ARRAY_BUFFER, NULL);
...
```

This renders an indexed set of vertices as a strip of triangles with shading and texturing information. First the buffers and pointers into them are set as well. The vertices are then passed down to the rendering pipeline. The state changes are undone after rendering to put the OpenGL back into its original state. It is clear this is not the simplest code to work with. If the rendering code was merged into the visualization code, all renderable objects would possess similar code chunks. This (1) makes the code harder to read and (2) produces a lot of repetitive code throughout the codebase.

Our system segregates this type of rendering code. We provide classes such as *TriangleRenderer* and *LineRenderer* which contain utility functions that simplify the rendering process. A typical usage of the triangle renderer is shown below.

```
...
TriangleRenderer::RenderTriangle_VBO(m_vboID,
                                     m_indexID,
                                     m_numberOfIndices,
                                     TRIANGLE_STRIP);
...
```

This call to the RenderTriangle_VBO function passes in the required buffers, the number of vertices to be rendered and the rendering mode. This approach allows the developer to take advantage of code re-use and makes the code much more readable.

4.3.2 State objects

We provide a *State* class that encapsulates various OpenGL states that are utilized by our visualization assets. The state class has the following members:

- (bool) m_lighting;
- (bool) m_texturing;
- (bool) m_blend;
- (uint) m_program;
- (int) m_stateBlendSrc;
- (int) m_stateBlendDst;
- (bool) m_render;

The first three bool members are flags indicating whether the matching OpenGL state will be enabled. The m_program member is the ID of the shader program that is used to render the asset. The blend members store the blending states when blending is enabled. The final member, m_render, indicates whether the asset is rendered or ignored. This member has no counterpart in the OpenGL state machine. It is included to allow the user to disable the rendering an asset without removing it from the scene graph. The state class has a member function, *SetState()*, which is called immediately before the asset is rendered.

```
void State::SetState()
{
   OGL_Renderer& renderer = OGL_Renderer::Instance();

   if(m_lighting)   renderer.Enable(LIGHTING);
   if(m_texturing)  renderer.Enable(TEXTURING);
   if(m_blend)
   {
      renderer.Enable(BLEND);
      renderer.SetBlendFunc(m_stateBlendSrc, m_stateBlendDst);
   }
   renderer.UseProgram(m_program);
}
```

After the asset has been rendered the OpenGL state is returned to its original state by calling the *UnsetState()* function of the state.

```
void State::UnsetState()
{
    OGL_Renderer& renderer = OGL_Renderer::Instance();

    if(m_lighting)   renderer.Disable(LIGHTING);
    if(m_texturing)  renderer.Disable(TEXTURING);
    if(m_blend)      renderer.Disable(BLEND);
    renderer.UseProgram(NULL);
}
```

These functions greatly simplify the rendering code and aid the developer in efficiently managing the OpenGL state machine and reduce unexpected behavior arising from incorrectly configures states. The state objects are utilized every time an asset is rendered. The code segment below outlines there usage within our application framework.

```
void AssetType::SendToRenderer()
{
    if(m_state.RenderingEnabled())
    {
        m_state.SetState();
        //Rendering Code
        ...
        m_state.UnsetState();
    }
}
```

4.3.3 Material objects and lights

Within OpenGL (and other rendering APIs), the currently bound material state affects how primitives that are passed to down the rendering pipeline interact with light sources. OpenGL lighting is comprised of various terms that approximate the behavior of light in the real-world. In computer graphics and visualization the aesthetics of the final rendering result are very important for high quality results. A research paper looks more polished and professional with high quality images. We recognize this importance and provide functionality that allows the user to adjust the various lighting and material parameters at run-time.

We allow the user to interactively add and remove light sources. The type of light source and its position can also be controlled by the user. The application also allows the user to set the values of each component of the light source (ambient, diffuse and specular). Likewise with materials we allow the user to adjust each component (ambient, diffuse, specular, emission and specular power). Allowing this level of control at run-time allows the user to receive immediate feedback of the results and prevents any unnecessary recompilation and re-generation of results.

Each asset has it's material object which encapsulates the state behavior. Prior to the asset being rendered it's material is bound by the OpenGL state machine. Once again, by separating the rendering code from the visualization asset code we are promoting code-reuse and not cluttering up the visualization asset classes with rendering code.

Note we omit a through discussion of how OpenGL approximates lighting and materials. Instead we refer the interested reader to [Woo et al. (2007)].

4.3.4 Textures, texture management and texture editing

As we have previously discussed, our application has served as a research platform for flow visualization techniques. More specifically we have focused on a sub-set of flow visualization techniques that fall into the geometry-based category. These methods compute a geometry that represents some behavior of a flow field. However, by color-mapping this geometry we can depict more information about the flow behavior than the geometry alone. For example, velocity magnitude is often mapped to color.

Color-mapping can be achieved in a variety of ways. A function may be provided that maps the color, although for complex mappings defining a suitable function may be difficult. A large lookup table may be produced, this is a flexible solution but can lead to the developer producing lots of code to produce large look up tables.

Our approach to color-mapping utilizes texture-mapping. Here the texture itself is the lookup table and all we have to do is provide the texture coordinate to retrieve the desired value from the texture. Textures are a very powerful tool in computer graphics and rendering APIs readily provide functionality for various interpolation schemes which we can utilize. They are also fast as they due to their hardware support. This system is also very flexible, new color-maps (in the form of images) can be dropped into the textures folder of the application and they will automatically be loaded the next time the application is run. Management of the texture is equally simple, the texture manager simply maintains a list of textures, the user can select the texture they wish to use from the GUI and the texture manager binds that texture to the OpenGL state.

Fig. 13. Some images from an interactive session with the color map editor. The top-left image shows the initial state of the editor. The top right image shows the result when the user inserts a new sample (black) in the center of the color map. The bottom-left image shows the result after the user has updated the color of the middle sample to yellow. Finally the bottom-right image shows the effect that dragging the middle sample to right has. The color values between each sample are constructed using interpolation.

We also provide a tool that allows the user to create their own color maps. This allows the user to customize the color-mapping at run-time to ensure that the mapping adequately represents the information they wish to present. Figure 13 shows some steps of an interactive session with the editor. The editor allows the user to insert (and remove) samples along the color map. The color of the samples can be altered and the position of the sample can be updated by dragging it around in the editor window. The colors values are interpolated between samples. An up-to-date preview of the color map is always displayed within the editor.

4.4 Simulation manager

The final major system in our application is the simulation manager. The simulation manager is responsible for loading the simulation data and managing the sub-sets of simulation data when it won't fit in core memory. The simulation provides a set of classes for 2D and 3D simulations. The simulation manager handles both discretely sampled data, such as the output from CFD simulations, and analytically defined data by providing the necessary parameters to a function to compute the vector information. Flow simulations are output in a variety of file formats using both ASCII and binary file output. Our application supports a range of formats and provides a simple interface for developers to add support for more formats in future.

The simulation manager is used whenever a vector field evaluation is requested by one of the visualization assets. It is responsible for determining whether a given position lies within the domain (both spatially and temporally). If the position is determined as valid, the simulation manager populates a cell object (of the corresponding grid type) with the appropriate vector values. The cell objects also belong to the simulation manager and are used to construct the final vector value at the desired position using interpolation.

4.4.1 Large-time dependent simulation data

As previously discussed, the output from time-dependent CFD simulations can be of the order of gigabytes or even terrabytes. Thus, we have to consider out-of-core methods. Our application handles such large amounts of data by only loading a sub-set of the simulation into memory. In order to perform a single integration step, only two time-steps need to be copied to main memory. For example if each our simulation output data for every second and we need to advect a particle at $t = 3.5s$, only time-steps 3 and 4 four are needed to interpolate the required vector values.

We employ a method similar to Bürger et al. [Bürger et al. (2007)]. We allocate a number of slots equal to the number of time-steps that fit into main memory. These slots are then populated with the data from a single time-step, starting with the first time-step and proceeding consecutively. For example, if we can fit 6 time-steps into memory we allocate 6 slots and populate them with time-steps 0-5. When we have passed through a time-step it's data is unloaded and the next time-step is loaded from file in it's place. For example, if we are constructing a pathline, when $t \geq 1$, the first slot (which holds the data for timestep 0) is overwritten with the data for timestep 6 – the next unloaded time-step in the simulation. Figure 14 illustrates an example.

Conceptually, a sliding window run over the slots, with the pair of slot covered by the window being used for the current vector field evaluations. When the sliding window has passed a slot, the slot is updated with the next unloaded time-step. When the sliding window reaches the last slot it wraps around to the first slot and the cycle is repeated. The sliding

Time-step	0	1	2	3	4	5
Slot	0	1	2	3	4	5

(a) $0 \leq t < 1$

Time-step	6	1	2	3	4	5
Slot	0	1	2	3	4	5

(b) $1 \leq t < 2$

Time-step	6	7	8	9	10	5
Slot	0	1	2	3	4	5

(c) $5 \leq t < 6$

Time-step	6	7	8	9	10	11
Slot	0	1	2	3	4	5

(d) $6 \leq t < 7$

Fig. 14. These four tables show the time-steps that are loaded into the simulation manager slots for given time periods. The grey cells show the time-steps that are used to perform any vector field evaluations for the stated time period. (a) Shows the first time period ($0 \leq t < 1$). (b) shows the next time period, the two slots used in the vector field evaluation have moved over – a sliding window. The previous slot has been updated with the subsequent unloaded time-step in the simulation (slot 0 is loaded with time-step 6). (c) The slots wrap around, when the sliding window reaches the last slot it switched back to the first slot. (d) The process repeats with the new time-steps in the slots.

window transition is triggered when a time greater than the current time period covered by the window is requested by the application.

For this method to be effective the simulation manager runs in a separate thread. Disk transfer operations are blocking calls and they halt the rest of the application if a single thread is used. Moving these blocking calls to a separate thread allows the application to proceed computing visualization results while data is loaded in the background. Note, there may be times where the visualization results are computed faster than the simulation manager can load the data. If the required time-steps are not present in memory the application has no option but to halt until they have been loaded. However, even in this case the multi-threaded simulation manager reduces the number and duration of halts compared to a single-threaded solution.

Another consideration that needs to be considered is how the visualization assets are constructed. If we were to generate 10 pathlines by computing the first pathline and then the second one and so on, the simulation manager would have to load all time-steps 10 times (one for each pathline). It is much more efficient to construct all pathlines simultaneously by iterating over them and computing successive points. This ensures that they all require the same sliding window position in the simulation slots and prevents unnecessary paging of data.

5. Conclusion

In a typical research paper many implementation details have to be omitted due to space restraints. It is rare to see literature that provides an in-depth discussion concerning the implementation of an entire visualization application. This chapter serves to provide such a discussion. The chapter provides an overview of the high-level application structure and provides details of key systems and classes and the reasoning why these were designed in this way. Many topics are covered ranging from multi-threaded data management for performance gains to GUI design and implementation with considerations both the developer and the user.

We demonstrate that using a good software engineering practices and design methodologies provide an enhanced experience for both software developers and end-users of the software.

This serves as proof that research code is not restricted to small 'one-off' applications and that implementing proof-of-concept algorithms into a larger framework has many benefits – not least of which is an easier comparison to other techniques.

6. References

Architecture Review Board, O. (2000). *OpenGL Reference Manual: The Official Reference Document to OpenGL, Version 1.2*, Addison Wesley. D. Schreiner, editor.

Bürger, K., Schneider, J., Kondratieva, P., Krüger, J. & Westermann, R. (2007). Interactive Visual Exploration of Unsteady 3D Flows, *Proc. EuroVis*, pp. 251–258.

Cabral, B. & Leedom, L. C. (1993). Imaging Vector Fields Using Line Integral Convolution, *Poceedings of ACM SIGGRAPH 1993*, Annual Conference Series, pp. 263–272.

Gamma, E., Helm, R., Johnson, R. & Vlissides, J. (1994). *Design Patters: Elements of Reusable Object-Oriented Software*, Addison Wesley.

Haller, G. (2001). Distinguished material surfaces and coherent structures in three-dimensional fluid flows, *Phys. D* 149: 248–277.
URL: *http://portal.acm.org/citation.cfm?id=370169.370176*

Haller, G. (2005). An objective definition of a vortex, *Journal of Fluid Mechanics* 525: 1–26.

Helman, J. L. & Hesselink, L. (1989). Representation and Display of Vector Field Topology in Fluid Flow Data Sets, *IEEE Computer* 22(8): 27–36.

Hultquist, J. P. M. (1992). Constructing Stream Surfaces in Steady 3D Vector Fields, *Proceedings IEEE Visualization '92*, pp. 171–178.

INI File (n.d.). http://en.wikipedia.org/wiki/INI_file.

Krishnan, H., Garth, C. & Joy, K. I. (2009). Time and streak surfaces for flow visualization in large time-varying data sets, *IEEE Transactions on Visualization and Computer Graphics* 15(6): 1267–1274.

Laramee, R., Hauser, H., Zhao, L. & Post, F. H. (2007). Topology Based Flow Visualization: The State of the Art, *Topology-Based Methods in Visualization (Proceedings of Topo-in-Vis 2005)*, Mathematics and Visualization, Springer, pp. 1–19.

Laramee, R. S. (2010). Bob's Concise Coding Conventions (C^3), *Advances in Computer Science and Engineering (ACSE)* 4(1): 23–36.

Laramee, R. S., Hauser, H., Doleisch, H., Post, F. H., Vrolijk, B. & Weiskopf, D. (2004). The State of the Art in Flow Visualization: Dense and Texture-Based Techniques, *Computer Graphics Forum* 23(2): 203–221.
URL: *http://www.VRVis.at/ar3/pr2/star/*

Laramee, R. S., Jobard, B. & Hauser, H. (2003). Image Space Based Visualization of Unsteady Flow on Surfaces, *Proceedings IEEE Visualization '03*, IEEE Computer Society, pp. 131–138.
URL: *http://www.VRVis.at/ar3/pr2/*

Lorensen, W. E. & Cline, H. E. (1987). Marching Cubes: a High Resolution 3D Surface Construction Algorithm, *Computer Graphics (Proceedings of ACM SIGGRAPH 87, Anaheim, CA)*, ACM, pp. 163–170.

Mallo, O., Peikert, R., Sigg, C. & Sadlo, F. (2005). Illuminated Lines Revisited, *Proceedings IEEE Visualization 2005*, pp. 19–26.

McLoughlin, T., Edmunds, M., Laramee, R. S., Chen, G., Max, N., Yeh, H. & Zhang, E. (2011). Visualization of User-Parameter Sensitivity for Streamline Seeding, *Technical report*, Dept. Computer Science, Swansea University.

McLoughlin, T., Jones, M. W. & Laramee, R. S. (2011). Similarity Measures for Streamline Seeding Rake Enhancement, *Technical report*, Dept. Computer Science, Swansea University.

McLoughlin, T., Laramee, R. S., Peikert, R., Post, F. H. & Chen, M. (2010). Over Two Decades of Integration-Based, Geometric Flow Visualization, *Computer Graphics Forum* 29(6): 1807–1829.

McLoughlin, T., Laramee, R. S. & Zhang, E. (2009). Easy Integral Surfaces: A Fast, Quad-based Stream and Path Surface Algorithm, *Proceedings Computer Graphics International 2009*, pp. 67–76.

McLoughlin, T., Laramee, R. S. & Zhang, E. (2010). Constructing Streak Surfaces for 3D Unsteady Vector Fields, *Proceedings of the Spring Conference on Computer Graphics (SCCG)*, pp. 25–32.

Meyers, S. (2005). *Effective C++: 55 Specific Ways to Improve Your Programs and Designs*, Addison-Wesley.

Peng, Z. & Laramee, R. S. (2009). Higher Dimensional Vector Field Visualization: A Survey, *Theory and Practice of Computer Graphics (TPCG '09)*, Cardiff, UK, pp. 149–163.

Post, F. H., Vrolijk, B., Hauser, H., Laramee, R. S. & Doleisch, H. (2003). The State of the Art in Flow Visualization: Feature Extraction and Tracking, *Computer Graphics Forum* 22(4): 775–792.
URL: *http://cs.swan.ac.uk/ csbob/research/*

van Heesch, D. (197-2004). *Doxygen, Manual for version 1.3.9.1*, The Netherlands.

van Wijk, J. J. (2003). Image Based Flow Visualization for Curved Surfaces, *Proceedings IEEE Visualization '03*, IEEE Computer Society, pp. 123–130.

Weiskopf, D., Hopf, M. & Ertl, T. (2001). Hardware-Accelerated Visualization of Time-Varying 2D and 3D Vector Fields by Texture Advection via Programmable Per-Pixel Operations, *Proceedings of the Vision Modeling and Visualization Conference 2001 (VMV 01)*, pp. 439–446.

Woo, M., Neider, J., Davis, T. & Shreiner, D. (2007). *OpenGL Programming Guide, The Official Guide to Learning OpenGL, Version 2.1*, 6 edn, Addison Wesley.

wxWidgets GUI Library (n.d.). `http://www.wxwidgets.org/`.

7

Simulations with Particle Method

Nobuhiko Mukai
Computer Science, Tokyo City University, Japan

1. Introduction

In computer graphics, one of the most exciting themes is visualization based on physical simulation, and visual simulation of fluid, which includes liquid and air, is the most challenging issue among them. In order to visualize fluid behavior, there are two major methods: Eulerian grid method and Lagrangian particle method. In Eulerian grid method, level set method is used to identify the boundary of the fluid. In Lagrangian particle method, Marching Cubes is used as the technique that generates the surface of the fluid, while some researches use level set method to generate it, which is called particle level set method.

(Greenwood & House, 2004) used particle level set method to visualize bubbles, especially splashing. (Zheng et al., 2006) used a regional level set method with semi-implicit surface tension model to simulate multi-manifold bubbles. (Kim et al., 2007) solved the volume error caused by level set method to visualize foamy bubbles. On the other hand, (Kim et al., 2010) used a spatial averaging and stochastic approach with particles to simulate sparse bubble flow.

In addition, there are two major methods for Lagrangian particle method: SPH (Smoothed Particle Hydrodynamics) and MPS (Moving Particle Semi-implicit) methods. Both methods use particles and calculate fluid behavior based on Navier-Stokes equation; however, the basic idea is different. SPH considers that the physical amount of a particle, which is mass density, velocity and so on, does not belong to the particle itself but it distributes smoothly around the particle, and kernel function is used to calculate the physical amount of each particle. On the other hand, MPS considers that the physical amount such as mass density or velocity belongs to the particle itself, and calculates the interaction between particles with weight function. MPS can also be applied to incompressive fluid by satisfying the condition of density constant.

(Selle et al., 2005) used hybrid techniques of Lagrangian particle method and Eulerian grid based method for vortex visualization. (Hong et al., 2008) also used hybrid method incorporating bubble model based on SPH into Eulerian grid based simulation to visualize bubbly water. In addition, (Chang et al., 2009) used SPH method for viscoelastic fluid simulation. On the other hand, (Yamamoto, 2009) used MPS method to construct momentum preserved two way coupling system between fluids and deformable bodies. The targets of the simulation based on particle method are diverse. The target of most researches mentioned above is bubbles; however, the target of (Chang et al., 2009) is viscoelastic fluids, and there are many researches on viscoelastic fluids. (Goktekin et al., 2004) used particle level set method to animate incompressible fluids, and visualized the viscoelastic behavior by adding elastic terms to Navier-Stokes equation. On the other hand, (Cavet et al., 2005) used SPH method for fluid simulation, but inserted or removed springs between particles to visualize the behavior of viscoelastic fluid. (Losasso et al., 2006) used separate particle level set method, which sets different levels for multiple regions, to visualize the interaction of different liquids such as viscous objects and water. In addition, (Qin et al., 2010) used a coupling technique of SPH and MSM (Mass Spring Model) to visualize the interaction between blood flow and blood vessel wall

There are many researches using particle method, which are mentioned above; however, the following issues have not been solved. 1) physical based visualization on disappearance of bubbles, 2) visualization of spinnability, which is a character that viscoelastic liquid stretches very thin and long such as a rubber string, and 3) simulation of bleeding out of blood vessel. In addition, SPH is more used than MPS for particle method although MPS can be applied to incompressible fluid. Therefore, in this chapter, MPS based simulation methods for the above unsolved three visualizations are explained.

2. Governing equations

The first basic equation of fluid is equation of continuity that is derived from the law of conservation of mass. Suppose that ρ and m are the density and the mass of fluid, which volume is V. Then, the following equation is true.

$$m = \int_V \rho dV \tag{1}$$

If mass is constant, the following equation is true since mass is invariant for time.

$$\frac{Dm}{Dt} = \frac{D}{Dt}\int_V \rho dV = 0 \tag{2}$$

Where, D/Dt is called Lagrange differential calculus that is defined as follows.

$$\frac{D}{Dt} := \frac{\partial}{\partial t} + \mathbf{u} \cdot \nabla \tag{3}$$

Where, $\mathbf{u}$ is the velocity of fluid and ∇ is gradient. They are defined as follows.

$$\mathbf{u}\left(u_x, u_y, u_z\right) := \left(\frac{\partial x}{\partial t}, \frac{\partial y}{\partial t}, \frac{\partial z}{\partial t}\right) \qquad \nabla := \left(\frac{\partial}{\partial x}, \frac{\partial}{\partial y}, \frac{\partial}{\partial z}\right) \tag{4}$$

Here, Eq. (2) is rewritten as the following by using Reynolds' transport theorem.

$$\int_V \left[\frac{D\rho}{Dt} + \rho \nabla \cdot \mathbf{u}\right] dV = 0 \tag{5}$$

Where, $\nabla \cdot$ is divergence that is defined as follows.

$$\nabla\cdot := \frac{\partial}{\partial x} + \frac{\partial}{\partial y} + \frac{\partial}{\partial z} \tag{6}$$

Eq. (5) should be approved for any volume so that equation of continuity is derived as the following (Nakamura, 1997).

$$\frac{D\rho}{Dt} + \rho\nabla\cdot\mathbf{u} = 0 \quad or \quad \frac{\partial\rho}{\partial t} + \nabla\cdot(\rho\mathbf{u}) = 0 \tag{7}$$

If fluid is incompressible, ρ is also invariant for time so that equation of continuity for incompressible fluid becomes Eq. (8).

$$\nabla\cdot\mathbf{u} = 0 \tag{8}$$

The next important equation is Cauchy's equation of motion that is derived from the law of conservation of momentum, which is defined as follows (Nakamura, 1997).

$$\frac{D}{Dt}\int_V \rho\mathbf{u}dV = \int_S \mathbf{n}\cdot\boldsymbol{\sigma}dS + \int_V \rho\mathbf{K}dV \tag{9}$$

Where, $\mathbf{n}$ is normal vector of the surface, $\boldsymbol{\sigma}$ is stress tensor, and $\mathbf{K}$ is body force per unit mass. Eq. (9) can be rewritten as follows by using Reynolds' transport theorem and Gauss' divergence theorem.

$$\int_V \left[\frac{D(\rho\mathbf{u})}{Dt} + \rho\mathbf{u}\nabla\cdot\mathbf{u}\right]dV = \int_V \nabla\cdot\boldsymbol{\sigma}dS + \int_V \rho\mathbf{K}dV \tag{10}$$

Then, Cauchy's equation of motion is derived as follows from Eq. (10) by considering equation of continuity (Eq. (7)).

$$\rho\frac{D\mathbf{u}}{Dt} = \nabla\cdot\boldsymbol{\sigma} + \rho\mathbf{K} \tag{11}$$

The last important equation of fluid is Navier-Stokes equation, which is derived from Cauchy's equation of motion. Here, stress tensor is described as follows by using pressure p, unit tensor $\mathbf{I}$ and stress deviation $\boldsymbol{\tau}$ (Nakamura, 1997).

$$\boldsymbol{\sigma} = -p\mathbf{I} + \boldsymbol{\tau} \tag{12}$$

In addition, stress deviation can be rewritten as follows for incompressible fluid.

$$\boldsymbol{\tau} = 2\mu\mathbf{D} \tag{13}$$

Where, μ is coefficient of viscosity, $\mathbf{D}$ is deformation rate tensor and written as follows with element expression.

$$D_{ii} := \frac{\partial u_i}{\partial x_i} := \frac{\partial u_1}{\partial x_1} + \frac{\partial u_2}{\partial x_2} + \frac{\partial u_3}{\partial x_3}, \qquad D_{ij} = D_{ji} = \frac{1}{2}\left(\frac{\partial u_i}{\partial x_j} + \frac{\partial u_j}{\partial x_i}\right) \tag{14}$$

Where, the suffix of i and j represents 1, 2 or 3, in turn, 1, 2 and 3 represents x, y and z, respectively. With the above equations (Eq. (8), (11), (12), (13) and (14)), Navier-Stokes equation is derived as the following (Nakamura, 1997)..

$$\rho \frac{D\mathbf{u}}{Dt} = -\nabla p + \mu \nabla^2 \mathbf{u} + \rho \mathbf{K} \tag{15}$$

Where, ∇^2 is Laplacian and defined as follows.

$$\nabla^2 := \frac{\partial^2}{\partial x_i^2} := \frac{\partial^2}{\partial x_1^2} + \frac{\partial^2}{\partial x_2^2} + \frac{\partial^2}{\partial x_3^2} = \frac{\partial^2}{\partial x^2} + \frac{\partial^2}{\partial y^2} + \frac{\partial^2}{\partial z^2} \tag{16}$$

3. MPS method

As mentioned above, there are two major particle methods: SPH and MPS. SPH considers that the physical amount of a particle distributes smoothly around the particle, while MPS considers that the physical amount of a particle belongs to the particle itself, and calculates the interaction between particles with weight function. If the calculation is performed for all particles, it takes huge amount of time so that MPS limits the area for the calculation of one particle, and considers that only particles within the area affect the interaction for the particle. The radius of the area, which is defined as a sphere, is called the radius of influence. Fig. 1 illustrates the radius of influence for particle i as r_e and one of particles affecting particle i as j. The quantity affecting from particle j to particle i is calculated with weight function shown in Eq. (17).

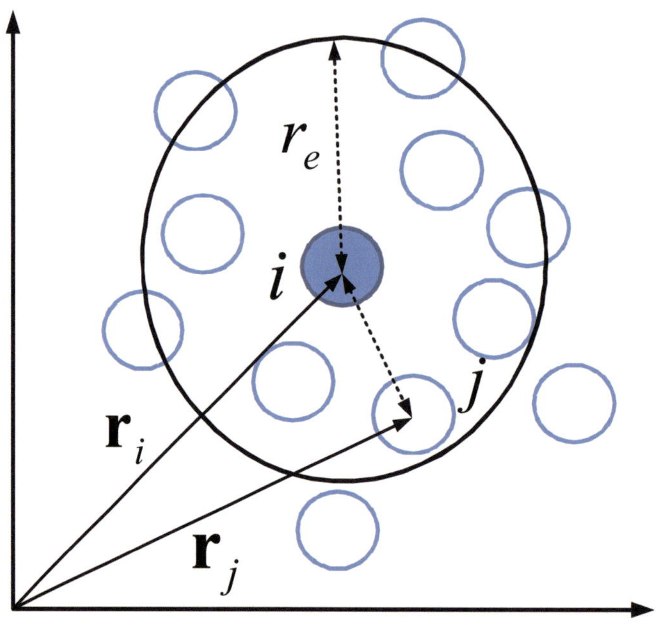

Fig. 1. Relation between a particle and the radius of influence

$$w\left(\left|\mathbf{r}_j-\mathbf{r}_i\right|\right)=\begin{cases}\dfrac{r_e}{|\mathbf{r}_j-\mathbf{r}_i|}-1 & \left(0<|\mathbf{r}_j-\mathbf{r}_i|<r_e\right)\\ 0 & \left(r_e\leq|\mathbf{r}_j-\mathbf{r}_i|\right)\end{cases} \tag{17}$$

Where, $|\mathbf{r}_j-\mathbf{r}_i|$ is the distance between particle i and particle j. In addition, the density n_i in the area, which is a sphere that has particle i as the center and the radius of influence r_e as its radius, is called particle number of density and calculated with the above weight function as follows.

$$n_i=\sum_{j\neq i}w\left(\left|\mathbf{r}_j-\mathbf{r}_i\right|\right) \tag{18}$$

Especially, the initial density is expressed as n^0, and this value is kept constantly for incompressive fluid during simulation. In MPS method, discrete operators for gradient, divergence and Laplacian are defined as follows in order to solve Navier-Stokes equation.

$$\text{Gradient: } \left\langle\nabla\phi\right\rangle_i=\frac{d}{n^0}\sum_{j\neq i}\left[\frac{\phi_j-\phi_i}{\left|\mathbf{r}_j-\mathbf{r}_i\right|^2}\left(\mathbf{r}_j-\mathbf{r}_i\right)w\left(\left|\mathbf{r}_j-\mathbf{r}_i\right|\right)\right] \tag{19}$$

$$\text{Divergence: } \left\langle\nabla\cdot\mathbf{u}\right\rangle_i=\frac{d}{n^0}\sum_{j\neq i}\frac{\left(\mathbf{u}_j-\mathbf{u}_i\right)\cdot\left(\mathbf{r}_j-\mathbf{r}_i\right)}{\left|\mathbf{r}_j-\mathbf{r}_i\right|^2}w\left(\left|\mathbf{r}_j-\mathbf{r}_i\right|\right) \tag{20}$$

$$\text{Laplacian: } \left\langle\nabla^2\phi\right\rangle_i=\frac{2d}{\lambda n^0}\sum_{j\neq i}\left[\left(\phi_j-\phi_i\right)w\left(\left|\mathbf{r}_j-\mathbf{r}_i\right|\right)\right] \tag{21}$$

$$\lambda=\frac{\sum_{j\neq i}\left|\mathbf{r}_j-\mathbf{r}_i\right|^2 w\left(\left|\mathbf{r}_j-\mathbf{r}_i\right|\right)}{\sum_{j\neq i}w\left(\left|\mathbf{r}_j-\mathbf{r}_i\right|\right)} \tag{22}$$

Where, ϕ_i and $\mathbf{u}_i$ are quantities of scalar such as density, and vector such as velocity for particle i respectively, and d is the space dimension number (Koshizuka, 2005).

MPS method treats incompressible fluid so that the density should be preserved, which means that particle number n_i should be kept to be the same as the initial particle number n^0. In order to perform it, all terms except for the pressure are calculated at first, and then, particles move to temporal positions according to the velocities that are also calculated temporarily. Next, the pressure term is calculated by solving Poisson equation of pressure. Then, particle velocities and positions are modified by calculating the velocity again with the pressure term. Finally, fluid is visualized by generating polygons from particles with some methods such as Marching Cubes or particle level set method.

Here, how to derive Poisson equation of pressure is explained. At first, all terms except for pressure are considered for Navier-Stokes equation so that only pressure term should be considered this time. Navier-Stokes equation with only the pressure term is written as Eq. (23).

$$\rho\frac{D\mathbf{u}}{Dt} = -\nabla p \tag{23}$$

In addition, MPS supposes incompressible fluid so that the density is constant. Then, the equation of continuity (Eq. (7)) is written as follows with the initial density of ρ^0.

$$\frac{D\rho}{Dt} + \rho^0 \nabla \cdot \mathbf{u} = 0 \tag{24}$$

In MPS, the density is calculated as particle number with Eq. (18). Then, Eq. (24) can be written as Eq. (25).

$$\frac{1}{n^0}\frac{n^0 - n^*}{\Delta t} + \nabla \cdot \mathbf{u} = 0 \tag{25}$$

Here, n^* is the temporal density. Eq. (23) can also be written as follows since Eq. (8) is satisfied for incompressible fluid.

$$-\nabla p = \rho\left(\frac{\partial \mathbf{u}}{\partial t} + \mathbf{u}\nabla \cdot \mathbf{u}\right) = \rho^0 \frac{\partial \mathbf{u}}{\partial t} \tag{26}$$

Then, the velocity can be expressed as follows.

$$\mathbf{u} = -\frac{\Delta t}{\rho^0}\nabla p \tag{27}$$

Finally, by substituting Eq. (27) for Eq. (25), Poisson equation of pressure is obtained as the following (Koshizuka, 2005).

$$\nabla^2 p = -\frac{\rho^0}{\Delta t^2}\frac{n^* - n^0}{n^0} \tag{28}$$

The simulation algorithm by MPS method is shown in Fig. 2.

4. Bubble simulation

This simulation supposes that fluid velocity is low and bubbles appear at a depth of about a few centimeters. Then, fluid is supposed to be incompressible so that MPS method is applied. In addition, the analysis method of two dimensional simulation is described for easy understanding. Fig. 3 shows the bubble model. There are many water particles in the water and some air particles make a bubble. The bubble in the water moves up to water surface by the pressure difference among particles. In Fig. 3, the pressure of a particle that constructs the lower part of the bubble, which is shown as P_B in Fig. 3, is higher than the pressure of a particle that constructs the upper part of the bubble, which is shown as P_A in Fig. 3, so that the bubble moves up to water surface. After it reaches water surface, a

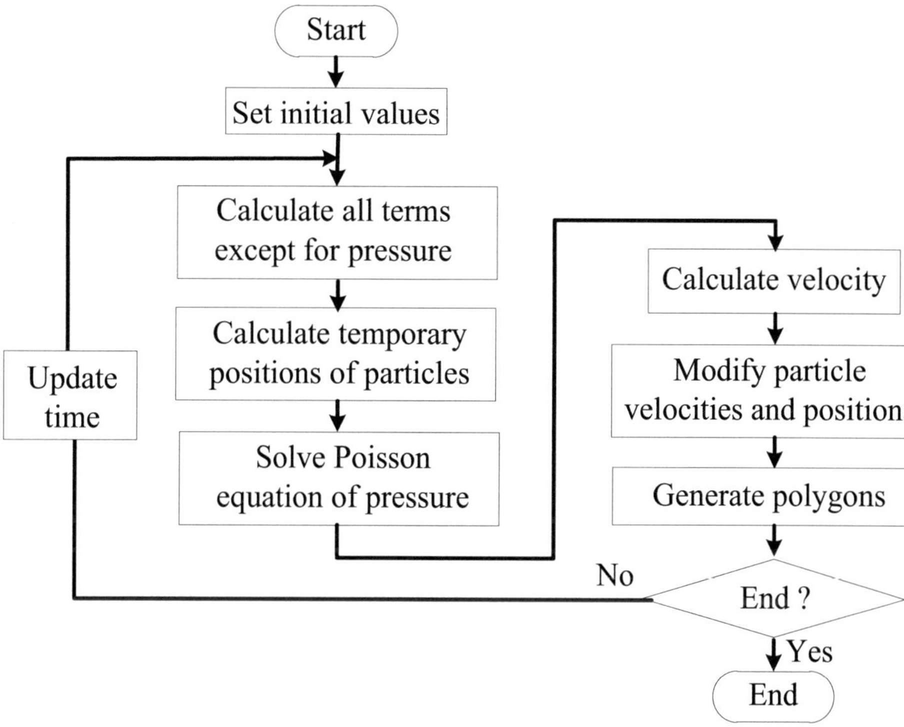

Fig. 2. Simulation algorithm using MPS

part of the bubble goes out of the water and this part is called water screen that is constructed with water screen particles. The bubble that has went out of the water still moves up by surface tension that works on water screen particle. Finally, the pressure difference between the inside and the outside of the bubble becomes larger than the surface tension. Then, the bubble is broken and dissappears. This is the bubble model of this simulation. Therefore, the governing equations of bubble simulation are equation of continuity (Eq. (7)) and Navier-Stokes equation with surface tension shown as the following.

$$\rho \frac{D\mathbf{u}}{Dt} = -\nabla p + \mu \nabla^2 \mathbf{u} + \rho \mathbf{K} + \gamma \kappa \delta \mathbf{n} \tag{29}$$

Where, γ is surface tension coefficient, κ is curvature, δ is delta function, $\mathbf{n}$ is normal vector of surface tension on water screen.

Water screen particle is different from a particle that is inside water particles, and is called free surface particle. It means that water screen particle is one of free surface particles. Then, free surface particle should be searched in order to find water screen particle. Free surface particle is not inside water particles but on the surface of water particles, so that particle number of density is low. In this simulation, fluid is supposed to be incompressible so that particle number of density is constant and the same as the initial one. Then, a particle, which particle number of density is less than 97% of the initial density, is defined as free surface particle.

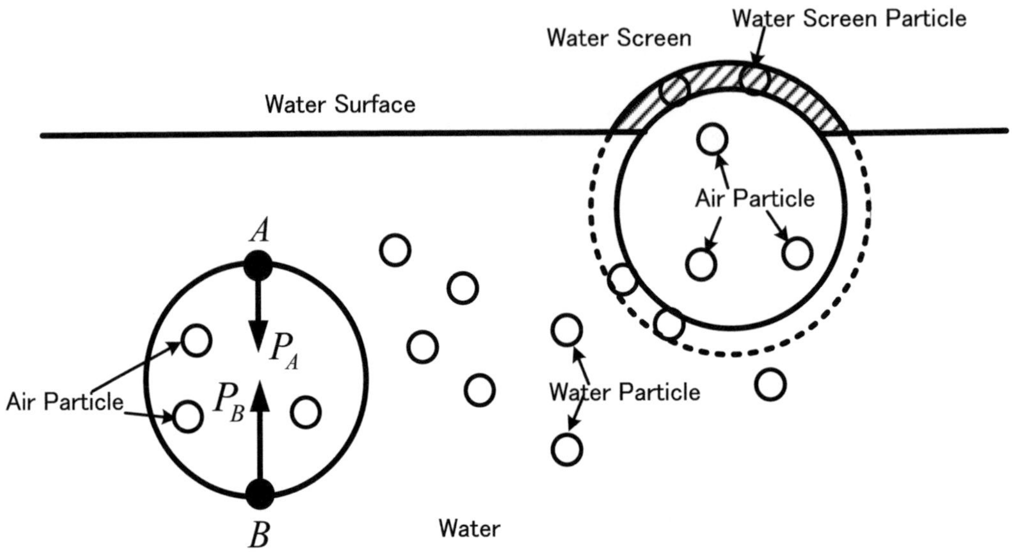

Fig. 3. Bubble model

Next, the calculation of surface tension is described. Surface tension is caused by bonding strength between water particles. Then, it is necessary to calculate the density of water screen, and the density in MPS is considered as the particle number so that particles that are within the radius of influence of a particle, should be counted to calculate the density. The particle density is calculated as follows.

$$w^{st}\left(\left|\mathbf{r}_j - \mathbf{r}_i\right|\right) = \begin{cases} 1 & \left(0 < \left|\mathbf{r}_j - \mathbf{r}_i\right| < r_e\right) \\ 0 & \left(r_e \le \left|\mathbf{r}_j - \mathbf{r}_i\right|\right) \end{cases} \tag{30}$$

$$+ n_i^{st} = \sum_{j \ne i} w^{st}\left(\left|\mathbf{r}_j - \mathbf{r}_i\right|\right) \tag{31}$$

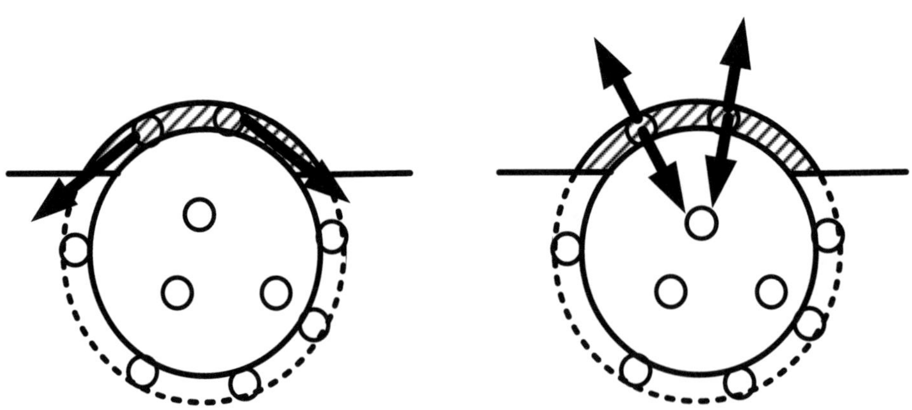

(a) Surface tension (b) Force to bring up a bubble

Fig. 4. Surface tension and force to bring up a bubble

Then, normal vector **n** of surface tension for a particle is calculated by the difference of the densities around the particle. The direction of surface tension, which is calculated with the above method, is shown in Fig. 4 (a). The surface tension is on water screen and facing out of the bubble. Bubbles move up out of the water and dissappear eventually; however, this force cannot bring up the bubble. Then, our method counts not only water particles but also air particles that are in the bubble for the calculation of particle density. By counting the air particles, the direction of surface tension faces the inside of water screen, and the reaction of this surface tension brings up the bubble (Fig. 4 (b)).

Fig. 5 shows a result of the simulation, where a bubble moves up to water surface from the bottom of the water. The model is constructed with 1,232 particles, where 756, 60, and 416 particles for water, air and wall, respectively. On the way to water surface, the shape of the bubble changes by the pressure from the water particles around the bubble. After the bubble

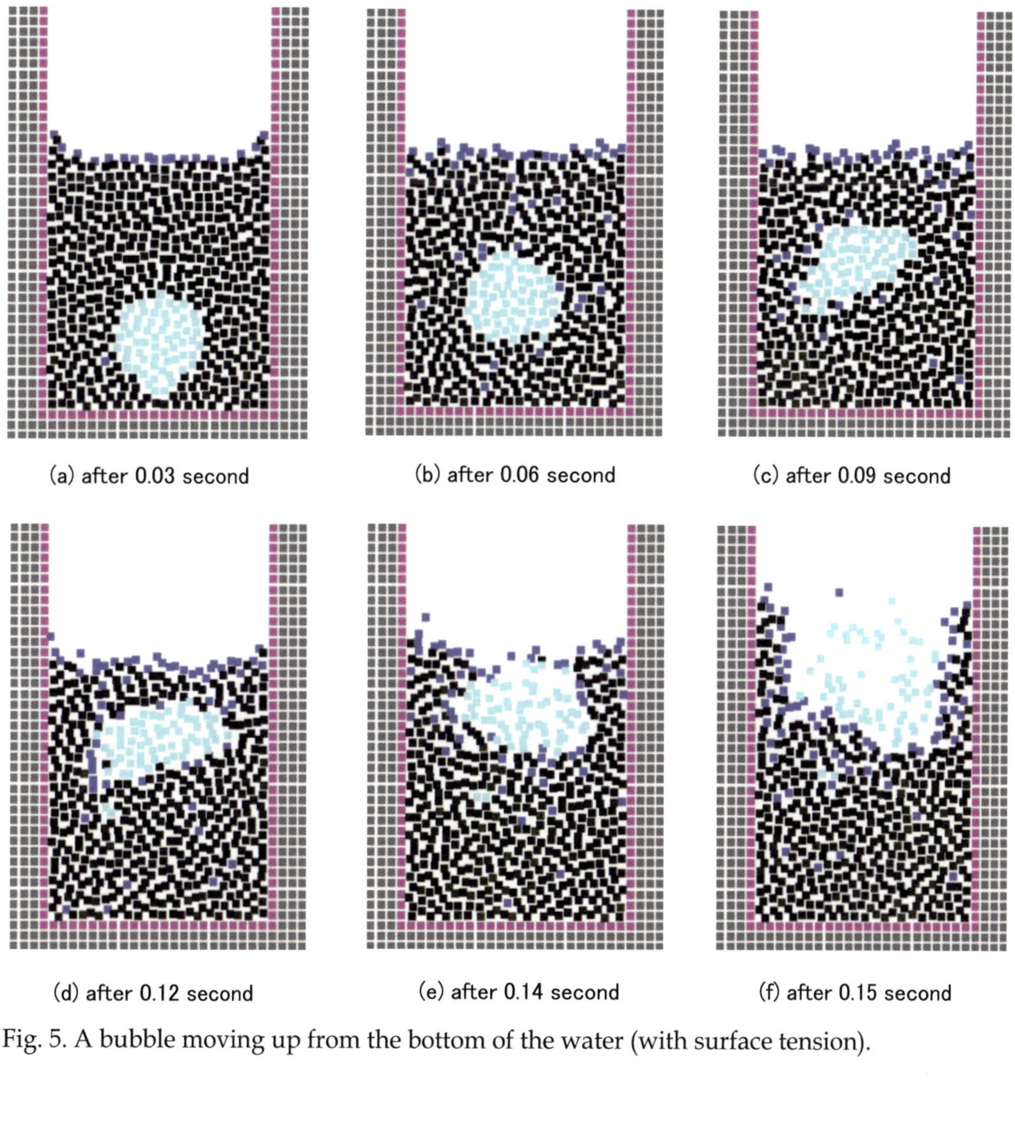

Fig. 5. A bubble moving up from the bottom of the water (with surface tension).

reaches water surface, the reaction of the surface tension brings up the bubble, and water screen is broken when the pressure inside the bubble is higher than the surface tension of water screen. Finally, the bubble disappears.

On the other hand, Fig. 6 shows another result of the simulation without surface tension. If there is no surface tension, the bubble cannot keep its shape, and air particles inside the bubble diffuse in the water. The bubble is broken before it reaches water surface (Kagatsume et al., 2011).

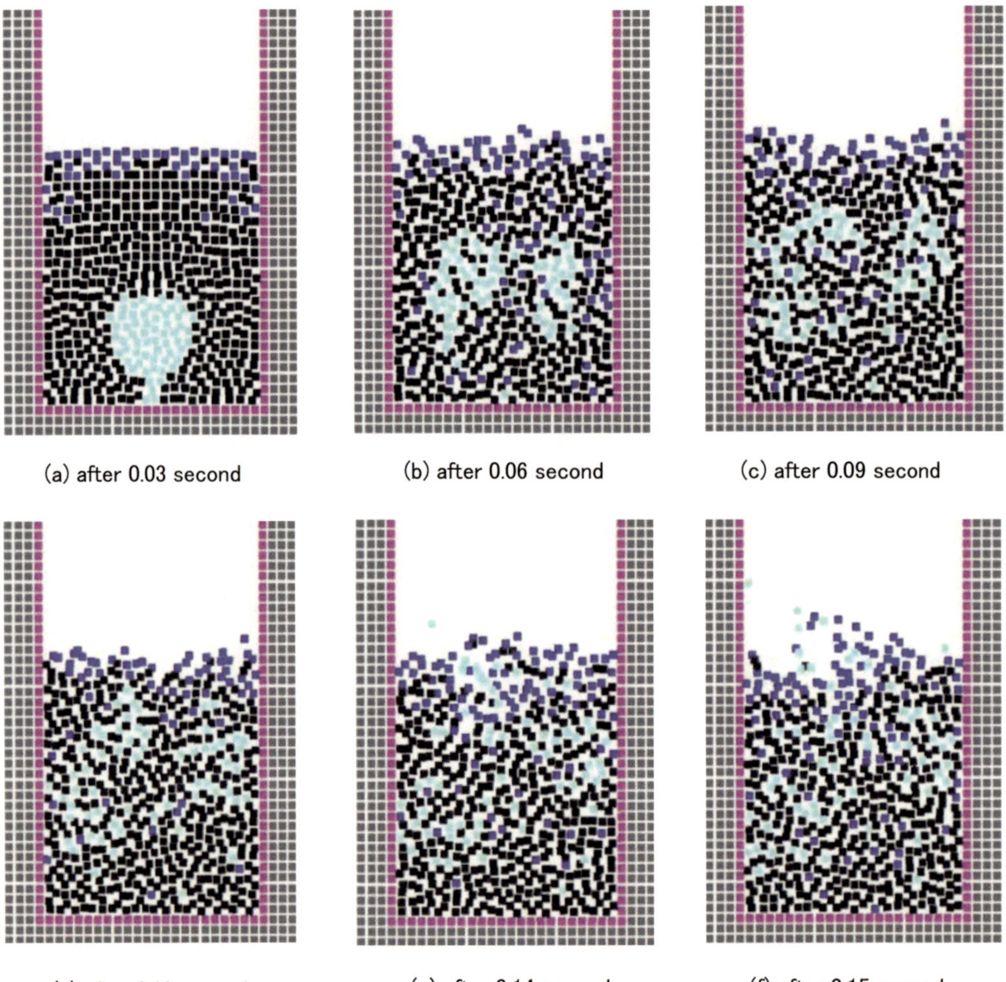

(a) after 0.03 second (b) after 0.06 second (c) after 0.09 second

(d) after 0.12 second (e) after 0.14 second (f) after 0.15 second

Fig. 6. A bubble moving up from the bottom of the water (without surface tension).

5. Spinnability simulation

Spinnability is one feature of viscoelastic fluid, which has a character of both viscosity and elasticity. When viscoelastic fluid is pulled, it stretches very thin and long such as a rubber string. This feature is called spinnability. For spinnability simulation, equation of continuity is necessary and also Navier-Stokes equation is used; however, constitutive equation of viscoelastic fluid should be taken into account for stress tensor of Cauchy's equation of motion. Then, in this section, governing equations are derived from Cauchy's equation of motion. In addition, when viscoelastic fluid is stretched, it has free surface so that surface tension should be considered. Then, Cauchy's equation of motion with surface tension is the following.

$$\rho \frac{D\mathbf{u}}{Dt} = \nabla \cdot \boldsymbol{\sigma} + \rho \mathbf{K} + \gamma \kappa \delta \mathbf{n} \tag{32}$$

Here, stress tensor can be written as $\boldsymbol{\sigma} = -p\mathbf{I} + \boldsymbol{\tau}$ (Eq. (12)). For viscoelastic fluid, stress deviation $\boldsymbol{\tau}$ is divided into two parts: viscoelastic fluid and solvent as follows because viscoelastic fluid is dissolved by solvent in order to have the feature of spinnability.

$$\boldsymbol{\tau} = \boldsymbol{\tau}_v + \boldsymbol{\tau}_s \tag{33}$$

Solvent is incompressible fluid so that the stress deviation is written as follows by Eq. (13).

$$\boldsymbol{\tau}_s = 2\mu_s \mathbf{D} \tag{34}$$

On the other hand, there are some models for stress deviation of viscoelastic fluid, and two models, which are Giesekus and Larson models, are adopted and compared in this section.

Giesekus model:

$$\boldsymbol{\tau}_v + \lambda \overset{\nabla}{\boldsymbol{\tau}}_v + \alpha \frac{\lambda}{\mu_v} \boldsymbol{\tau}_v \cdot \boldsymbol{\tau}_v = 2\mu_v \mathbf{D} \tag{35}$$

Larson model:

$$\boldsymbol{\tau}_v + \lambda \overset{\nabla}{\boldsymbol{\tau}}_v + \frac{2\zeta\lambda}{3G} \mathbf{D} : \boldsymbol{\tau}_v \left(\boldsymbol{\tau}_v + G \right) = 2\mu_0 \mathbf{D} \tag{36}$$

Where, λ is relaxation time, α is influence coefficient of nonlinear term, ζ is model parameter, G is relaxation modulus, μ_0 is zero shear viscosity, : is inner product of tensor. In addition, ∇ in the above equations (Eq. (32) and (33)) is called upper convective difference and defined as follows.

$$\overset{\nabla}{\boldsymbol{\tau}}_v = \frac{d\boldsymbol{\tau}_v}{dt} - \mathbf{L} \cdot \boldsymbol{\tau}_v - \boldsymbol{\tau}_v \cdot \mathbf{L}^t \tag{37}$$

$$\mathbf{D} = \frac{1}{2}\left(\mathbf{L} + \mathbf{L}^t \right), \quad \mathbf{L} = \nabla \mathbf{u} \tag{38}$$

Fig. 7 shows particle model expression of spinability simulation with Giesekus model. Fig. 7 (a) shows the initial state. The model is composed of 2,744 particles for viscoelastic fluid and 5,007 particles for solid objects, which are just attached with the viscoelastic fluid and pulled. Then, the viscoelastic fluid is stretched according to the movement of solid objects. Fig. 7 (b) shows the middle state, where the viscoelastic fluid is stretching such as a rubber string. The middle part of the fluid is gradually thinner. Fig. 7 (c) shows the state just before it is broken so that there are only a few particles at the thinnest part. Fig. 7 (d) shows the state just after it is broken, then the fluid shrinks rapidly as if it is a rubber string. In turn, Fig. 8 shows the surface model expression of the same particle model from the different point of view. Surface model is generated from the particle model with Marching Cubes (Mukai et al., 2010).

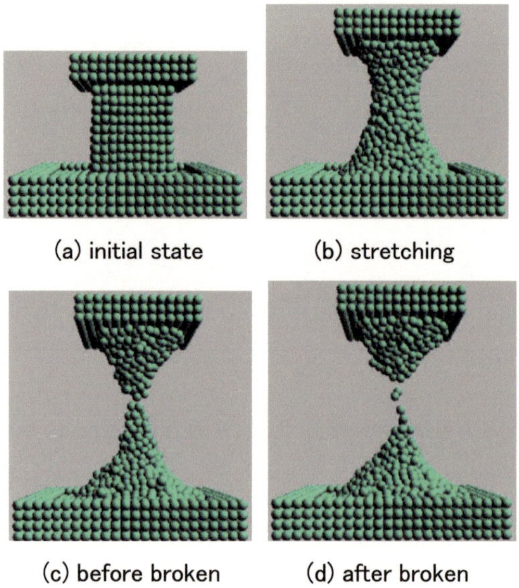

Fig. 7. Particle model expression of spinability simulation with Giesekus model

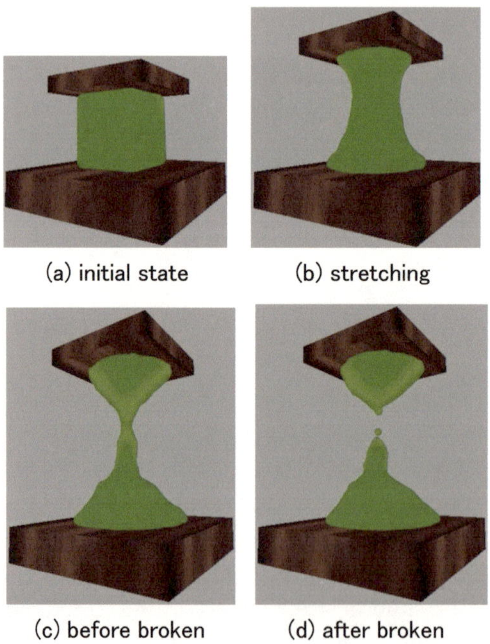

Fig. 8. Surface model expression of spinability simulation with Giesekus model

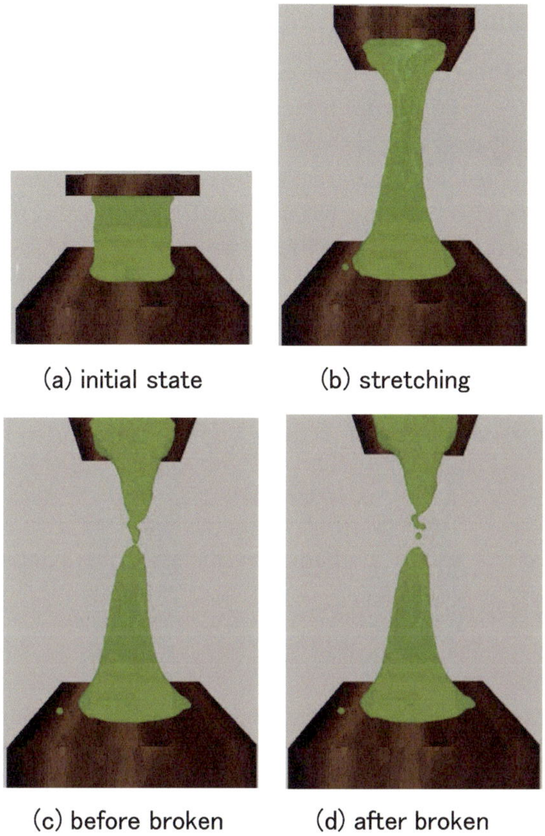

Fig. 9. Surface model expression of spinability simulation with Larson model

On the other hand, Fig. 9 shows surface model expression with Larson model. The viscoelastic fluid with Larson model is more stretching than that with Giesekus model. The stretching length depends on the velocity of viscoelastic fluid. Table 1 shows the comparison of the stretching length for Giesekus and Larson models according to its velocity. The viscoelastic fluid with Giesekus model does not stretch so much for the velocity, while the fluid with Larson model stretches longer for the velocity (Arimatsu et al., 2011).

Velocity [m/s]	Stretching length [mm]	
	Giesekus model	Larson model
0.018	2.3	14.7
0.068	2.3	21.4
0.100	2.4	22.8
0.140	2.4	25.8
0.180	2.4	28.4

Table 1. Comparison of the stretch length

6. Blood flow simulation

This section explains the method of blood vessel deformation and bleeding simulation by using MPS. Blood itself is fluid so that it should be simulated with particle model. On the other hand, blood vessel is not fluid but solid that deforms very easily, which is elastic body. In addition, we have to consider the interaction between blood flow and blood vessel. Then, in this section, blood vessel is decomposed into small particles and the interaction between blood itself and blood vessel is calculated with particle method. The governing equations are equation of continuity (Eq. (7)) and Cauchy's equation of motion (Eq. (11)). For incompressible fluid, the stress tensor $\boldsymbol{\sigma}$ is expressed as follows with Eq. (12) and (13).

$$\boldsymbol{\sigma} = -p\mathbf{I} + 2\mu\mathbf{D} \tag{39}$$

On the other hand, the stress tensor $\boldsymbol{\sigma}$ for elastic body is expressed as follows.

$$\boldsymbol{\sigma} = -\lambda tr(\boldsymbol{\varepsilon})\mathbf{I} + 2G\boldsymbol{\varepsilon} \tag{40}$$

Where, $\boldsymbol{\varepsilon}$ is strain tensor, λ and G are Lame parameters that are defined as follows.

$$\lambda = \frac{\nu E}{(1+\nu)(1-2\nu)}, \quad G = \frac{E}{2(1+\nu)} \tag{41}$$

Where, ν is Poisson's ratio and E is Young's modulus. Trace of strain tensor $tr(\boldsymbol{\varepsilon})$ is calculated as the difference between particle number of density and initial one as follows.

$$\langle tr(\boldsymbol{\varepsilon})\rangle_i = -\frac{n_i - n^0}{n_i} \tag{42}$$

In addition, non-slip boundary condition is satisfied for the boundary between the blood vessel and blood particles that touch the blood vessel. The interaction force $\mathbf{F}$ between particles is calculated with Hooke's law as follows.

$$F_{\mathbf{i}} = \begin{cases} \sum_{i \neq j} k \dfrac{\left(|\mathbf{r}_j - \mathbf{r}_i|\right)}{2r} & \left(|\mathbf{r}_j - \mathbf{r}_i| < 2r\right) \\ 0 & \left(r \leq |\mathbf{r}_j - \mathbf{r}_i|\right) \end{cases} \tag{43}$$

Where, k is spring constant and r is the radius of a particle.

Fig. 10 shows the simulation result of blood vessel deformation. Fig. 10 (a) shows the initial state, where two surgical tools are supporting a blood vessel model lying horizontally. The number of particles for the blood vessel, blood and surgical tools are 9,568, 5,852 and 1,365, respectively. Fig. 10 (b) shows the case that the inside of the blood vessel is filled with elastic particles so that the blood vessel is not deformed so much when two surgical tools push the blood vessel. On the contrary, Fig. 10 (c) shows the case that the inside of the blood vessel is empty so that the blood vessel is deformed largely; however, it is not real because there is blood flow inside the blood vessel. Then, Fig. 10 (d) shows the case that the inside of the blood vessel is filled with blood particles so that the blood vessel is deformed moderately, since there is blood flow inside the blood vessel and the blood flow pressure pushes back the force that comes from the surgical tools.

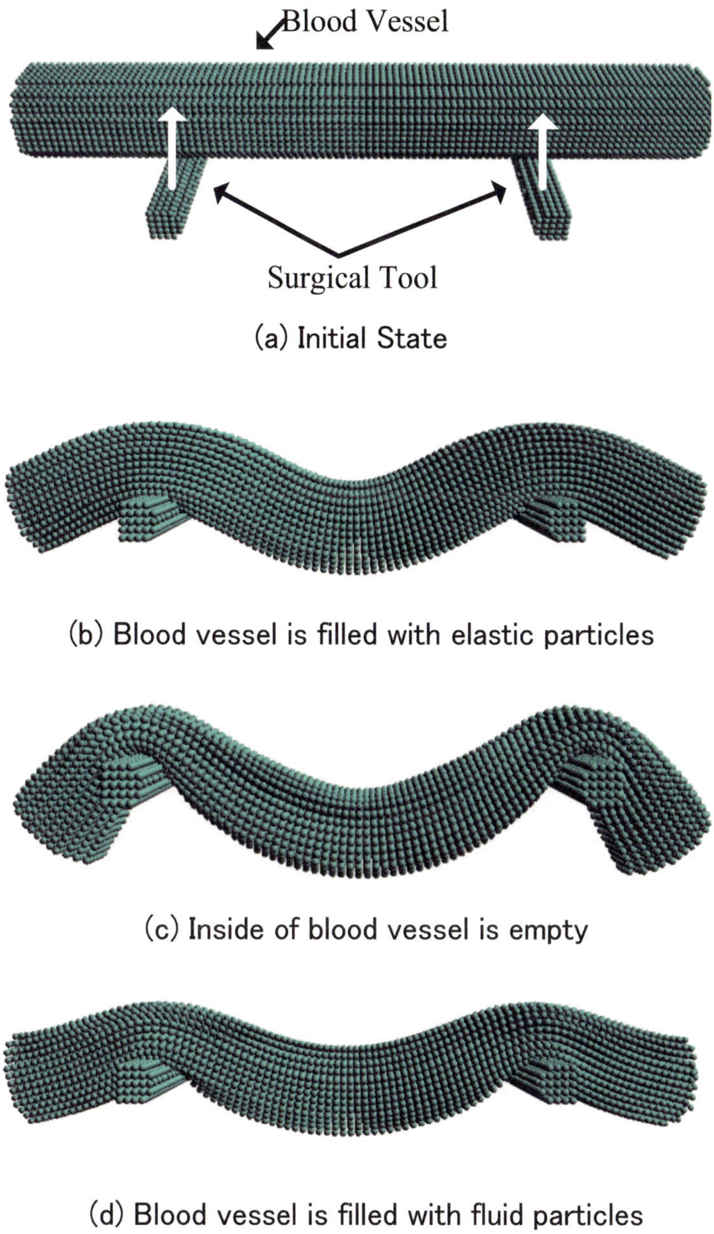

Fig. 10. Blood vessel deformation with particle method

On the other hand, Fig. 11 shows another simulation of blood vessel deformation and bleeding with the aorta model. Fig. 11 (a) shows the initial state. The model is constructed with 15,000 and 7,000 particles for blood vessel and blood itself, respectively. The aorta model is generated from image data of a real patient. The aorta is extracted from volume data, which is constructed with multiple image data, and it is converted into polygon data by using Marching Cubes. Then, the polygon data is converted into particle data, which is used for this simulation. Blood flows into the blood vessel from the upper part of the aorta, and it flows out of the lower part of it. When two surgical tools push the blood vessel, it is deformed by considering the interaction between blood vessel and blood flow (Fig. 11 (b)). In addition, if a part of the blood vessel is broken, bleeding occurs (Fig. 11 (c)). (Nakagawa et al., 2010, 2011)

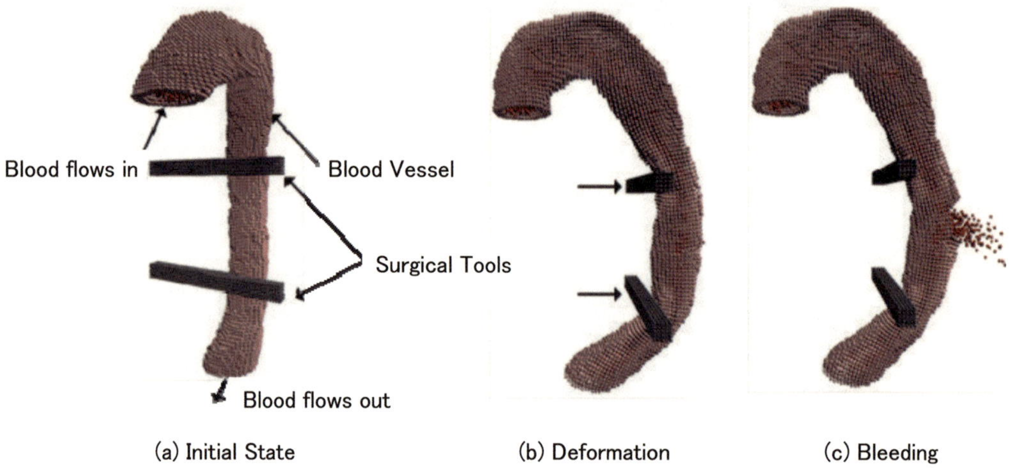

Fig. 11. Simulation of blood vessel deformation and bleeding

7. Conclusion

In this section, three kinds of simulation with particle method were explained. For all simulations, the basic equations are equation of continuity and Cauchy's equation of motion, which leads Navier-Stokes equation. There are two types of particle methods: SPH and MPS, and in this chapter these simulations use MPS method since MPS treats incompressible fluid such as water, viscoelastic fluid and blood. In bubble simulation, surface tension is added to Navier-Stokes equation so that the bubble moves up to water surface keeping its shape, and it is broken by the pressure from the inside of the bubble. In spinnability simulation, stress deviation of Cauchy's equation of motion is divided into two kinds: viscoelastic fluid and solvent. For stress deviation of viscoelastic fluid, two types of models, which are Giesekus and Larson models, were used to compare its stretching length. As the result of the simulation, stretching length with Larson model was longer than that of Giesekus's. Finally, blood vessel deformation and bleeding simulations were performed. Blood itself is fluid; however, blood vessel is elastic body so that the different equations of stress tensor were used for fluid and elastic body. Simulation result says that the blood vessel filled with blood flow is deformed moderately and bleeding simulation can be also visualized.

In the future, there are some issues to be solved. 1) three dimensional simulation of bubble moving, changing its shape, and disappearance, 2) considering a new model of stress deviation for viscoelastic fluid, which model stretches viscoelastic fluid longer and expresses good spinnability, and 3) verification of the simulation of blood vessel deformation and bleeding. The simulation result should be evaluated by surgeons. In addition, visualization of the blood flow and stress distribution inside the blood vessel will be also useful for the preoperative planning of real surgeries.

8. Acknowledgment

This research was supported by JSPS KAKENHI (21500125).

9. References

Arimatsu K.; Nakagawa M & Mukai N. (2010). Particle Based Expression of Spinability of Viscoelastic Fluid, *Proceedings of the Media Computing Conference,* DVD, 4 pages

Chang Y.; Bao K.; Liu Y.; Zhu J. & Wu E. (2009). A Particle-based Method for Viscoelastic Fluids Animation, *Proceeding of the 16th ACM Symposium on Virtual Reality Software and Technology,* pp.111-117

Clavet S.; Beaudoin P. & Poulin P. (2005). Particle-based Viscoelastic Fluid Simulation, *Proceeding of the 2004 ACM SIGGRAPH/Eurographics Symposium on Computer Animation,* pp.219-228

Goktekin T. G.; Bargteil A. W. & O'Brien J. F. (2004). A Method for Animating Viscoelastic Fluids, *Proceeding of the 2004 ACM SIGGRAPH,* pp.463-468

Greenwood, S.T. & House D.H. (2004). Better with Bubbles : Enhancing the Visual Realism of Simulated Fluid, *Proceeding of the 2004 ACM SIGGRAPH/Eurographics Symposium on Computer Animation,* pp.287-296

Hong J. M.; Lee H. Y.; Yoon J. C. & Kim C. H. (2008). Bubbles Alive, *Proceeding of the 2008 ACM SIGGRAPH,* pp.48:1-48:4

Kagatsume N.; Nakagawa M. & Mukai N. (2011). Bubble Disappearance Simulation Using Particle Methods, *ITE Technical Report,* Vol. 35, No.32, pp.13-16

Kim B.; Liu Y.; Llamas I.; Jiao X. & Rossignac J. (2007). Simulation of Bubbles in Foam With The Volume Control Method, *Proceeding of the 2007 ACM SIGGRAPH,* pp.98-1-98-10

Kim D.; Song O. & Ko H. (2010). A Practical Simulation of Dispersed Bubble Flow, *Proceeding of the 2010 ACM SIGGRAPH,* pp.70:1-70:5

Koshizuka S. (2005), Particle Method, Maruzen Co. Ltd.

Losasso F.; Shinar T.; Selle A. & Fedkiw R. (2007). Multiple Interacting Liquids, *Proceeding of the 2006 ACM SIGGRAPH,* pp.812-819

Mukai N.; Ito K.; Nakagawa M. & Kosugi M. (2010). Sinnability Simulation of Viscoelastic Fluid, *the 2010 ACM SIGGRAPH posters*

Nakamura K. (1997), Non-Newtonian Fluid Mechanics, Corona Publishing Co. Ltd.

Nakagawa M.; Mukai N. & Kosugi M. (2010), A Blood Vessel Deformation Metho Considering Blood Stream for Surgical Simulations, *Proceeding of 2010 IWAIT,* CDROM, 6 pages

Nakagawa M.; Mukai N.; Tatefuku Y.; Niki K. & Takanashi S. (2011), Simulation of the Aorta Deformation and Bleeding by Using Particle Method, *Trans. of IIEEJ,* Vol. 40, No.5, pp.761-767

Qin J.; Pang W. M.; Nguyen B. P.; Ni D. & Chui C. K. (2010). Particle-based Simulation of Blood Flow and Vessel Wall Interaction in Virtual Surgery, *Proceeding of the 2010 Symposium on Information and Communication Technology,* pp.128-133

Selle A.; Rasmussen N. & Fedkiw E. (2005). A Vortex Particle Method for Smoke, Water and Explosions, *Proceeding of the 2005 ACM SIGGRAPH,* pp.910-914

Yamamoto K. (2009). Real Time Two-Way Coupling of Fluids to Deformable Bodies using Particle Method on GPU, *the 2009 ACM SIGGRAPH ASIA posters*

Zheng W.; Yong J. H. & Paul J. C. (2006). Simulation of Bubbles, *Proceeding of the 2006 ACM SIGGRAPH/Eurographics Symposium on Computer Animation,* pp.325-333

8

Fast Local Tone Mapping, Summed-Area Tables and Mesopic Vision Simulation

Marcos Slomp, Michihiro Mikamo and Kazufumi Kaneda
Hiroshima University
Japan

1. Introduction

High dynamic range (HDR) imaging is becoming an increasingly popular practice in computer graphics, bringing unprecedented levels of realism to computer-generated imagery and rich detail preservation to photographs and films. HDR imagery can embrace more accurately the wide range of light intensities found in real scenes than its counterpart, low dynamic range (LDR), which are tailored to the limited intensities of display devices. Simply put in computer terminology, think of HDR as a *very large, continuous* range of intensities encoded in a floating-point representation (but not necessarily), while LDR translates to *coarse, quantized* ranges, usually encoded as 8-bit integers and thus limited to 256 *discrete* intensities.

An important term in HDR imaging is the *dynamic range* or *contrast ratio* of a scene, representing the distance between the lowest and highest intensity values. Luminance in the real world typically covers 14 orders of magnitude (dynamic range of $10^{14} : 1$), ranging from direct sunlight (10^5 up to $10^8 cd/m^2$) to shallow starlight (10^{-3} down to $10^{-6} cd/m^2$), while typical image formats and commodity display devices can cope with only 2 up to 4 orders of magnitude (maximum contrast ratio of $10^4 : 1$) [Ledda et al. (2005)].

A challenging task on HDR imaging consists in the proper presentation of the large range of intensities within HDR imagery in the much narrower range supported by display devices while still preserving contrastive details. This process involves intelligent luminance (dynamic range) compression techniques, referred to as *tone reproduction operators* or, more commonly, *tone mapping operators* (TMO). An example is depicted in Figure 1.

The process of tone mapping shares similarities with the light adaptation mechanism performed by the Human Visual System (HVS), which is also unable to instantly cope with the wide range of luminosity present in the real world. Even though the HVS is only capable of handling a small range of about 4 or 5 orders of magnitude at any given time, it is capable of dynamically and gradually shift the perceptible range up or down, appropriately, in order to better enclose the luminosity range of the observed scene [Ledda et al. (2004)]. Display devices, on the other hand, are much more restrictive, since there is no way to dynamically improve or alter their inherently fixed dynamic range capabilities.

Tone mapping operators can be classified as either *global* (spatially-uniform) or *local* (spatially-varying). Global operators process all pixels uniformly with the same parameters, while local operators attempt to find an optimal set of parameters for each pixel individually, often considering a variable-size neighborhood around every pixel; in other words, the

(a) No Tone-Mapping (clamped) (b) Global Operator (c) Local Operator

Fig. 1. A comparison between the global and the local variants of the photographic operator of Reinhard et al. (2002). Local operators are capable of preserving more contrastive detail.

amount of luminance compression is locally adapted to the different regions of the image. Determining such local vicinities is not straight-forward and may introduce strong haloing artifacts if not handled carefully. Although all local tone-mapping operators are prone to this kind of artifacts, good operators try to minimize their occurrence. Overall, local operators retain superior contrast preservation over global operators, but at much higher computational costs. Figure 1 illustrates the visual differences between each class of operator.

Due to the prohibitive performance overhead of local operators, current HDR-based real-time applications rely on either global operators or in more simplistic exposure control techniques. Such exposure mechanisms can be faster than global operators, but are not as automatic, often requiring extensive manual intervention from artists to tailor the parameters for each scene and vantage point; worse yet, if objects or light sources are modified, this entire tedious process would have to be repeated.

Apart from contrast preservation and performance issues, most tone-mapping operators focus exclusively on luminance compression, ignoring chromatic assets. The HVS, however, alters color perception according to the overall level of luminosity, categorized as *photopic*, *mesopic* and *scotopic*. The transition between these ranges is held by the HVS, stimulating visual cells – cones and rods – according to the overall lighting conditions. Cones are less numerous and less responsive to light than rods, but are sensitive to colors, quickly adapt to abrupt lighting transitions and provide sharper visual acuity than rods.

(a) without mesopic vision simulation (b) with mesopic vision simulation (proposed)

Fig. 2. An evening urban scene (a) without mesopic vision simulation and (b) with the mesopic vision strategy later described in Section 4. As it can be seen the sky changes from purple to a more blueish tone, while distant artificial lights shift from red to orange/yellow.

At photopic conditions (think of an outdoor scene at daylight) color perception is accurate since *only* cones are being stimulated. When the lighting conditions turn to scotopic (think of starlight), colors can no longer be discerned because cones become completely inhibited while rods become fully active. *Mesopic vision* is a transitory range in-between where rods and cones are both stimulated simultaneously. At this stage colors can still be perceived, albeit in a distorted fashion: the responses from red intensities tend to fade faster, thus producing a peculiar *blue-shift* phenomenon known as Purkinje effect [Minnaert (1954)].

Moonlit scenes, for example, present a blueish appearance even though the light being reflected by the moon from the sun is not anywhere close to blue in nature, but it is actually *redder* than sunlight [Khan & Pattanaik (2004); van de Hulst (1957)]. Besides this overall blueish appearance at extreme mesopic vision conditions, the same phenomenon also causes otherwise red features to appear in a much darker tone, or in an *orangeish* or *yellowish* tone; similarly, purple tonalities tend to be noticed in dark blue colorations. Refer to Figure 2 for a depiction of a scene with and without the proposed mesopic vision filter.

The explanation of such effect comes from the fact that in mesopic conditions rods respond better to short wavelengths (blue) stimuli than long and medium wavelengths (red, yellow, green). As the overall luminosity conditions dim, but *before* rods completely take over the visual system (scotopic vision), color perception shifts towards the currently most sensible rod's wavelengths, that is, around blue.

Mesopic vision reproduction for computer-generated images has immediate application on artistic assets and architectural lighting design. Perhaps an even more relevant application is on road engineering and signalization planning, by reproducing the overall experience of drivers subjected to adverse lighting conditions.

This chapter focuses on an efficient GPU-based implementation of the local-variant of the photographic operator introduced by Reinhard et al. (2002) that achieves real-time performance without compromising image quality. The presented approach approximates the costly variable-size Gaussian convolutions with efficient box-filtering through Summed-Area Tables (SAT) [Crow (1984)], as suggested earlier by Slomp & Oliveira (2008). This work, however, utilizes a technique based on balanced-trees for the SAT generation [Blelloch (1990)] instead of the originally employed (and more widely spread) recursive-doubling algorithm [Dubois & Rodrigue (1977)]. This algorithmic change vastly improves performance, in particular for large-sized images, at the expense of a more involved implementation.

More importantly, a novel, fast and universal perceptually-based method to reproduce color shifts under mesopic vision conditions is introduced. Unlike previous works, the present work can deal with the *entire* mesopic vision range. The method builds upon initial investigations of Mikamo et al. (2009), who suggested the use of perceptual metrics for mesopic vision reproduction derived from psychophysical experiments performed by Ikeda & Ashizawa (1991). The proposed *uniform* mesopic filter is not bound exclusively to the aforementioned photographic operator, but can in fact suit *any* other existing TMO, since the chromatic adjustment stage is *decoupled* from the luminance compression stage. Finally, this chapter also describes how to exploit the foundations of the local photographic operator to further extend the proposed uniform filter in a *spatially-varying* manner and achieve more plausible mesopic vision results without performance penalties. Only a tiny performance footprint is incurred to the overall tone-mapping process, hence being friendly to real-time applications.

External resources

The demo program is available for download at the following URL:

`http://www.eml.hiroshima-u.ac.jp/demos/fast-mesopic-tmo`

2. Related work

A proper sound review on tone-reproduction operators would consume several pages of this document, since the available literature is vast and rich. Therefore, this background review section will focus on pertinent research related to *real-time local tone-mapping* as well as *mesopic vision simulation*. The curious reader is referred to Reinhard et al. (2010) for an extensive survey on tone-mapping and HDR imaging techniques.

2.1 Real-time local tone-mapping

Local operators, due to the varying-size filtering and halo-avoidance requirements, impose great challenge for faithful real-time implementations, even with parallel power of modern programmable graphics hardware (GPU). From all existing TMOs, the photographic operator introduced by Reinhard et al. (2002) has received special attention from researchers and practitioners, mainly due to its simplicity (few parameters), automaticity (no user intervention), robustness (extreme dynamic ranges) and perceptually-driven approach (local adaption is guided by an HVS-based brightness perception model). There are two variants of the operator, a global and a local one. The photographic operator is reviewed in Section 2.3.

The local variant of the photographic operator, at its core, makes use of differences of Gaussian-filtered (DoG) luminance images at various scales. Unfortunately, convolving an image with variable-size Gaussian kernels is a computationally demanding operation. Several attempts were made to accelerate this filtering to provide real-time frame rates.

Goodnight et al. (2003) investigated the implementation of local operators on GPU. Their best result was with the photographic operator, where they implemented the 2D Gaussian convolution using separable 1D kernels in a two-stage approach. Their implementation is by no means naïve, but makes clever use of the efficient 4-component vector dot product instruction provided by GPU architectures. This reduces the number of required filtering passes and thus achieves better performance. Despite all their optimization efforts, the technique only runs at interactive rates when using a small subset of the originally required adaptation scales (i.e., the first few Gaussian-filtered luminance images at small convolution profile sizes; see Section 2.3). A limited number of adaptation zones gradually causes the operator to fall-back to the global variant case, thus sacrificing important contrastive details (see Figure 3-b).

Krawczyk et al. (2005) proposed an approximation for the local photographic operator on the GPU. The Gaussian-filtered luminance images are downsampled to $1/4$, $1/16$, and $1/64$ of their original size. Convolutions are then performed using smaller approximate Gaussian kernels of fixed size (always 7 pixels wide), with intermediate filtered results being reused. The blurred images are then upsampled back to the original size prior to evaluating the DoG model. This strategy significantly speeds up the operator, but not without inherent limitations: there is excessive blurring across high contrast edges being caused by the downsampling-upsampling process, potentially introducing noticeable halo artifacts (see

Figure 3-c). Besides these shortcomings, their main contributions concentrate on reproducing perceptual effects such as temporal luminosity adaptation, glare and loss of vision acuity.

Slomp & Oliveira (2008) replaced the expensive variable-size Gaussian convolutions of the operator with box-filtering powered by Summed-Area Tables (SAT) [Crow (1984)]. Summed-Area Tables allow arbitrary rectangular portions of an image to be efficiently box-filtered in constant time $O(1)$. Although box-filtering provides a very crude approximation of Gaussian-filtering, within the context of the photographic operator results are nearly indistinguishable from the original operator, as demonstrated in Figure 3-d. It is worth mentioning that box-weighted kernels were also used in the context of tone mapping by Pattanaik & Yee (2002) in their bilateral-filtering algorithm. The process of SAT generation can be efficiently implemented on the GPU, thus not only mitigating the occurrence of halos, but also substantially accelerating the operator, even when compared against the fast method of Krawczyk et al. (2005). A review on SAT and their generation is provided in Sections 2.4, 3.2 and 3.3.

(a) Reinhard et al. (2002) (b) Goodnight et al. (2003) (c) Krawczyk et al. (2005) (d) Slomp & Oliveira (2008)

Fig. 3. Comparison between different implementations of the local photographic operator. Note that words vanished from the book in (b), and halos appeared around the lamp in (c).

This Chapter describes a more attractive method for SAT generation based on balanced-trees [Blelloch (1990)]. The originally employed recursive-doubling algorithm [Dubois & Rodrigue (1977)] requires less passes, but performs more arithmetic operations and is more sensitive to cache thrashing. In spite of the advantages and readily availability since long, the adoption of the balanced-tree approach by the computer graphics community was oddly timid.

2.2 Mesopic vision simulation

Despite luminance compression, many tone mapping operators have concentrated efforts on reproducing perceptual effects recurrent from the HVS, most notably: temporal luminosity adaption, scotopic vision simulation, loss of visual acuity, and glare. The literature on these topics is broad; refer to Reinhard et al. (2010) for examples of each category. However, and quite surprising, very little has been done on reproducing mesopic vision; below is a summary of the most remarkable research related to mesopic vision in tone reproduction.

Durand & Dorsey (2000) have specialized the rod-cone interaction model of Ferwerda et al. (1996) to better suit night scenes, adding support for chromatic adaptation and color shifts, among other effects. Even though the method does not explicitly address mesopic vision, the underlying framework can be tunned to handle specific *subranges* of mesopic vision with some degree of fidelity, but not without some user interaction. The technique is fast and runs at interactive rates since it inherits the same *global* characteristics of Ferwerda et al. (1996).

Khan & Pattanaik (2004) have also proposed a blue-shift filter based on rod-cone interaction. Their technique is designed primarily for moonlit scenes, without the intervention of artificial light sources. Overall, the method tends to introduce very strong blue hues on the scene, almost completely mitigating other color tones. This is due to their hypothesis that *only* short wavelength cones (blue) would respond to light in a naturally moonlit scene. The technique itself does not rely on HDR imagery and therefore can not be classified as a TMO.

Kirk & O'Brien (2011) have proposed a color shift model for mesopic vision, building upon the biological model and fitting experiments of Cao et al. (2008). Their model can be combined with existing TMO since chrominance adaptation is decoupled from luminance compression. The chrominance adaption strategy itself is spatially-uniform (global), but nonetheless computationally demanding and incompatible with interactive frame rates. The overhead comes from the fact that *spectral* information is required; in other words, the input images must be capable of approximating the continuous distribution of energy at every pixel using some higher dimensional representation. Moreover, the method assumes that the spectral sensitivity of the camera is known; if not provided by the manufacturer, a calibration procedure is required to estimate the sensitivity. Traditional HDR imagery can also be targeted, although not without first estimating the unknown spectral distribution.

The mesopic vision reproduction strategy to be introduced in this Chapter takes a more generic avenue than the methods above. Chrominance adaptation is also decoupled from luminance compression, thus suitable to co-exist with nearly any available TMO. The *entire* mesopic vision range is handled systematically without special conditions. The technique is targeted for widely available HDR imagery, hence unconventional spectral information is not required. The performance overhead introduced is most likely negligible. Two variants of the proposed filter are presented: a more generic spatially-uniform one and a spatially-varying one that uses the infrastructure available from the local photographic operator. The technique, however, should *not* be misunderstood as a definitive replacement to the more specialized aforementioned approaches, but rather as an accessible framework that does not incur into prohibitive performance penalties, acquisition and development costs or image quality degradation.

2.3 Review of the photographic tone reproduction operator

Reinhard et al. (2002) digital photographic operator uses a photographic technique called Zone Systems [Adams (1983)] as a conceptual framework to manage luminance compression. The goal is to map the *key-value* (subjective predominant intensity) of a scene to the *middle-gray* tone of the printing medium (*middle-intensity* of the display device in this case) and then linearly rescaling the remaining intensities accordingly. This can be intuitively thought as setting an exposure range in a digital camera. An overview of the operator is shown in Figure 4.

Given an HDR image, a good estimation for its key-value is the *geometric average* (*log-average*) of its luminances, which is less susceptible to small outliers than plain arithmetic average:

$$\widetilde{L} = exp\left(\frac{1}{N}\sum_{x,y} log(L(x,y)+\delta)\right) \quad (1)$$

where N is the number of pixels in the image, $L(x,y)$ is the luminance at the pixel with coordinates (x,y), and δ is a small constant (i.e., $\delta = 0.00001$) to prevent the undefined $log(0)$.

Each pixel luminance is then *scaled* based on the Zone System printing zones, with the estimated key-value $\widetilde{L}$ being mapped to the middle-grey range:

$$L_r(x,y) = L(x,y)\frac{\alpha}{\widetilde{L}} \quad (2)$$

where $\alpha = 0.18$ for average-key scenes (akin to automatic exposure control systems present in digital cameras [Goodnight et al. (2003)]). For high-key and low-key scenes, the parameter α has to be tweaked, but an automatic estimation strategy is described by Reinhard (2003).

For the global-variant of the operator, each relative luminance $L_r(x,y)$ is mapped to a normalized displayable range $L_d(x,y) \in [0,1)$ as follows:

$$L_d(x,y) = \frac{L_r(x,y)}{1+L_r(x,y)} \quad (3)$$

This global operator is prone to conceal contrastive detail. A better approach is to locally adapt the contrast of each region, individually, similar to photographic *dodging-and-burning*:

$$L_d(x,y) = \frac{L_r(x,y)}{1+L_r^{s_{max}}(x,y)} \quad (4)$$

where $L_r^{s_{max}}(x,y)$ is the Gaussian-weighted average of the largest isoluminant region s_{max} around each isolated pixel where no substantial luminance variation occur. The term $L_r^{s_{max}}(x,y)$ can be more intuitively thought as a measurement of *local area luminance* around a pixel. It is imperative to judiciously determine these isoluminant regions because otherwise strong haloing artifacts are prone to appear around high-contrast edges of the image.

The dodging-and-burning approach of the local photographic operator uses *differences of Gaussian*-filtered (DoG) portions of the scaled luminance image $L_r(x,y)$ at increasing sizes to iteratively search for these optimal isoluminant regions, according to the following expression:

$$V_s(x,y) = \frac{L_r^s(x,y) - L_r^{s+1}(x,y)}{2^{\phi}\alpha/s^2 + L_r^s(x,y)} \quad (5)$$

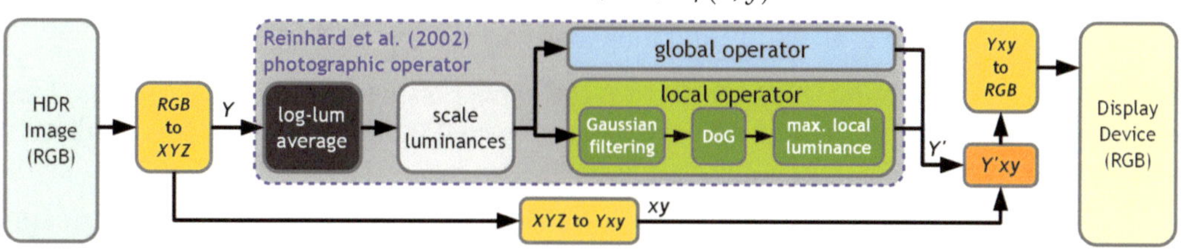

Fig. 4. Overview of the photographic tone mapping operator of Reinhard et al. (2002). The input Y is the HDR luminance ($L(x,y)$) and the output Y' is the compressed luminance ($L_d(x,y)$).

where ϕ is a sharpening factor, and defaults to $\phi = 8$. The term $L_r^s(x,y)$ corresponds to a center-surround Gaussian-blurred image, formally:

$$L_r^s(x,y) = L_r(x,y) \otimes Gaussian_s(x,y) \tag{6}$$

where the operator $\otimes$ denotes the kernel convolution operation and $Gaussian_s(x,y)$ is a Gaussian convolution profile of some scale s centered at pixel coordinates (x,y). The choice for this DoG-based model is not arbitrary and closely follows the human brightness perception model and psychophysical experiments of Blommaert & Martens (1990).

Finally, the largest isoluminant scale s_{max} is found by thresholding the Gaussian differences $V_s(x,y)$ obtained from Equation 5 against the following expression:

$$s_{max} : |V_{s_{max}}(x,y)| < \epsilon \tag{7}$$

where $\epsilon = 0.05$ proved to be a good thresholding choice through empirical experimentation, according to Reinhard et al. (2002).

Starting from the initial scaled luminance image $L_r(x,y)$ of Equation 2, subsequent blurred images $L_r^s(x,y)$ are produced according to Equation 6 with a kernel about 1.6 times larger than the previous one. As the differences $V_s(x,y)$ are computed according to Equation 5, they are thresholded against Equation 7, stopping as soon as the condition fails. The largest scale is selected if the threshold condition is never reached. In the end, the estimated local area luminance $L_r^{s_{max}}(x,y)$ is plugged back into Equation 4 for tone mapping.

In general, a total of eight scales (and therefore a total of seven DoG) is sufficient for most situations. The suggested kernel *length* (*not radius*) in pixels, at both horizontal and vertical directions, of the first eight center-surround profiles are: $1, 3, 5, 7, 11, 17, 27$ and 41.

Color information can be removed prior to luminance compression and inserted back afterwards by using the Yxy deviation of the $CIE\ XYZ$ color space [Hoffmann (2000)]. The Yxy color space is capable of separating luminance and chrominance components. This decolorization and recoloring process is also depicted in the diagram of Figure 4.

2.4 Review of Summed-Area Tables (SAT)

Although originally introduced as a texture-mapping enhancement over mip-mapping, precision constraints made Summed-Area Tables inviable for the graphics hardware to follow at that time. Since their original conception by Crow (1984), SAT were successfully employed on a wide range of tasks ranging from face and object recognition[1] [Viola & Jones (2004)], depth-of-field and glossy reflections [Hensley et al. (2005)], shadows [Díaz et al. (2010); Lauritzen (2007); Slomp et al. (2010)] and tone-mapping [Slomp & Oliveira (2008)].

A SAT is simply a *cumulative table*, where each cell corresponds to *the sum of all elements above and to the left of it, inclusive*, in the original table, as depicted in Figure 5-ab. More formally:

$$SAT(x,y) = \sum_{i=1}^{x} \sum_{j=1}^{y} Table(i,j) \tag{8}$$

[1] Summed-Area Tables are also referred to as *integral images* in some image processing, computer vision and pattern recognition contexts.

where $1 \leq x \leq c$ and $1 \leq y \leq r$, with c and r representing the number of columns and rows of the source table, respectively. A SAT therefore has the *same* dimensions of its input table.

The usefulness of SAT comes from the fact that any *rectangular* region (axis-aligned) of the input table can be *box-filtered*[2] (or integrated) with *only four* lookups on the associated SAT (see Figure 5-cd). This gives the same *constant* filtering complexity $O(1)$ to *any* kernel size.

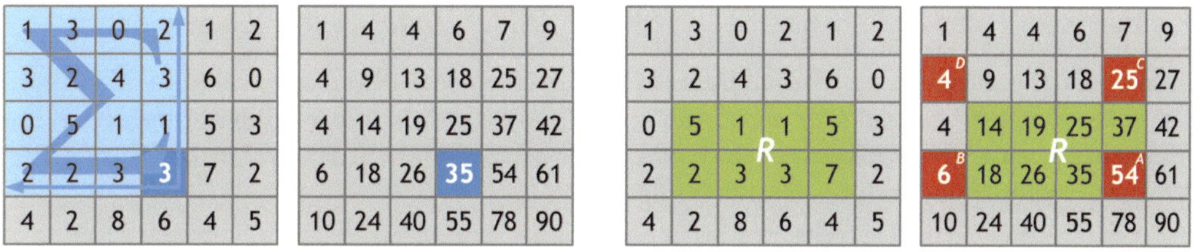

(a) input table (b) Summed-Area Table (c) filtering region (d) SAT-based filtering

Fig. 5. A small 6×5 table (a) and its corresponding SAT (b). The highlighted blue cell on the SAT is the sum of all the highlighted blue cells in the input table (all cells up and to the left, inclusive). In order to filter the 8 elements marked in green in the input table (c), only the four red elements A, B, C and D need to be fetched from the SAT (d), a fact that holds true for arbitrary sizes. The filtering result is given by: $\frac{A-B-C+D}{area} = \frac{54-6-25+4}{4*2} = \frac{27}{8} = 3.375$.

Fetching cells outside the boundaries of the SAT, however, requires special attention: elements out of the upper or left boundary are assumed to evaluate to *zero*, while elements out of the bottom or right boundary should be redirected back to the closest element at the respective boundary (analogous to the *clamp-to-edge* mode in OpenGL). Bilinear filtering can also be used to sample the SAT at non-integer locations if necessary.

Note that the original table could be entirely discarded: the SAT alone is capable of restoring the original values of the table from which it was built from. Depending on the application, if the input table is to be used constantly along with the SAT, it is a good idea to keep the input table at hand. This is specially true if the underlying numerical storage representation is prone to introduce precision errors due to arithmetic operations (i.e., floating-point).

Summed-Area Tables can be efficiently generated in a purely sequential fashion in $O(n)$, as shown by Crow (1984). Parallel implementations on the GPU are reserved to the next Section.

3. Photographic local tone reproduction with summed-area tables

The approximation proposed by Slomp & Oliveira (2008) to the local photographic operator of Reinhard et al. (2002) suggests the replacement of the costly variable-size Gaussian-filtering by box-filtering. This means that the Equation 6 of Section 2.3 gets replaced by:

$$L_r^s(x,y) \approx L_r(x,y) \otimes Box_s(x,y) \tag{9}$$

Box-filtering can be efficiently performed through Summed-Area Tables at a fraction of the cost of Gaussian convolutions, requiring only four SAT lookups for any kernel scale s. The

[2] Higher-Order Summed-Area Tables [Heckbert (1986)] can extend plain SAT beyond box-filtering, allowing for triangular and spline-based filtering, at the expense of increased constant time overhead and numerical issues. Although compelling, a more in-depth discussion on the subject is out of the scope of this text since plain SAT are sufficient for the tone mapping technique used in this document.

input table is, in this case, L_r from Equation 2, and the corresponding SAT will be referred to as $SAT[L_r]$. Equation 9 is then rewritten as:

$$L_r^s(x,y) \approx SAT[L_r]_s(x,y) \tag{10}$$

where $SAT[L_r]_s(x,y)$ box-filters a square-shape region of L_r centered around the pixel location (x,y) at some scale s using only the contents of the $SAT[L_r]$ itself; in other words, the four pertinent cells of the SAT are fetched and filtering follows as depicted in Figure 5-cd.

The set of differences $V_s(x,y)$ from Equation 5 are performed without any structural alteration, the only change being that $L_r^s(x,y)$ and $L_r^{s+1}(x,y)$ now amount to box-filtered portions of the scaled luminance image instead of the Gaussian-filtered regions. An overview of the modified local photographic operator is shown in Figure 6.

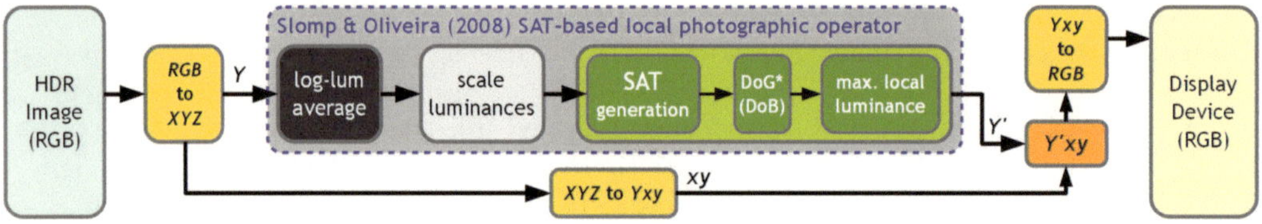

Fig. 6. Overview of the SAT-based local photographic operator of Slomp & Oliveira (2008).

Visually, results produced with this box-filtering approximation proved to be comparable to the original operator (see Figure 3-ad). Quantitative analysis using the S-CIELAB metric of Zhang & Wandell (1997) was also evaluated in the paper by Slomp & Oliveira (2008). Typically, the same originally devised filtering scales (listed at the end of Section 2.3) and threshold $\epsilon = 0.05$ from Equation 7 can be used. However, since box filters weight the contributions equally, they are more prone to noticeable halos than Gaussian filters of the same scale, which gradually reduces the weights towards the limits of the profiles. If such artifacts become apparent, the authors suggest reducing the threshold ϵ down to 0.0025.

3.1 Generating the scaled luminance image on the GPU

Prior to SAT generation, the scaled luminance image L_r should be computed. This process is fairly straight-forward and can be mapped entirely to the GPU. Initially, the input HDR image is placed into a *float-precision RGB* texture (in the case of synthesized 3D scenes, the entire scene is rendered in such texture target), as depicted in Figure 7-a.

Following that, the *RGB* texture is re-rendered into a *luminance-only* (single-channeled) float-precision texture using a full texture-aligned quad. At this stage, each *RGB* pixel is converted to the *XYZ* color space, but only the *logarithm* of the *luminance* component Y (plus some δ) is stored in this new texture. This corresponds precisely to the internal summation component of Equation 1. The summation and average can be evaluated with a full mip-map reduction of this log-luminance image: the single texel of the last mip-map level will be the key-value $\widetilde{L}$ from Equation 1, *except* for the *exponentiation*. These steps are shown in Figure 7-bc.

Finally, a final full texture pass is performed and targeted to yet another luminance-only float-precision texture, this time evaluating Equation 2. The term $L(x,y)$ is obtained by once again sampling the *RGB* texture and converting the pixels to the *XYZ* color space. The key-value $\widetilde{L}$ is accessible through the last log-luminance mip-map level, remembering to take

(a) input HDR *RGB* image (b) log-luminance (c) mipmap (d) scaled luminance L_r

Fig. 7. Efficient generation of the scaled luminance image L_r on the GPU. The logarithm of the luminance (b) of the input image (a) is submitted to a mip-mapping reduction stage (c) and then used to produce the scaled luminance image (d).

the exponentiation once the texel is fetched. The parameter α is an application-controlled uniform shader parameter. In fact, the base log-luminance texture can be used here as the render target, since it is no longer required by the operator, thus alleviating memory requirements. Refer to Figure 7-d for a depiction of the resulting scaled luminance image.

At this point, the scaled luminance texture L_r can be either used directly on the global operator or submitted to an efficient SAT generation stage to be later used to approximate the local operator, a topic reserved for Section 3.2.

3.2 Fast Summed-Area Table generation on the GPU

Summed-Area Tables can be seen as the 2D equivalent of 1D array prefix-sums. A prefix-sum is a cumulative array, where each element is the sum of all elements to the left of it, inclusive, in the original array. There are two types[3] of prefix-sum: *prescan* and *scan*. A prescan differs from a scan by a leading zero in the array and a missing final accumulation; refer to Figure 8 for an example. As a matter of fact, prefix-sums are not limited to addition operation, but can be generalized to any other operation (neutral element is required for prescans). In the context of SAT generation, however, scans under the addition operation suffices.

1	3	0	2	1	2	4	3

(a) input array

0	1	4	4	6	7	9	13	16

(b) prescan

1	4	4	6	7	9	13	16

(c) scan

Fig. 8. An example of a prescan (b) and a scan (c) under addition on some input array (a).

The process of generating a SAT can be break down into a two stage array scan. First, each row of the input table is independently submitted to a 1D array scan. The resulting table, to be referred to here as a *partial SAT*, is then submitted to another set of 1D scans, this time operating on each of its columns. The resulting table this time is the complete SAT itself. The process is illustrated in Figure 9.

Prefix-sum generation is a straight-forward $O(n)$ procedure using a purely sequential algorithm. Prefix-sums, however, comprise a versatile and fundamental building block for many parallel algorithms. Therefore, efficient methods that harness parallelism from

[3] A prescan may also be referred to as an *exclusive* prefix-sum, while a scan can be referred to as either an *inclusive* prefix-sum or as an *all*-prefix-sum [Blelloch (1990)].

1	3	0	2	1	2
3	2	4	3	6	0
0	5	1	1	5	3
2	2	3	3	7	2
4	2	8	6	4	5

(a) input table

1	4	4	6	7	9
3	5	9	12	18	18
0	5	6	7	12	15
2	4	7	10	17	19
4	6	14	20	24	29

(b) partial SAT

1	4	4	6	7	9
3	5	9	12	18	18
0	5	6	7	12	15
2	4	7	10	17	19
4	6	14	20	24	29

(c) partial SAT

1	4	4	6	7	9
4	9	13	18	25	27
4	14	19	25	37	42
6	18	26	35	54	61
10	24	40	55	78	90

(d) complete SAT

Fig. 9. SAT generation as a set of 1D array scans. Each row of the input table (a) is submitted to an 1D array scan, leading to a partial SAT (b). Each column of this partial SAT (c) is then submitted to another 1D array scan, resulting in the complete SAT (d).

prefix-sum generation also exist. Two of these algorithms are based on multi-pass parallel gathering patterns that map particularly well to the GPU: recursive-doubling [Dubois & Rodrigue (1977)] and balanced-trees [Blelloch (1990)].

The approach based on balanced-trees perform less arithmetic operations than recursive-doubling, but requires twice as much passes. This trade-off, however, quickly starts to pay-off for moderately larger inputs, with balanced-trees being much more work-efficient and faster than recursive-doubling on a GPU-based implementation. As far as the parallel complexity goes, the balanced-tree approach is $O(n/p + log(p))$ while recursive-doubling is $O(n/p\ log(n))$. The interested reader is redirected to Harris (2007) and Blelloch (1990) for a more in-depth complexity analysis.

Until recently the computer graphics community has curiously favored the recursive-doubling approach, despite the attractive performance gains and readily availability since long of the method based on balanced-trees. There are already plenty of resources available related to recursive-doubling implementations on the GPU [Harris (2007); Hensley et al. (2005); Lauritzen (2007); Slomp & Oliveira (2008)]. For this matter, this section will refrain in reviewing recursive-doubling and will instead focus on the balanced-tree-based approach.

3.3 Fast parallel scan generation on the GPU based on balanced-trees

Prefix-sum surveys on the literature that mention the balanced-tree approach usually describe it as a method for producing prescans only [Blelloch (1990); Harris (2007)]. Although prescans can be easily converted into scans in a few different ways (if the input is still available), this additional computation is not necessary since it is actually possible to modify the plain balanced-tree approach slightly in order to produce a scan directly. This section will focus only on this direct scan generation since it is more useful for SAT generation. Only 1D scan will be detailed, but its extension for SAT generation should be clear from Figure 9: all rows/columns can be processed simultaneously at the same pass with exactly the same shader.

There are two stages involved in the balanced-tree technique: a reduction stage (up-sweep) and an expansion stage (down-sweep). The reduction stage is straight-forward and consists on successively accumulating two nodes in $log_2(n)$ passes. Starting from the input array, each pass produces a set of partial sums on the input array; the last pass produces a single node (the root) comprising the sum of all elements of the input array. This resembles an 1D mip-map reduction, except that averages are not taken. The left side of Figure 10 depicts the process.

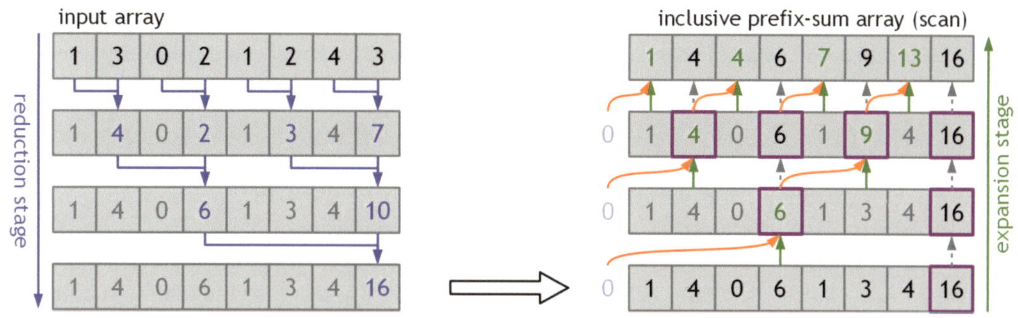

Fig. 10. An walk-through on scan generation using the balanced-tree approach.

The expansion stage is less intuitive and challenging to put into words. The reader is directed to Figure 10-right for the explanation to follow. Expansion starts from the root node of the reduction stage, referred to here as the first *generator* node (outlined in magenta). The generator node itself is its own rightmost child (dashed gray arrows). The left child is computed by adding its own value from the reduction tree (green arrows) with the value of its *uncle* generator node immediately to the left (orange arrows). If there is no such *uncle* node, a *ghost* zero-valued uncle is assumed (violet zero-valued nodes). Both children now become generator (parent) nodes (again outlined in magenta) for the next pass and the process repeats. After $log_2(n)$ passes the resulting array will be the scan of the input array.

The process illustrated in Figure 10 is memory-efficient since all computations are performed successively on the same input array without the need of any auxiliary memory. Unfortunately, a GPU-based implementation would suffer from the impossibility of performing simultaneous read and write operations on the same texture memory. The intermediate reduction and expansion stages, therefore, require additional memory to store their computations. A depiction of the suggested layout for this extra memory is presented in Figure 11.

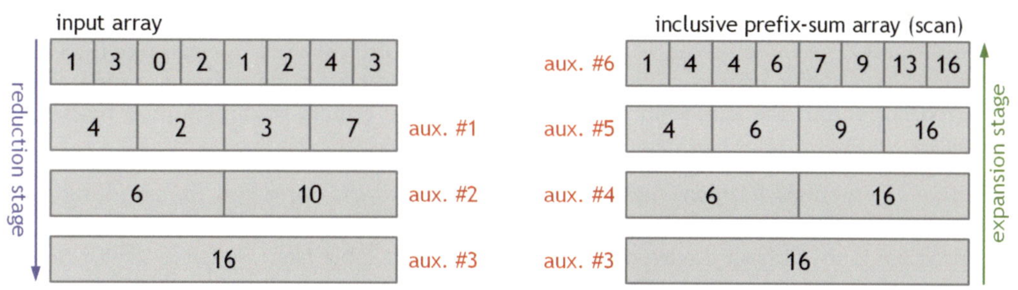

Fig. 11. Suggested layout for the auxiliary GPU memory during the scan. Simultaneous read/write from/to a same buffer never happens. In order to expand aux.#4 the expanded parent buffer aux.#3 and the reduced *sibling* buffer aux.#2 must be accessed. Similarly, expanding aux.#5 needs access to aux.#4 and aux.#1. The final expansion uses aux.#5 and the input buffer itself. The extra memory amounts to about three times the size of the input.

Even though the amount of necessary auxiliary memory with this layout is substantially large ($\approx 3n$), the memory access patterns becomes more cache-coherent than the ones from the memory-efficient version of Figure 10 since the data in each buffer is laid out together instead of sparsely distributed in a single array. This cache-coherence is also another attractive advantage that a GPU-based scan with balanced-trees has over a recursive-doubling one.

There is no need to limit the computations to two nodes per pass. Reducing and expanding a fixed number of k ($2 \leq k \leq n$) nodes per pass requires just a few modifications and can substantially improve the performance and lower the amount of extra memory. The optimal value for k is dependent on several architectural details of the GPU in question, such as memory latency and cache efficiency, and is open for experimentation. In the hardware profiles investigated it was found that $k = 4$ provided the overall best performance (see Section 5). GPU-based implementations of recursive-doubling can also benefit from a higher number of accumulations per pass as demonstrated by Hensley et al. (2005).

A reduction phase with $k > 2$ is straight-forward to implement, but the expansion phase is again more involved. Each generator node will now span k children per pass. To compute the expanded value of any child, the respective child value from the reduction tree is added together with its expanded uncle node, just as when $k = 2$. However, the values of *all* their *reduced siblings* immediately to the *left* have to be added together as well. For example, if $k = 8$ then the expanded value of the 5th child will be the sum of its expanded uncle node with its own respective node in the reduction tree, plus the sum of all of its siblings to the left in the reduction tree, namely, the 1st, 2nd, 3rd and the 4th.

This process works seamlessly even when the array length n is not a multiple of k. Note that the value of the generator node is no longer propagated. One could propagate it to its kth child (if any), but this is less systematic since special cases need to be accounted in the shader.

Equipped with such an algorithm, a GeForce GTX 280 is capable of generating a 2048x2048 SAT in about 2*ms*. In comparison, recursive-doubling would take nearly 6*ms*. In general, the overall speedup is of roughly 3x. Performance results are summarized in Section 5.

3.4 A Note on precision issues with Summed-Area Tables

Luminances are positive quantities, which makes the SAT of luminance images grow monotonically. The values in the SAT can quickly reach overflow limits or run out of fractional precision due to ever increasing accumulations. Depending on the dynamic range of the involved scene and the dimensions of the image, these critical situations may be hastily reached.

When such situations happen, high-frequency noise artifacts appear in the resulting tone mapped image, thus compromising the quality as shown in Figure 12-a. One way to mitigate this problem is to subtract the average value of the input table from the table itself prior to SAT generation [Hensley et al. (2005)]. This simple procedure has two main implications: first, the SAT allots an additional bit of precision, the signal bit, due to introduction of negative quantities, and second, the SAT is no longer monotonic and thus the range of the values within it should have much lower magnitude.

After filtering with this non-monotonic SAT, keep in mind that the average input table value should be added back. The average value can be computed using the same mip-mapping reduction strategy described earlier for the log-luminance average (see Section 3.1). The performance overhead incurred is small and well worth for the extra robustness. There is no need for additional memory for this average-subtracted scaled luminance image: the average can be subtracted onto the original scaled luminance texture using subtractive color blending.

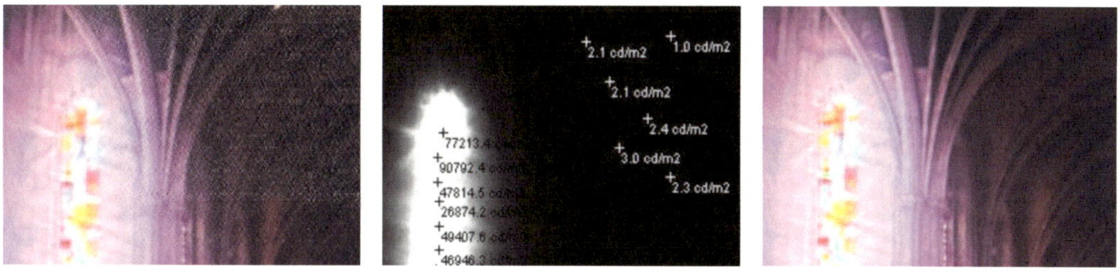

(a) plain monotonic SAT (b) luminance magnitude range (c) non-monotonic SAT

Fig. 12. Summed-Area Tables of luminance images are inherently monotonic and prone to unpleasing noise artifacts (a) if the quantities involved have a wide dynamic range (b). Making the SAT non-monotonic by first subtracting the average luminance mitigates such artifacts.

4. Mesopic vision simulation

In order to reproduce Purkinje's blue-shift effect, it is necessary to have some quantitative estimation on how individual color responses tend to change under mesopic vision conditions. Following that, it is important to be able of reproducing such changes in some HVS-compatible and perceptually-uniform fashion. Therefore, before the proposed mesopic vision operators are properly introduced in Sections 4.3- 4.5, a discussion on psychophysical subjective luminosity perception and opponent-color spaces will be presented in Sections 4.1 and 4.2.

4.1 Equivalent lightness curve

Ikeda & Ashizawa (1991) have performed a number of subjective luminosity perception experiments under various lighting conditions. In these experiments, subjects were exposed to a special isoluminant room where different glossy colored cards[4] were presented to them. Once adapted to the different levels of luminosity, the subjects were asked to match the brightness of the colored cards against particular shades of gray distributed in a scale[4]. From the data analysis, several curves of *equivalent lightness* were plotted, depicting how the experienced responses of different colors varied with respect to the isoluminant room conditions. The results can be compiled into a single equivalent lightness response chart, as shown in Figure 13.

As can be observed in the curves, as the overall luminosity decreases, red intensities produce much lower lightness responses than blue intensities, which only slightly varies. This behavior implicitly adheres to the expected characteristics of the Purkinje's effect, that is, the tendency of the HVS to favor blue tonalities at low lighting conditions. Since blue responses are barely affected, finding adequate lowering factors mainly for red responses should be a sufficient approximation, which is the key idea behind the proposed mesopic filters.

The red response curve of Figure 13 can be approximated by the following expression:

$$E(I) = \frac{70}{1 + (10/I)^{0.383}} + 22 \tag{11}$$

[4] Standard, highly calibrated color/gray chips and scale produced by Japan Color Research Institute.

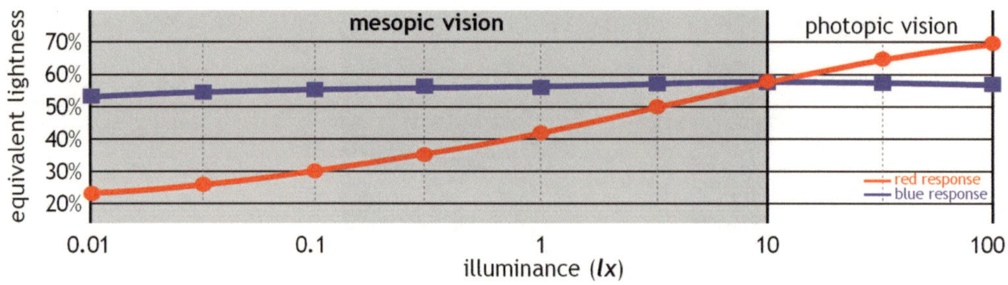

Fig. 13. Equivalent lightness curve for red and blue according to the experiments of Ikeda & Ashizawa (1991). These curves summarize the experienced relative brightness from several colored cards against gray-scale patterns in different isoluminant environment conditions.

The range of interest is the mesopic vision range, that is to say, between 0.01 lx and 10 lx. If the equivalent lightness of some overall luminosity $E(\lambda)$ is normalized against the equivalent lightness of the triggering luminance of the mesopic vision range $E(10)$, then the result will yield a coefficient ρ that indicates, in relative terms, how much the response coming from red intensities at such lighting conditions lowers with respect to the starting range $E(10)$:

$$\rho(\lambda) = \frac{E(\lambda)}{E(10)} \tag{12}$$

In other words, if $\rho(\lambda) \geq 1$, the overall luminosity offers photopic conditions and chrominances *do not* need to be altered. However, if $\rho(\lambda) < 1$ then the overall luminosity lies in the mesopic vision range, and $\rho(\lambda)$ gracefully provides a normalized relative measurement of how much red components should be scaled down in order to reproduce the expected experienced response. These two conditions can be handled uniformly by *clamping* $\rho(\lambda)$ to $[0, 1]$.

4.2 Opponent-color theory and the L*a*b* color space

Recent physiological experiments by Cao et al. (2008) have shown that mesopic color-shifts happen in the opponent-color systems of the Human Visual System, and that these shifts change linearly with the input stimuli. The initial hypothesis behind opponent-color theory in the HVS was proffered by German physiologist Karl Ewald Konstantin Hering and later validated by Hurvich & Jameson (1955). The key concept is that particular pairs of colors tend to nullify each other responses in the HVS and thus can not to be noticed simultaneously.

Color perception in the HVS is guided by the joint activity of two independent opponent systems: red versus green and yellow versus blue. A plot of these opponent response curves is shown in Figure 14-a, based on the experiments of Hurvich & Jameson (1955). Interestingly, luminance perception is also controlled by another opponent system: white versus black.

Physiologically speaking, these systems are dictated by opponent neurons which appropriately produce a chain of excitatory and inhibitory responses between the two components of each individual system. Numerically this models to positive feedbacks at some wavelengths being interfered concurrently by negative impulses at their counterparts.

Several color spaces were established based upon opponent-color schemes. The *CIE* $L^*a^*b^*$ (Figure 14-b) is remarkably one of the best known and widely used of such color spaces since

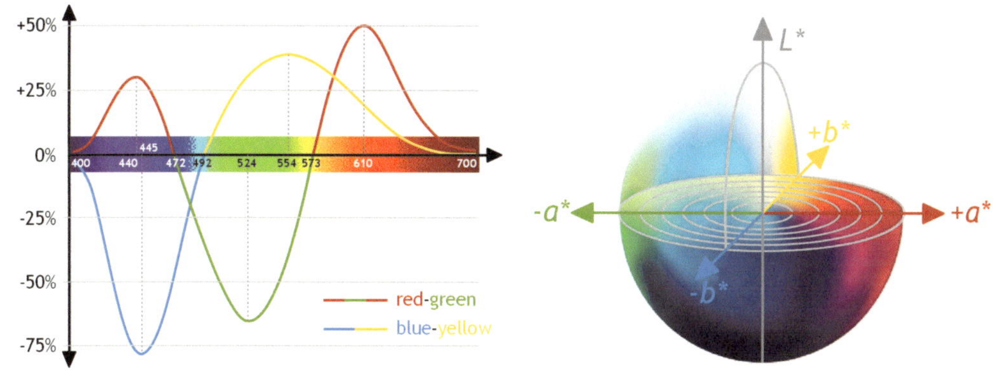

(a) HVS opponent-colors: wavelength × response (b) L*a*b* opponent-color space

Fig. 14. Opponent chromatic response curves of the HVS (a), and the L*a*b* color space (b).

it gauges color distances in a compatible perceptually-uniform (linear) fashion with respect to the Human Visual System. The L^* component represents a *relative* measurement of luminance (thus can not be expressed in cd/m^2), while a^* relates to a red-green opponent system and b^* to a blue-yellow opponent system. For simplicity, throughout the remaining of this Section the $CIE\ L^*a^*b^*$ color space will be shortly referred to as *Lab*.

The proposed mesopic vision filters to be introduced in the following Sections make use of the *Lab* color space. The choice for an opponent-color system to apply the color-shifts is supported by the physiological observations of Cao et al. (2008); the *Lab* space itself was selected because it offers the desired perceptually linear characteristics. Even though external light stimuli is directly *received* by red-green-blue cone-shaped sensors in the retina, the experienced *perceived* color comes from the activity of opponent-color systems wired to these primaries.

4.3 Overview of the mesopic vision reproduction operator

The proposed mesopic vision filter for digital images is derived directly from the lightness response curve specialized for mesopic vision of Equation 11 and from the perceptually-uniform *Lab* color space. Given a pixel represented in some color space (i.e., *RGB*), the process begin by promoting the pixel to the *Lab* color space.

A *Lab* pixel holding a *positive* quantity at its a component is actually holding some red intensity (negative a means green, see Figure 14). Now, if the overall luminosity condition suggests mesopic vision (that is, $\rho(\lambda) < 1$) then this red (positive-a) component should modulated by the normalized coefficient $\rho(\lambda)$ obtained from Equation 12, as below:

$$a' = a\,\rho(\lambda) \tag{13}$$

and this modified quantity a' replaces the original a in the *Lab* triplet, yielding to $La'b$. This can then be converted back to the initial color space (i.e., *RGB*) for presentation purposes.

In order to integrate these chrominance adjustments with HDR luminance compression, another color space must be used as an intermediate, preferentially one that can decouple luminance from chrominance. The *Lab* space itself is one of such spaces, but since the component L comprises only a relative measurement of luminance, this may cause incompatibilities with tone mapping operators that require proportionally equivalent absolute quantities. The Yxy deviation of the $CIE\ XYZ$ color space is up to this task [Hoffmann (2000)].

The general algorithm for the filter can be summarized in the following steps:

1. obtain a measurement of the overall luminosity – λ – (Sections 4.4 and 4.5)
2. compute the red response coefficient for this luminosity – $\rho(\lambda)$ – (Equation 12)
3. transform the original HDR pixels to the *Lab* color space
4. perform the blue-shift by altering the red (positive-a) component – a' – (Equation 13)
5. transform the modified $La'b$ pixels to the Yxy color space
6. compress the HDR pixel luminance Y using some TMO, yielding to Y'
7. replace the HDR pixel luminance Y by the compressed pixel luminance Y'
8. transform the modified Yxy pixels to the color space of the display device

The proposed mesopic vision filter offers two variants to determine the average isoluminant for the step 1 above: one that is spatially-uniform (per-scene, global) and another that is spatially-varying (per-pixel, local). They are introduced in Sections 4.4 and 4.5, respectively.

4.4 Spatially-uniform mesopic vision reproduction operator

One way to determine the overall luminosity of a scene is through the log-average luminance, as reviewed in Section 2.3. This log-average is a suitable candidate, but it was observed that it has a tendency of placing relatively bright images very low into the mesopic range scale. Simple arithmetic average of the luminances was found to produce more plausible indications for the global mesopic scale, which is also more compatible with the equivalent lightness curve of Section 4.1 that is plotted based on absolute luminosity quantities.

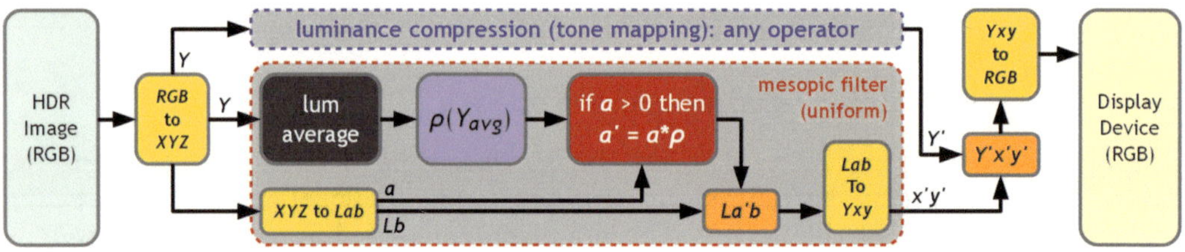

Fig. 15. Overview of the spatially-uniform mesopic vision reproduction filter.

Computing the arithmetic average of the luminances is straight-forward on GPU by using the same mip-map reduction strategy described in Section 3.1. It is possible to produce this average in advance along with the log-average by reformatting the base log-luminance texture with an additional channel to hold the absolute luminance (`GL_LUMINANCE_ALPHA32F`).

Once evaluated, the average serves as a measurement for the overall luminosity of the entire scene and the algorithm follows as listed in Section 4.3, applying the *same* response coefficient $\rho(Y_{avg})$ to all pixels, uniformly. The process is illustrated in Figure 15. An example of this spatially-uniform mesopic filter is shown in Figure 16-b. Refer to Section 5 for more examples.

The advantage of such uniform filter is that it is independent of luminance compression and hence can be integrated with any existing TMO. The disadvantage becomes clear when strong red-hued light sources are present in the scene, as is the case of Figure 16. When the overall luminosity suggests mesopic vision, the intensity coming from such light sources will be inadvertently suppressed, regardless of their own local intensity; even worse, the higher the intensity, the larger the shift will be. Red light traffic semaphores, neon lights and rear car lights, for example, still hold perceptually strong red intensities which are not noticed as yellow by an external observer, even at the dimmest surrounding lighting conditions. An even more extreme example would be a digital alarm clock equipped with red LEDs: even in complete darkness the LEDs are still perceived as red. This leads to the design of a variant filter that is capable of reproducing mesopic vision in a local, spatially-varying fashion.

(a) without mesopic simulation (b) spatially-uniform mesopic (c) spatially-varying mesopic

Fig. 16. Comparison between an image without mesopic simulation (a), with global mesopic filter (b) and per-pixel mesopic filter (c). All red intensities shift toward orange/yellow in (b), while only those not sufficiently bright enough change in (c) like the light reflex in the leftmost wall. Also note that purple tones shifted towards a more blueish hue in the mesopic images.

4.5 Spatially-varying mesopic vision reproduction operator

In order to counter-act the effects described at the end of Section 4.4, per-pixel local area luminance must be inspected. The good news is that such local measurement is already available from the local variant of the photographic tone mapping operator ($L_r^{s_{max}}(x,y)$). The bad news is that this quantity is based on the relative *scaled* luminance image L_r of Equation 2, and thus incompatible with the *absolute* scale of the equivalent lightness curve from Section 4.1.

Fortunately, the scale can be nullified with the inverse function of the scaled luminance L_r:

$$L_r^{-1}(x,y) = L_r(x,y)\frac{\widetilde{L}}{\alpha} = L(x,y) \tag{14}$$

The expression above can be generalized to filtered versions of $L_r(x,y)$ at any scale s:

$$L_r^s(x,y)\frac{\widetilde{L}}{\alpha} = L^s(x,y) \tag{15}$$

Hence, plugging the *scaled* local area luminance $L_r^{s_{max}}(x,y)$ in the expression above yields to $L^{s_{max}}(x,y)$, which is the *absolute* local area luminance. This quantity is now compatible with the equivalent lightness curve, and it is now possible to determine individual response coefficients $\rho(L^{s_{max}}(x,y))$ for each pixel (x,y), thus enabling localized mesopic adjustments.

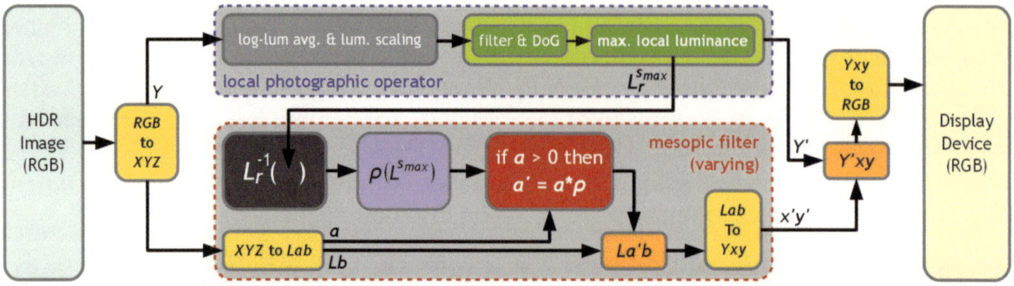

Fig. 17. Overview of the spatially-varying mesopic vision reproduction filter.

An overview of this spatially-varying mesopic filter is depicted in Figure 17. The application of the filter on a real image in shown in Figure 16-c; more examples are provided in Section 5.

The spatially-varying mesopic filter is structurally simpler than the spatially-uniform one since no additional data need to be assembled. The filter is, however, strongly attached to the framework provided by the photographic operator. Although no other local TMO was explored, most local operators perform estimations of local pixel averages and hence should be able to offer such information and feed it through the filter pipeline of Figure 17.

An advantage of using the local photographic operator over other local operators for the localized mesopic reproduction is the fact that per-pixel local area luminances are searched through an HVS-based brightness perception model [Blommaert & Martens (1990)]. This means that the chromatic adjustments follow some perceptual guidelines, while other operators may not rely at all on HVS features and thus become less suitable for a proper mesopic reproduction.

5. Results

This Section summarizes the performance achievements of balanced-trees over recursive-doubling for GPU-based SAT generation, as well as the performance of the mesopic filters. Additional examples of the mesopic filters are also available in Figures 23 and 24.

The system configurations and hardware profiles investigated are listed below:

1. Windows 7 Enterprise 32bit SP1 running on an Intel(R) Core(TM)2 Quad CPU Q9499 2.66GHz with 4GB RAM equipped with a NVIDIA GeForce GTX 280 with 1GB VRAM (240 shader cores at 1107MHz, memory at 1296MHz, WHQL Driver 280.26)
2. Windows 7 Enterprise 32bit SP1 running on an Intel(R) Core(TM)2 Quad CPU Q8200 2.33GHz with 4GB RAM equipped with a NVIDIA GeForce 9800 GT with 512MB VRAM (112 shader cores at 1500MHz, memory at 900MHz, WHQL Driver 280.26)
3. Windows XP Professional x64 Edition SP2 running on an Intel(R) Xeon(R) CPU W3520 2.67GHz with 8GB RAM equipped with an ATI FirePro 3D V3700 with 256MB VRAM (40 shader cores at 800MHz, memory at 950MHz, WHQL Catalyst Driver v8.85.7.1)

The main program was implemented in C++, compiled and linked with Visual C++ Professional 2010. The graphics API of choice was OpenGL and all shaders were implemented in conformance to the feature-set of the OpenGL Shading Language (GLSL) version 1.20. A

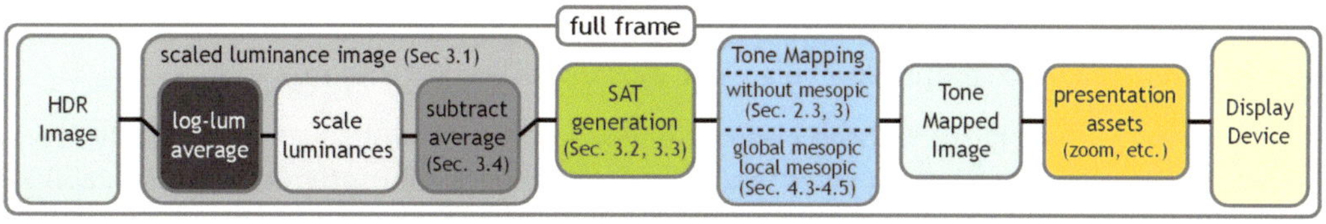

Fig. 18. Overview of all the stages implemented in the program for a complete frame display.

diagram depicting all the stages of the program for the display of a complete frame on the screen is presented in Figure 18.

All performance times in this Section are given in *milliseconds*. Full-frame times were captured with performance counters from the Win32 API and double-checked with the free version of Fraps 3.4.6. Intra-frame performance was profiled using OpenGL Timer Query Objects (`GL_ARB_timer_query`). Performance results were recorded through multiple executions of the program from which outliers were removed and the average was taken.

Summed-Area Table generation times for typical screen/image resolutions using recursive-doubling and balanced-trees are presented in Figures 19-a and 19-b, respectively. The speed-up achieved with the balanced-tree approach is shown in Figure 20.

Performance times for the tone mapping stage alone with and without the mesopic simulation are shown in Figure 21-a. The overhead introduced to the operator by the spatially-varying mesopic filter is shown in Figure 22. Complete frame times are shown in Figure 21-b, accounting for all the stages depicted in Figure 18 with the spatially-varying mesopic filter activated.

From Figure 20 it can be seen that SAT generation with the balanced-tree outperforms recursive-doubling by a factor of 2.5x$\approx$3x (or 4x on the ATI FirePro 3D V3700) as the image size increases. From Figure 22 one can see that the overhead introduced by the spatially-varying mesopic filter tends to amount to about 16% up to 19% of the original execution time of the operator without the filter (8% for the ATI FirePro 3D V3700). Most of this overhead is coming from the non-linear Yxy to *Lab* color conversions (and vice-versa) inside the tone mapping shader. Note that this overhead is being measured relative to the tone mapping stage alone; putting it on a full-frame scale the overhead is most likely negligible.

6. Limitations and future work

The main drawback with SAT generation on the GPU is the fact that it requires a considerable amount of intermediate memory. This is due to the simultaneous read-write texture (global) memory restrictions and the lack of adequate inter-fragment synchronization and communication directives of GPU architectures. As the expected clash between GPU and multi-core CPU architectures comes to a close, such memory access constraints tend to disappear. Current development on general-purpose GPU computing technologies such as CUDA, OpenCL, DirectCompute and C++Amp already started to address these limitations and are paving the road for exciting new prospects. The interoperability overhead between such technologies and regular graphics API is also expected to diminish with future advances.

It must be noticed that the introduced mesopic filters decrease responses from red intensities only, as suggested by the curves of equivalent lightness that were studied. A future opportunity is to investigate how the response coming from of other colors (green and yellow, namely, for the assumed opponent-system) behave according to different levels of luminosity, leading to a much more robust and believable mesopic vision experience.

Another limitation of the introduced mesopic filters is that color-shifts happen instantly. It is a known fact that chrominance changes in the HVS do not occur abruptly, but instead stabilize gradually on due time, just like with luminosity adaptation. Temporal luminance adaptation is a topic already studied extensively, but little is known about temporal chromatic adaptation, which still remains as a fascinating open field for further research.

The local averages used by the spatially-varying mesopic filter come directly from the brightness perception model used implicitly by the local photographic operator. Such local averages are convenient since they are already part of the luminance compression framework that was utilized and are efficient to be computed. The estimation of such local averages is based on psychophysical brightness perception experiments and the obtained results look plausible; however, they may not be the most suitable candidate for local averages under mesopic conditions. Additional physiological evidence must be researched in order to validate the accuracy of the employed brightness perception model for mesopic vision.

An implicit assumption made over the length of this document was that the source HDR imagery was properly calibrated. In other words, the HDR images were expected to be

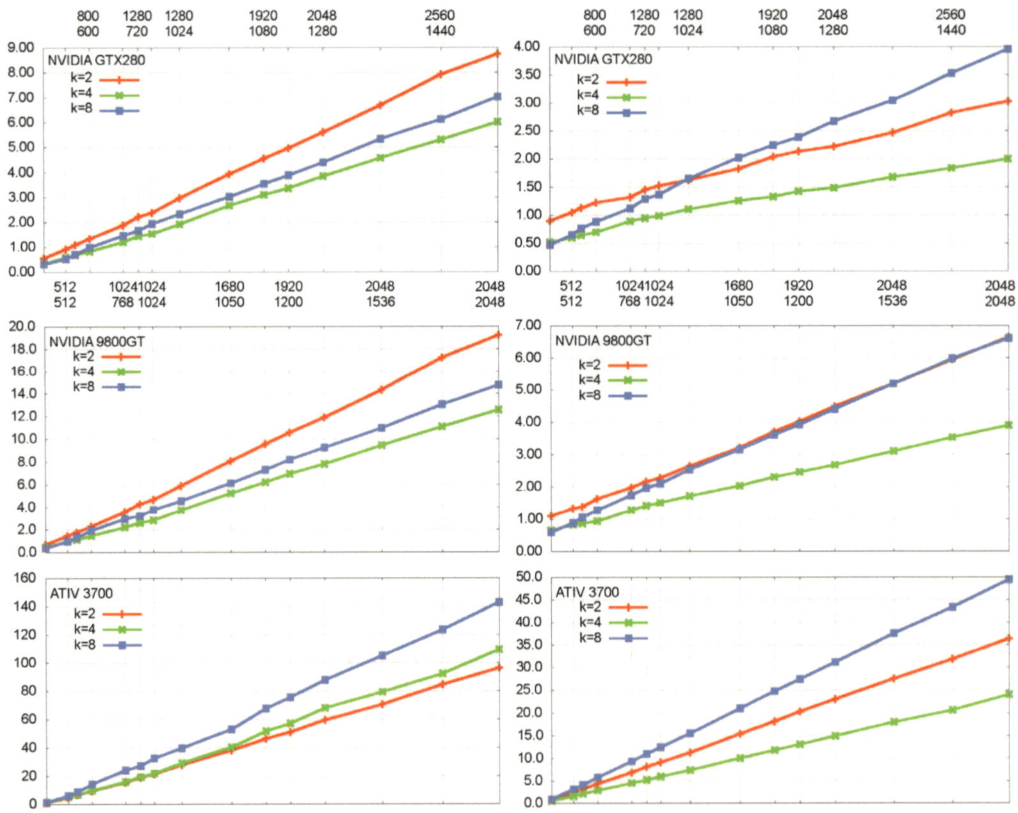

a) SAT generation time for recursive-doubling. b) SAT generation time for balanced-trees.

Fig. 19. SAT generation time

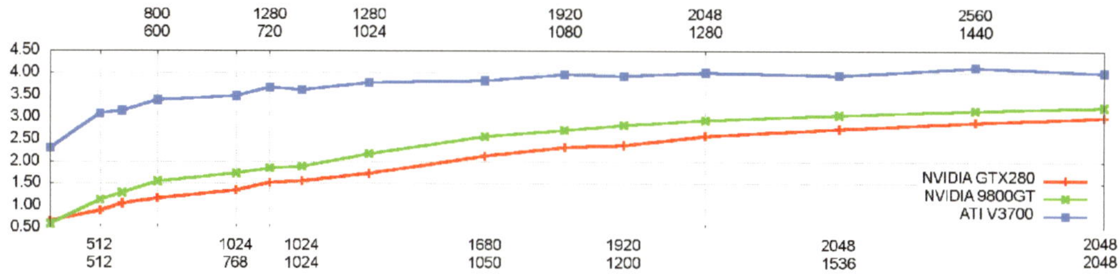

Fig. 20. Relative speed-up between balanced-trees and recursive-doubling for SAT generation based on the best (fastest k) times recorded for each algorithm for each image size, according to the performance results of Figures 19-a and 19-b.

holding physically accurate quantities. This may not be always the case, but HDR images should supposedly contain proportionally equivalent quantities at least, differing to real quantities only by some constant, uniform scaling factor. In the context of the proposed mesopic reproduction filters, any HDR image that infringes this constraint is considered an ill-formed image.

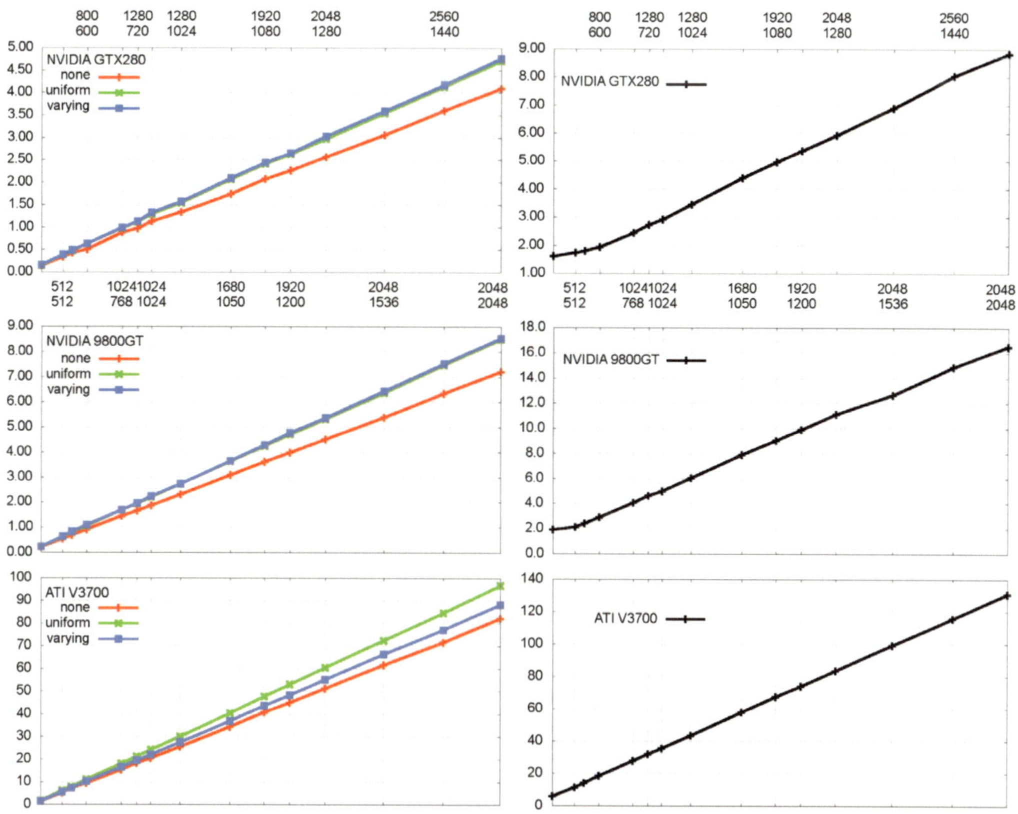

a) Performance of the tone mapping stage alone, with and without the mesopic filters.

b) Full frame times accounting for all the stages presented in Figure 18.

Fig. 21

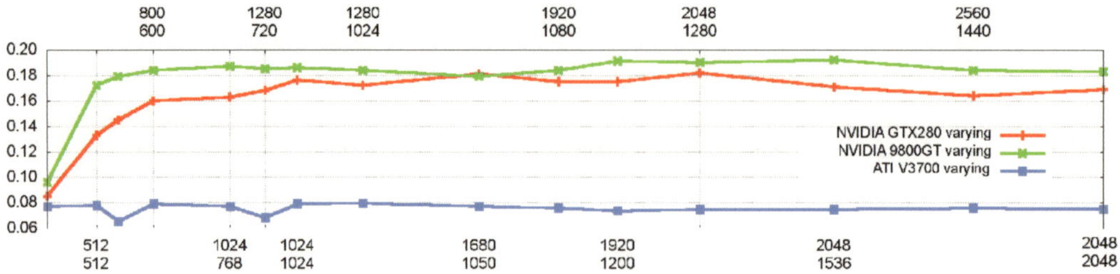

Fig. 22. Overhead of the spatially-varying mesopic filter to the tone mapping stage.

Fig. 23. Examples of the proposed mesopic filters. The first row of the top images is without the filter, the second row is the global filter and the third row is the local filter; similarly for the images at the bottom, but arranged in columns instead of in rows.

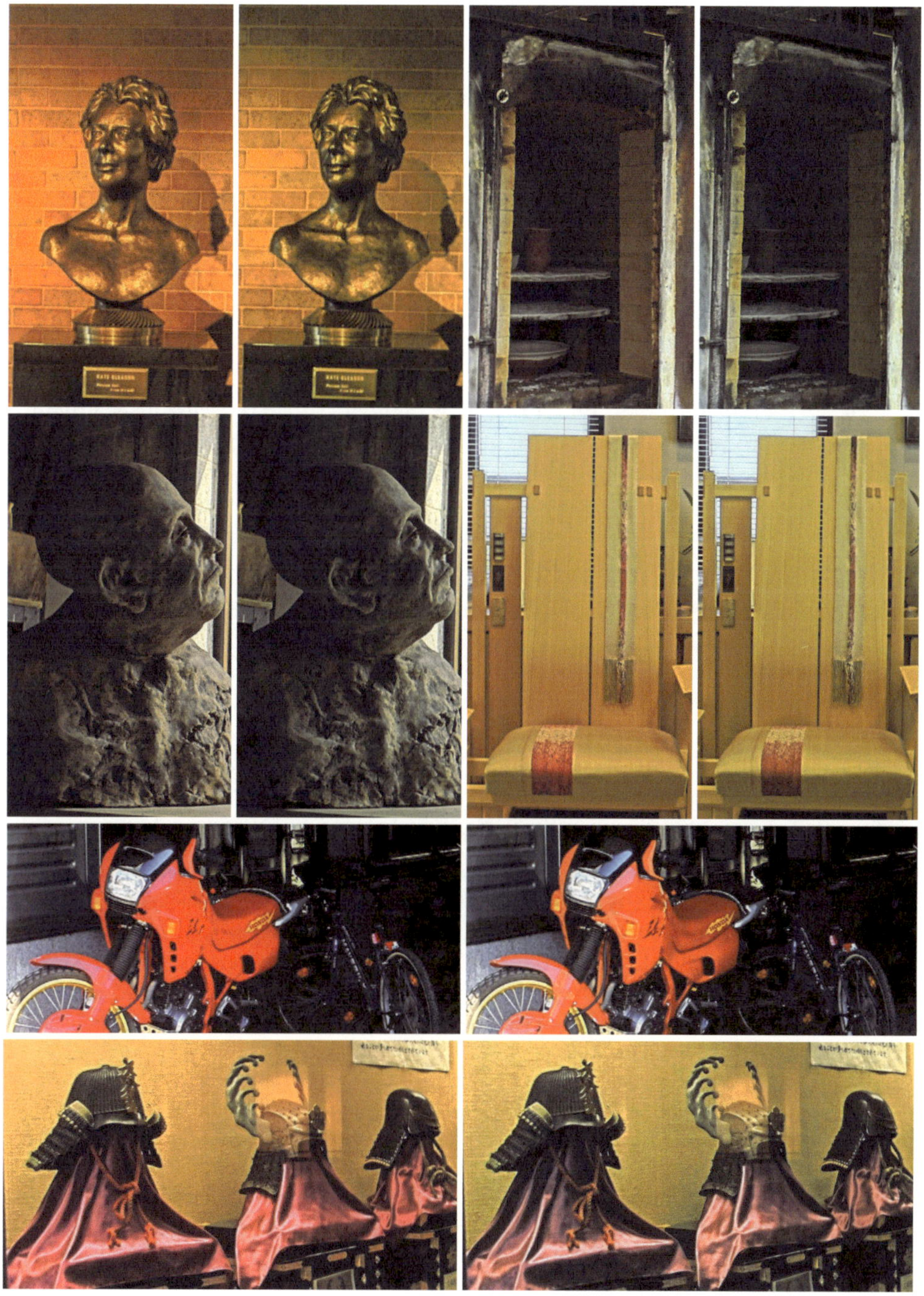

Fig. 24. Examples of the proposed mesopic filters. The leftmost image of each image set is without the filter; the rightmost is the varying filter. For these images, either the global or the local mesopic filter produces very similar results because there are no strong light intensities in the images, which makes the local averages to be somewhat close to the global average.

Finally, adapting other local operators to function along with the proposed spatially-varying mesopic filter is a possible direction for future work. However, not all local operators are guided by perceptual characteristics of the Human Visual System and thus may be less suitable for a proper mesopic vision reproduction experience.

7. Conclusion

This chapter described a faster method based on balanced-trees to accelerate the Summed-Area Table generation stage for local photographic tone reproduction. The balanced-tree approach not only has a lower computational complexity than the more widely known recursive-doubling technique, but has also memory access patterns that are more cache-friendly to common GPU architectures. Substantial improvements of about 3x in the SAT generation time were achieved on the inspected hardware profiles and image resolutions.

A balanced-tree implementation on GPU is more involved than a recursive-doubling one, but can still be accomplished with any GPU architecture that supports at least the Shader Model 2.0 feature set. Even though parallel algorithms for prefix-sum generation based on balanced-trees were readily available since long, the computer graphics community has just recently started to acknowledge and appreciate its advantages, and so far only a handful of resources exist on the subject in the graphics literature.

A novel, general and efficient approach to reproduce the Purkinje effect under mesopic vision conditions was also introduced. The method was designed to work with popular, widely-spread HDR imagery formats. The blue-shift is simulated by suppressing the responses coming from red intensities according to either global or local luminosity conditions. These red responses are smoothed based on an equivalent-lightness curve recovered through psychophysical experiments performed on real subjects. The smoothing is applied in an HVS-compatible, perceptually-linear fashion through the $CIE\ L^*a^*b^*$ opponent-color space, and this linearity conforms to recent physiological evidence.

The spatially-uniform mesopic filter is completely decoupled from luminance compression, thus allegedly suitable for any existing tone mapping operator. The more interesting spatially-varying filter exploits the foundations and perceptually-based characteristics of the local photographic operator to perform mesopic adjustments in a per-pixel basis. The filters are simple to be implemented entirely on the GPU and the overhead introduced is negligible and should not hurt the performance of existing real-time applications.

8. Acknowledgments

We would like to sincerely thank the Munsell Color Science Laboratory, Gregory Ward, Mark Fairchild (Mark Fairchild's HDR Photographic Survey), Erik Reinhard, Paul Debevec, Jack Tumblin, Yuanzhen Li, Dani Lischinski, Laurence Meylan and others for generously making their HDR imagery data-set freely available for researchers. We also thank the initiatives of GLEW (OpenGL Extension Wrangler Library), DevIL (Developer's Image Library, former OpenIL), Scilab, LibreOffice and gnuplot for the excellence of their open-source contributions, as well as to Microsoft for providing Visual Studio Professional and Windows 7 Enterprise free of charge for students through their academic alliance program, and to Fraps for the freeware version of their real-time video capture and benchmarking tool. This research was supported by Japan's Ministry of Education, Culture, Sports, Science and

Technology (Monbukagakusho/MEXT) and Japan Society for the Promotion of Science (JSPS) - KAKENHI No. 2310771.

9. References

Adams, A. (1983). *The Print*, Little, Brown and Company.

Blelloch, G. E. (1990). Prefix sums and their applications, *Technical report*, Synthesis of Parallel Algorithms.

Blommaert, F. J. & Martens, J.-B. (1990). An object-oriented model for brightness perception, *Spatial Vision* 5(1): 15–41.

Cao, D., Pokorny, J., Smith, V. C. & Zele, A. (2008). Rod contributions to color perception : linear with rod contrast, *Vision Research* 48(26): 2586–2592.

Crow, F. C. (1984). Summed-area tables for texture mapping, *Proceedings of SIGGRAPH 84* 18: 207–212.

Díaz, J., Vázquez, P.-P., Navazo, I. & Duguet, F. (2010). Real-time ambient occlusion and halos with summed area tables, *Computers & Graphics* 34(4): 337 – 350.

Dubois, P. & Rodrigue, G. (1977). An analysis of the recursive doubling algorithm, *High Speed Computer and Algorithm Organization* pp. 299–307.

Durand, F. & Dorsey, J. (2000). Interactive tone mapping, *Proceedings of the Eurographics Workshop on Rendering Techniques 2000*, Springer-Verlag, London, UK, pp. 219–230.

Ferwerda, J. A., Pattanaik, S. N., Shirley, P. & Greenberg, D. P. (1996). A model of visual adaptation for realistic image synthesis, *Proceedings of SIGGRAPH 96*, ACM, New York, NY, USA, pp. 249–258.

Goodnight, N., Wang, R., Woolley, C. & Humphreys, G. (2003). Interactive time-dependent tone mapping using programmable graphics hardware, *Proceedings of the 14th Eurographics workshop on Rendering*, EGRW '03, Eurographics Association, Aire-la-Ville, Switzerland, Switzerland, pp. 26–37.

Harris, M. (2007). *Parallel Prefix Sum (Scan) with CUDA*, NVIDIA Corporation. URL: `http://developer.download.nvidia.com/compute/cuda/1_1/Website/projects/scan/doc/scan.pdf`

Heckbert, P. S. (1986). Filtering by repeated integration, *Proceedings of of SIGGRAPH 86*, ACM, New York, NY, USA, pp. 315–321.

Hensley, J., Scheuermann, T., Coombe, G., Singh, M. & Lastra, A. (2005). Fast summed-area table generation and its applications, *Computer Graphics Forum* 24: 547–555.

Hoffmann, G. (2000). CIE color space, *Technical report*, University of Applied Sciences, Emden. URL: `http://www.fho-emden.de/~hoffmann/ciexyz29082000.pdf`

Hurvich, L. & Jameson, D. (1955). Some quantitative aspects of an opponent-colors theory. ii. brightness, saturation, and hue in normal and dichromatic vision, *Journal of the Optical Society of America* 45: 602–616.

Ikeda, M. & Ashizawa, S. (1991). Equivalent lightness of colored objects of equal munsell chroma and of equal munsell value at various illuminances, *Color Reserch and Application* 16: 72–80.

Khan, S. M. & Pattanaik, S. N. (2004). Modeling blue shift in moonlit scenes by rod cone interaction, *Journal of VISION* 4(8): 316a.

Kirk, A. G. & O'Brien, J. F. (2011). Perceptually based tone mapping for low-light conditions, *ACM SIGGRAPH 2011 papers*, SIGGRAPH '11, ACM, New York, NY, USA, pp. 42:1–42:10.

Krawczyk, G., Myszkowski, K. & Seidel, H.-P. (2005). Perceptual effects in real-time tone mapping, *Proceedings of the 21st Spring conference on Computer Graphics*, New York, NY, USA, pp. 195–202.

Lauritzen, A. (2007). *Summed-Area Variance Shadow Maps*, Addison-Wesley Professional, pp. 157–182.

Ledda, P., Chalmers, A., Troscianko, T. & Seetzen, H. (2005). Evaluation of tone mapping operators using a high dynamic range display, *ACM Trans. Graph.* 24: 640–648.

Ledda, P., Santos, L. P. & Chalmers, A. (2004). A local model of eye adaptation for high dynamic range images, *Proceedings of the 3rd international conference on Computer graphics, virtual reality, visualisation and interaction in Africa*, AFRIGRAPH '04, ACM, New York, NY, USA, pp. 151–160.

Mikamo, M., Slomp, M., Tamaki, T. & Kaneda, K. (2009). A tone reproduction operator accounting for mesopic vision, *ACM SIGGRAPH ASIA 2009 Posters*, New York, NY, USA, pp. 41:1–41:1.

Minnaert, M. (1954). *The Nature of Light and Colour in the Open Air*, Dover Publications.

Pattanaik, S. & Yee, H. (2002). Adaptive gain control for high dynamic range image display, *Proceedings of the 18th spring conference on Computer graphics*, SCCG '02, ACM, New York, NY, USA, pp. 83–87.

Reinhard, E. (2003). Parameter estimation for photographic tone reproduction, *Journal of Graphics Tools* 7(1): 45–52.

Reinhard, E., Heidrich, W., Debevec, P., Pattanaik, S., Ward, G. & Myszkowski, K. (2010). *High Dynamic Range Imaging: Acquisition, Display, and Image-Based Lighting (2nd Edition)*, Morgan Kaufmann Publishers Inc., San Francisco, CA, USA.

Reinhard, E., Stark, M., Shirley, P. & Ferwerda, J. (2002). Photographic tone reproduction for digital images, *ACM Transactions on Graphics* 21: 267–276.

Slomp, M. & Oliveira, M. M. (2008). Real-time photographic local tone reproduction using summed-area tables, *Computer Graphics International 2008*, Istambul, Turkey, pp. 82–91.

Slomp, M., Tamaki, T. & Kaneda, K. (2010). Screen-space ambient occlusion through summed-area tables, *Proceedings of the 2010 First International Conference on Networking and Computing*, ICNC '10, IEEE Computer Society, Washington, DC, USA, pp. 1–8.

van de Hulst, H. C. (1957). *Light Scattering by Small Particles*, Wiley & Sons.

Viola, P. & Jones, M. (2004). Robust real-time object detection, *International Journal of Computer Vision* 57(2): 137–154.

Zhang, X. & Wandell, B. (1997). A spatial extension of CIELAB for digital color image reproduction, *Journal of the Society for Information Display (SID)* 5: 61–63.

9

Volume Ray Casting in WebGL

John Congote[1], Luis Kabongo[1], Aitor Moreno[1], Alvaro Segura[1], Andoni Beristain[1], Jorge Posada[1] and Oscar Ruiz[2]
[1]*Vicomtech Research Center*
[2]*EAFIT University*
[1]*Spain*
[2]*Colombia*

1. Introduction

Real-time 3D computer graphics systems usually handle surface description models (i.e. B-Rep representations) and use surface rendering techniques for visualization. Common 3D model formats such as VRML, X3D, COLLADA, U3D (some intended for the Web) are based entirely on polygonal meshes or higher order surfaces. Real-time rendering of polygon models is straightforward and raster render algorithms are implemented in most graphics accelerating hardware. For many years several rendering engines, often via installable browser plug-ins, have been available to support 3D mesh visualization in Web applications.

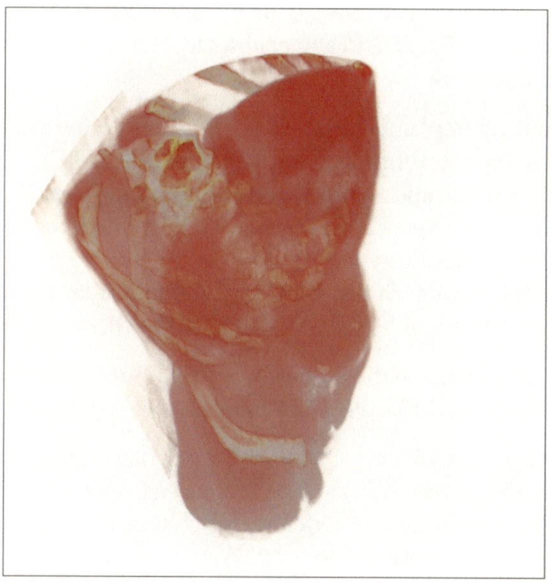

Fig. 1. Medical data rendered with volume ray-casting

However, some scientific fields (e.g. medicine, geo-sciences, meteorology, engineering) work with 3D volumetric datasets. Volumetric datasets are regular or irregular samples of either scalar ($f : \mathbb{R}^3 \rightarrow \mathbb{R}$) or vector ($f : \mathbb{R}^3 \rightarrow \mathbb{R}^3$) fields. For the purpose of this chapter, we will use the term *volumetric data sets* to refer to scalar fields and will ignore for the time being vector fields. Surface-based raster rendering techniques are obviously not suitable for visualizing such datasets and specific Direct Volume Rendering algorithms are needed, which are not available for the Web. Ray Casting is a common technique for volume visualization which displays the saliend characteristics of the volume set, although it is not photo-realistic.

Therefore, our work uses *Volume Ray-Casting,* which is a common technique in Computer Graphics for volume visualization. Originally presented by Kajiya Kajiya & Von Herzen (1984) as an extension of *Ray-tracing* algorithm, then Levoy Levoy (1988) defines the volume rendering. This has been further studied in Hadwiger et al. (2009). The aforementioned rendering is not photo-realistic, however it shows important characteristics of the dataset.

In medical imaging, diagnostic techniques, such as computer tomography (CT), magnetic resonance imaging (MRI) and positron emission tomography (PET), produce sets of parallel slices that form a volumetric dataset. Volume rendering is a common technique for visualizing volumetric datasets along with multi-planar reconstructions (MPR). Storage and distribution of these 3D images usually requires a Picture Archiving and Communication Systems (PACS), which normally uses specialized workstation software (Meyer-Spradow et al. (2009), Fogal & Kruger (2010)) for interactive visualization (Mahmoudi et al. (2009)). Reference Kabongo et al. (2009) presents on some of the few implementations of volumetric data displays.

WebGL is a new standard for accelerated 3D graphics rendering on the Web that complements other technologies in the future HTML5 standard (Marrin (2011)). Some of the major Web browsers, including Google Chrome, Mozilla Firefox, WebKit, Safari and Opera have already implemented WebGL in their latest releases or release candidates. WebGL is basically a JavaScript binding of the OpenGL ES API and enables low level imperative graphics rendering based on programmable shaders.

We present in this chapter an implementation of a volume rendering system for the Web, based on the Volume Ray-casting algorithm and implemented on WebGL. The system is capable of obtaining interactive visualization with diverse volume datasets (Figure 1). The original Volume Ray-casting algorithm was slightly modified to work with the input structures needed for the Web environment. Special care was taken to avoid the use of dynamic server content. This avoidance allows for the algorithm to be used without increasing the demands on the server and shifts, as much as possible, the processing to the client.

This work was tested in bioinformatic scenarios with volumetric datasets such as medical imaging. Also, a metereological prototype was developed to visualize doppler radar datasets.

This chapter is organized as follows. Section 2 presents a brief status of the different technologies present in this work: Volume Rendering, Web rendering, medical and confocal visualization. Section 3 presents our methodology for volume rendering with special attention to the modifications of the algorithm for the Web environment. Section 4 shows the implementation of volume rendering for doppler wheather radars. Section 5 presents the output obtained by the implemented algorithm and the performance values in different conditions. Section 7 presents the conclusions of our work and future directions.

2. Related work

2.1 Direct volume rendering techniques

In 3D scalar field interactive visualization, two solutions prevail: Surface Rendering and Direct Volume Rendering. Surface Rendering, which has the advantage of being easy to compute due to its low geometric complexity. It's main disadvantages are: i. A surface must be synthesized first, which is not a trivial task as it depends on the quality of the sample; ii. Since it must be precalculated, the result is static and cannot be easily adjusted in real time.

Recent advances in Direct Volume Rendering and graphic card capabilities allow the representation of volumes with good quality by projecting volumetric data into a 2D image, depending on the position of a virtual camera. *The main advantage of this technique is the visualization of all inner characteristics at once.*

Preprocessing of images does not intervene in the images since there is no part of the DVR of the computations even when the camera is displaced. In order to project the volumetric data, several methods exist (Meißner et al. (2000)). Westover Westover (1991) discusses *Volume Splatting* and represents each scalar value by a simple geometrical shape that will face the camera, allowing fast rendering. It's main disadvantage is the loss of quality. A technique called *Shear Warping* (Lacroute & Levoy (1994)), consists of applying shear warp transformations to the volume slices to imitate the real orientation of the camera. Since the technique is based on simple transformations, the method is quite fast, but it's main drawback is a low sampling power. With the constant improvement in graphic card capabilities, the *Texture Mapping* method has been popularized in video-games. It consists of re-slicing the volume depending on the orientation of the camera viewpoint, and representing all of the slices at once taking advantage of eventual occlusion optimizations (Hibbard & Santek (1989)), *, but the lack of specialized visualization methods in this algorithm has made it unussable for profesional appliactions such as medical imaging.*

Volume Ray-casting was initially presented by Kajiya Kajiya & Von Herzen (1984) as an extension of the Ray-Tracing algorithm for volumetric shapes. Later the methodology was formalized by Levoy Levoy (1988). Since then, Volume Ray-casting has become one of the most common methods for volume rendering. The set of rays from the camera reach the 3D scene and hit the objects, generating parametric (scalar) landmark values. By defining a blending function it is possible to give priorities to the different values encountered along the ray, allowing the visualization of different internal structures. Additional modifications to the algorithm, such as *transfer functions*, and *Phong illumination* (Phong (1975)) were developed in order to improve the perception and make the volume look realistic. Compared to the other techniques, this one is older and more accurate in sampling. However, the computational power required makes it's usage initially difficult in real-time interactive representations, allowing other approximations to establish. Nowadays, the increasing computational power of graphic cards allows fast calculations (Kruger & Westermann (2003)) which give new interest to Volume Ray-casting. Reference Hadwiger et al. (2009) presents a tutorial with all the basic explanation on volume ray-casting. We used this tutorial as a starting point for the theoretical foundations in our implementation and for technical details. Open Source implementations such as Meyer-Spradow et al. (2009) and Fogal & Kruger (2010) were also used.

2.2 Web 3D rendering

The fact that the Web and 3D graphics are currently ubiquitous in desktop and handheld devices makes their integration urgent and important. Several standards and proprietary solutions for embedding 3D in the Web have been devised, such as VRML, X3D or vendor-specific Web browser plug-ins, and implementations on general purpose plug-ins, etc. A review of these techniques can be found in Behr et al. (2009).

In the case of Medical Imaging and other computing-intensive visualization scenarios, a partial solution has been the use of on-server rendering (Blazona & Mihajlovic (2007)). In this approach, the rendering process is performed in the server and its resulting image is sent to the client. This solution increases the load on the server when many clients are present. In addition, the high latency times make the system unresponsive and unsuitable for smooth interactive visualization.

Unresolved issues among solutions for Web 3D graphics are: dedicated languages, plug-in requirements for interpretation, portability across browsers, devices and operating systems, and advanced rendering support. While writing this chapter, the Khronos Group released the WebGL 1.0 specification, which has been under development and testing. In practice, the WebGL 1.0 is a Javascript binding of the OpenGL ES 2.0 API. Calls to the API are relatively simple and serve to set up vertex and index buffers, to change rendering engine state such as active texture units, or transform matrices, and to invoke drawing primitives. Most of the computation is performed in vertex and fragment shaders written in the GLSL language, which run natively on the GPU hardware. Unlike previous Web 3D standards which define declarative scene description languages, WebGL is a low-level imperative graphic programming API. It's imperative model enables great flexibility and exploits the advanced features of modern graphics hardware.

The WebGL 1.0 standard takes advantage of already existing OpenGL-based graphics applications, such as accurate iso-surface computation (Congote et al. (2010)) or optimized shader programming (Marques et al. (2009)). The usage of an interpreted language to manage the behavior of scene elements and animations might be considered as a drawback, due to their low speed. However, the performance of JavaScript interpreters are constantly improving. Current optimized just-in-time compilation in the latest engines provides performance not far from that of natively compiled languages.

2.3 Medical visualization

Across different scientific fields, Medical Visualization is one of the most challenging since the user interpretation directly translates into clinical intervention. Quality is one of the most important factors, but fast interactive response is also important in this domain. Medical Visualization has already produced several implementations of volumetric visualization on the Web, mainly for educational purposes (John et al. (2008)John (2007)). These approximations require third party systems for the correct visualization, or the presence of a rendering server (Poliakov et al. (2005), Yoo et al. (2005)), which limits the scalability of the application. Using standards such as VRML and Texture Mapping (Behr & Alexa (2001)), visualization of volumes in the Web has been achieved.

3. Methodology

Direct Volume Rendering is a set of Computer Graphics algorithms to generate representations of a 3D volumetric dataset. The produced image is a 2-dimensional matrix $I : [1,h] \times [1,w] \rightarrow \mathbb{R}^4$ (w: width and h: height in pixels). A pixel has a color representation expressed by four-tuple (R,G,B,A) of red, green, blue and alpha real-valued components, $(R,G,B,A \in [0,1])$.

(a) Front Faces (b) Back Faces

Fig. 2. Color cube map coordinates

The volume is a 3-dimensional array of real values $V : [1,H] \times [1,W] \times [1,D] \rightarrow [0,1]$ (H: Height, W: Width, D: Depth of the represented volume, in positive integer coordinates). Therefore, $V(x,y,z) \in [0,1]$. The volume-rendering algorithm is a projection of a 3D model into a 2D image. The projection model used in this work is known as a pin-hole camera (Hartley & Zisserman (2003)). The pin-hole camera model uses an intrinsic $K \in M_{3\times4}$ and an extrinsic $R \in M_{4\times4}$ real-valued matrices. These matrices project a 3D point $p \in \mathbb{P}^3$ onto a 2D point $p' \in \mathbb{P}^2$.

A volume is normally represented as a set of images. Each image represents a slice of the volume. Usually slices are parallel and evenly-spaced, but this is not always the case. For example, volumes can also be sampled in spherical coordinates with the angular interval being variable. Both cases (cartesian and spherical samples) are handled by our algorithm.

Volume ray-casting is an algorithm which defines the color for each pixel (i,j) in the image or projection screen I, calculated in function of the values of a scale field $V(x,y,z)$ associated with the points (x,y,z) visited by a ray originated in such a pixel. The ray is casted into the cuboid that contains the data to display (i.e the scalar field V). The ray is equi- parametrically sampled. For each sampled point p_s on the ray an approximation of the scalar field $V(p_s)$ is calculated, usually by calculating a tri-linear interpolation. In addition, a shade might be associated to p_s, according to the illumination conditions prevailing in the cuboid. The color associated to p_s might be determined by axis distances as shown in figure 2. As the last step, the pixel in the image which originated the ray is given the color determined by the sampled point p_s nearest to the screen in such a ray.

Alternatively, the samples on the ray may also cast a vote regarding the color that their originating pixel will assume by using a composition function (Eq:1-4), where the accumulated color A_{rgb} is the color of the pixel (i,j), and A_a is the alpha component of the pixel which is set to 1 at the end of the render process. Given an (x,y,z) coordinate in the

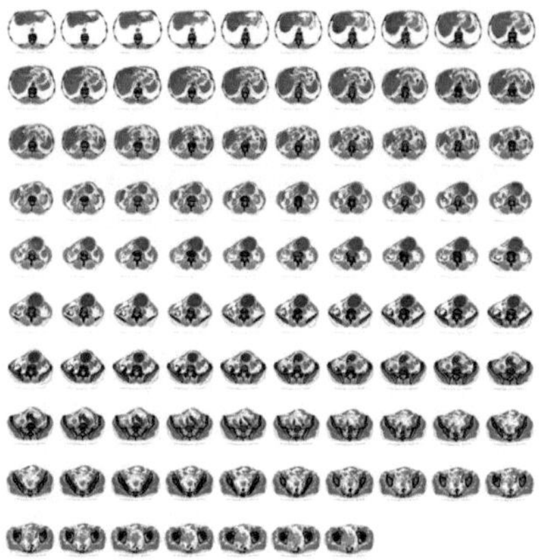

Fig. 3. Aorta dataset in mosaic form to be read by the shader

volume and a step k of the ray, V_a is the scalar value of the volume V, V_{rgb} is the color defined by the transfer function given V_a, S are the sampled values of the ray and O_f, L_f are the general Opacity and Light factors.

$$S_a = V_a * O_f * \left(\frac{1}{s}\right) \tag{1}$$

$$S_{rgb} = V_{rgb} * S_a * L_f \tag{2}$$

$$A^k_{rgb} = A^{k-1}_{rgb} + \left(1 - A^{k-1}_a\right) * S_{rgb} \tag{3}$$

$$A^k_a = A^{k-1}_a + S_a \tag{4}$$

3.1 Data processing and volume interpolation

The images for one volume are composed into a single image containing all slices that will be stored in a texture as shown in Figure 3. This texture is generated by tilling each slice beside the other in a matrix configuration, this step was implemented as a preprocessing step in our algorithm. The size of the texture in GPU memory could change from 4096×4096 in PC to 1024×1024 for handheld devices. The reduction in the quality in the image is explained in Figure 9. The number of images per row, the number of rows, and the total number of slices, must be given to the shader.

In medical images the sample bit depth is commonly greater than 8 bits per pixel. This is dificult to handle in Web applications where commonly supported formats are limited to 8 bits per sample. In this chapter, medical data sets were reduced to 8 bits.

Higher depths could be supported using more than one color component to store the lower and higher bits of each pixel, but this representation is not currently implemented in our shader.

For the correct extraction of the value of the volume, two equations were implemented. The equations 5-17 show how to obtain the value of a pixel in coordinates x, y, z from images presented in an cartesian grid. s is the total number of images in the mosaic and M_x, M_y are the number of images in the mosaic in each row and column as the medical dataset shows in Figure 3.

The functions presented in the equations are defined by the GLSL specification. This allow us to manipulate the images as continuous values because the functions of data extraction from the texture utilize interpolation.

$$s_1 = \text{floor}(z * S) \tag{5}$$

$$s_2 = s_1 + 1 \tag{6}$$

$$dx_1 = \text{fract}(\frac{s_1}{M_x}) \tag{7}$$

$$dy_1 = \frac{\text{fract}\left(\frac{s_1}{M_y}\right)}{M_y} \tag{8}$$

$$dx_2 = \text{floor}(\frac{s_2}{M_x}) \tag{9}$$

$$dy_2 = \frac{\text{fract}\left(\frac{s_2}{M_y}\right)}{M_y} \tag{10}$$

$$tx_1 = dx_1 + \frac{x}{M_x} \tag{11}$$

$$ty_1 = dy_1 + \frac{y}{M_y} \tag{12}$$

$$tx_2 = dx_2 + \frac{x}{M_x} \tag{13}$$

$$ty_2 = dy_2 + \frac{y}{M_y} \tag{14}$$

$$v_1 = \text{tex2D}\,(tx_1, ty_1) \tag{15}$$

$$v_2 = \text{tex2D}\,(tx_2, ty_2) \tag{16}$$

$$V_a(x, y, z) = \text{mix}\,(v_1, v_2, (x \times S) - s_1) \tag{17}$$

3.1.1 Identification of ray coordinates

The geometry of a cube is generated with coordinates from $(0,0,0)$ to $(1,1,1)$. This cube represents the boundary of the volumetric dataset and is painted with colors representing the coordinates at each point x, y, z. Coordinates (Figure 2)are stored in the r, g, b color component of each pixel. The cube is then rendered in the scene from the desired view point. The rendering process has several steps. The first two steps are the rendering of the color cube with the depth function change. Then, one of the passes presents the closest region of the cube to the camera (Figure 2(a)), and the second pass presents the far region (Figure 2(b)).

With these two renders a ray is calculated from each point in the cube for the render with the faces closest to the eye, and the end of the ray with the point of the back region. The colors in the cube represent the exact coordinates of the ray for each pixel in the image. We store the color information of the cube as 24 bit RGB values. This range of values seems to be small and not precise enough for big images, but color interpolation gives enough precision for the ray coordinates.

Most voxel-based volume datasets are arranged in a cartesian uniform grid. A medical CT or MRI scanner, computes parallel slices of the specimen at different positions with a normally constant spacing. Each image contains a matrix of samples of relative to the specific signal measured by the equipment. By stacking all slices aligned together, a discretely sampled volume is defined. Each sample can be addressed by cartesian x, y, z coordinates, one being a slice selector and the other two coordinates of a point in that slice image.

3.1.2 Ray generation

The ray is generated for each pixel in the image I, geometrically the start and end positions of the ray are extracted from the previous render passes with the information of the color cube. The ray is divided by S steps, which indicates the number of samples of the volume. For each sample the x, y, z inside the volume is calculated and the value of that position is interpolated from the texture.

3.1.3 Transfer function

Transfer functions (TF) assign optical properties (color and opacity) to the original volume data values i, $F_{rgb\alpha}(i) = (r, g, b, \alpha)$, in order to improve the visualization of the internal parts of the volume data. In volume ray-casting, when the ray traverses the data, TF are used to obtain the optical properties of the volume data resulting representation at each ray step. These are then blended using the composition function. In general, two transfer functions are defined, the color transfer function, which obtains an RGB value and the opacity transfer function, which obtains an $Alpha$ value. For a recent review on transfer functions, the reader is referred to Arens & Domik (2010); Pfister et al. (2001).

Transfer functions can have many dimensions. One-dimensional transfer functions, like the one presented in this section, make a direct mapping between the original voxel data scalar values and the resulting optical values. On the other hand, multidimensional transfer functions do not only use the volume data values, but also additional information such us first and second derivatives Kniss et al. (2002) of the volume data, or even the position (based on a segmentation mask). This additional information allows a better separation between materials, and thus, better visualizations. The order of interpolation in the discrete space and the application of the TF defines the difference between *pre-* and *post-classification*. In pre-classification, TF values for the closest neighbors to the input raw data are obtained and then an interpolation is performed on the different TF color and opacity values. Using post-classification on the other hand, first the raw data is interpolated to sample voxel data and then the TF is applied on it. Both approaches produce different results, whenever the interpolation does not commute with the transfer functions. As the interpolation is usually non-linear, it will only commute with the TF if the TF are constant or the identity. Post-classification is the "right" approach in the sense of applying the transfer functions to a continuous scalar field defined by a mesh together with an interpolation prescription. Nevertheless, some works try to achieve the correctness of post-classification in pre-classification approaches with a lower computational burden, like in Engel et al. (2001).

Independently of the TF dimensions, creating a suitable TF in order to highlight the most meaningful data for the user and an specific data set is a difficult, and usually an ad-hoc task which requires experienced users, and where an a-priori knowledge about the specific data-set is important too. The most common approach is to have a generic TF definition and then adapting or tuning it manually in an iterative trial and error process, until the meaningful data becomes visually salient. This is a time comsuming task completely dependant on the user's expertise and is why many contributions have been proposed in order to improve this workflow Pfister et al. (2001). Some improve the GUI tools to perform this manual tuning which simplify the procedure, like those present in the latest versions of the OsiriX Imaging software for DICOM visualization, while others include some kind of semiautomatic TF tunning based on the underlying data set, like in Wu & Qu (2007). Finally, some papers even present automatic TF tunning approaches, like in Zhou & Takatsuka (2009), but they are only valid for generic tasks since they are not specifically tailored to each particular need of the user.

All these works stand on the assumption that there is a correspondence between the cells formed by the TF input parameters and the different materials in the volume data. It is important to take this fact into account when selecting the TF input parameters and for a possible preliminary data processing step. Multidimensional functions permit a better separation between materials, since they consider more input variables, at the expense of being more difficult to tune and increased storage and computation requirements.

In practice, TF are usually precomputed and stored as lookup tables. This raises two issues: dynamic range and dimensionality. Ideally, the TF should store one resulting value per possible value in the input parameter space. Therefore, for one-dimensional 8-bit input data, the TF should have 256 entries, and for 16-bit input data, the TF should have 65536 different entries. In the same sense, a bidimensional TF with both parameters being in the range of 256 would require 256^2 values. The current hardware limitations, especially in GPU based implementations, require the reduction in size of the TF lookup tables, which in turn affects to the accuracy of the TF or requires methods to compress the TF. Finally, as stated by Kniss et al. (2003), it is not enough to sample the volume with the Nyquist frequency of the data field, because undersampling artifacts would still become visible. This problem is exacerbated if non-linear transfer functions are allowed. That is, the narrower the peak in the transfer function, the more finely we must sample the volume to render it without artifacts. Similarly, as more dimensions are added to the transfer function we must also increase the sampling rate of the volume rendering.

In GPU based direct volume rendering, the color and opacity TF are stored in the GPU as one or more textures $t_{x,y,z}$. Then, the value of the texture $t_{x,y,z}$ is used to identify the color and alpha to be used in the composition function (Eq:1), usually in a post-classification scheme, such as the one presented in this section. When the composition function reaches the end of the ray in the cube or the accumulated alpha A_a reaches its maximum, early termination, the ray is interrupted and the resulting color A_{rgb} for the ray in the corresponding pixel is the cumulated value.

4. Meteorology

Doppler wheather radars are a type of remote sensing device used in meteorology. This use case scenario is described in its own section due to the particular issues it raises and the modifications required in the general volume rendering algorithm. A weather radar scans the space around it measuring several physical variables useful for the study of the current state of the local atmosphere (Segura et al. (2009)). A full scan of a Doppler radar produces a discretely sampled volume in which each sample contains several scalar values, namely reflectivity, differential reflectivity, radial velocity and spectral width. The distribution of samples in space is not uniform which poses specific challenges for analysis and visualization. Reflectivity in particular is linked to the amount of water present in the atmosphere and is especially representative of hydrometeors. Volume rendering of this variable may provide insight into the spatial shape of water masses in the air affecting different meteorological phenomena.

4.1 Radar visualization challenges

Even if the dataset is volumetric radar data is usually visualized in 2D representations, such as the *plan position indicator* (PPI) extracted at constant angular elevation, or the *constant altitude plan position indicators* (CAPPI) extracted at a constant altitude above sea level. 3D visualization is less common, but has even been presented in Web applications, for example in Sundaram et al. (2008). In this case, all rendering was precomputed in the server using OpenGL and Nvidia's Cg shading language and remotely displayed in the client by a VNC client applet. The authors mention a problem with scalability as a lot of processing is centralised. Also obviously, depending on network performance animations and interaction may not be smooth in such a setup.

Radar data visualization also poses new challenges as the data are acquired in a spherical coordinate system (Riley et al. (2006)) producing non-uniform sampled grids in space unlike the regular voxel volumes commonly found in medical datasets. This problem was Goenetxea et al. (2010) by rendering textured conic surfaces corresponding to each elevation. That method is only an approximation that does not fill the space between the cones. In order to represent the entire space using a ray-casting algorithm, the data set can be previously resampled in a uniform cartesian grid producing a voxel-based representation suitable for the common rendering algorithm. But given that resolution is not uniform in the radar data, resampling has its problems: if all detail is to be kept the resampled volume is huge, if memory use is to be limited, detail is lost. The method described below does not require preprocessing for resampling and does not suffer from said problems.

4.1.1 Spherical coordinates

A weather radar scans the surrounding sky in successive sweeps. Beginning at a low angular elevation, the radar performs a 360° azimuth scan (Figure 4). At each one-degree space direction a ray is emitted and a number of samples along the ray are measured back from its echoes (here 400 samples called buckets). The radar then proceeds step by step increasing elevation at each successive swept scan. Elevation angles are not normally uniformly incremented because most data of interest is at the lower levels. Our datasets use 14 such elevations from which only 5 had relevan information.

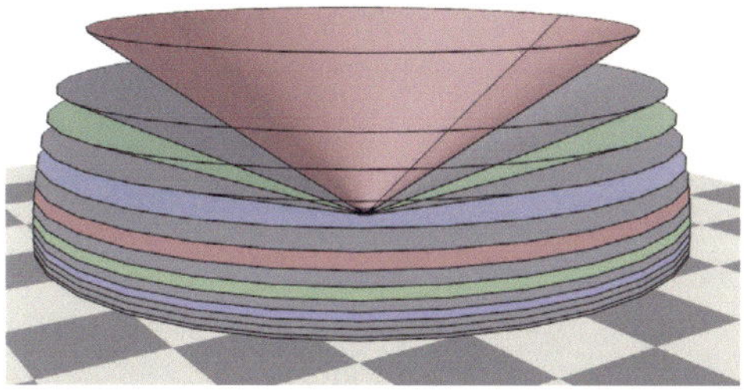

Fig. 4. Simplified geometry of a radar scan. Each scan can be approximated as a cone. Therefore, a radar volume dataset is approximated as a set of co-axial conic slices with the radar in the common apex.

The real process is more complicated because rays do not follow a straight line in the atmosphere. Salonen et al. (2003) and Ernvik (2002) explain this double phenomenon. Due to refraction, rays suffer changes in direction when crossing atmospheric layers with different index of refraction. In a standard atmosphere this makes beams bend downwards. On the other hand, as the Earth has a curved surface, a straight line leaving a radar has its altitude increasing non-linearly. If our vertical coordinate axis represents altitude, then straight rays in space appear to bend upwards in our coordinate system. Also, radar movement is slow so that the time at which the first and last elevation are scanned differ in several minutes.

For the purposes of our visualization radar rays will be considered straight, which is not a bad approximation for our limited range as both mentioned phenomena have an opposite effect. But in more accurate, larger scale scenarios, or when integrating data from more than one radar, they should be taken into account.

Such a scanning process results in a discrete sampling of the sky volume in which each sample has *elevation*, *azimuth* and *range* coordinates. Thus, samples can be addressed by spherical coordinates. In the conversion of raw radar data into input images suitable for the WebGL implementation the sample values become pixel values. Each swept scan for a fixed elevation angle forms one image in which columns correspond to azimuth directions (there are 360 columns spaced an angle of one degree), and rows correspond to distance along each ray (400 rows spaced 250 m in range). Each image maps to a conical surface in space as shown in figure 4. In order to store the entire volume as one image, the images from consecutive elevations are stacked vertically as seen in figure 5 (the figure is rotated 90° for presentation).

$$r = \sqrt{(x-0.5)^2 + (y-0.5)^2 + (z-0.5)^2} \tag{18}$$

$$\varphi = \arctan(y, x) + \pi \tag{19}$$

$$\theta = \arccos(z/\varphi) \tag{20}$$

For the spherical coordinates volume dataset from a radar the following Equations 18-20 where used. The interpolation process used for the identification of the volume value in an arbitrary point is presented in Equations 5-17. We use a simple interpolation method because the data is expected to be normalized from the capture source. The problems presented in this topic were explained by Segura et al. (2009).

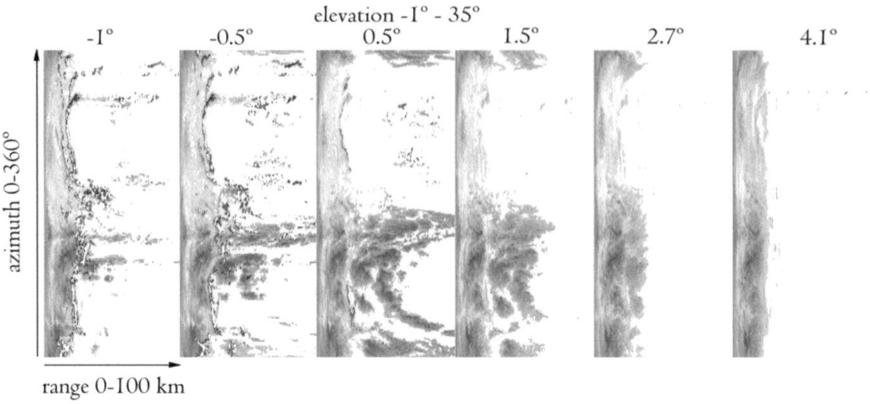

Fig. 5. Original Doppler radar image. Each vertical band represents data along a cone from figure 4 corresponding to an elevation angle

4.2 Weather radar volume rendering implementation

Our method extends the general volume ray casting algorithm previously presented in order to take into account the specific spherical coordinate system of the samples, and the layout of the dataset in memory. Thus, when traversing the volume, at each step the point's cartesian coordinates are transformed into spherical coordinates with 18. These coordinates are used to look up the volume value in the dataset. The non-uniform separation of elevations adds further complexity as it prevents a direct elevation to slice number conversion and imposes the use of a search process. As in the general algorithm, after the two slices above and below the sample are found, a value is interpolated from them.

It is important to note that each ray is traversed in tens to hundreds of steps, so this method requires a very high number of non-trivial computations and loops for each pixel, considerably more than in the general case. All of this conversion and search takes place in the programmed shader and results in very complex compiled shaders. At the time of writing only some WebGL implementations are capable of compiling and running them, specifically *Mozilla Firefox* in native OpenGL mode and *Opera*, and relatively powerful hardware is needed to achieve smooth rendering. Again, the technique would not be feasible for real-time use without the advent of modern programmable GPUs.

4.2.1 HTML user interface

We implemented a simple HTML user interface using jQuery UI (Figure 6) to interact with the volume rendering shader. It allows the tuning of parameters such as the window (zoom and offset), the quality (number of steps) and the transfer function (adapted specifically for this weather radar information), with immediate visual feedback.

The zoom and pan controls allow users to conveniently navigate the radar data, which is not as regular as medical images. For instance, the useful information is found in the bottom of the volume (i.e. near the ground). In addition, the resolution in outer areas is lower than near the radar source. Due to their geometrical configuration, the large area directly over radars is rarely scanned. Therefore, additional navigation controls for zooming and panning have been

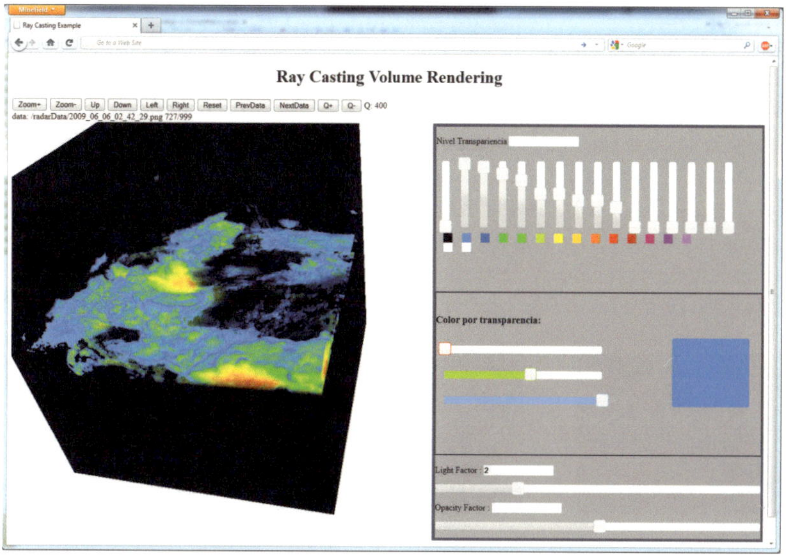

Fig. 6. Radar reflectivity visualization Web application with support for interactive definition of transfer functions.

implemented in the sample Web page, allowing user interaction of zooming in and out, and panning the view.

Additional controls have been added to the user interface to allow users to modify the number of steps, a variable directly linked to the shader, and its modification triggers a recompilation. This option has been added only for scientific purposes, since final users should not be aware of such a concept.

A very simple HTML-based editor for transfer functions was implemented, which allows the proper inspection of the radar data by changing the values and colors with the provided sliders. Figure 7 shows different visualization of the same radar sample, obtained by changing the transfer function (affecting colors and opacity for different reflectivity values). The figure also shows the effect of variations in camera parameters (zoom, pan and view orientation). The chosen number of steps was high enough to display a 800×800 canvas with high quality images and yet to keep the visualization frame rate above 26 frames/second.

4.2.2 Animation support

The visualization of a single radar volume is useful for static analysis, but the nature of the atmosphere is essentially dynamic. As the radar scans the atmosphere every 10 minutes, a collection of continuous 3D information is available for visualization. Animated series of CAPPI images are useful to visualize the evolution of a storm, or to analyze the generation process.

The utilization of volume rendering in animated series is referred as 4D data visualization, as it adds the time variable. In this case, the volumetric visualization of the radar data is used in combination with specific values of the transfer function, chosen to highlight specific parts of the volume. It is quite common to use these techniques to filter the more intense zones of the data, normally associated with the more dangerous rain or hail types.

In the Web GUI implemented, simple temporal navigational functionality has been added to enable users to access the next or previous volume in the sequence. One of the possible problems to allow a smooth visualization is the loading time, as the whole load and visualization process has to be made for each individual volumetric dataset. Fortunately, the loading time is rather short and the possibility to create fully interactive 4D animations is open. Additional tests have shown that the limit is normally imposed by the size of the dataset and the bandwidth of the network, since the data must be downloaded from the server.

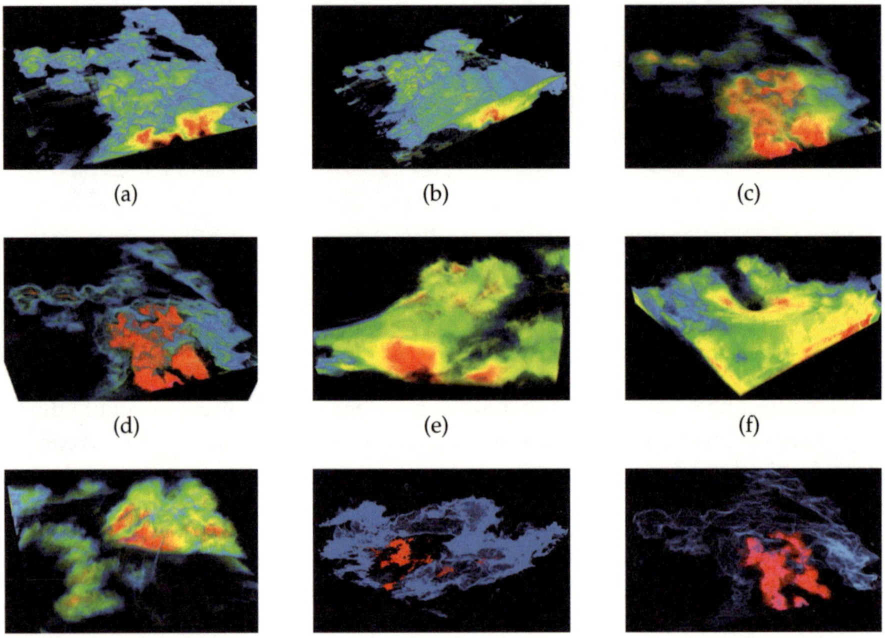

(a) (b) (c)

(d) (e) (f)

(g) (h) (i)

Fig. 7. Different weather radar volume renderings. Images (a) and (b) use typical color mapping for reflectivity scans (measured in decibels, dBZ). Images (c), (d), (e), (f), (g), (h) and (i) have been generated by varying the transfer function (color and transparency) and the window zoom and pan.

5. Results

The proposed GPU implementation of the Volume Rendering technique presented in the previous sections has been tested with different settings and with different datasets. As the interactive and real-time results depend on both hardware and software, it is very important to begin with the platform specification used for the testing. In the following sections, medical volumetric datasets and weather radar volume samples are used to validate that WebGL is a valid and promising technology for real-time and interactive applications.

5.1 Hardware and software configuration

The tests for this chapter have been conducted using an Intel Quad Core Q8300 processor, 4GB of RAM and a GeForce GTX 460, Windows 7 PRO 64 bits (Service Pack 1) with the latest stable graphics drivers. Amongst all of the Web browsers with full implementation of WebGL standard, we selected FireFox 6.0.2 for the test, other browsers are know to work with the implementation like Chrome 9.0.597.98[1] and Opera 11.50 labs (build 24661[2]).

It is worth while pointing out that both Chrome and Firefox, in default configuration, use Google's Angle library [3] to translate WebGL's native GLSL shaders to Microsoft's HLSL language and compile and run them through the DirectX subsystem. This procedure improves compatibility with lower-end hardware or older graphics drivers. Firefox Minefield has been configured with two different settings by modifying some keys in the configuration page *about:config*: (1) the default value of *webgl.prefer-native-gl* was set to `TRUE`. (2) The default value of *webgl.shader_validator* was `TRUE`. These changes basically disable Angle as the rendering back-end end validator of shaders, thus directly using the underlying native OpenGL support.

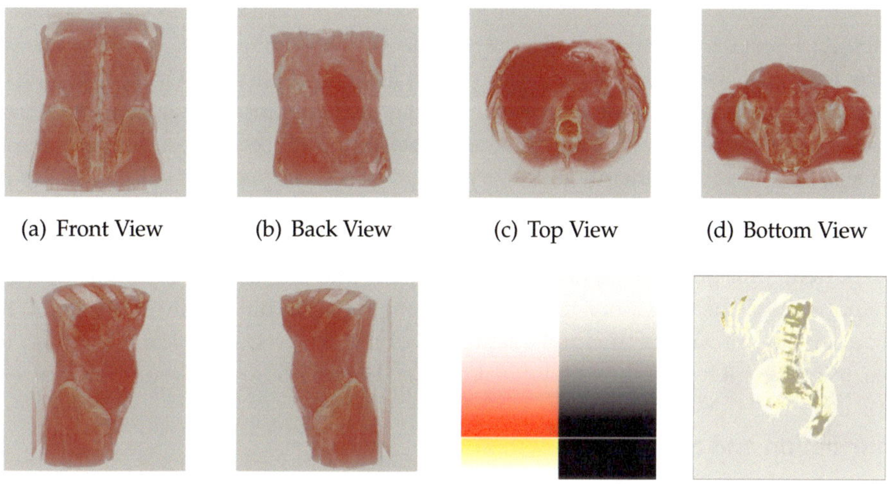

(a) Front View (b) Back View (c) Top View (d) Bottom View

(e) Left Side View (f) Right Side View (g) Used Transfer Function (h) Applying Other TF

Fig. 8. Subfigures (a), (b), (c), (d), (e) and (f) illustrate renderings of the axial views of the sample volume dataset. The output was generated in 800×800 with 200 steps. Subfigure (g) depicts the applied transfer function, where the left side represents the color and the right side the transparency (black=opaque, white=transparent). With different transfer functions other outputs are obtained, as subfigure (h) shows.

A LightTPD Web server[4] was installed and configured in the same computer, to serve the dataset images, the sample webpages (HTML and JavaScript files) and the vertex and fragment shaders.

[1] http://www.google.com/chrome

[2] http://snapshot.opera.com/labs/webgl/Opera_1150_24661_WebGL_en.exe

[3] http://code.google.com/p/angleproject

[4] http://www.lighttpd.net

5.2 Medical dataset

Figure 8 shows some graphical output for the medical dataset introduced in the previous section. The 6 different axial views have been generated using 200 steps in the shaders implementation (800×800 canvas rendered in Firefox).

5.2.1 Dataset resolution

This qualitative test was intended to show how the input dataset resolution affects the final rendering quality. Using the same dataset, a modified version was created by reducing the input resolution per slice from 4096^2, 2048^2, 1024^2m 512^2. The number of steps in the shaders were also varied, using 30, 80, 140 and 200 steps with *Firefox*. A selection of the results are shown shown in Figure 9. If the number of steps is small the banding artifacts of the algorithm are noticiable, which is a problem. Some aproximations could be implemented to resolve this as show by Marques et al. (2009).

5.3 Medical dataset in portable devices

The Mozilla Firefox Development Group has released a mobile version of the browser for ARM devices called Fennec[5]. We have tested it on 2 Android-based devices: Samsung Galaxy Tab[6] and Samsung Galaxy S smartphone[7]. Taking into account the hardware limitations of such devices, we have scaled down the *Aorta* dataset to half resolution, reduced the HTML canvas size and chosen a suitable number of steps to obtain quality results with the highest possible interactivity. The test using this browser was quite straight-forward. No further modification in the implementation of the shaders, Glue JavaScript code or HTML Web page were required. Although we achieved a low frame rate (about 2 or 3 frames per second), this demonstrated the possibilty to render volume datasets on handheld devices. Further optimizations in the data or the implementation of the shaders, specifically oriented to such devices, might result in better overall performance. We set aside such issues for future work.

6. Contribution and complexity analysis

Our contribution is an implementation of a volume rendering system for the Web. The system is based on the Volume Ray-Casting algorithm with a complexity of $O(M * S)$, where M is the number of pixels to be drawn and S is the number of steps of the ray that traverses the volume. Since the algorithm is implemented in WebGL, its visualization speed is similar to native applications because it uses the same accelerated graphic pipeline. The original algorithm has been slightly modified to work with the input structures due to the lack of Volume Textures in WebGL. Therefore, our algorithm simulates the 3D data by using a 2D tilling map of the slices of the volume maintaining the tri-linear interpolation, so there is no real loss in quality because the interpolation is the same as that used in the GPU. Although a slight impact in performance could be generated for this interpolation, this is minimal and very difficult to perceive because the browsers are not capable of handling such fast events. This is due to the browsers been heavily dependent on several layers such as the shader

[5] http://www.mozilla.com/en-US/mobile
[6] http://galaxytab.samsungmobile.com/2010/index.html
[7] http://galaxys.samsungmobile.com

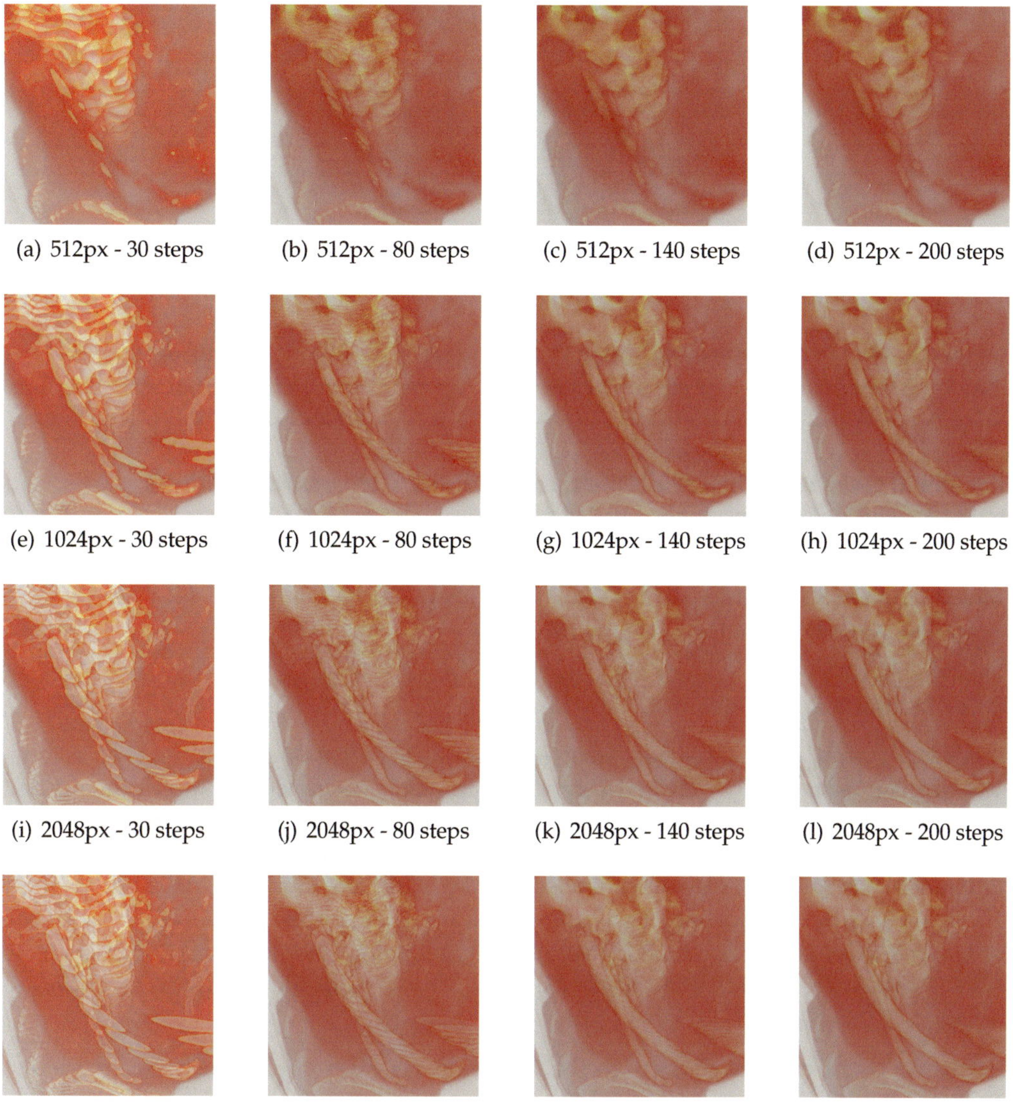

(a) 512px - 30 steps (b) 512px - 80 steps (c) 512px - 140 steps (d) 512px - 200 steps

(e) 1024px - 30 steps (f) 1024px - 80 steps (g) 1024px - 140 steps (h) 1024px - 200 steps

(i) 2048px - 30 steps (j) 2048px - 80 steps (k) 2048px - 140 steps (l) 2048px - 200 steps

(m) 4096px - 30 steps (n) 4096px - 80 steps (o) 4096px - 140 steps (p) 4096px - 200 steps

Fig. 9. Resolution qualitative test. Even with the dramatic reduction of the resolution, the volume render allows identification of the main structures.

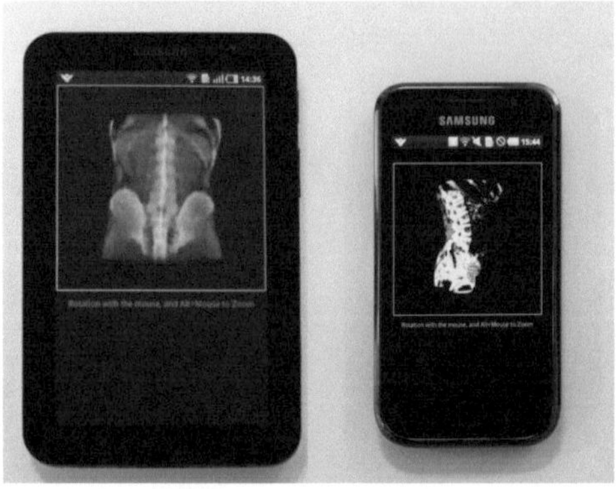

Fig. 10. A Samsung Galaxy Tab (left) and a Galaxy S Smartphone (right) volume - rendering medical datasets.

compilers, hardware architecture, graphic drivers, etc. Our algorithm was designed to run entirely in the client (which is the novelty of our proposal). Some delays are expected because of the network performance, and the interpreted nature of JavaScript. Our implementation[8] does not show a significant overhead for the server to present the data in 3D as occurs in Mahmoudi et al. (2009), therefore allowing more clients to be connected simultaneously. As a logical conclusion, more powerful clients are required to handle this approximation.

The limitations in our method, even been WebGL compilant, stem from the fact that some browsers do not adequately provide powerful enough shader language implementations to even allow compilation of larger shader programs.

7. Conclusions and future work

A medical application presented here illustrates the capabilities of complex volume rendering visualization in Web browsers. Although many performance improvements and optimizations are still needed, the material discussed here indicates that rendering volumetric data with Web standard technology is applicable to many other technical fields. Such an initiative also re-ignites interest for visualization functions implemented in the past for high-end desktop visualization applications. The integration of our implemented software in the Web follows the upcoming HTML5 standard, namely a JavaScript API and the new WebGL context for the HTML5 canvas element. The implementation of the algorithm in declarative languages as X3DOM is planned.

The scope of the present chapter does not include the integration of different rendering styles. However, interactive and complex lighting integration are promising ways to improve render quality. The use of multi-dimensional interactive transfer functions is also a promising direction to explore. The minor optimizations applied to this work allow us to expect a mathematically-planned negotiation between speed performance and quality will be a promising research field. An additional goal for optimization time-varying datasets using videos instead of images as a render input, since video formats already minimize transmitted data by reducing temporal redundancy.

[8] http://demos.vicomtech.org/volren

Another important evolution will be the integration of surface rendering within volume-rendered scenes in order to visualize, for example, segmented areas in medical images or terrain surfaces. Some tests have already been performed on desktop prototypes. This chapter lays the technical ground that would make the integration of surface render in volume-rendering (via WebGL) possible and reasonable.

8. Acknowledgments

This work was partially supported by the Basque Government's ETORTEK Project (ISD4) research programme and CAD/CAM/CAE Laboratory at EAFIT University and the Colombian Council for Science and Technology –COLCIENCIAS–. Radar datasets were provided by the Basque Meteorology and Climatology Department.

9. References

Arens, S. & Domik, G. (2010). A survey of transfer functions suitable for volume rendering., *in* R. Westermann & G. L. Kindlmann (eds), *Volume Graphics*, Eurographics Association, pp. 77–83.
URL: *http://dblp.uni-trier.de/db/conf/vg/vg2010.html#ArensD10*

Behr, J. & Alexa, M. (2001). Volume visualization in vrml, *Proceedings of the sixth international conference on 3D Web technology*, ACM New York, NY, USA, pp. 23–27.

Behr, J., Eschler, P., Jung, Y. & Zöllner, M. (2009). X3dom: a dom-based html5/x3d integration model, *Proceedings of the 14th International Conference on 3D Web Technology*, ACM, pp. 127–135.

Blazona, B. & Mihajlovic, Z. (2007). Visualization service based on web services, *Journal of Computing and Information Technology* 15(4): 339.

Congote, J., Moreno, A., Barandiaran, I., Barandiaran, J. & Ruiz, O. (2010). Extending marching cubes with adaptative methods to obtain more accurate iso-surfaces, *Computer Vision, Imaging and Computer Graphics. Theory and Applications International Joint Conference, VISIGRAPP 2009, Lisboa, Portugal, February 5-8, 2009. Revised Selected Papers*, Springer Berlin / Heidelberg, pp. 35–44.

Engel, K., Kraus, M. & Ertl, T. (2001). High-quality pre-integrated volume rendering using hardware-accelerated pixel shading, *Proceedings of the ACM SIGGRAPH/EUROGRAPHICS workshop on Graphics hardware*, HWWS '01, ACM, New York, NY, USA, pp. 9–16.
URL: *http://doi.acm.org/10.1145/383507.383515*

Ernvik, A. (2002). *3d visualization of weather radar data*, Master's thesis. LITH-ISY-EX-3252-2002.

Fogal, T. & Kruger, J. (2010). Tuvok, an Architecture for Large Scale Volume Rendering, *in* M. Dogget, S. Laine & W. Hunt (eds), *Proceedings of the 15th International Workshop on Vision, Modeling, and Visualization*, pp. 57–66.
URL: *http://www.sci.utah.edu/ tfogal/academic/tuvok/Fogal-Tuvok.pdf*

Goenetxea, J., Moreno, A., Unzueta, L., Galdós, A. & Segura, A. (2010). Interactive and stereoscopic hybrid 3d viewer of radar data with gesture recognition, *in* M. G. Romay, E. Corchado & M. T. García-Sebastián (eds), *HAIS (1)*, Vol. 6076 of *Lecture Notes in Computer Science*, Springer, pp. 213–220.

Hadwiger, M., Ljung, P., Salama, C. R. & Ropinski, T. (2009). Advanced illumination techniques for gpu-based volume raycasting, *ACM SIGGRAPH 2009 Courses*, ACM, pp. 1–166.

Hartley, R. & Zisserman, A. (2003). *Multiple View Geometry in Computer Vision*, second edn, Cambridge University Press, Cambridge, UK.
URL: *http://dx.doi.org/10.2277/0521540518*

Hibbard, W. & Santek, D. (1989). Interactivity is the key, *Proceedings of the 1989 Chapel Hill workshop on Volume visualization*, VVS '89, ACM, New York, NY, USA, pp. 39–43.
URL: *http://doi.acm.org/10.1145/329129.329356*

John, N., Aratow, M., Couch, J., Evestedt, D., Hudson, A., Polys, N., Puk, R., Ray, A., Victor, K. & Wang, Q. (2008). MedX3D: standards enabled desktop medical 3D., *Studies in health technology and informatics* 132: 189.

John, N. W. (2007). The impact of web3d technologies on medical education and training, *Computers and Education* 49(1): 19 – 31. Web3D Technologies in Learning, Education and Training.
URL: *http://www.sciencedirect.com/science/article/B6VCJ-4GNTFHN-1/2/038248c7a389ba900e10bef7249450da*

Kabongo, L., Macia, I. & Paloc, C. (2009). Development of a commercial cross-platform dicom viewer based on open source software, *in* P. H. U. Lemke, P. P. K. Inamura, P. P. K. Doi, P. P. M. W. Vannier, P. P. A. G. Farman & D. PhD (eds), *International Journal of Computer Assisted Radiology and Surgery; CARS 2009 Computer Assisted Radiology and Surgery Proceedings of the 23rd International Congress and Exhibition*, Vol. 4, International Foundation of Computer Assisted Radiology and Surgery, Springer, Berlin, Germany, pp. S29–S30.

Kajiya, J. T. & Von Herzen, B. P. (1984). Ray tracing volume densities, *SIGGRAPH Comput. Graph.* 18: 165–174.
URL: *http://doi.acm.org/10.1145/964965.808594*

Kniss, J., Kindlmann, G. & Hansen, C. (2002). Multidimensional transfer functions for interactive volume rendering, *Visualization and Computer Graphics, IEEE Transactions on* 8(3): 270 – 285.

Kniss, J., Premoze, S., Ikits, M., Lefohn, A., Hansen, C. & Praun, E. (2003). Gaussian transfer functions for multi-field volume visualization, *Proceedings of the 14th IEEE Visualization 2003 (VIS'03)*, VIS '03, IEEE Computer Society, Washington, DC, USA, pp. 65–.
URL: *http://dx.doi.org/10.1109/VISUAL.2003.1250412*

Kruger, J. & Westermann, R. (2003). Acceleration techniques for gpu-based volume rendering, *VIS '03: Proceedings of the 14th IEEE Visualization 2003 (VIS'03)*, IEEE Computer Society, Washington, DC, USA, p. 38.

Lacroute, P. & Levoy, M. (1994). Fast volume rendering using a shear-warp factorization of the viewing transformation, *Proceedings of the 21st annual conference on Computer graphics and interactive techniques*, SIGGRAPH '94, ACM, New York, NY, USA, pp. 451–458.
URL: *http://doi.acm.org/10.1145/192161.192283*

Levoy, M. (1988). Display of surfaces from volume data, *IEEE Comput. Graph. Appl.* 8(3): 29–37.

Mahmoudi, S. E., Akhondi-Asl, A., Rahmani, R., Faghih-Roohi, S., Taimouri, V., Sabouri, A. & Soltanian-Zadeh, H. (2009). Web-based interactive 2d/3d medical image processing and visualization software, *Computer Methods and Programs in Biomedicine* In Press,

Corrected Proof: –.
URL: *http://www.sciencedirect.com/science/article/B6T5J-4XYB3W7-1/2/7068a72bb5a9b0c62a3819562ab176f5*

Marques, R., Santos, L. P., Leškovský, P. & Paloc, C. (2009). Gpu ray casting, *in* A. Coelho, A. P. Cláudio, F. Silva & A. Gomes (eds), *17Âž Encontro Português de Computaçao Gráfica*, En Anexo, Covilha, Portugal, pp. 83–91.

Marrin, C. (2011). *WebGL Specification*, Khronos WebGL Working Group.
URL: *http://www.khronos.org/webgl/*

Meißner, M., Huang, J., Bartz, D., Mueller, K. & Crawfis, R. (2000). A practical evaluation of popular volume rendering algorithms, *Proceedings of the 2000 IEEE symposium on Volume visualization*, Citeseer, pp. 81–90.

Meyer-Spradow, J., Ropinski, T., Mensmann, J. & Hinrichs, K. H. (2009). Voreen: A rapid-prototyping environment for ray-casting-based volume visualizations, *IEEE Computer Graphics and Applications (Applications Department)* 29(6): 6–13.
URL: *http://viscg.uni-muenster.de/publications/2009/MRMH09*

Pfister, H., Lorensen, B., Bajaj, C., Kindlmann, G., Schroeder, W., Avila, L., Raghu, K., Machiraju, R. & Lee, J. (2001). The transfer function bake-off, *Computer Graphics and Applications, IEEE* 21(3): 16 –22.

Phong, B. T. (1975). Illumination for computer generated pictures, *Commun. ACM* 18(6): 311–317.

Poliakov, A. V., Albright, E., Hinshaw, K. P., Corina, D. P., Ojemann, G., Martin, R. F. & Brinkley, J. F. (2005). Server-based approach to web visualization of integrated three-dimensional brain imaging data, *Journal of the American Medical Informatics Association* 12(2): 140 – 151.
URL: *http://www.sciencedirect.com/science/article/B7CPS-4FJT8T8-7/2/1ec1f4078ec3bf48810583ea08227b32*

Riley, K., Song, Y., Kraus, M., Ebert, D. S. & Levit, J. J. (2006). Visualization of structured nonuniform grids, *IEEE Computer Graphics and Applications* 26: 46–55.

Salonen, K., Järvinen, H. & Lindskog, M. (2003). Model for Doppler Radar Radial winds.

Segura, Á., Moreno, A., García, I., Aginako, N., Labayen, M., Posada, J., Aranda, J. A. & Andoin, R. G. D. (2009). Visual processing of geographic and environmental information in the basque country: Two basque case studies, *in* R. D. Amicis, R. Stojanovic & G. Conti (eds), *GeoSpatial Visual Analytics*, NATO Science for Peace and Security Series C: Environmental Security, Springer Netherlands, pp. 199–208.

Sundaram, V., Zhao, L., Song, C., Benes, B., Veeramacheneni, R. & Kristof, P. (2008). Real-time Data Delivery and Remote Visualization through Multi-layer Interfaces, *Grid Computing Environments Workshop, 2008. GCE'08*, pp. 1–10.

Westover, L. A. (1991). *Splatting: a parallel, feed-forward volume rendering algorithm*, PhD thesis, Chapel Hill, NC, USA. UMI Order No. GAX92-08005.

Wu, Y. & Qu, H. (2007). Interactive transfer function design based on editing direct volume rendered images, *Visualization and Computer Graphics, IEEE Transactions on* 13(5): 1027 –1040.

Yoo, S., Key, J., Choi, K. & Jo, J. (2005). Web-Based Hybrid Visualization of Medical Images, *Lecture notes in computer science* 3568: 376.

Zhou, J. & Takatsuka, M. (2009). Automatic transfer function generation using contour tree controlled residue flow model and color harmonics, *Visualization and Computer Graphics, IEEE Transactions on* 15(6): 1481 –1488.

10

Motion and Motion Blur Through Green's Matrices

Perfilino E. Ferreira Júnior[1] and José R. A. Torreão[2]
[1]*Universidade Federal da Bahia*
[2]*Universidade Federal Fluminense*
Brazil

1. Introduction

Green's functions are powerful tools for solving differential equations. They arise in the resolution of boundary value problems (Stakgold, 1998) and heat diffusion equations (Folland, 1995), being also applied to economic modeling (Oppenheim & Willsky, 1996), and for deriving numerical approximations to integral equations (Jerri, 1999).

In the computer vision context, Green's functions of image matching equations have been introduced for solving the shape-from-shading problem (Torreão, 2001), and later used for edge detection (Torreão & Amaral, 2002; 2006), disparity estimation (Torreão, 2007), motion synthesis (Ferreira Júnior et al., 2008), and video interpolation (Ferreira Júnior et al., 2005).

If we consider a dynamic $3D$ scene imaged by a single camera, a pair of captured images, f_1 and f_2, can be related through the image matching equation (Jahne et al., 1999),

$$f_2(x+U, y+V) = f_1(x,y), \tag{1}$$

where U and V denote, respectively, the horizontal and vertical components of the optical flow. Several models have been used for describing the pair (U,V), among them the uniform model (which allows only for translational motions), the affine model (which incorporates planar rotation, shear, and dilation), and the projective model (which also incorporates perspective distortions).

Here, we will initially consider one-dimensional matching equations of the form

$$f_2(x+U) = f_1(x), \tag{2}$$

where $U \equiv U(x)$ follows the affine model $U(x) = u_0 + u_1 x$, for u_0 and u_1 constants. The $2D$ case will be tackled later. Expanding the left-hand side of Eq. (2) into a second-order Taylor series, we obtain the approximation

$$\frac{U^2(x)}{2} f_2''(x) + U(x) f_2'(x) + f_2(x) = f_1(x) \tag{3}$$

The solution to Eq. (3), via the Green's function method, can be obtained as

$$f_2(x) = f_1(x) \star G(x) = \int_{\mathcal{D}} G(x,\xi) f_1(\xi) d\xi \tag{4}$$

where $\mathcal{D}$ is the domain of interest, and where $G(x,\xi)$ is the Green's function, whose form, when considering an unbounded domain, has been obtained in (Ferreira Júnior et al., 2005), and employed for video interpolation. There, the possible existence of singular points of Eq. (3) – which are points where U(x) vanishes (Stakgold, 1998) – has not been considered, an issue that will be taken up here.

Motion synthesis with the simultaneous introduction of motion blur is another task which has been approached through the $1D$ affine Green's function model, proving it superior to competing techniques (Ferreira Júnior et al., 2008). Also, in (Ferreira Júnior et al., 2009), the second-order matching model of Eq. (3) has been compared to first-order variants, having been shown to generally yield more realistic motion effects.

In the present chapter, we propose to consider the following issues: i) that of improving our motion synthesis approach by using a matrix formulation, instead of a filtering one, to obtain the solutions to the affine matching equation; ii) that of solving the related problem of motion reversal. The chapter is organized as follows: in Section 2, we model the Green's function image matching problem, considering its discretization and its solution via the matrix approach. In Section 3, we apply the Green's function method to the problems of video interpolation and motion reversal. Finally, in Section 4, we present our concluding remarks.

2. Green's matrices

Let us start by considering some properties of the general matching equation (Eq. (2)), in the affine flow case. That equation can be formally rewritten as

$$f_2(x) = M_U\left[f_1\right](x), \tag{5}$$

where $U(x) = u_0 + u_1 x$, for u_0 and u_1 constants, with $u_1 \neq 0$ (the case $u_1 = 0$ reduces to the uniform flow, and will not be considered here), and where M_U denotes the linear transformation

$$M_U\left[f\right](x) = f\left(\frac{x-u_0}{1+u_1}\right) \tag{6}$$

The affine vector field $U(x)$ vanishes at the point $x_U = \frac{-u_0}{u_1}$, for which we have $f_2(x) = f_1(x)$, i.e., a fixed point. Fig. 1 illustrates the behavior of the matching operator in the neighborhood of x_U. Its effect consists in the combination of a translation by $\frac{u_0}{1+u_1}$, and a scaling by $\frac{1}{1+u_1}$. When $u_1 > 0$, we obtain an expansion, and when $u_1 < 0$, a contraction results. Fig. 2 depicts the overall effect of applying M_U to the function $f_1(x) = \frac{sin(x^2)}{x}$. If we consider a second-order Taylor series expansion of the left-hand side of Eq. (2), we obtain the approximation in Eq. (3), whose solution can be expressed in terms of the Green's function, as in Eq. (4). This will be treated next.

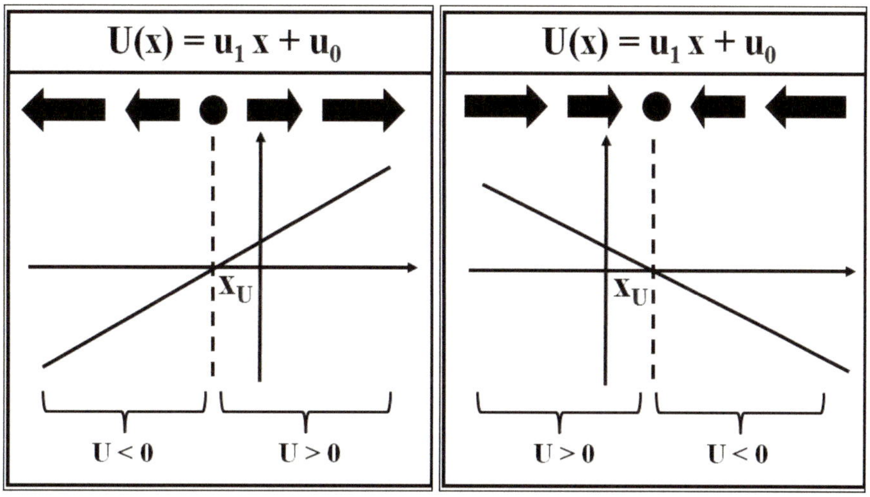

Fig. 1. Illustrating the behavior of the affine matching operator. Left: Expansion ($u_1 > 0$). Right: Contraction ($u_1 < 0$).

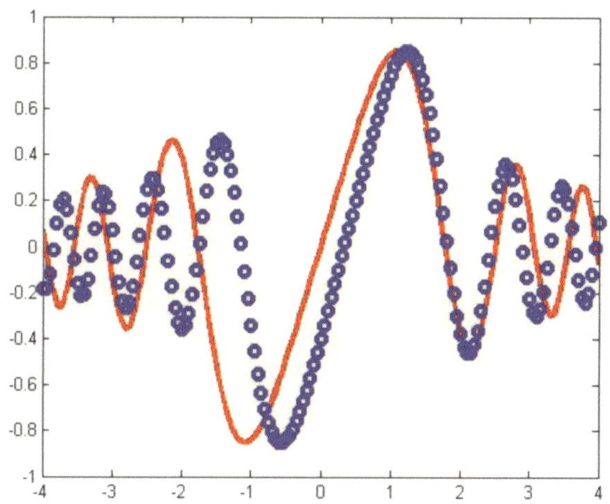

Fig. 2. Application of the operator M_U, with $(u_0, u_1) = (0.31, -0.155)$, to the function $f_1(x) = \frac{sin(x^2)}{x}$ (solid line). The circles represent the resulting signal, $f_2(x) = M_U[f_1](x) = \frac{sin\left(\frac{x-u_0}{1+u_1}\right)^2}{\left(\frac{x-u_0}{1+u_1}\right)}$. The fixed point, in this case, is at $x = 2$.

2.1 Continuous Green's functions

Assuming an unbounded domain $\mathcal{D}$, a limited Green's function can be obtained under two different guises. The form

$$G_+(x,\xi) = \frac{2}{u_1{}^2\beta(\xi - x_U)} \left[\frac{x - x_U}{\xi - x_U}\right]^\alpha \sin\left\{\beta \log\left[\frac{x - x_U}{\xi - x_U}\right]\right\}, \tag{7}$$

for $x > \xi$, with $G_+(x,\xi) = 0$, otherwise, will be bounded over the domain $\mathcal{D} \subset (x_U, +\infty)$, as long as we take $u_1 > 0$. On the other hand, a bounded Green's function over the domain $\mathcal{D} \subset (-\infty, x_U)$ can be obtained, assuming $u_1 < 0$, as

$$G_-(x,\xi) = \frac{2}{u_1{}^2\beta(x_U-\xi)}\left[\frac{x_U-x}{x_U-\xi}\right]^{\alpha} \sin\left\{\beta \log\left[\frac{x_U-x}{x_U-\xi}\right]\right\}, \tag{8}$$

for $x < \xi$, with $G_-(x,\xi) = 0$, otherwise. In either case, the parameters α and β are given as

$$\begin{cases} \alpha = -\frac{1}{u_1} + \frac{1}{2} \\ \beta = \frac{1}{u_1}\sqrt{1 + u_1 - \frac{u_1^2}{4}} \end{cases} \tag{9}$$

Over finite domains, both forms will remain valid for $2(1-\sqrt{2}) < u_1 < 2(1+\sqrt{2})$. Fig. 3 shows plots of G_+ and G_-, and it can be noted that the Green's function forms are mirror reflections of one another about the axis $x = \xi$.

Fig. 4 illustrates the roles of the filters G_+ and G_- as approximations of the affine matching operator. For instance, let us consider the expansion case (left-hand panel). When considering a point x on the interval $(x_U, +\infty)$, we see that the value of the matching function $f_2(x)$ will depend on the values of $f_1(\xi)$ for all $\xi < x$. Each of these values will be weighted by the corresponding Green's function, $G_+(x,\xi)$, to yield $f_2(x)$ by the linear combination in Eq. (4). Similarly, the values of $f_1(\xi)$ for all $\xi > x$ will be weighted by $G_-(x,\xi)$, in order to yield $f_2(x)$ whenever $x \in (-\infty, x_U)$. The contraction case (right-hand panel in the figure) can be similarly treated. Fig. 5 illustrates the effects of the exact matching operator, M_U, and of its

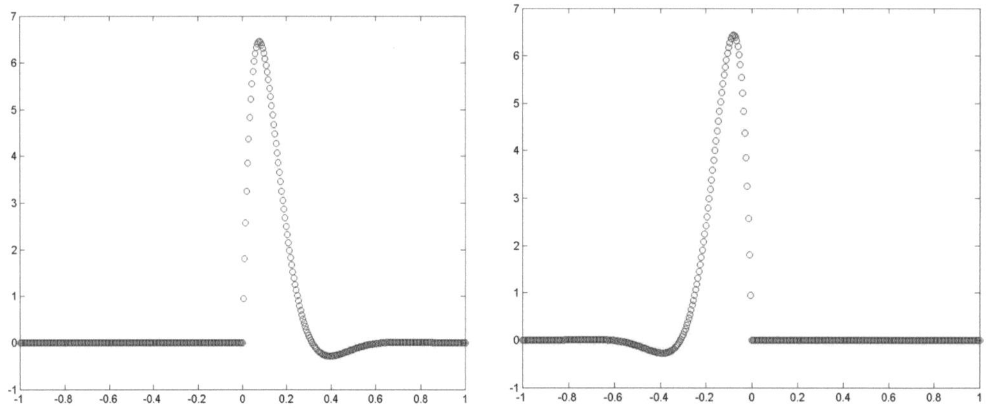

(a) G_+ filter plotted as function of x, for $\xi = 0$. Parameter values: $u_0 = 0.1$ and $u_1 = 0.005$.

(b) G_- filter plotted as function of x, for $\xi = 0$. Parameter values: $u_0 = -0.1$ and $u_1 = 0.005$.

Fig. 3. Plots of the G_+ and G_- filters.

approximation by the Green's filters, $G_\pm$, when applied to the same test signal as considered in Fig. 2. The discretization of both operators will be discussed in the following subsection.

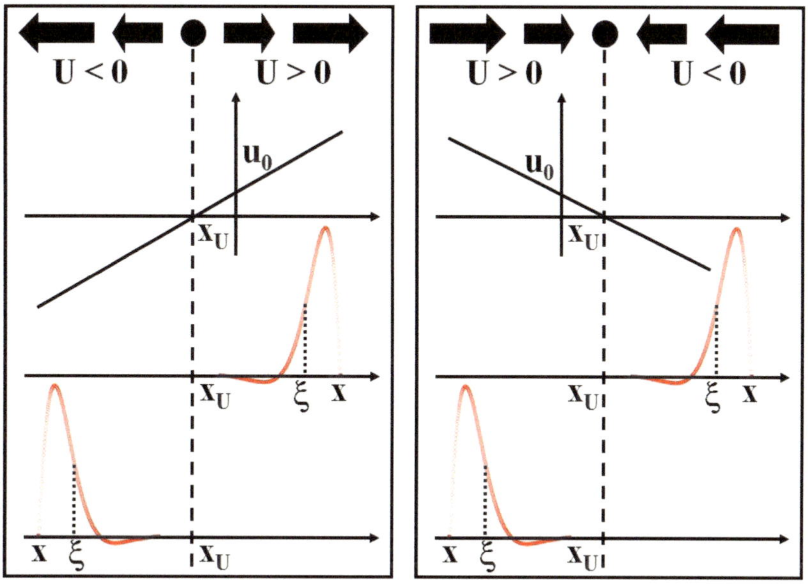

(a) Expansion, with $u_0 > 0$ and $u_1 > 0$: The central plot shows $G_+(x, \xi)$, and the lower plot shows $G_-(x, \xi)$, as functions of ξ, for a fixed x.

(b) Contraction, with $u_0 > 0$ and $u_1 < 0$: Similarly as in (a), but with G_+ in the lower plot and G_- in the central one.

Fig. 4. Illustrating the roles of the G_+ and G_- filters.

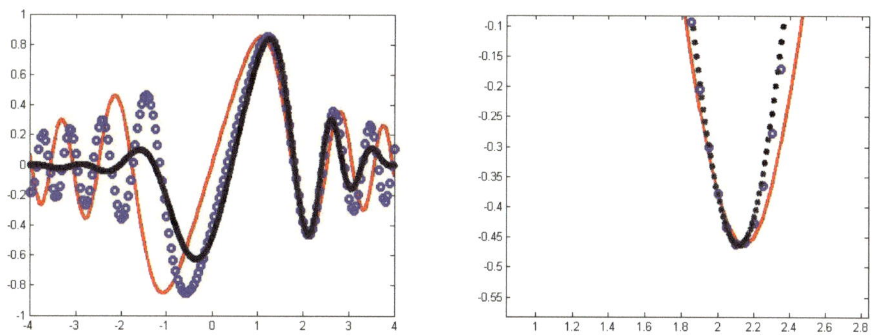

(a) Curves f_1, $M_U[f_1]$ and $f_1 \star G_\pm$

(b) The property of the fixed point

Fig. 5. Illustrating the action of the operator M_U, and of its approximations $G_\pm$. Plots of $f_1(x) = \frac{\sin(x^2)}{x}$ (solid line), $f_2(x) = M_U[f_1](x) = \frac{\sin\left(\frac{x-u_0}{1+u_1}\right)^2}{\left(\frac{x-u_0}{1+u_1}\right)}$ (circles), and $f_1 \star G_\pm$ (crosses). The parameter values were $u_0 = 0.31$ and $u_1 = -0.155$, leading to a fixed point at $x_U = 2$.

2.2 Discrete Green's functions

In the discrete case, Eq. (4) will reduce to the form

$$f_2(x) = \sum_k G(x,k) f_1(k) \tag{10}$$

where $G = G_{\pm}$. Since $x = x_U$ is a singular point of the Green's operator, we found it necessary to use stratified sampling for its discretization, with the sampling frequency increasing as we approach x_U (Ferreira Júnior et al., 2009). We consider this below.

2.2.1 Samples of the Green's function

We have adopted a non-weighted area sampling (Foley et al., 1995), for computing G at an image point. At each scanline, the area of a given pixel is partitioned along the horizontal direction, and the value of G is computed there. The discretized value $G(x,k)$ is then obtained by considering a Haar basis $\{\varphi(x)\}$, such that

$$G(x,k) = \sum_j G_j \varphi(k-j), \tag{11}$$

where k plays the role of an index inside the pixel at coordinate x, and where the coefficients G_j are computed as

$$G_j = \int_j^{j+1} G(x,\bar{\xi}) d\bar{\xi}. \tag{12}$$

Thus, the normalization condition

$$\int_{\mathcal{D}} G(x,\xi) d\xi = 1, \tag{13}$$

will also hold in the discrete case, where $\mathcal{D}$ is the considered domain. Fig. 6 illustrates the sampling process.

The stages for the computation of $G(x,k)$ can be summarized as follows:

1. At each scanline, an image pixel is partitioned into n subpixels (cells).
2. At the subpixel level, numerical integration is performed for determining the value of G_j (see Eq. (12)).
3. Each G_j value will then contribute to the expansion of $G(x,k)$, in terms of the Haar basis (see Eq. (11)).
4. A larger sampling frequency, $f_s^* > f_s$, is employed when $|U(x)| < T_U$.

As we show next, the discretization of the Green's function becomes more efficient if a matrix representation is used. In this case, we need to compute the Green's function samples only once, and a single matrix product per line is required for yielding the transformed image. The complexity of the original filtering process, as described in (Ferreira Júnior et al., 2008; 2009) , is of order $O(M.N^2)$ per each image line, and since the filtering along the image columns is also required, we have a total complexity of order $O(M.N^2) + O(N.M^2)$. With the matrix approach, this will be reduced to $O(M) + O(N)$.

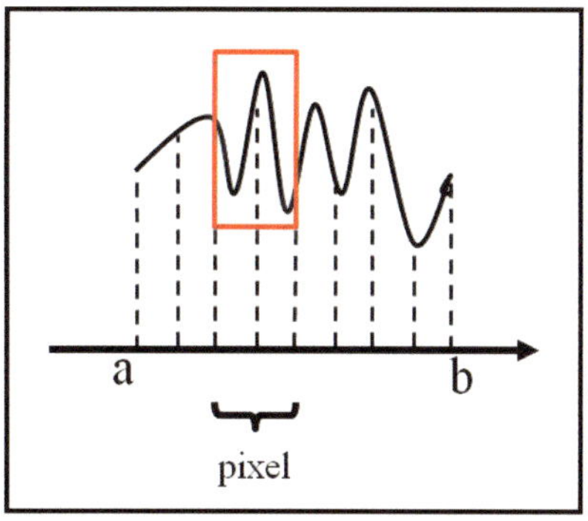

(a) An uniform partitioning is performed along a scanline.

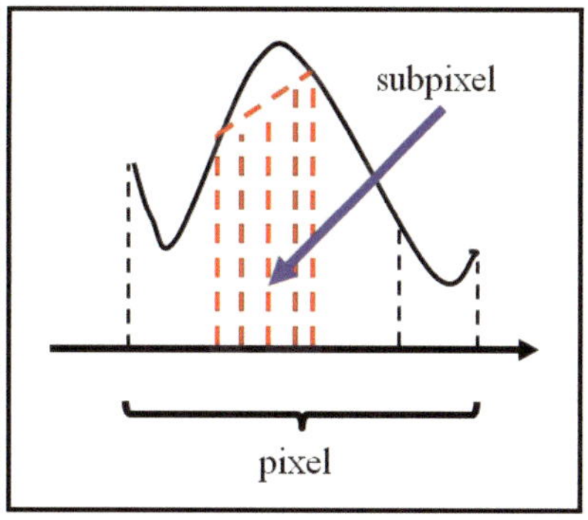

(b) Each pixel is subdivided and sampled at a frequency f_s, contributing to the value G_j.

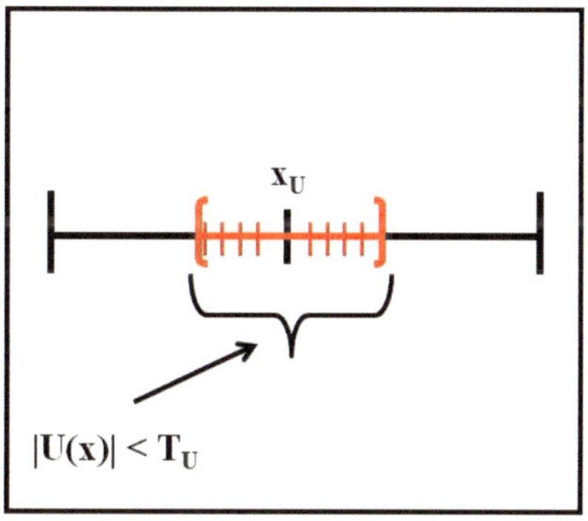

(c) The sampling frequency increases to f_s^* ($f_s^* > f_s$), when $|U(x)| < T_U$, where T_U is a threshold value.

Fig. 6. Unweighted area sampling of the Green's function

2.2.2 Constructing the Green's matrix

Here we undertake the construction of the Green's matrix for the expansion case, as in Fig. 4(a) (the contraction case can be similarly treated). Let us consider Eq. (4), with $g = f_2$ and $f = f_1$, and let us partition the intervals $(x_U, +\infty)$ and $(-\infty, x_U)$ in n subintervals, each of length $\Delta\xi = 1$. Thus, at each pixel x_j, Eq. (4) can be rewritten as

$$g(x_j) = \Delta\xi \left\{ \frac{1}{2} G_\pm(x_j, \xi_0) f(\xi_0) + G_\pm(x_j, \xi_1) f(\xi_1) + \cdots \right.$$
$$\left. + G_\pm(x_j, \xi_{j-2}) f(\xi_{j-2}) + G_\pm(x_j, \xi_{j-1}) f(\xi_{j-1}) \right\} \quad (14)$$

assuming $x_j > \xi_i > x_U$, for $\xi_i > \xi_{i+1}$ ($j = 1, 2, \cdots, n$ and $i = 0, 1, \cdots, j-1$), with $x_j \in (x_U, +\infty)$, when considering $g = G_+ \star f$, and $x_j < \xi_i < x_U$, for $\xi_i < \xi_{i+1}$ ($j = 1, 2, \cdots, n$ and $i = 0, 1, \cdots, j-1$), with $x_j \in (-\infty, x_U)$, when considering $g = G_- \star f$.

Thus, at each domain, $(x_U, +\infty)$ and $(-\infty, x_U)$, Eq. (14) yields $2n$ equations, n of which will be given as

$$\begin{cases} g_1 = \frac{1}{2}G_{10}f_0 \\ g_j = \frac{1}{2}G_{j0}f_0 + G_{j1}f_1 + ... + G_{j,i-1}f_{i-1}, \end{cases} \tag{15}$$

where $g_j = g(x_j)$ $(j = 1, 2, \cdots, n)$, $f_i = f(\xi_i)$ $(i = 0, 1, ..., j-1)$ and $G_{ji} = G_+(x_j, \xi_i)$, for $x_j \in (x_U, +\infty)$. The other n equations will be similarly given, but for $G_{ji} = G_-(x_j, \xi_i)$, with $x_j \in (-\infty, x_U)$. In matrix form, this corresponds to the product

$$\begin{bmatrix} \frac{1}{2}G_{n,0} & G_{n,1} & \cdots & G_{n,n-1} & 0 & 0 & 0 & \cdots & 0 \\ 0 & \frac{1}{2}G_{n-1,0} & \cdots & G_{n-1,1} & 0 & 0 & 0 & \cdots & 0 \\ \vdots & \vdots & \ddots & \vdots & \vdots & \vdots & \vdots & \vdots & \vdots \\ 0 & 0 & \cdots & \frac{1}{2}G_{1,0} & 0 & 0 & 0 & \cdots & 0 \\ 0 & 0 & \cdots & 0 & 1 & 0 & 0 & \cdots & 0 \\ 0 & 0 & \cdots & 0 & 0 & \frac{1}{2}G_{n+1,0} & 0 & \cdots & 0 \\ 0 & 0 & \cdots & 0 & 0 & G_{n+2,1} & \frac{1}{2}G_{n+2,0} & \cdots & 0 \\ \vdots & \vdots & \vdots & \vdots & \vdots & \vdots & \vdots & \ddots & \vdots \\ 0 & 0 & \cdots & 0 & 0 & G_{2n,n+1} & G_{2n,n+2} & \cdots & \frac{1}{2}G_{2n,0} \end{bmatrix} \begin{bmatrix} f_0 \\ f_1 \\ \vdots \\ f_{n-1} \\ f_U \\ \bar{f}_{n-1} \\ \bar{f}_{n-2} \\ \vdots \\ \bar{f}_0 \end{bmatrix} = \begin{bmatrix} g_1 \\ g_2 \\ \vdots \\ g_n \\ g_U \\ \bar{g}_n \\ \bar{g}_{n-1} \\ \vdots \\ \bar{g}_1 \end{bmatrix} \tag{16}$$

or, equivalently,

$$\mathcal{A}\hat{\mathbf{f}} = \hat{\mathbf{g}} \tag{17}$$

with

$$\mathcal{A} = \left[\begin{array}{c|c} \mathbf{G}_- & \bigcirc \\ \hline \bigcirc & \mathbf{G}_+ \end{array}\right] \tag{18}$$

being the Green's matrix, and the vectors $\hat{\mathbf{f}} = (f_0, \ldots, f_{n-1}, f_U, \bar{f}_{n-1}, \ldots, \bar{f}_0)^T$ and $\hat{\mathbf{g}} = (g_1, \ldots, g_n, g_U, \bar{g}_n, \ldots, \bar{g}_1)^T$ denoting, respectively, the lines of the input and of the output images. Note that $(f_0, f_1, \ldots, f_{n-1})^T$ will be the input pixels actuated on by G_- and $(\bar{f}_{n-1}, \bar{f}_{n-2}, \ldots, \bar{f}_0)^T$ will be those actuated on by G_+. Also note that the value 1 appearing at the center of the matrix $\mathcal{A}$ expresses the fixed point property

$$f(x_U) = g(x_U) \tag{19}$$

When implementing consecutive horizontal and vertical filterings, as in(Ferreira Júnior et al., 2009), separate kernels can be used, such that

$$\mathcal{B}\hat{\mathbf{f}} = \hat{\mathbf{g}} \tag{20}$$

where $\mathcal{B} = \mathcal{A}_Y.\mathcal{A}_X$, with $\mathcal{A}_X$ and $\mathcal{A}_Y$ implementing the filtering along the directions x and y, respectively. Thus, the whole computational cost will be that of performing the multiplication of each image line by the Green's matrix.

In the following section, we present the application of the above strategy to the problems of video interpolation and motion reversion.

3. Experimental results

Motion synthesis with the simultaneous generation of blur is obtained here by the use of Eq. (17), where $\mathcal{A}$ denotes the Green's matrix, and where we are considering $\hat{\mathbf{f}}$ and $\hat{\mathbf{g}}$ as image rows. In the interpolation of zoom sequences, Eq. (17) is applied twice, once over rows and once over columns.

3.1 Motion estimation and reconstruction quality

For the video interpolation experiments, we take the output of a motion estimation algorithm as input parameters to the Green's function, similarly as in (Ferreira Júnior et al., 2009). The general $2D$ affine model for motion estimation can be expressed as

$$\begin{bmatrix} \tilde{U} \\ \tilde{V} \end{bmatrix} = \begin{bmatrix} \tilde{u_0} \\ -\tilde{v_0} \end{bmatrix} + \begin{bmatrix} \tilde{u_1} & -\tilde{u_2} \\ \tilde{v_1} & \tilde{v_2} \end{bmatrix} \cdot \begin{bmatrix} x - c_x \\ y - c_y \end{bmatrix}, \qquad (21)$$

where $(c_x, c_y)^T$ denotes the image center. In our interpolation experiments, we considered combined horizontal and vertical motions, such that our affine model will be separable, i.e.,

$$\begin{bmatrix} U \\ V \end{bmatrix} = \begin{bmatrix} u_0 \\ v_0 \end{bmatrix} + \begin{bmatrix} u_1 & 0 \\ 0 & v_2 \end{bmatrix} \cdot \begin{bmatrix} x \\ y \end{bmatrix} \qquad (22)$$

Note that we are using the tilde in Eq. (21), but not in Eq. (22), to distinguish the *estimated* motion components from *generated* ones.

The signs of the components u_1 and v_2, in Eq. (22), allow the classification of the singular (fixed) points of the generated vector field (Verri et al., 1989). Thus, the singular point (x_U, y_V) (here, $x_U = -\frac{u_0}{u_1}$ and $y_V = -\frac{v_0}{v_2}$ denote the fixed points for the horizontal and the vertical motion components, respectively) will be a focus of expansion when $u_1, v_2 > 0$, a focus of contraction, when $u_1, v_2 < 0$, and a saddle point , if u_1 and v_2 have different signs. Comparing equations (21) and (22), we obtain

$$\begin{cases} u_0 = \tilde{u_0} - \tilde{u_1} c_x + \tilde{u_2} c_y \equiv u_0^* \\ u_1 = \tilde{u_1} \\ 0 = -\tilde{u_2} \\ v_0 = -\tilde{v_0} - \tilde{v_1} c_x - \tilde{v_2} c_y \equiv v_0^* \\ 0 = \tilde{v_1} \\ v_2 = \tilde{v_2} \end{cases} \qquad (23)$$

For estimating the motion components from a given image sequence, we have used an optical flow algorithm based on affine regression, kindly made available to us by Professor Michael Black (Black & Anandan, 1996). Using the estimated components in the relations above, the Green's function parameters $(u_0, u_1, u_2, v_0, v_1, v_2)$ were then obtained. Similarly as in (Ferreira Júnior et al., 2005), we here usually work with fractions of the translation components, $(r.u_0, r.v_0)$, where r is the proportion of movement desired at each frame (e.g., $1/2$, $1/3$, etc.). As for the scaling components, u_1 and v_2, they are usually chosen as fractions of u_0 and v_0, respectively.

In what follows, we present results of the experimental analysis of the Green's matrix affine matching approach.

3.2 Results

We have considered here the effects of camera zoom-in and camera zoom-out (actually, both processes can be construed as a single one, just differing on the order of presentation of the frames). The Green's function approach will give rise to the fixed point

$$(x_U, y_V) = (-\frac{u_0}{u_1}, -\frac{v_0}{v_2}) \quad (24)$$

corresponding, respectively, to an expansion focus, in the zoom-in case, and to a contraction focus, in the zoom-out case.

3.2.1 Application 1: Video interpolation

Ideally, since we are considering an affine model instead of a full projective one, we should work with scenes depicting flat objects on a frontoparallel plane, such that there would be little change in depth. It is also known that depth discontinuities increase the complexity of the motion estimation process (Li, 2006).

The interpolated frames have here been obtained according to the following steps: **(a)** we estimate the affine optical flow between a pair of original frames; **(b)** from this, the corresponding Green's function components are calculated through Eq. (23); finally **(c)**, each interpolation frame is generated through Eq. (17).

The example illustrated in Fig. 7 corresponds to a synthetic motion sequence, over which we performed a zooming-in operation. It should be noted that the intermediate, interpolated frame in the figure presents appreciable blur, as expected from the Green's function approach. The full sequence appears as Example 1 in our website (`http://www.graphics.ufba.br/intechpage`), and simulates an optical zoom operation.

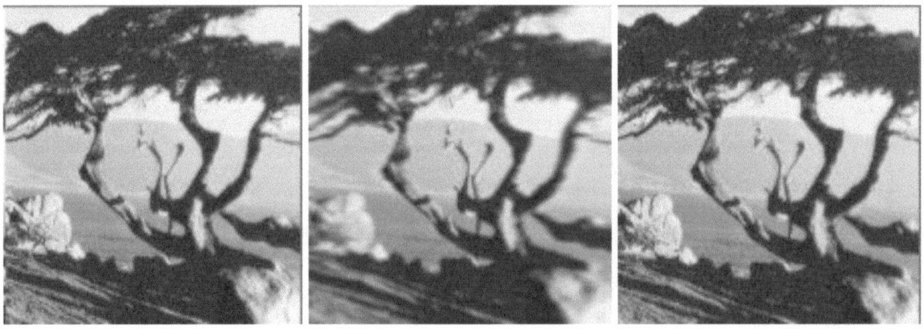

(a) A frame of reference - 150 × 150 pixels. (b) Interpolated frame with our Green's Matrix from the reference image in (a). (c) A second frame of reference - 150 × 150 pixels.

Fig. 7. Motion parameters were $(u_0, u_1, v_0, v_2) = (-3, 0.040, -1, 0.013)$. A focus of expansion appears at $(x_U, y_V) = (75, 75)$.

Table 1 presents the optical flow components estimated from the reference frames depicted in Fig. 7(a) and (c). Fig. 8 presents a different pair of frames from the same video considered

Motion Estimation Parameters					
u_0	u_1	u_2	v_0	v_1	v_2
6.226374	0.009514	0.005162	−1.119647	−0.014769	−0.014783

Table 1. Optical flow components obtained through Black's algorithm (Black & Anandan, 1996).

above, along with the interpolated frame now obtained through a zooming-out operation. The full generated sequence also appears, as Example 2, in our website.

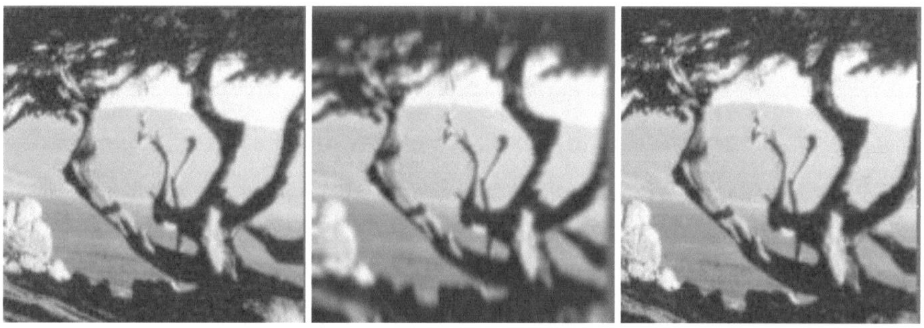

(a) A frame of reference - 150 × 150 pixels.

(b) Interpolating frame, obtained from the image in (c) through the Green's Matrix approach.

(c) A second frame of reference - 150 × 150 pixels.

Fig. 8. Motion parameters were $(u_0, u_1, v_0, v_2) = (2, -0.027, 3, -0.040)$. A focus of contraction appears at $(x_U, y_V) = (75, 75)$.

Table 2 presents the optical flow components estimated from the reference frames depicted in Fig. 8(a) and (c). We also performed an interpolation test with a fragmented sequence

Motion Estimation Parameters					
u_0	u_1	u_2	v_0	v_1	v_2
−0.112766	0.022996	−0.007487	2.169647	−0.013922	0.054095

Table 2. Optical flow components obtained through Black's algorithm (Black & Anandan, 1996).

from a real video (an old Three Stooges picture). It appears in Fig. 9 , and as Example 3 in our website. In the original sequence, the camera recedes, leading to a sudden discontinuity between frames (see the website), due to the appearance of new objects in the field of view. The net visual effect is that of an elastic deformation of the scene, which in this case is much more complex than in the previous examples, and not very amenable to our affine approach.

Table 3 presents the optical flow components obtained from the reference frames in Fig. 9(a) and (c).

(a) A frame of reference - 280 × 210 pixels.

(b) Interpolating frame, obtained from the image in (a) through the Green's Matrix approach.

(c) A second frame of reference - 280 × 210 pixels.

Fig. 9. Motion parameters were $(u_0, u_1, v_0, v_2) = (-0.015, 0.000, -3, 0.029)$. A focus of expansion appears at $(x_U, y_V) = (140, 105)$.

Motion Estimation Parameters					
u_0	u_1	u_2	v_0	v_1	v_2
−0.142945	−0.002325	−0.001457	−6.492826	−0.009811	0.026797

Table 3. Optical flow components obtained through Black's algorithm (Black & Anandan, 1996).

Our next experiment is based on a sequence created by Chad Soriano, which can be found at `http://www.chadsorianophotoblog.com/2011_03_11_archive.html`. It presents a more favorable situation for the application of the Green's function approach, by showing a single object on a dark background. In Fig. 10, we display two reference frames in the sequence, and the interpolated one.

(a) A frame of reference - 240 × 131 pixels.

(b) Interpolated frame with our Green's Matrix from the image in (a).

(c) A second frame of reference - 240 × 131 pixels.

Fig. 10. Motion parameters were $(u_0, u_1, v_0, v_2) = (2, -0.008, 1, -0.008)$. A focus of contraction appears at $(x_U, y_V) = (120, 66)$.

Table 4 presents the optical flow components obtained from the reference frames of Fig. 10(a) and (c).

Next, we will illustrate the use of the Green's matrix approach for the removal of motion effects.

Motion Estimation Parameters					
u_0	u_1	u_2	v_0	v_1	v_2
−10.093081	0.016620	−0.000431	0.104955	−0.002782	0.106368

Table 4. Optical flow components obtained through Black's algorithm (Black & Anandan, 1996).

3.2.2 Application 2: Motion reversion

Here, as a means of validation of the obtained results, the mean reconstruction error and the similarity measure, defined respectively as

$$\epsilon = \frac{\sum_{j=1}^{M-1}\sum_{k=1}^{N-1} \|f(j,k) - f_R(j,k)\|}{M.N.P} \tag{25}$$

and

$$(1-\epsilon) * 100\% \tag{26}$$

have been used for assessing the quality of the restorations. In the first equation, f denotes the original image, f_R is its restored version, M and N stand for image width and height, respectively, and P for the number of gray levels.

Fig. 11 (also Example 5 in our website) shows an example of reversal of motion effects.

(a) The original input - 270 × 250 pixels. (b) The result of applying the Green's matrix over the original input. (c) The result of motion reversal.

Fig. 11. Motion Reversal Experiment. Here the Green's Matrix has been applied to each image line. Motion parameters for generating (b) were $(u_0, u_1) = (-7, 0.052)$. A focus of expansion appears at $x_U = 135$.

In this case, through the Green's matrix approach, the image in Fig. 11 (a) underwent an expansion along the x direction (we used $u_1 > 0$), generating the image in Fig. 11(b). Next, both images were used for estimating the optical flow, and for computing the Green's matrix parameters as in Section 3.1. We finally obtained the inverse to that matrix and used it to generate Fig. 11(c). As shown, this has the effect of removing most of the blur and motion components. The quality measures of the reconstructed image are presented in Table 5. We also performed another test, where we reversed the Green's matrix separately, in the horizontal and in the vertical directions. Fig. 12 (Example 6 in our website) shows more

Quality Measures		
Figures	Mean error	Similarity (%)
Figs. 11(a) and (c)	0.089303	91.07

Table 5. Mean error and similarity results.

results of reversal of motion effects. The image of Fig. 12(b) was obtained by consecutively

(a) The original input - 280 × 210 pixels.

(b) The result of applying the Green's matrix over the original input.

(c) The result of motion reversal.

Fig. 12. Motion Reversal Experiment. The motion parameters were empirically chosen as $(u_0, u_1, v_0, v_2) = (0.03, -0.0002, 6.5, -0.062)$. A focus of contraction appears at $(x_U, y_V) = (140, 105)$.

applying the Green's matrix over the lines and columns of Fig. 12(a) (the matrix parameters were empirically chosen). The restored image in Fig. 12(c) was then generated by inverting both processes. It can be seen that the motion and blur components are substantially reduced, but the edges are substantially enhanced. Also, there appear some artifacts at the image boundary, which are probably due to boundary conditions which have not been appropriately considered here (Hansen et al., 2006) . Table 6 shows the quality measures of the restoration.

Quality Measures		
Figures	Mean error	Similarity (%)
Figs. 12(a) and (c)	0.046797	95.32

Table 6. Mean error and similarity results.

4. Conclusions and future works

Here we have proposed a matrix formulation for the Green's function affine matching approach. Such formulation leads to reduced computational costs, and affords application to complex problems, such that of interpolating video sequences including camera zoom-in and camera zoom-out. We have also proposed an inverse filtering scheme for the reversal of motion effects. This has so far yielded promising results, allowing the partial removal of both motion and blur components introduced by the Green's function itself. We are now testing its application to real motion sequences.

As future developments of our work, we envision a better treatment of the boundary problem associated with the Green's function, and also its regularization. A possible application could lie in super-resolution for synthetic zooming. The robustness under noise of our approach should also be assessed.

5. References

Black, M. & Anandan, P. (1996). The robust estimation of multiple motions: Parametric and piecewise-smooth flow fields, *Computer Vision and Image Understanding*, CVIU 63(1), pp. 75-104

Ferreira Júnior, P., E.; Torreão, J., R., A.; Carvalho, P.,C.,P.; and Velho, L. (2005). Video Interpolation Through Green's Functions of Matching Equations, *Proc. of IEEE International Conference on Image Processing*, Vol. 3, pp. III-1080-3. doi:10.1109/ICIP.2005.1530583 Key: citeulike:2804665

Ferreira Júnior, P.,E.; Torreão, J.,R.,A.; Carvalho, P.,C.,P.; and Vieira, M.,B. (2008). Motion Synthesis Through 1D Affine Matching, *Pattern Analysis and Applications* 11, pp. 45-58

Ferreira Júnior, P.,E.; Torreão, J.,R.,A.; and Carvalho, P., C., P. (2009). A Comparative Analysis of Green's Functions of 1D Matching Equations for Motion Synthesis, *Pattern recognition Letters* 30(14),pp. 1321–1334

Foley, J.; Van Dam, A.; Feiner, S.; Hughes, J. (1995). Computer Graphics: Principles and Practice in C, *Addison-Wesley Professional*, 2nd Edition.

Folland, G., B. (1995). Introduction to Partial Differential Equations, *Princeton University Press*, 2nd edition

Hansen, P. C.; Nagy, J,; O'Leary, D. (2006). Deblurring Images: Matrices, Spectra, and Filtering, *Society for Industrial and Applied Mathematics*, 1st edition

Jahne, B.; Hausseker, H.; Geissler, P. (1999). In: Handbook of Computer Vision and Applications, Vol. 2, *Academic Press*

Jerri, A. (1999). Introduction to Integral Equations with Applications, *Wiley-Interscience*, 2nd edition

Li, X. (2005). Super-Resolution for Synthetic Zooming, *Journal on Applied Signal Processing*, Volume 2006, Article ID 58195, pp. 1–12, DOI 10.1155/ASP/2006/58195

Oppenheim, A.,V.; and Willsky, A.,S. (1996). Signals and Systems, *Prentice Hall*, 2nd edition

Sondhi, M. (1972). The Removal of Spatially Invariant Degradations, *Proc. of IEEE* 60(7), pp. 842–853

Stakgold, I. (1998). Green's Functions and Boundary Value Problems, *A Wiley-Interscience Pub.*, 2nd edition

Torreão, J., R.,A. (2001). A Green's Function Approach to Shape from Shading, *Pattern Recognition* 34, pp. 2367-2382

Torreão, J.,R.,A. and Amaral, M.,S. (2002). Signal Differentiation Through a Green's Function Approach, *Pattern Recognition Letters* 23(14), pp. 1755–1759

Torreão, J.,R.,A. and Amaral, M.,S. (2006). Efficient, recursively implemented differential operator, with application to edge detection, *Pattern Recognition Letters* 27(9), pp. 987–995

Torreão, J.,R.,A. (2007). Disparity Estimation Through Green's functions of Matching Equations, *Biol. Cybernetics* 97, pp. 307–316

Verri, A.; Girosi, F.; Torre, V. (1989). Mathematical Properties of the 2*D* Motion Field: from Singular Points to Motion Parameters, *Journal of the Optical Society of America A* 6(5), pp. 698–712

11

Maxine: Embodied Conversational Agents for Multimodal Emotional Communication

Sandra Baldassarri and Eva Cerezo
Advanced Computer Graphics Group (GIGA), Computer Science Department, Engineering Research Institute of Aragon (I3A), Universidad de Zaragoza, Spain

1. Introduction

Emotions are fundamental to human experience, influencing cognition, perception and everyday tasks such as learning, communication and even rational decision-making. Human-computer interaction (HCI) systems capable of sensing user affective state and giving adequate affective feedback are, therefore, likely to be perceived as more natural, persuasive and trustworthy (Cassell & Bickmore, 2000). Affective Computing (Picard, 1997) is the research area concerned with computing that relates to, arises from, or deliberately influences emotion. Affective computing expands HCI by including emotional communication together with appropriate means of handling affective information. Last scientific researches indicate that emotions play an essential role in perception, decision making abilities, problem-solving process and learning.

During the last years, a considerable amount of researchers have become interested in the development of new interfaces that follow the human-human model of communication. These interfaces must be able to receive and analyze affective information that comes from different input channels: image, video, audio, tactile, position trackers, biological sensors, etc. In this way, affective multimodal interfaces extend the traditional channels of human perception to better mach the natural communication of human beings (Gunes et al., 2008).

Within this context, embodied conversational agents (ECAs) offer a natural and intuitive interface to perform social interaction. The benefits of interacting through 3D human–like virtual agents able to express their emotions have been widely proved (Cassell & Bickmore, 2000) (Pantic & Bartlett, 2007).

Credible ECAs should be able to properly move and communicate taking into account that human communication is based on speech, facial expressions, body language and gestures. In fact, social psychologists argue that more than 65% of the social meaning of a person-to-person conversation relies on the non-verbal band (Morris et al., 1979) highlighting the importance of emotions and body language in the communication and comprehension of information (Birdwhistell, 1985). Emotions are induced through all body language (Picard, 1997), nevertheless, most of the work in this area is focused in the facial expression of emotions (Cowie et al., 2001) (deRosis et al., 2003) (Raouzaiou et al., 2004) (Zhang et al., 2010) (Gunes et al., 2011). There is a lack of research works that include animation and synthesis of emotions through the body, probably because of the inherent complexity of determining the characteristics of each emotion. Some researchers include gestures in their work, but only in order to emphasize a verbalized message (Noma & Baldler, 1997) (Haviland, 2004) (Cassell, 2007). There are, however, some applications that include emotional virtual humans but that are usually developed for specific and delimited environments like the tutor Steve (Rickel & Johnson, 2000), an agent used for education and training that has the ability to give instant praise or express criticism depending on the succeed or failure of students' answers. Unfortunately Steve only express gestures through the hands and the head and, although it makes gestures as nodding, refusing or pointing, it doesn't establish any relationship between emotions and gestural behavior. In the work of Prendinger and Ishizuka's (Prendinger & Ishizuka, 2001) emotional virtual agents are used to interact with the users and other agents, but are not very expressive. On the other hand Caridakis et al. (Caridakis et al., 2006) work with more expressive agents but their expressions are limited to gestures captured from video and only hand and head gestures are considered.

There are other very interesting works that focus in non-verbal gestures and also consider the emotional state of the virtual agent (Hartmann et al., 2005) (Mancini & Pelachaud, 2009) (Raouzaiou et al., 2004) to express specific gestures. Su et al. (Su et al., 2007) go further developing a virtual story-teller endowed with personality. The personality influences gestures and the expression of the emotions through the whole body, but, unfortunately, only positive and negative emotions are considered in the final body animation.

With all this in mind we have developed Maxine, a powerful engine to manage embodied animated characters that support multimodal and emotional interaction and that are capable of responding appropriately to the users with affective feedback. The aim is to establish more effective communication with the user, recognizing the user's emotional state, and using a virtual character capable of expressing its emotional state. In this chapter we will focus in the novel features recently added to the Maxine engine: the addition of non-verbal communication capabilities to the virtual characters so that they can express emotions through body postures and gestures. Maxine virtual characters have been used in different domains: a young virtual character that helps special needs children to play with a customizable multimodal videogame; a virtual butler to control a remote domotic hall; and an interactive tutor that helps university students to practice Computer Graphics concepts. In this chapter we will focus in an application in which body language becomes essential: a virtual interpreter that translates from Spanish spoken language to Spanish Sign Language taking emotions into account.

The chapter is organized as follows. In Section 2, Maxine, the platform for managing virtual agents is briefly described. Section 3 details the implementation of the new features added to Maxine virtual characters: the expression of emotions through body postures and gestures. Section 4 presents the affective virtual interpreter to Spanish Sign Language developed focusing in affective issues and, finally, in Section 5, conclusions are presented and current and future work is outlined.

2. Maxine: An animation engine for multimodal emotional communication through ECAs

Maxine is a powerful multimodal animation engine for managing virtual environments and virtual actors. The system is capable of controlling virtual 3D characters for their use as new interfaces in a wide range of applications. One of the most outstanding features of the system is its affective capabilities. The system supports real-time multimodal interaction with the user through different channels (text, voice, mouse/keyboard, image, etc.) and it is able to analyze and process all this information in real-time for recognizing the user's emotional state and managing the virtual agent's decisions. Virtual characters are endowed with facial animation, lip synchronization, and with an emotional state which can modify character's answers, expressions and behaviours. The new features added to Maxine provide virtual characters with full expressive bodies.

The overall architecture of the system, shown in Figure 1, is composed of 4 main modules described in detail in previous works (Baldassarri et al., 2008) (Cambria et al., 2011): the Perception Module, the Affective Analysis Module, the Deliberative/Generative Module and the Motor Module.

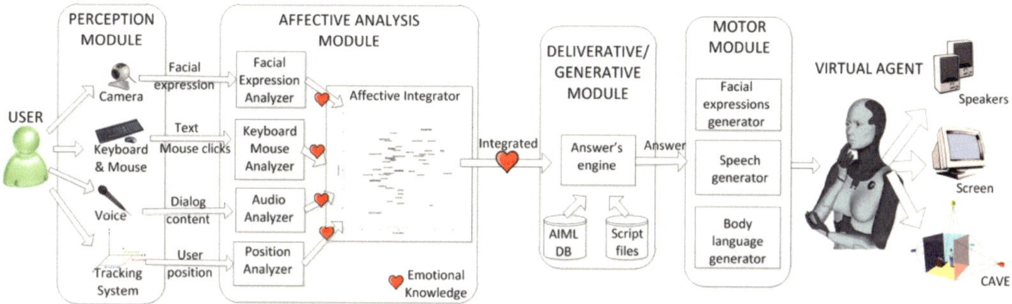

Fig. 1. Maxine's architecture.

The Perception Module consists of the hardware and software necessary to gather the multimodal information obtained during the interaction between the user and the virtual agent: via keyboard, mouse, tactile screens, voice (natural language conversation), communicators, webcam, background microphones, positioning tracker, etc.

Then, from these inputs, the Affective Analysis Module (Cambria et al., 2011) extracts emotional information that it is integrated by a multimodal fusion technique (Hupont et al., 2011). Besides recognizing the user's facial expressions with a webcam (Cerezo et al., 2007) new modules have being added to the system for the detection of affective information. In particular, affective cues are extracted from user's typed-in text, and right now a keyboard pulses and mouse clicks analyzer is being developed to detect states of boredom, confusion, frustration and nervousness of the user. The audio analyzer evaluates the text contents and provides an affective point in the Whissell's space (Whissell, 1989) for each sentence with emotional load. We are also considering the analysis of prosody in speech in a near future.

After gathering and analyzing the multimodal input information and taking into account the dialogue contents, the system has to manage the appropriate virtual agent's reactions and generate the answers to the user's questions. Two kinds of reactions can be distinguished: generative and deliberative. Generative actions are purely reactive: for example, should the user key something in, the virtual presenter will interrupt the presentation; should the user changes his/her position, the 3D actor look/orientation will change; if a lot of background noise is detected, it will request silence, etc. Deliberative character's reaction calls for a more complex analysis which elicits an answer through the user's voice interaction (dialogue contents) and the user's detected emotional state. The Deliberative/Generative Module basically generates an answer for the user's questions in text mode, and they are based on the recognition of patterns associated to fixed answers. These answers, however, vary according to the virtual character's emotional state (e.g. if the user insults the actor, the later will reply with an angry voice and facial expression), the detected emotional state of the user (captured from video, typed-in text, emoticons), or may undergo random variations so that the user does not get the impression of repetition should the conversation goes on for a long time. The development of this part of the system is based on chatbot technology under GNU GPL licenses: ALICE (ALICE, 2011) and CyN (CyN Project, 2001), and has been modified to include commands or calls to script files which results are returned to the user as part of the answer, when they are executed. This makes it possible, for example, to check the system time, log on to a website to check what the weather is like, etc.

Finally, the Motor Module is in charge of generating the system's outputs and the final animation of the 3D virtual character. The animations which the system works with are derived from two sources: animations from motion capture and animations generated by means of commercial software. Besides general animations that can be regular, cyclic and pose animations, our system allows to work with background and periodic animations, which are secondary animations executed automatically at certain established intervals. One typical example of this kind of animation is used to make an actor blink or register breathing motions. The implementation of secondary animations was done using Perlin's algorithms, based on coherent noise, and using random variation in the execution frequency in order to avoid unnatural movements.

For facial animation, we work with the six basic expressions defined by Ekman: anger, disgust, fear, happiness, sadness and surprise (Ekman, 1999), and animation blending is achieved with the help of the Cal3D library (CAL3D, 2011). The voice synthesis is made using SAPI5 (Long, 2002), a set of libraries and functions that enables to implement a voice synthesizer (in English), and, additionally, the Spanish voices offered by the Loquendo packages. SAPI gives information about the visemes (visual phonemes) that occur when delivering the phrase to be synthesized, what allows to solve the problem of labial synchronization. Visemes are used to model the actor's mouth movements. As the voice generated by text-voice converters usually sounds artificial, is was decided to provide Maxine virtual characters with an emotional voice by modifying the tone, frequency scale, volume and speed (Baldassarri et al., 2009). Script-files-based commands containing the facial expression, the speech and body parameters are generated and executed in real-time to achieve the appropriate body and facial animation (lip-synch and facial expressions) and emotional voice synthesis.

The additions made to the Motor Module in order to achieve more realistic and natural virtual characters improving their body non verbal communication capabilities are described in detail in next section.

3. Body language: Expressing emotions through the virtual agent body

As it has been said before, in order to obtain a more natural interaction with the users, similar to human face-to-face-communication, it is very important that virtual characters can be capable of expressing their emotions in a realistic way. In the early versions of Maxine, emotions were managed basically at a facial level: through the animation of the facial expressions, the modulation of the voice and the lip synchronization, as it was briefly described in Section 2. Here we present the work done to convert Maxine's virtual agents in credible and humanized characters capable of expressing their emotions through their bodies. For this purpose, the Motor Module of Maxine has been expanded with new features that take into account body language: the generation of emotional body expressions and gestures.

3.1 Emotions through body postures and movements

In Maxine, 3D virtual characters have improved their affective capabilities with the possibility of expressing their emotions through the animation of postures and movements of the whole body. The emotions expressed by the virtual humans' bodies can either be basic or mixed emotions. The basic ones are based on a discrete approach (the six emotions defined by Ekman) while the mixed ones are based in a continuous approach, more suitable for working with the wide range of emotions that can be usually found in social interaction.

3.1.1 Basic emotions

The **basic emotions** considered to be expressed by the virtual characters' bodies are those used in Maxine for facial animation, that is, the six universal emotions proposed by Ekman: anger, disgust, fear, happiness, sadness and surprise, plus the neutral one. Although the problem of facial expression of emotions has been widely studied, there are only few works about the body expression of emotions; probably because of some outward expressions of emotions (body language) have different meanings in different cultures. However, there are some ergonomic studies that establish the more common body postures adopted when one of the six basic emotions is felt. These studies specify the changes in the weight of the body (forward, backward, neutral) and the values of the more important positions and angles of the bones. Our work is based on the study carried out by Mark Coulson (Coulson, 2004) about the expression of emotions through body and movement.

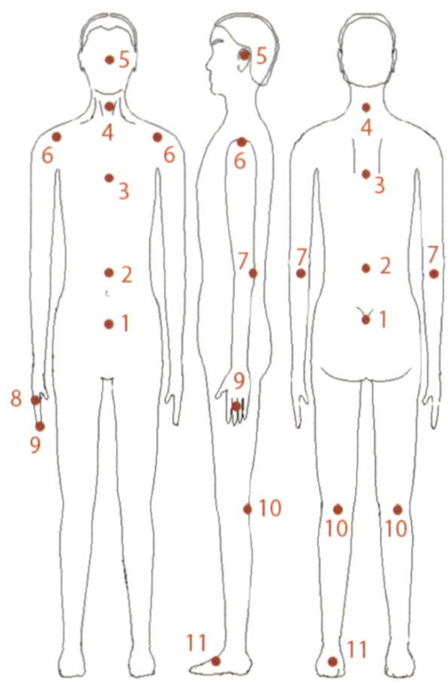

Fig. 2. MPEG4 reference points.

However, for the integration in our system, the values of Coulson had to be adapted to the MPEG4 standard (MPEG4, 2011) (see the positions of the MPEG4 reference points in Figure 2) and, in some cases, they have also been slightly modified, as it is explained later in this section.

The final values of the rotations and movements of each point for showing the different basic emotions can be seen in Table 1. All the values in the table are in degrees refered to the bones' rotations and positive values are considered when the rotation is forward.

	PELVIS (pelvis) ●1	SPINE 4 (abdomen) ●2	SPINE 3 (backbone) ●3	SPINE 2 (neck) ●4	SPINE 1 (head) ●5	RIGHT&LEFT ARM 1(shoulders) ●6		RIGHT&LEFT ARM 1(elbows) ●7		RIGHT&LEFT ARM 2 (hands) ●8		RIGHT&LEFT HAND (fingers) ●9	RIGHT&LEFT LEG 1 (back of the knees) ●10		RIGHT&LEFT LEG 2 (feet) ●11	
						Rotation(1)	Turn(2)	Right	Left	Right	Left		Right	Left	Right	Left
Anger	0°	0°	14°	17°	8°	6°	13°	80°	18°	16°	0°	closed	0°	10°	-	forward
Disgust	6°	20°(3)	0°	0°	-15° - 20°(3)	11°	0°	55°	65°	-30°	-50°	opened	0°	11°	-	backward (tiptoe)
Fear	10°	0°	10°	30°	12°	25°	5°	50°	80°	0°	-22°	closed	22°	24°	-	forward
Happiness	8°	-12°	-10°	0°	-5°	-13°	0°	100°		0°		closed	0°		forward	-
Sadness	12 - 14°	0°	20°	30°	25°	-20°	0°	30°		30°		half closed	0°	5°	-	forward
Surprise	0°	-17°	-12°	-5°	-13°	10°	0°	90°		0°		opened	25°	0°	backward (tiptoe)	-

* Shoulder's rotation taking collarbone as turn point: positive values indicate up rotation and negative values indicate down rotation.

** Turn of the bone over itself, positive if the turn is forward

***Turn is considered to the sides.

Table 1. Values of the MPEG4 reference point positions in the body expression of the six basic emotions.

Following, some images of different basic emotions generated by our system considering the values described in Table 1, are shown. Figure 3 shows the body of a virtual character expressing the emotions of sadness (left) and fear (right).

It must be said that in some cases, such as in the emotion of anger, the values extracted from Coulson's work give a body posture too masculine (see Figure 4 left). So, for representing animating a female virtual character, some changes have been done and new body postures have been generated (Figure 4 right).

3.1.2 Mixed emotions: From a discrete to a continuous space

The first version of the system was based on the six emotions defined by Ekman (Ekman, 1999) but, in order to add more natural expressions to the virtual agents, the system has been enriched with the possibility of working with mixed emotions, changing from a discrete to a continuous approach.

The Ekman's *categorical* approach, where emotions are a mere list of labels, fails to describe the wide range of emotions that occur in daily communication. There are a few tentative efforts to detect non-basic affective states from deliberately displayed facial expressions, including "fatigue" (Ji et al., 2006), and mental states such as "agreeing", "concentrating", "interested", "thinking", "confused", and "frustrated" (Kaapor et al., 2007) (Yaesin et al.,

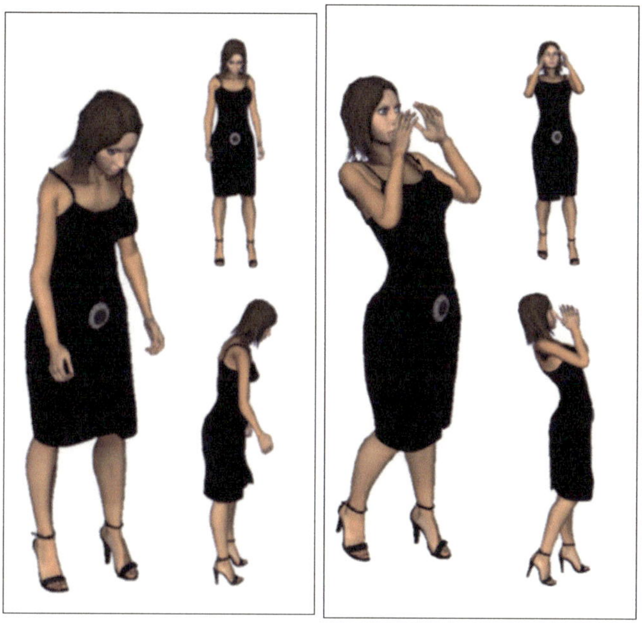

Fig. 3. Body expression of sadness (left) and fear (right).

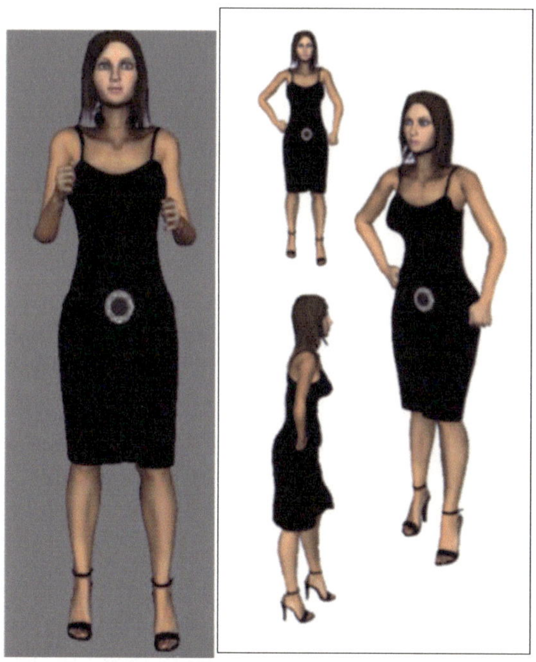

Fig. 4. Body expression of anger considering Coulson's values resulted in a too masculine posture (left). Body posture of anger adapted for a female virtual character (right).

2006). In any case, *categorical* approach presents a discrete list of emotions with no real link between them. To overcome this problem, some researchers, such as Whissell (Whissell, 1989) and Plutchik (Plutchik, 1980) prefer to view affective states not independent but rather related to one another in a systematic manner. In this work we decided to use one of the most influential evaluation-activation 2D models in the field of psychology: that proposed by Cynthia Whissell (Whissell, 1989). She considers emotions as a continuous 2D space whose dimensions are evaluation and activation. The evaluation dimension measures how a human feels, from positive to negative. The activation dimension measures whether humans are more or less likely to take some action under the emotional state, from active to passive. In her study, Whissell assigns a pair of values <evaluation, activation> to each of the approximately 9000 carefully selected affective words that make up her "Dictionary of Affect in Language". Figure 5 shows the position of some of these words in the evaluation-activation space.

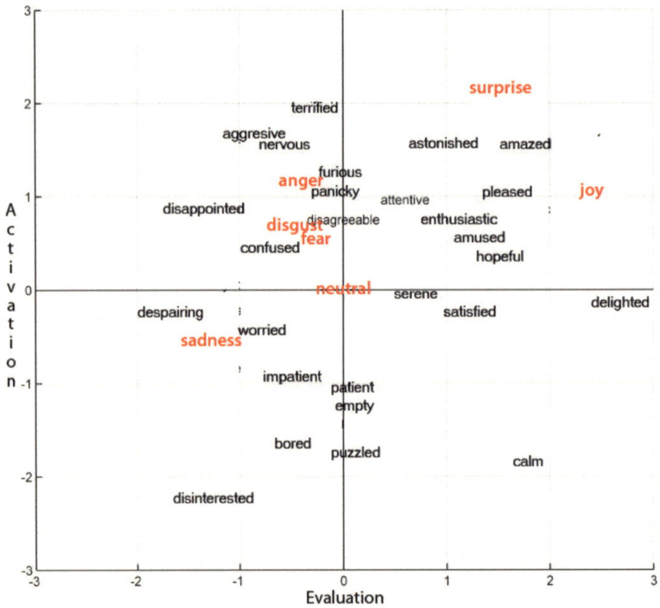

Fig. 5. Simplified Whissell's evaluation-activation space.

It can be seen that the emotion-related words corresponding to each one of Ekman's six emotions have a specific location (x_i, y_i) in the Whissell space (in bold in Figure 5). The final

(x, y) coordinates of a mixed emotion can be calculated as the centre of mass of the seven weighted points (corresponding with the Ekman's six basic emotions plus "neutral") in the Whissell's space following (1). In this way the output of the system is enriched with a larger number of intermediate emotional states.

$$x = \frac{\sum_{i=1}^{7} w_i * x_i}{\sum_{i=1}^{7} w_i} \quad \text{and} \quad y = \frac{\sum_{i=1}^{7} w_i * y_i}{\sum_{i=1}^{7} w_i} \tag{1}$$

In order to show the power of our system, we present images of the synthesis of the some specific mixed emotions, defined as combinations of weighted points of the basic ones. Following the equations defined in (1), the "astonishment" emotion shown in Figure 6 (left) can be represented in the 2D Whissell's space as a weighted combination of surprise, happiness and neutral while the emotion of "displeasure" results of considering a weighted mixed between disgust and happiness (see Figure 6 right).

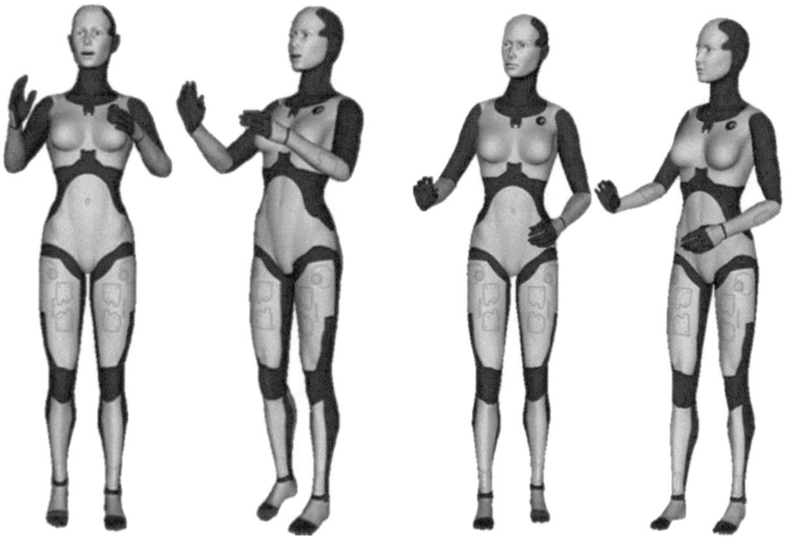

Fig. 6. Virtual character's expression of astonishment (left) and displeasure (right).

3.2 Gestures

Gestures are other way of non verbal communication, and usually comprise different parts of the body like arms, hands, fingers, legs, and feet movement. Gestures allow individuals to communicate a variety of feelings and thoughts, from contempt and hostility to approval and affection, often together with body language in addition to spoken words. However, the meaning of each gesture can vary across cultures, status, occupation, age or gender (Brislin, 1993). In our work we exclude these complex factors and deploy well-known and commonly used gestures in order to be used and understood everywhere. On the other hand, there are many gestures that are performed during social interaction in order to express or reinforce an emotion, such as self-touching gestures. Therefore, we decide to allow the addition of body gestures to the previously generated mixed emotions, based in the work of Su *et al.* (Su et al., 2007).

Summing up, our Gesture module allows the generation of the most commonly used gestures, such as nodding, shaking the head, hiding the face, clenching the fists, saying O.K., or greeting someone with the hand; or allows adding gestures to other body postures and movements, in order to improve the expression of emotions.

Following, some examples are shown. Figure 7 shows a virtual character expressing negation by moving the forefinger, while in Figure 8 the virtual agent is greeting with her hand.

Figure 9 presents a virtual character performing the "astonishment", "confusion" and "displeasure" emotions after having improved them with the gestures of touching the neck, the forehead and folding the arms, respectively.

Fig. 7. Virtual character refusing something by moving the forefinger.

Fig. 8. Virtual character greeting with the hand.

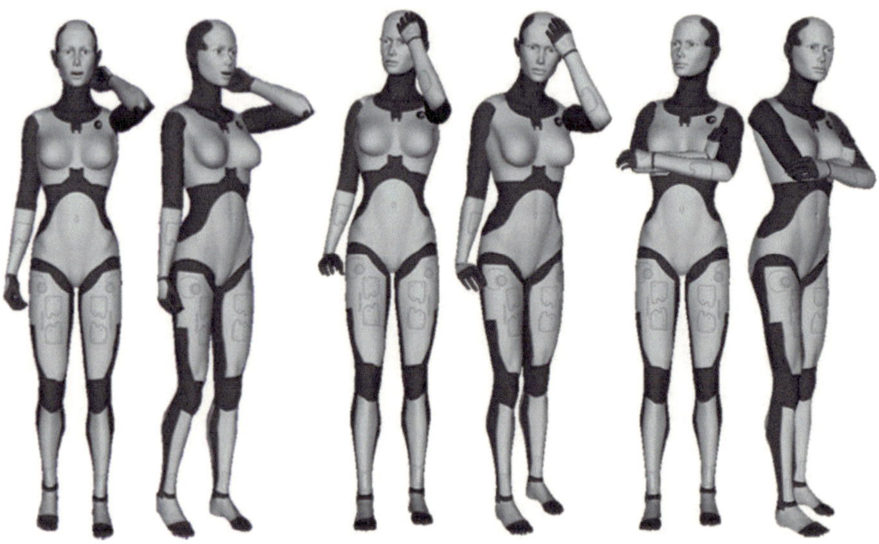

Fig. 9. "Astonishment" emotion was improved with the touch one self's neck gesture (left), "confusion" emotion was improved with the touch one self's forehead gesture (middle), and "displeasure" emotion was improved with the arms-folded gesture.

4. An affective virtual interpreter to Spanish Sign Language

The features previously described have been used in the development of an application that uses emotional virtual characters as virtual interpreters, capable of translating from written or spoken Spanish language to Spanish Sign Language (LSE).

In the last few years, the design of computer application interfaces has evolved in order to guarantee the accessibility of applications to everyone. Regarding the deaf community, a considerable amount of work has been done in the automatic translation into sign languages. These languages, unfortunately, are not universal and each country has its own variety. In fact, most of the work done (Ong & Ranganath, 2005) is based on English grammar. This is the case of the works derived from ViSiCAST (Visicast, 2011) and eSIGN (ESIGN, 2011) projects. Regarding Spanish Sign Language (LSE), San-Segundo et al. (San-Segundo et al., 2008) have developed a translator based on Spanish grammar that uses VGuido, an eSIGN avatar, but their application domain is very restricted (sentences spoken by an official when assisting people who are applying for their Identity Card). None of the previous works take into account emotional states. But, as in face-to-face communication, mood, emotions and facial expressions are an integral part of sign languages (Olivrin, 2008). Words can considerable change their meaning depending on the mood or emotion of the speaker. Moreover, communicating in sign language without facial expressions would be like speaking in a monotonic voice: more boring, less expressive and, in some cases, ambiguous. The system presented in this paper is based on Spanish grammar, takes the emotional state into account and emotions are reflected in the signs performed by an affective virtual character.

4.1 The automatic translation system

An automatic translation system from phrases in Spanish into LSE was developed as an independent module in C++ language. The system considers the syntactical and morphological characteristics of words and also the semantics of their meaning. The translation of a sentence or phrase is carried out by four modules (see Figure 10).

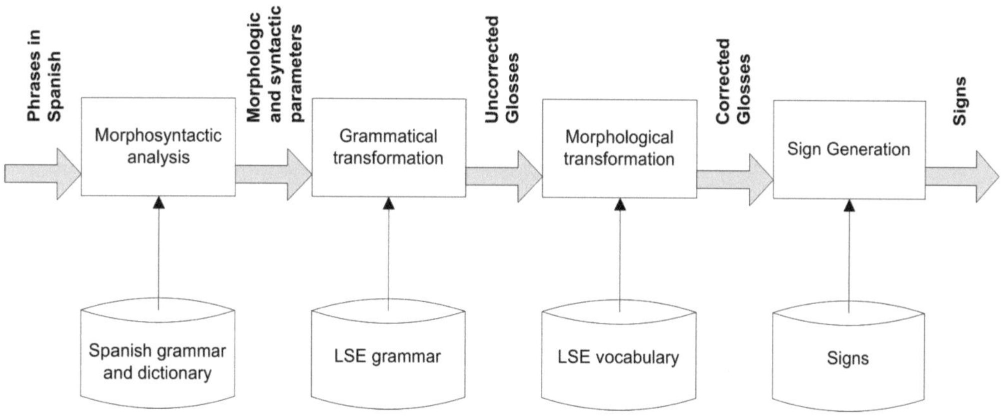

Fig. 10. Automatic translation system developed.

- **Morphosyntactic analysis**: A phrase in Spanish is used as input. A series of parameters containing all the morphological information of the words as well as the relations and syntactical dependencies among them are drawn from it. This module uses the FreeLing analyzer (FreeLing, 2011), which was migrated to the Windows system.

- **Grammatical transformation**: On the basis of the syntactic information gathered during the previous step, and through the application of grammatical rules, this module generates a series of glosses.
- **Morphological transformation**: Some of the glosses resulting from the previous step could be incorrect. This may occur when the original word in Spanish has no direct correlation to a term in LSE. Sometimes a synonym of that term will correlate directly to a term in LSE, but it can also occur that several signs are required in LSE to render a single word in Spanish. Or sometimes in Spanish several words can be used to express an idea that LSE expresses in a single sign. So, in this step, all the changes in the words are implemented, resulting in grammatically correct glosses.
- **Sign generation**: Once the appropriate glosses have been produced (those which correspond directly to signs), in this step they are translated into a representation format that allows to generate the appropriated animations.

4.2 Adding emotions to the translation process

The emotional state of deaf person influences the way that that person will communicate, just like anyone else. On the one hand, the construction of phrases and the signs that make them up are modified and on the other hand, the final realization of the signs is also modified. In the fully developed system, the inclusion of the user's emotional state provokes changes in two translation phases: grammatical rules are modified, and so is the final transformation of the signs.

- **Grammatical transformation:** As we have seen, each type of block is associated to a series of rules pertaining to its form and function. These procedures are modified to change the way of generating the translations according to emotional swings. Emotion influences meaning and leads to the repetition of certain words, such as the nucleus, or to the appearance of new ones (similar to question tags or pet expressions). However, it can also be the case that certain blocks alter the order of the words within them to emphasize some of them.
- **Sign generation:** Emotion also influences the way in which specific words are signed. Thus, for example, the word "*no*" can be accompanied by different gestures. When the person signing is happy, he or she will move their finger, but if the person is angry, he or she usually resorts to dactylology and signs "N-O". In order to take these cases into account, the dictionary used for final translation of the glosses into the chosen language of representation has been modified, allowing one and the same word to be translated differently depending on the emotional state parameter.

4.3 Managing the virtual interpreter

The automatic translation system previously described has been incorporated in Maxine's system within the Deliberative/Generative Module. The final management of the virtual interpreter is carried out by the Motor Module generating animations that take the face, body, gestures and emotions into account.

The inputs of Maxine can be either written or spoken Spanish, generating phrases, that are passed to the translation system, which returns the signs that must be animated. Thanks to

Maxine's capabilities, the user's emotional state can be captured by a webcam be supplied to the automatic translator to be taken into account. The output consists in an affective virtual interpreter playing the final signs (animations) corresponding to the translation into Spanish Sign Language.

Figure 11 shows images of the virtual interpreter signing interrogative particles in LSE (how, which, how many, why, what and who), in which not only the facial expressions but the position and movement of the hands, and the posture of other parts of the body are involved.

The results of considering the emotional state in the translated signs can be seen in next figures. Figure 12 and 13 show the different ways to sign the word "NO": if happy she/he just moves the head (Figure 12 left) or the head and the forefinger (Figure 12 right), but when she/he is very angry, the face reflect the emotional state and dactylology is used in order to reaffirm the message, signing N-O (see Figure 13).

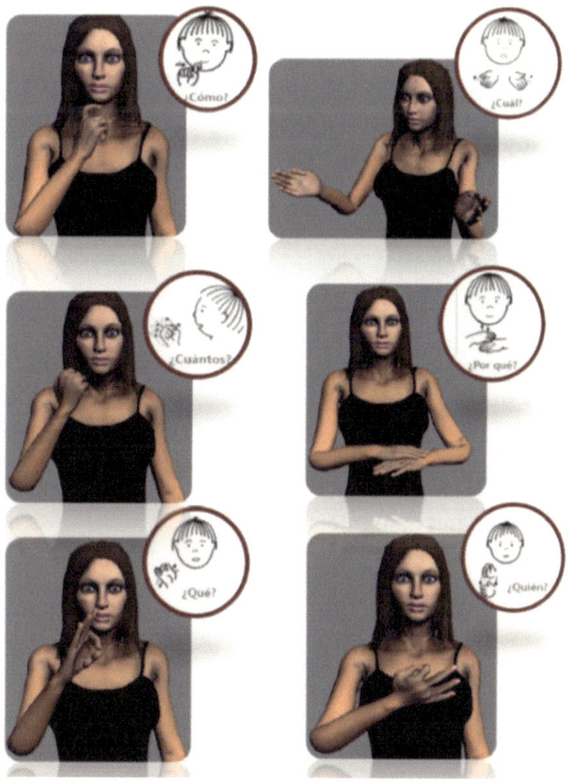

Fig. 11. Affective virtual interpreter signing different interrogative particles: how, which, how many, why, what and who (from left to right and from up to bottom).

Usually, affirmation is also signed in different ways depending on the emotional state of the person: if happy she/he just nods (see Figure 14), but if she/he is very angry, dactylology is used, signing S-I (YES in Spanish), as it is shown in Figure 15.

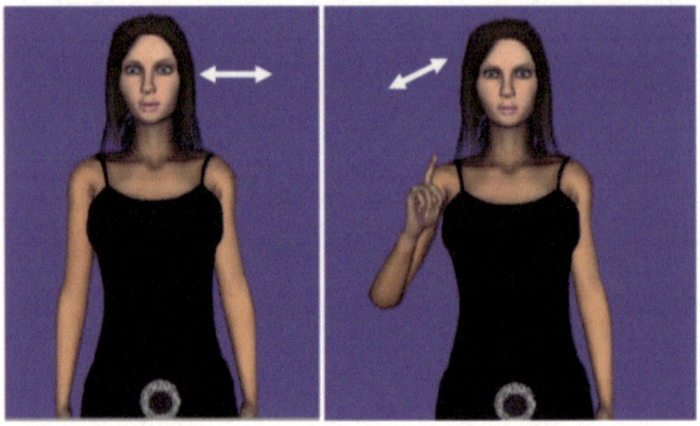

Fig. 12. The affective virtual interpreter says NO, when she is happy, shaking her head (left) or moving the forefinger (right).

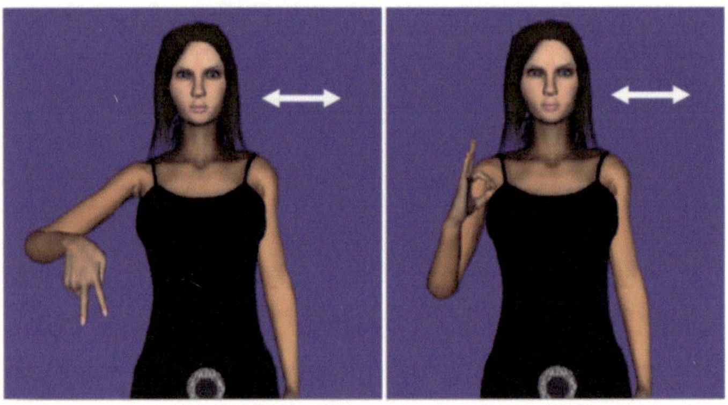

Fig. 13. The affective virtual interpreter says NO, when she is angry, shaking her head, through her facial expression and using dactylology.

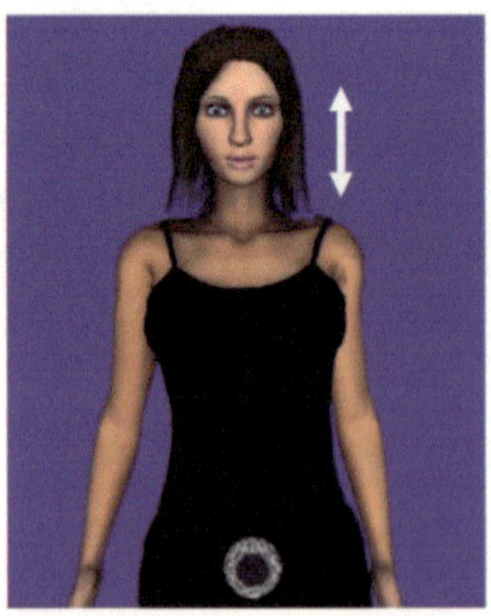

Fig. 14. The affective virtual interpreter says YES, when she is happy, nodding her head.

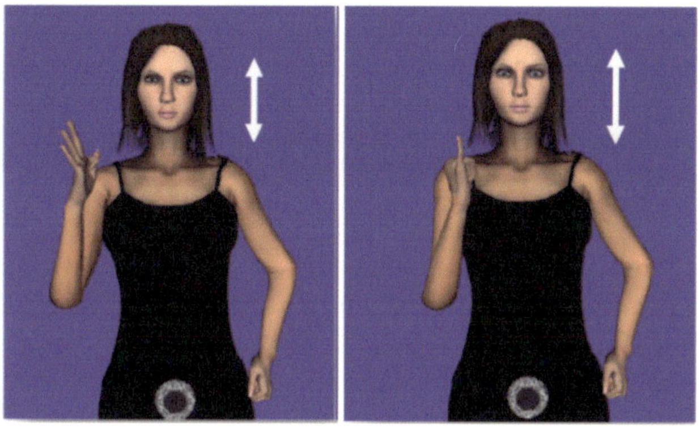

Fig. 15. The affective virtual interpreter says YES, when she is angry, nodding her head, changing her facial expression and using dactylology S-I (in Spanish).

The results generated with our system have been validated video-recording a real interpreter signing different sentences and comparing them with the same sentences performed by the virtual interpreter in order to verify the visual quality of the sign animations[1], as can be seen in Figure 16.

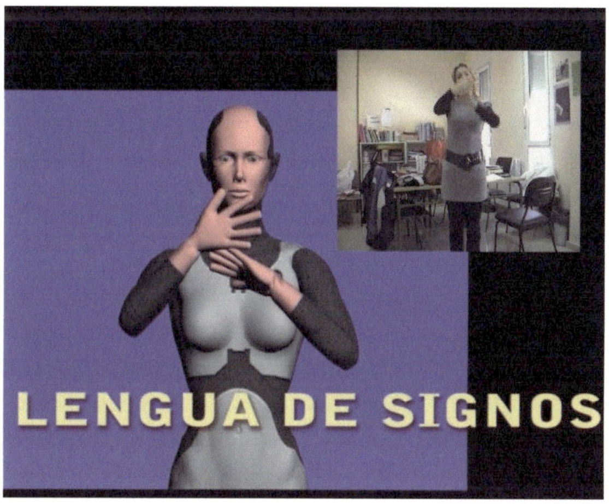

Fig. 16. Virtual and Real interpreters, signing the words "Sign Language" (in Spanish).

5. Conclusion

In this paper we have described the new features added to the Maxine system that allows multimodal interaction with users through affective embodied conversational agents. The virtual characters were already provided with facial expressions, lip-synch and emotional voice. However, in order to improve and obtain more natural human-computer interaction, Maxine virtual characters have now been endowed with new non-verbal communication capabilities: they are able to express their emotions through their whole body, by means of body postures and movements (considering basic and mixed emotions) and/or by corporal gestures.

[1] Videos of the animations can be found at our web page: http://giga.cps.unizar.es/affectivelab/video2.html

The potential of the affective agents provided with these new body language capabilities is presented through an application that uses virtual characters in order to enhance the interaction with deaf people. An emotional virtual interpreter translates from written or spoken Spanish language to Spanish Sign Language (LSE). The final signs performed take into account the interpreter's emotional state.

In the near future we will focus on enriching the interaction between the virtual character and the users including personality models for the virtual character and modifying the expression of emotions accordingly.

6. Acknowledgment

This work has been partly financed by the University of Zaragoza through the "AVIM-Agentes Virtuales Inteligentes y Multimodales" project and the Spanish DGICYT Contract Nº TIN2011-24660.

The authors want to thank the collaboration in this work of Lorena Palacio and Laura Sanz.

7. References

ALICE. (2011). Artificial Intelligence Foundation, Available from http://www.alicebot.org/

Baldassarri, S.; Cerezo, E. & Seron, F. (2008). Maxine: A platform for embodied animated agents. *Computers & Graphics* 32(3): pp. 430-437.

Baldassarri, S.; Cerezo, E. & Anaya, D. (2009). Emotional Speech Synthesis in Spanish for Natural Interaction. *New Trends on Human-Computer Interaction*, Chapter 15, pp. 151-160, Springer-Verlag.

Birdwhistell, R. L. (1985). *Kinesics and context: essays on body motion communication*. 4th Ed. Philadelphia: UPP. University of Pensylvania Press.

Brislin, R. (1993). *Understanding culture's influence on behavior*. Hartcout Brace College Publishers, New-York.

CAL3D. (2011). Character Animation Library. Available from http://cal3d.sourceforge.net

Cambria, E.; Hupont, I.; Hussain, A.; Cerezo, E. & Baldassarri, S. (2011). Sentic Avatar: Multimodal Affective Conversational Agent with Common Sense, *Lecture Notes in Computer Science, LNCS 6456: Toward autonomous, adaptive, and context-aware multimodal interfaces: theoretical and practical issues*. Springer-Verlag, pp. 81-95

Caridakis, G; Raouzaiou, A.; Karpouzis, K. & Kollias, S. (2006). Synthesizing Gesture Expressivity Based on Real Sequences. *LREC Conference. Workshop on multimodal corpora: from multimodal behaviour theories to usable models.*

Cassell, J. & Bickmore, T. (2000). External manifestations of trustworthiness in the interface. *Communications of the ACM*, 43(12), pp. 50-56.

Cassell, Justine (2007). "Body Language: Lessons from the Near-Human" In J. Riskin (ed.) *Genesis Redux : Essays in the History and Philosophy of Artificial Intelligence* . Chicago: University of Chicago Press., pp 346-374.

Cerezo, E.; Hupont, I.; Manresa, C.; Varona, J.; Baldassarri, S.; Perales, F. & Seron F. (2007). Real-time Facial Expression Recognition for Natural Interaction. *Lecture Notes in Computer Science, LNCS 4478: Pattern Recognition and Image Analysis*. Springer-Verlag, pp. 40-47.

Coulson, M. (2004). Attributing emotion to static body postures, *Journal of Nonverbal behavior* 28 (2), pp. 117-139

Cowie, R.; Doublas-Cowie, E.; Tsapatsoulis, N.; Vostis, G.; Kollias, S.; Fellenz, W. & Taylor, J.G. (2001). Emotion recognition in human computer interaction. *IEEE Signal Processing Magazine*, 1, pp. 32-80.

CyN Project. (2011). Available from http://www.daxtron.com/cyn.htm

de Rosis, F.; Pelachaud, C.; Poggi, I.; Carofiglio, V. and De Carolis, B. (2003). From Greta's mind to her face: modeling the dynamics of affective states in a Conversational Embodied Agent. *International Journal of Human- Computer Studies*, 59, 81-118.

Ekman, P. (1999). *Facial Expression, The Handbook of Cognition and Emotion*. John Wiley & Sons

ESIGN. (2011). Available from http://www.sign-lang.uni-hamburg.de/esign/

FreeLing. (2011). Available from http://garraf.epsevg.upc.es/freeling

Gunes, H.; Piccardi, M. & Pantic, M. (2008). From the lab to the real world: Affect Sensing recognition using multiples cues and modalities. *Affective Computing: Focus on Emotion Expression, Synthesis and Recognition*, pp. 185-218

Gunes, H.; Schuller, B.; Pantic, M. & Cowie, R. (2011). Emotion representation, analysis and synthesis in continuous space: A survey. *Proceedings of IEEE International Conference on Automatic Face and Gesture Recognition (FG'11), EmoSPACE 2011*, pp.827-834

Hartmann, B.; Mancini, M. & Pelachaud, C. (2005). Implementing expressive gesture synthesis for embodied conversational agents. *In Gesture Workshop (GW'2005)* pp. 188-199

Haviland J. B. (2004). Pointing, gesture spaces, and mental maps. In *Language and gesture*. Cambridge University Press.

Hupont, I; Ballano, S; Baldassarri, S. & E. Cerezo. (2011). Scalable Multimodal Fusion for Continuous Affect Sensing. *IEEE Symposium Series in Computational Intelligence 2011, (SSCI 2011)*, pp. 1-8.

Ji, Q., Lan, P. & Looney, C. (2006). A probabilistic framework for modeling and real-time monitoring human fatigue, *IEEE Transactions on Systems, Man and Cybernetics, Part A*, vol. 36, pp. 862–875.

Kapoor, A.; Burleson, W. & Picard, R. (2007). Automatic prediction of frustration. *International Journal of Human-Computer Studies*, vol. 65, pp. 724–736.

Long. B. (2002). Speech Synthesis and Speech Recognition using SAPI 5.1. In: *European Borland Conference*, London.

Mancini, M. & Pelachaud, C. (2009). Implementing distinctive behavior for conversational agents, *in Gesture-Based Human-Computer Interaction and Simulation*, Lecture Notes in Computer Science, pp. 163-174.

Morris, D.; Collett, P.; Marsh, P. & O'Shaughnessy M. (1979). *Gestures, their origin and distribution*, Jonahtan Cape, London UK.

MPEG4 (2011). http://cordis.europa.eu/infowin/acts/analysys/products/thematic/mpeg4/coven/coven.htm

Noma, T. & Badler, N. (1997). A virtual human presenter. *Proceedings of IJCAI, Workshop on Animated Interface Agents*. pp. 45-51.

Olivrin, G. (2008). Composing Facial expressions with signing avatars, *Speech and Face-to-Face Communication Workshop*, Grenoble, France.

Ong, S. & Ranganath, S. (2005). Automatic sign language analysis: A survey and the future beyond lexical meaning, *IEEE Trans Pattern Analysis and Machine Intelligence*, Vol 27 (6), pp. 873-891

Pantic, M. & Bartlett, M. (2007). Machine Analysis of Facial Expressions. *Face Recognition*, In-Tech Education and Publishing, Vienna, Austria, pp 377-416.

Picard, R.W. (1997). *Affective Computing*. The MIT Press.

Plutchik R. (1980). *Emotion: a psychoevolutionary synthesis.* New York: Harper & Row.

Prendinger, H. & Ishizuka M. (2001). Simulating Affective Communication with Animated Agents. *Proceedings of the Eighth IFIP TC.13 Conference on Human-Computer Interaction*, pp. 182-189

Raouzaiou, A.; Karpouzis, K. & Kollias, S. (2004). Emotion Synthesis in Virtual Environments. *In Proceedings of 6th International Conference on Enterprise Information Systems.*

Rickel, J. & Johnson W. L. (2000) Task-oriented collaboration with embodied agents in virtual worlds, In J. Cassell, S. Prevost, E. Churchill and J. Sullivan (eds.), *Embodied Conversational Agents*. MIT Press, pp. 95-122.

San-Segundo, R.; Barra, R.; Córdoba, R.; D'Haro, L.F.; Fernández, F.; Ferreiros, J.; Lucas, J.M.; Macías-Guarasa, J.; Monero, J.M. & Pardo, J.M. (2008). Speech to sign language translation system for Spanish, *Speech Communication*, Vol 50, pp. 1009-1020

Su, W.; Pham, B. & Wardhani, A. (2007). Personality and emotion-based high-level control of affective story character. *IEEE Transactions on Visualization and Computer Graphics* 13, pp. 284–287

Visicast. (2011). Available from http://www.visicast.sys.uea.ac.uk/

Whissell C. M. (1989). The dictionary of affect in language, *Emotion: Theory, Research and Experience*, vol. 4, The Measurement of Emotions, New York: Academic Press.

Yeasin, M.; Bullot, B. & Sharma, R. (2006). Recognition of facial expressions and measurement of levels of interest from video. *IEEE Transactions on Multimedia*, vol. 8, pp. 500–508.

Zhang, S.; Wu, Z.; Meng, H. & Cai, L.(2010). Facial Expression Synthesis Based on Emotion Dimensions for Affective Talking Avatar. In *Modeling Machine Emotions for Realizing Intelligence.* Springer Berlin Heidelberg, pp. 109-132

12

To See the Unseen – Computer Graphics in Visualisation and Reconstruction of Archaeological and Historical Textiles

Maria Cybulska
Institute of Architecture of Textiles, Technical University of Łódź, Poland

1. Introduction

Computer graphics is widely applied in many areas of science, engineering, education, advertising and entertainment. More and more often computer art can be seen in museums, both as individual works of art and as a supplement to museum exhibitions. The latter includes animation often used as a background enriching an exhibition or being simply an element of scenography. However, sometimes it can have a more important function. Specialized software and interactive devices permitting users to interact with a virtual world by manipulating objects can play an educational role. Multimedia presentations are sometimes used in interactive museum kiosks with touch-sensitive screens or on museum websites, permitting the looking of objects, some detail of their structure, rotating them or even looking inside. They can show a method of manufacturing, or natural and historical context.

Virtual artefacts we can see in museums or on the Internet are, in most cases, virtual copies or imitations of real historical objects. In most cases they are based on 3D scanning. However, these methods do not give satisfactory results, even when applied in the case of ceramic or metal sculptures, which are much easier to imitate than textiles. Despite the progress in 3D graphics, 360^0 photography still gives much better effects (Johansen, 2010).

The purpose of the research presented in this chapter is different. Methods of computer graphics are applied not to imitate or copy anything but to show what is hidden, what we can't see because of indirect contact with the object in the museum or because the object due to ageing is destroyed or sometimes even doesn't exist in any form but a short description (Andersson & Cybulska).

Computer graphics presented in the chapter were made with the use of *3ds max* software offering variety of tools, but also "maxscript" programming language. It allows the development of its own procedures that can be applied in the case of textiles.

2. Computer graphics in modelling textiles

2.1 Appearance of textiles

The appearance of textiles is a very complex phenomenon. It is the combined effect of many different factors: raw material, yarn and fabric structure, finishing and many other parameters resulting in a different properties as width, areal weight, stiffness, and so on. These parameters determine some other factors, as fabric texture or drapeability. On the other hand, the appearance of textiles is determined by light reflection and refraction, translucency, colour, etc. All these parameters should be taken into account in modelling and simulation of the textile object. (Cybulska & Florczak, 2006)

Fibres used in historical and contemporary textiles can be characterised by different cross-section and surface properties. For instance, cotton fibres have a form of twisted ribbon with a bean-like cross-section. A triangular cross-section of silk results in semigloss in contrast to circular polyester filament giving the thread or woven fabric a full gloss. Modern fibres are designed to have some particular properties, such as a good heat insulation or capilarity, which can be achieved mainly due to geometrical properties of the cross-section.

Fibres can be grouped together to create a coherent, continuous object called yarn or thread by wrapping, twisting or nodding them, according to yarn technology. Two or a higher number of yarns can be also twisted together creating plied structure. The appearance of yarn depends on the kind of fibres used: their length, diameter, luster and colour. Yarns made from filaments are smooth and glossy while these made from staple fibres are lustreless and hairy.

Woven fabrics are created from two sets of threads - the warp and the weft, which overlap and interlace with one another in a variety of ways called weave. The weave can be presented in the form of a diagram on squared paper, where squares filled with black mean the warp overlaps the weft, while white squares denote the overlaping weft. In mathematical terms it is simply a binary matrix which allows the controll of the loom mechanisms during the weaving.

The weave together with warp and weft structural parameters, colour and their spacing in the fabric result in the fabric patterning and appearance.

2.2 Modelling the fibres and yarns

The basic element of modelling is a grid object. Its shape depends on the geometric properties of the modelled element. In the case of fibre or yarn we can assume it is a kind of cylinder with different types of cross-section. Then the object can be modified using a variety of tools, which can change the structure according to specified parameters of the object or technology used, for instance by twisting, wrapping or bending the elements or by adding the noise to reflect the object's unevenness. To create the effect of reality we need to use some tools to determine the texture of the object - smoothness, hairiness, relief, translucency, glossiness, reflection and refraction of light.

Using software tools one can create models of fibre characterised by a different cross-section, diameter and length.We can start from a cylinder of an assumed cross-section. All fibre parameters can be further modified by extruding or twisting, according to the material characteristics. Procedures of the material editor can be used to determine some surface properties, like colour, roughness or smoothness, translucency, etc. This approach is correct if we want to visualise the fibre for educational purposes. For modelling the yarn we need to use much simplier models of fibres.

Fig. 1. Modelling the cotton fibre.

One can use two different methods of yarn modelling. The first one consists in giving the linear object the texture determined by the structural properties of the yarn. The presence of fibres is reflected by concavities and convexities on the cylindrical yarn surface. The effect can be achieved by some procedures of material editor. This method can be used in the visualisation of multifilaments.

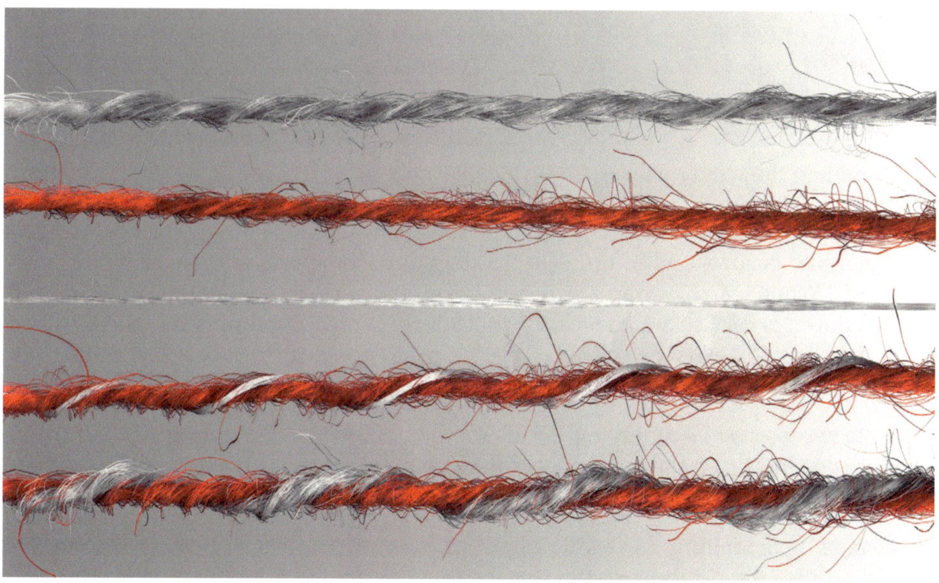

Fig. 2. Modelling the yarn. From the top: staple yarns, multifilament, plied yarns

In the case of staple yarn the method is not sufficient to create a realistic model. Thus the second method consists in forming the yarn from previously created 3D models of fibres, by distributing them along the yarn axis. The method allows the setting of some predetermined features, such as yarn unevenness or yarn hairiness for staple yarn (Cybulska & Florczak, 2006).

2.2 Modelling the woven fabric

Simulation of the woven fabric proceeds in two stages. The first one consists in forming the fabric from previously modelled linear elements. One can use both the exact simulation of yarn or yarn modelled by a simplified method. In the first case one can get a magnified image of fabric with clearly seen fibres. It is also possible to use the elements plied from two or more linear elements such as a warp or weft.

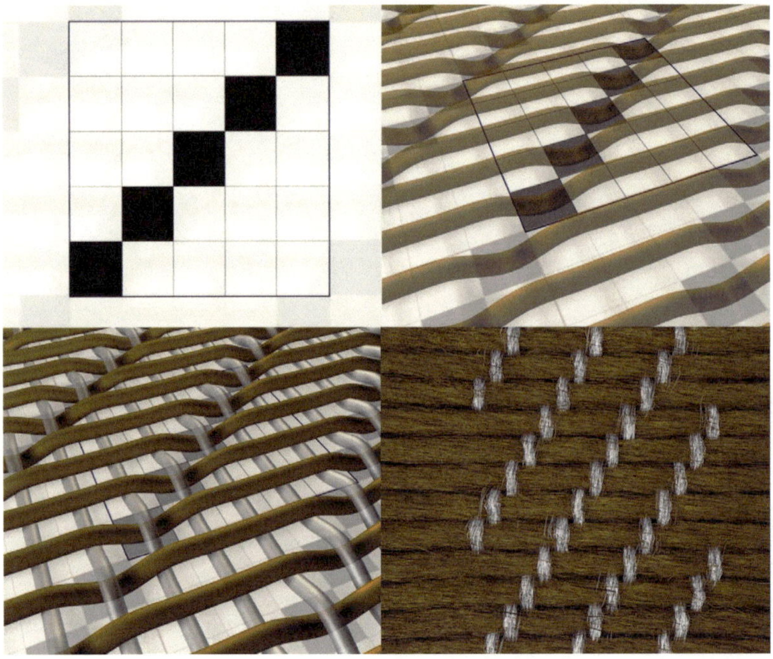

Fig. 2. Modelling the woven fabric

The elements are interlaced accordingly to the previously chosen weave presented in Fig.1 (top left). The number of rows and columns in the diagram correspond to the number of weft and warp threads. White warp overlap green weft if the appropriate square in the diagram is filled with black, thus it is very easy to develop a procedure for creating simplified models of woven fabric on the basis of binary matrix. The relative positioning of threads is determined by the diameter and spacing of warp and weft in the fabric we want to visualise.

The next stage consists in simplifying the 3D model of fabric by converting it to the flat object with texture depending on the properties of the raw material one wants to use. The calculation window allows one to determine some physical properties of fabric, such as areal weight.

The last stage of modelling the textile object of interest consists in placing the previously designed and visualised fabric on the surface of different kinds of 3D objects (Cybulska & Florczak, 2006).

3. Virtual reconstruction of textiles

3.1 Methodology

Textiles represent a variety of structures, materials and technologies, sometimes complex and often distorted, which makes them especially difficult to analyse by archaeologists or historians of art. In many cases documentation of textile collections is incomplete, using traditional, manual methods and thus not precise. It doesn't give us any idea of how the object originally looked. AIt is especially important in the case of archeological textiles which are often fragmentary preserved, colourless, and thus hard to appreciate and understand by the unprepared visitor. Reconstruction of these textiles on the loom can be done. However, this approach is not always possible and sometimes not even reasonable. Reconstructed this way object needs proper storage, exhibiting and conservation, and is rather costly[1]. In 2003 at the Institute of Architecture of Textiles, Technical University of Lodz, the idea arose to apply quite new tools in reconstructing textiles, using the method of computer graphics.

Reconstruction of textiles on the basis of excavated residues or fragments from museum collections, both real on the loom and virtual using 3D graphics methods, needs knowledge of historical manufacturing methods and the data concerning the reconstructed object. It requires complex analysis, including iconography, historical context, dyes applied, structure and the technology of threads, woven fabric and other components.

Among many available methods of modern analysis of textiles one can mention optical microscopy and image analysis for determination of structure; scanning electron microscopy (SEM), infrared spectroscopy (IR Spectroscopy) and atomic absorption or atomic emission spectroscopy (AAS/AES) for determination of the materials; high performance liquid chromatography (HPLC) for dyes analysis (Cybulska et al., 2008).

The whole procedure of reconstruction includes the following stages:

1. Documentation of the object including photographic documentation of the whole object and its components, sampling the material for further physical and chemical analysis, acquisition of microscopic images of the material.
2. Determination of the raw material and dyes.
3. Structural analysis including the processing of registered images, determination of structural parameters of fibres, yarns and fabric and determination of the object technology, structure and ornaments.
4. Virtual reconstruction of all components of the object, i.e. fibres, yarns and woven structures and reconstruction of the whole object.

3.2 Reconstruction using 3D graphics

The first stage of virtual reconstruction of the textile object is a careful analysis of the structure. In Fig.3. we can see a fragment from the Roman period made on weighted and tablet looms. According to archaeological experience it is a fragment of a parade cloak.

---

[1] Attempts to reconstructing textiles have been undertaken since a long time. Among the most interesting are the works of dr Karl Schlabow – founder and director of Textilmuseum Neumünster. On reconstructed warp-weighted loom he wove two beautiful Prachtmantels - replicas of those found in offering deposits in Thorsberg and Vehnemoor bogs. However this kind of reconstruction is difficult and time-consuming (it took several months) and, first of all, it requires skills in weaving on an ancient loom. (Schlabow 1976).

Fig. 3. Fragment of parade cloak from Odry, Poland

We need to visualise all identified structures using described in section 2 methods, taking into account all the results of structural analysis of yarns and woven fabrics. In Fig.4 we can see the main fabric of the cloak and two kinds of border made on tablets.

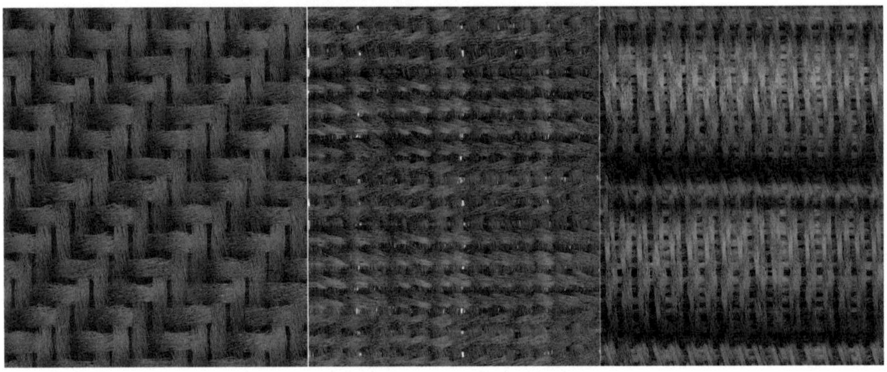

Fig. 4. Visualisation of different types of woven structures

We need to know how many tablets were used, what was their shape and what way they were rotated. In the case of patterned object we additionally need to determine the pattern and the colour of threads. In the case of the pattern presented in Fig.5. it is necessary to determine what is the order and the number of warp and weft threads in each identified colour.

At the end we need to determine the shape and size of the original object. Sometimes it possible to determine this on the basis of analysis of preserved fragments, however in most cases we use similar archaeological finds which are better preserved or analogical objects from museum collections.

3.3 Reconstruction using raster graphics

In museum collections there are numerous textiles which are partly destroyed. For many reasons conservation of these textiles rarely consists in reconstructing their original appearance. There is no way to bring back the original intensity of faded colours. Sometimes it can be hazardous to apply new materials on fragile, weakened silks or linens. However,

Fig. 5. Visualisation of the pattern

Fig. 6. Fragment of wall hanging (embroidery and appliqué work). Top from the left: before conservation, after conservation, after virtual conservation. Bottom from left: wall hanging before and after virtual conservation

we can make an attempt to reconstruct their appearance using computer graphics. This process we call "virtual conservation" permitting not only the correction of faded colours, but also the "replacement" of missing threads or larger fragments of fabric or embroidery, or to "remove" the results of improper conservation of the object.

On the basis of materials we need, we can organise the collection of patterns reflecting different kinds of threads and woven fabrics and apply them using brushes, stamps and many other tools. Although it looks quite easy, this approach also needs careful analysis of the object to determine all materials which were originally used and the whole decoration we need to restore.

4. Exemplary applications of computer graphics in the visualisation and reconstruction of historical and archaeological textiles

4.1 Woven fabric from the "princess" grave, Leśno, Poland

In the grave dated from the 2nd century and called the "princess" grave due to the rich equipment and a young woman buried there, the numerous fragments of wool fabric were found. (Kanwiszerowa & Walenta 1985). Most of them were probably residues of clothing, because they were found just near the skeleton. However, several fragments were found in, under and on the edges of a bronze pot. The arrangement gave the impression that the pot was wrapped with the fabric and deposited as burial goods for the women for her journey to the other world. (Maik 2005, 98-112).

The fabric was initially classified as an open work. However, microscopic and chemical analysis showed the residues of putrefied fibres (probably linen) and traces of crimp on the survived wool threads. It caused one to assume the fabric was originally made from wool and linen. The fabric was made with 2/2 twill weave. Using image analysis it was possible to determine the diameter, crimp and spacing of the yarn, the number of existing woollen yarns and previously existing linen ones. Analysis of dyes indicated the presence of indigotin, giving the blue colour of wool (Walton, 1993). The flax, as a cellulose fibre, was not yet dyed in that time, so it was assumed the linen threads were in natural colour. The reconstruction of fabric can be seen in Fig. 8 (Cybulska et al., 2009).

4.2 Parade cloak from Gronowo, Poland

In the male grave in Gronowo, dated from the 4th century, numerous fragments of two fabrics and fringes were found next to the man's feet. They were all compacted into one ball with the metal spur inside. After cleaning the find it occurred the fabrics are residues of two prachtmantels with tablet woven borders and fringes. One of the cloaks was monochrome, the second was polychrome chequered from dark and light brown threads (Fig. 5). They were probably used to wrap the dead men body (Maik, 1979). The analysis of dyes was made for polychrome fabric only. Tannin was found in the dark threads indicating brown colour. As there was no dye found in the light threads, they were probably in natural wool colour (Walton, 1993). Further analysis allowed to determine the object structure. The main fabric was made on a weighted loom using twill weave 2/2 S. Borders were made on 30 tablets, with density 13 tablets per 1 cm, all from the light thread used as warp. Fringes were in different colours, depending on their position in relation to the main fabric.

Fig. 7. Fragment of textile found inside the bronze pot in Leśno

Fig. 8. Reconstruction of the woven fabric from the "princess" grave from Lesno

In the next stage all elements were virtually reconstructed, including the main fabric, borders, corners and fringes. All these elements were used to reconstruct the whole cloak (Fig. 9) (Cybulska et al., 2009).

4.3 Orphrey from Tum

Fragments of embroidery found during the excavation in 1955 in the grave dated from the 16th century in the collegiate church in Tum, Poland, were placed under the hips and thighs of the buried body. The position of the textile, the fact that it was clergyman buried in the grave and the analysis of the fragments, makes one assume that the object is a fragment of a chasuble. The whole object includes a number of fragments of figural embroidery, which was the orphrey decorating the back of the chasuble. We can not be sure that the fragments include all the material that survived to our time. In the 1950's of the 20th century textiles were not treated as carefully as today. The object was moved from one place to another approximately sixty years after excavation. Thus some fragments could hale been overlooked or become lost.

Fig. 9. Textile fragments and reconstruction (at the bottom and on right) of the parade cloak from Gronowo

In its current state it includes a number of separated pieces of embroidery. Five fragments represent the heads in different positions: one head with nimbus and one with nimbus and curled hair, two heads with no nimbus in half-profile, both with curled hair and one head with crown. The other fragments represent the second crown, regular fragment of embroidery resembling the cloth, the nimbus attached to the long fragment of embroidery, which was probably the background for the figures and the long piece of embroidery in a form of a meander. The best preserved fragments are the beautifully elaborated figure with raised hands, one foot and no head and the coat of arms of three gold fish in a red field.

Fig. 10. Orphrey from the Tum collegiate church. On the left – the arrangement of surviving fragments, on the right – reconstruction of the orphrey by means of computer graphics

On the basis of analogical historical objects and analysis of the surviving fragments we made an attempt to reconstructing the orphrey. At the beginning we had to carefully analyse all fragments and their hypothetical positioning in the orphrey. We prepared the background in the form of the back of the chasuble with the orphrey in the shape of cross approximately 20 cm wide. We carefully placed all fragments on the drawn orphrey. Analysis of the surviving fragments allowed to associate them with a presentation of the tree of Jesse and the scene of the Crucifixtion.

In Fig. 10 and 11 one can see the embroidery as it would look if the whole object had survived to our time. In the virtual reconstruction we used only images of original elements of the preserved fragments (Cybulska et al., 2012).

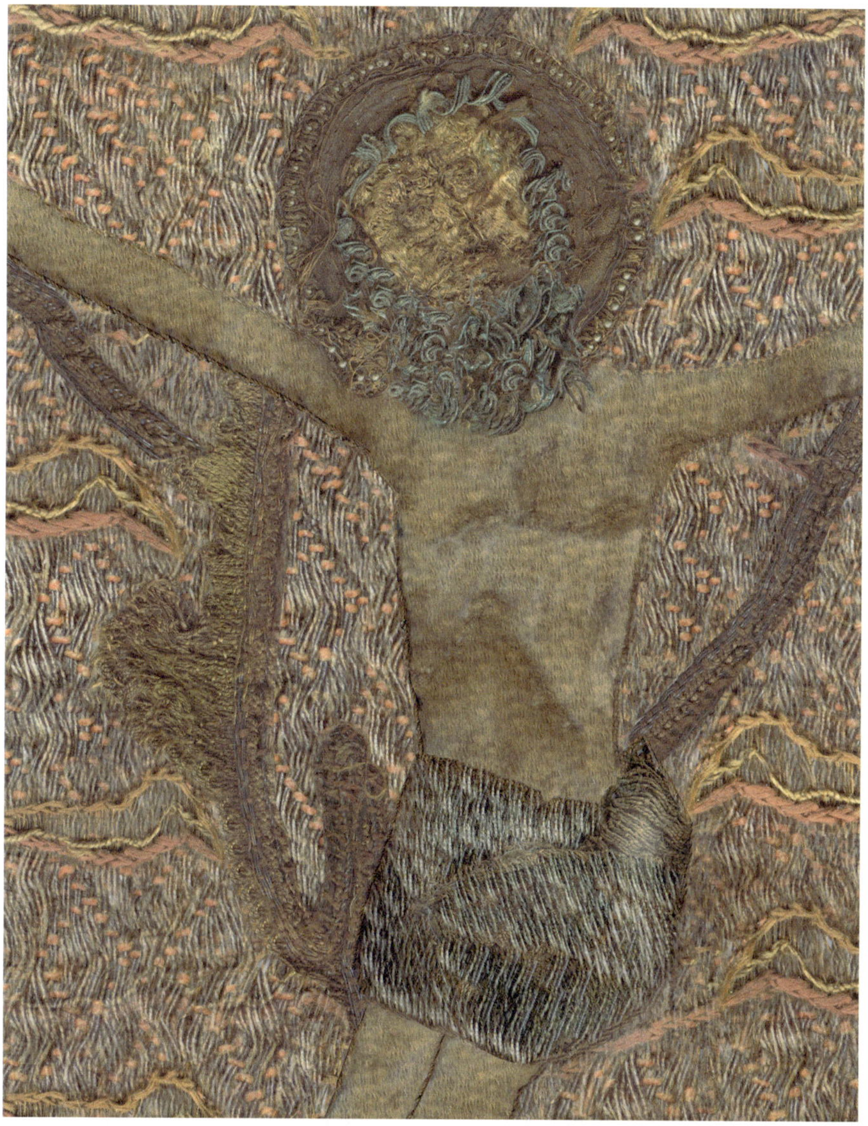

Fig. 11. Orphrey from the Tum collegiate church. Detail of the reconstruction of orphrey

4.4 Visualisation of the complex structures

The 18th century chasuble from the Lowicz cathedral represents a complex textile structure with two independent layers. The background is from pink silk taffeta. On the top is placed the hand-made silver net. The net was made on the basis of the four-cross silk leno fabric. Metal thread consists of a silver strip wrapped around a linen core. Silver threads (two in one course) are put onto the leno and sewn together with a white silk thread. The successive stages of the fabric formation are visualized and presented in Fig.11. In the last stage the net is laid on the pink taffeta background. This kind of visualisation can be a part of object documentation and support its conservation.

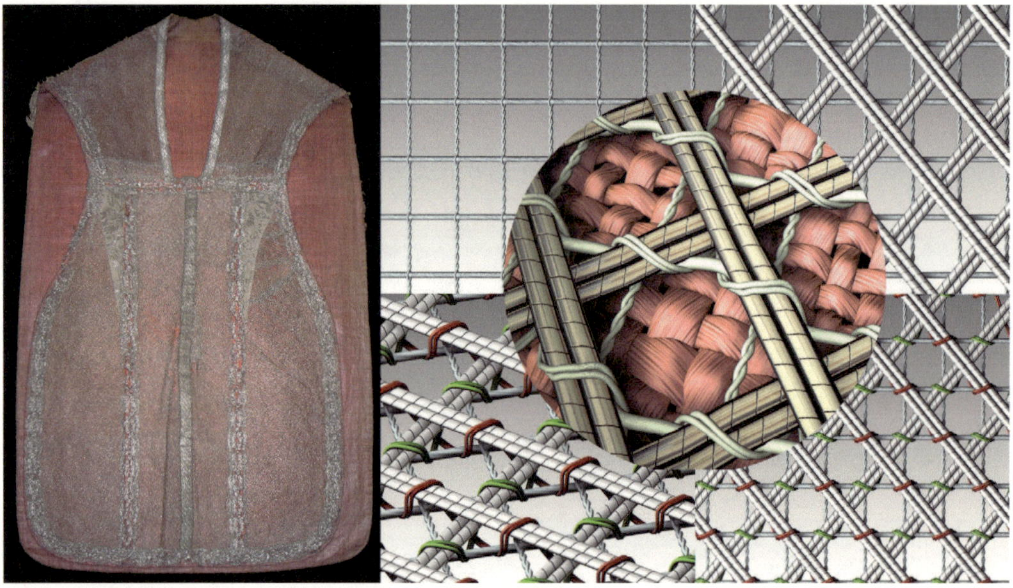

Fig. 12. Chasuble form the pink taffeta decorated with silver net. Visualization of the structure.

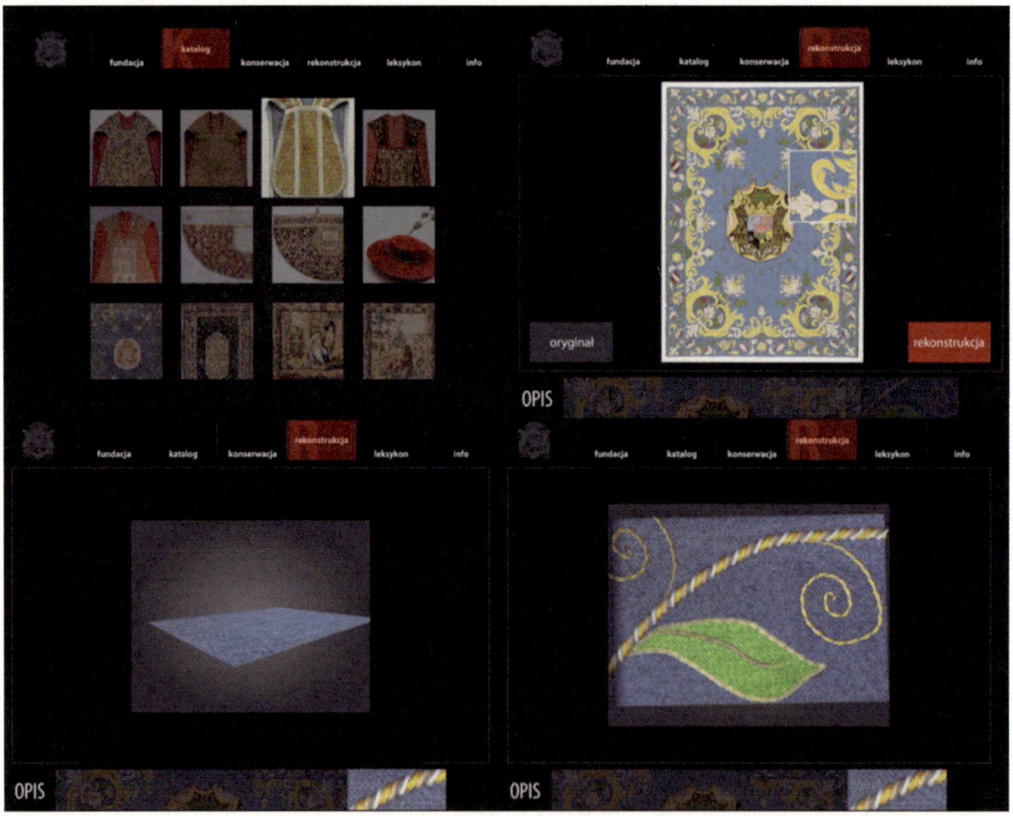

Fig. 13. Exemplary screens from kiosk presentation for the exhibition "Feast of Baroque"

4.5 Multimedia presentation in the museum

People visiting museums often complain about the way objects are exhibited. A long distance from the object, darkness, glass show-cases reflecting external light, not allowing one even to clearly see the objects, not talking about direct contact. The solutions that one uses to preserve works of art do not at the same time really allow one to appreciate them. Thus more and more often exhibitions of works of art are supported by multimedia presentations with easy access to knowledge concerning the objects. Using multimedia we can provide not only the text and images of the objects as they look now. We can also show some details of the structure, present what is hidden, what we can't see in the museum because of indirect contact with the object or because the object due to ageing is has been destroyed. Reconstruction by means of computer graphics can be one of the elements of multimedia presentation, which can offer also a closer look at the details of the object which can't be directly seen. It can present the conservation the object was treated with and the knowledge for visitors who want to know more, in the form of on-line lexicons of technical and artistic terms. In the presentation for the museum kiosk we can use all kinds of digital works: photographs, movies and computer works, as animations, visualisations and reconstructions. Flash presentation made for the exhibition "Feast of Baroque" in Wilanow Royal Palace, included all above mentioned elements.

5. Conclusions

The main advantage of virtual reconstruction is their accessibilty not only in the museum, but also on the Internet, both for professionals interested in the subject and society as a whole. Apart from the way they are presented they can clearly show the whole reconstructed object and some details of the structure. The educational role of reconstruction is also very important. When studying any archaeological object in its current state, a chance to know its original structure and appearance is very valuable. Archaeological textiles are very good example - colour and shapeless residuals can get back their form and beauty.

Virtual reconstructions of textiles can also serve as a good and interesting supplement to museum collections. It is well known that as much as we know is as much as we can see and understand and thus more appreciate the merits of the objects we watch. Textiles are very good examples. They are often treated the same way as paintings, however the closer one looks at complicated structures and the variety of techniques and material used in one object the more enchanted even indifferent or sceptical spectators can become.

6. References

Andersson E. & Cybulska M. (2012). Textile production, tools and technology - how to make textiles visible on the basis of an interpretation of an UR III text. In: *Textile Production and Consumption in the Ancient Near East. Archaeology, Epigraphy, Iconography*. Koefoed, H., Nosch, M.-L & Andersson Strand, E. (Ed.), Ancient Textiles Series, Oxbow Books, Oxford, England (in print)

Cybulska, M. and Florczak, T. (2005) Application of 3D graphics methods in textile designing, *Proceedings of VII International Conference ArchTex 2005*, pp. 182-186

Cybulska M. & Maik J (2007). Archaeological textiles - a need of new methods of analysis and reconstruction. *FIBRES & TEXTILES in Eastern Europe,* Vol. 18, No. 3 (80) pp. 100-105

Cybulska M., Jedraszek-Bomba A., Kuberski S. & Wrzosek H. (2008). Methods of Chemical and Physicochemical Analysis in the Identification of Archaeological and Historical Textiles. *FIBRES & TEXTILES in Eastern Europe,* Vol. 16, No. 5 (70) pp. 67-73.

Cybulska M., Florczak T. & Maik J. (2009). Virtual reconstruction of archaeological textiles. In: *NESAT X,* Oxbow Books, Oxford, England, ISBN-13: 978-1-84217-370-1

Cybulska M., Florczak T. (2009). Multimedia presentation for the exhibition "Celebration of Baroque. The Artistic Patronage of Primate Michał Stefan Radziejowski (1645-1705)", Wilanow Royal Palace, May 12 - September 15, 2009, Warsaw, Poland

Cybulska M. (2010). Reconstruction of Archaeological Textiles. *FIBRES & TEXTILES in Eastern Europe,* Vol. 18, No. 3 (80) pp. 100-105

Cybulska M., Maik J., Orlińska-Mianowska E., Kuberski S. (2012). Figural Embroidery from Tum Collegiate Church - Analysis, Reconstruction and Identification, In: *NESAT XI,* VML Verlag (in print)

Kanwiszerowa, M. and Walenta, K. (1985) Grób książęcy nr 1 z Leśna na Pomorzu Wschodnim, *Prace i Materiały Muzeum Archeologicznego i Etnograficznego w Łodzi, seria archeologiczna,* 29, 101-127

Johannes K. (2010). Digital Costume Display, *Proceedings of Textile Society of America Symposium " Textiles & Settlement: From Plains Space to Cyber Space",* Lincoln, Ne, USA, October 2010, Retrieved from http://digitalcommons.unl.edu/

Kanwiszerowa, M. & Walenta, K. (1985) Grób książęcy nr 1 z Leśna na Pomorzu Wschodnim, *Prace i Materiały Muzeum Archeologicznego i Etnograficznego w Łodzi, seria archeologiczna,* 29, pp. 101-127

Maik, J. (1979) Tkaniny wykopaliskowe z cmentarzyska w Gronowie, woj. koszalińskie, *Materiały Zachodniopomorskie, 22: 1976,* pp.111-121.

Schlabow, K. (1976) *Textilfunde der Eisenzeit in Norddeutschland,* Göttinger Schriften zur Vor- und Frühgeschichte, 15, Neumünster, Karl Wachholtz Verlag.

Walton, P. (1993) Wools and Dyes in Northern Europe in the Roman Iron Age, *Fasciculi Archaeologiae Historicae,* 6, 61-68.

13

Developing an Interactive Knowledge-Based Learning Framework with Support of Computer Graphics and Web-Based Technologies for Enhancing Individuals' Cognition, Scientific, Learning Performance and Digital Literacy Competences

Jorge Ferreira Franco[1,2] and Roseli de Deus Lopes[1]
[1]*Laboratory of Integrated Systems, Polytechnic School of the University of São Paulo,*
[2]*Ernani Silva Bruno, Primary School, Municipal Secretary of Education, São Paulo,*
Brazil

1. Introduction

The knowledge related to computer graphics principles, virtual reality, web3D and other advanced information visualization tools and techniques as well as low cost, but high quality hardware and software facilities has gained growing accessibility over the last decade. However, there have been the challenges of influencing and supporting individuals' skills, cognitive competencies and learning performance enhancements based on the mentioned principles and technologies (Dede, 2009); (Franco et al., 2009); (O' Connor & Cohn, 2010); (Osberg, 1997 a, b); (Winn, 1997); (Youngblut, 1998). It includes improving citizens' traditional and digital literacy skills and scientific competences related to reading, writing, mathematics and sciences (Franco & Lopes, 2009, 2011); (OECD/PISA in focus 2, 2011); (PISA, 2010); (Mervis, 2011); (UNESCO, 2008); (Wilson et al., 2010).

Hence, there has been the necessity of improving educational policy actions for decreasing the digital divide (Nachira et al., 2007); (UNESCO, 2008); (Ronchi, 2009) and enhancing learning performance (OECD/PISA in focus 6, 2011). These problems include improving educators' professional skills and competencies (OECD, 2011) for dealing with information visualization tools such as virtual reality, interactive media and electronic technologies (Fundação Victor Civita, 2010); (Lopes et al. 2010); (Osberg, 1997a); (Winn, 1997).

In addition, it has been necessary investigating mechanisms for promoting social innovation and development, and how these can be achieved from the top down or the bottom up, involving collaboration that can be enhanced based in a context of dialogue, mutual knowledge and respect (Huws, 2011). For instance, as demonstrated on the development of the educational theory and practice related to alphabetizing citizens within a critical way in order that they can become lifelong learners with autonomy (Freire, 1996).

The development of this long-term empirical work (Franco and Lopes, 2011) and its research material (Bricken & Byrne, 1992); (Dede, 2009); (O'Connor & Cohn, 2010); (Winn, 1997) have showed that using low cost, but high quality desktop virtual reality and other advanced information visualization techniques and tools on individuals' education have the potential for supporting a culture of promoting social innovation and development as well as influencing individuals' lifelong learning attitudes with sustainability.

However, using virtual reality and computer graphics techniques for supporting individuals' education has been explored in small scale in ordinary schools and citizens' daily lives. So, this work development has contributed for decreasing the problem of influencing empirical uses of computer graphics and information visualization techniques beyond academic research to "*solve a real-world (non-computer graphics) problem*" (Potel, 2004).

Bates (1992) has investigated the concept that virtual reality can "*let us go anywhere and do anything*" and as "*language of presentation will develop over time*" (Bates, 1992).

Ahead of virtual reality allow virtual world builders enriching the experience for participants, the current state of the art of digital technology has supported going "*beyond the visual, and it seems clear that music, speech, and other sound will be similarly important to the broad success of virtual reality*" (Bates, 1992) and inspire interactive experience. For instance, this learning possibility was explored in the creative, collaborative and interactive educational information visualization experience, which integrated through VRML, video, still images and sound files at k-12 education (Franco et al., 2008).

So, based on information visualization technology potential for improving citizens' lifelong education and professional lives, this work has faced the mentioned challenges through the strategy of influencing and supporting recursively and incrementally citizens' cognitive, scientific, learning and performance enhancements related to their traditional/digital literacy competences since k-12 education (Franco, Machado & Lopes, 2011).

This work includes training citizens for dealing with the growing amount of information and computing resources in the knowledge based society of the 21st century (Computing in the Core, 2011); (CORDIS Work Programme, 2010); (UNESCO, 2008). And addressing the industry needs of a skilled workforce for dealing with simple and advanced contemporary technologies within digital ecosystems (Digital Ecosystems, 2011); (Nachira et al., 2007).

An example of such needs is the collaborative project Virtual and Interactive Environments for Workplaces of the Future, (VIEW of the Future), which has investigated how the state of the art of "*virtual environment (VE) concepts, practices, methodologies, systems and relevant application guidelines*" (Wilson, 2002) can support the industrial market. And has analyzed VE e virtual reality influence on human development (Crosier et al., 2004), considering the growing use of emerging technologies on industrial and academic research and development R&D work and in training such as in the military field (Skinner et al., 2010).

The potential for supporting individuals to deal with the challenges highlighted on this introduction via using information visualization technologies, such as virtual reality (Bates, 1992), has indicated that educational policies need to be reconsidered and/or improved, as investigated in (OECD, 2010); (U.S. DE, 2010). For instance, there has been the necessity of amplifying investments for influencing an increase on individuals' grasping and using computer science and information visualization technologies at k-12 education within more effective ways (Camera, 2011); (Dede, 2009); (Fundação Victor Civita, 2010). And supporting educators' lifelong high quality knowledge and professional development because they are *"expected to be able to adapt to new knowledge and demands during their careers"* (OECD, 2011).

Such expectative has pointed investigating and applying at k-12 education daily work a recursive and consistent educational policy involving institutions (government, universities, k-12 schools) collaborative work from the top down and or the bottom up to enhance educators' knowledge and cognition for using advanced contemporary technologies (ACT) with fluency (Franco et al., 2009); (Fundação Victor Civita, 2010); (U.S.DE, 2010).

It includes improving disadvantaged students' ACT skills and scientific knowledge competencies both at school and surrounding community accordingly to Pont (2004) in (Davis 2008). *"This involves curriculum development, teacher training and development, contributing to community development, out-of-school support, and parental support. It involves community-wide programmes that empower the students"* (Pont, 2004, p. 179) in (Davis, 2008).

1.1 An interdisciplinary and interactive knowledge-based learning framework

A way for empowering students and educators' digital literacy knowledge and skills as well as supporting a school surrounding community development can and has been through carrying out an *interdisciplinary and interactive knowledge-based learning framework* (IIK-BLF) process with support of emerging and advanced information visualization technologies. It has brought about a culture of influencing individuals' cognitive, digital literacy, scientific and learning competences enhancements. This IIK-BLF has been carried out within a multilevel approach as in (McLoughlin, Kaminski & Sodagar, 2008); (Rueda et al., 2001).

This IIK-BLF development process has attempted to combine an increase on individuals' mentioned competences and stimulate ones' performance enhancements in the context of learning and teaching sciences concepts (Franco & Lopes, 2010 and 2011). It has used as motivation and sustainable support information visualization technologies, such as web-based and virtual reality (VR) techniques and computer graphics (CG) principles as in (Dede, 2009); (Franco, Farias & Lopes, 2010); (Osberg, 1997b); (Youngblut, 1998).

So, this IIK-BLF has focused on the problem of sharing knowledge related to information visualization technologies and on how-to-integrate and use recursively and incrementally, these and other diverse adaptive technologies (Digital Ecosystems, 2011) such as interactive media and virtual environments (NATE/LSI, 2011); (Skinner et al, 2010) within k-12 education curriculum development for enhancing individuals' computer literacy competencies as well as the teaching and learning of sciences (Davis, 2008).

For applying this IIK-BLF integration process, we have considered the growing influence of visual culture on citizens' daily life (Hernández, 2000) and on business communication processes (Bresciani, Tan & Eppler, 2011). These factors have brought about the necessity of improving citizens' visual alphabetization (Donis, 2007).

We have addressed this necessity through using interactive media and virtual environments in teaching/learning and training at k-12 education, employing lessons, which have been transferrable (Mestre, 2002), for instance, from the military training practices and reflections with virtual environments in (O'Connor & Cohn, 2010). So, this long-term IIK-BLF has applied educational actions beyond descriptions related to the necessity of improving STEM (science, technology, engineering, and mathematics) education at K-12 schools (Mervis, 2011). It includes the growing number of assessments and reflections about them such as in (PISA, 2010) and rhetorical policy and competencies guidelines in (UNESCO, 2008).

Hence, this IIK-BLF practical development has added value to investigations and reflections in contemporary R&D literature and practices related to using information visualization technologies since k-12 education (Dede, 1995, 2009); (Osberg, 1997a, b).

Both literature and practices have showed the necessity of putting into practice a long term, recursive and inclusive experiential learning work using advanced information visualization tools and techniques (Dede, 2009); (O'Connor & Cohn, 2010); (Youngblut, 1998). And influencing citizens' digital knowledge, skills and competencies enhancements, which can support individuals dealing with and learning STEM concepts (CORDIS Work Program, 2010) as well as improving their visual alphabetization processes (Donis, 2007).

1.2 This IIK-BLF long term contributions through using information visualization

This IIK-BLF has supported individuals' direct manipulating (Preece et al., 1994) interactive media technologies through influencing individuals programming computers and visualizing 2D and 3D web-based content during educational activities. It has been a long-term, recursive, incremental and spiral development strategic process, which has contributed for reducing the problem of enhancing individuals' digital literacy tacit knowledge, as exemplified in (Franco & Lopes, 2010, 2011); (Dede, 2009); (Osberg, 1997a).

This IIK-BFL development has showed that integrating low cost, but high quality information visualization systems, such as desktop virtual reality on individuals' formal and informal education has made an effective difference for influencing citizens' learning attitudes, cultural knowledge improvements and lives development in diverse ways.

So, this IIK-BFL has been an inclusive approach required for *"the interdisciplinary nature of human performance research to understanding the brain-body-environment intersection"* (Fiore, Salas & Palvas, 2010) and as a way of influencing ordinary individuals' cognitive and learning competences (Franco et al., 2009) through general and specific knowledge enhancements based on using interactive media and virtual environments (Del Nero, 1997).

Evidences for such reflections are that school and surrounding community have taken part of lifetime opportunities. For instance, the community has participated on the one-to-one learning model project from the Non Governmental Organization One Laptop per Child (OLPC), which in Brazil is called 'Um Computador por Aluno' (UCA) and carried out collaborative work with the Laboratory of Integrated Systems (LIS) from the Polytechnic School of the University of São Paulo. These actions have resulted on institutions as well as researchers and educators' cooperative work, including technical and human sustainability for developing innovative learning projects based on interactive media and information visualization technologies (Franco et al., 2009); (Franco & Lopes, 2011); (Lopes et al., 2010).

Another contribution is that this IIK-BLF has inspired individuals' development of problem solving competencies based on Wing's computational thinking concept (NRCC, 2011); (Wing, 2010) and conscious use of emerging and advanced information visualization technologies such as VRML (Nadeu, Moreland & Heck, 1998), X3D (Brutzman, 2008); HTML5/X3D (Behr, J et al. 2009, 2011) and Scratch™ (Resnick et al. 2009); (Scratch, 2011).

These contributions have supported individuals' growing awareness related to information technology (IT) marketing "demand for a variety of skills in areas ranging from website development to upgrading internal systems and meeting the needs of mobile users". Ones' computer programming (CP) skills and digital literacy knowledge enhancements have been key points for this. These skills have the potential of preparing citizens for better working life opportunities since CP will be first in line for IT jobs, accordingly to a survey (Saia, 2011).

Cognitive sciences investigation related to the ability of inventing and transmitting cultural objects has suggested that human brain is preadapted to cultural transmission, which requires minding other minds (Dehaene, 2009). Our reflections involving this IIK-BLF development and contribution have showed that this empirical work has gone beyond providing accessibility to advanced contemporary technologies such as virtual reality.

Key factors for that and this work sustainability have been ordinary individuals' mental models and cultural transformations. Citizens' have reflected and understood that dominating and using interactive media and technologies have brought about adding value to their education, citizenship, school and surrounding community development.

In addition, using contemporary information visualization technologies on individuals' interactive knowledge development processes have happened through growing collective conscience that *"a base of tacit knowledge is frequently a pre-requisite for making use of any particular bit of codified knowledge"* (Cortright 2001).

2. Individuals' tacit knowledge development based on interactive media and electronics environments and sciences support

Individuals' tacit knowledge has increased through a culture of direct manipulating, disseminating and integrating emerging visualization technologies related to interactive electronics environments (NATE/LSI, 2011) in educational activities with sustainability.

The sustainability has come from using accessible web-based technologies in this inclusive project and providing to individuals, for instance, boy and girls, equity opportunities for learning and using advanced information visualization technologies through ESB computers lab and beyond (Franco & Lopes, 2009, 2011). Examples that have supported this mood of influencing individuals' digital, scientific and tacit knowledge development with simulations are in (Dede, 2009). And in a R&D work, which has used VR, considering individuals' culture and creating a new way for engaging people with computers so that they can practice, learn and perform better (Belman, 2011); (ICT Cultural Awareness, 2011).

Another foundation that has supported influencing citizens' tacit knowledge development is that this IIK-BLF has integrated engineering, pedagogy and cognitive sciences diverse concepts, methods and epistemologies. This integration has brought about individuals' collaboration and cognition development through stimulating human to human and human computer interactions (HCI) as well as provoking research, create and visualize digital content (Rogers, Brignull & Scaife, 2002).

As in (O´ Connor & Cohn, 2010) such digital and human systems and sciences integration and interactions have caused opportunities for developing multidisciplinary and interdisciplinary learning through individuals' collaborative work. It includes ones' experiencing the concept of cognitive interactivity, which *"refers to interactions between internal and external representations when performing cognitive tasks (e.g learning)"* (Rogers, Scaife & Rizzo, 2005).

In practice, cognitive interactivity has been achieved through coding virtual environments via computer programming VRML scripts and visualizing them with support of individuals' collaborative, cognitive and human computer interactions (Franco et al., 2008). In addition, sciences, HCI interactions and digital systems integration within this IIK-BLF have contributed for developing an interdisciplinary, flexible and open pedagogic and technical architecture, which has been useful at k-12 education formal learning and educators' professional development (Franco & Lopes, 2008, 2009) and on citizens' informal learning and entertaining activities (Franco, Cruz & Lopes, 2006); (Franco et al., 2009).

Such engineering, pedagogy and cognitive sciences integration has also supported advanced R&D work such as a new research model called '*convergent research model*' (Sharp et al. 2011) and practical work related to learning sciences and developing psychological and social studies based on virtual reality within a cross-disciplinary environment (ICT, 2011).

Similarly, this IIK-BLF development has used such sciences and digital integration with support of VR and interactive media electronics (NATE/LSI, 2011), including advanced information visualization technology evolutionary R&D work (Instant Realty, 2011); (X3DOM, 2011) for influencing citizens' digital literacy skills and competences as well as cultural and scientific learning and performance enhancements processes (Franco et al., 2009); (Franco, Farias & Lopes, 2010); (O' Connor & Cohn, 2010) as in figure-1.

Fig. 1. An example of how this IIK-BLF has contributed for improving individuals' tacit knowledge through direct manipulating interactive media and technologies (such as text editor, VRML code, and a web3D-based browser as BS Contact™) for programming, visualizing and reflecting about the processes of enhancing knowledge and competences.

In the above example, at the end of 2009, in the computers lab of a Primary School called Ernani Silva Bruno (ESB), students from the 7th grade level presented to a geography educator, who was finishing her initial education course, how they were using web-based virtual reality technologies for learning and doing symbolic representation (Osberg, 1997b).

Through experiential learning activities students and educators practiced their cognitive abilities such as logical reasoning skills, with support of computational thinking paradigm (NRCC, 2011); (Wing, 2010). They used computer graphics principles and information visualization tools as problem solving instruments for creating scientific visualization (Cunningham, 2007) related to cultural and spatial data acquired on ESB School surrounding community nature and researched on the web.

The data was integrated in the virtual environment through VRML textual code and its related symbolic visualization as the panoramic view showed in figure-2, with support of both, a vision that "*a virtual reality system as producing surface level phenomena via the inter-face and associated software, then the organization and content of software well behind the interface constitute a\deep structure for the virtual world*" (Bates, 1992) and of the metadata approach

(Pocsai et al., 1998). So, ones experienced *"the arrangement of code and data that produces the essential meaning of the interactive experience"* (Bates, 1992).

Paraphrasing (Pocsai et al., 1998), the metadata approach has been recognized as a feasible technique, which in bibliography has worked since years. As showed on figure-2, *"metadata is represented as a set of facts about the resource"* (e.g. language (VRML). Each fact is represented as an attribute (or element). *"An attribute contains a type identifying what information the attribute contains and one or more values"* (e.g. **PointLight { location** 0.0 500.0 0.0, **radius** 3000.0, **ambientIntensity** 0.5**}** and **# Commentaries** in Portuguese language **(#controle da iluminação do mundo virtual / 'controling the virtual world lighting'))**. *"Metadata may be part of the resources themselves"* (e.g. information inside of a VRML <{meta}> tag) or *"kept separately from them (e.g. index information of www-search-engines, file creation date-information in UNIX file systems"*) figure-2 on the left (Pocsai et al., 1998).

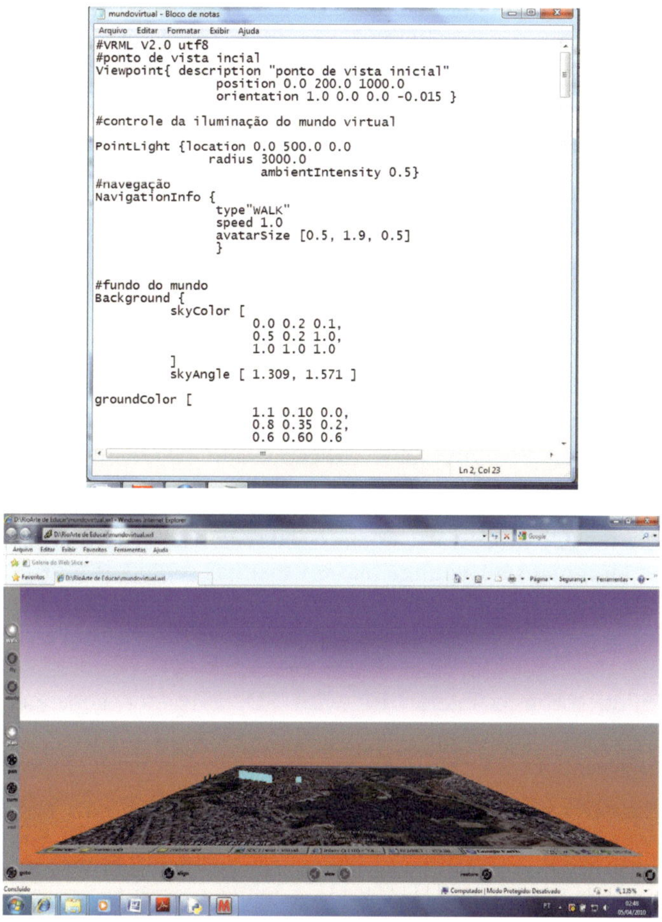

Fig. 2. VRML textual code and its symbolic representation using the concept of metadata in (Pocsai et al., 1998) and supporting individuals' tacit knowledge, digital literacy skills and cognition improvements such as attention, planning, critical thinking and memory through programming, saving and debugging the VRML file as well as enhancing ones' writing, reading and visualization abilities and competences.

Beyond the interactive learning processes of researching, reading, writing, creating the virtual environment and improving individuals' tacit knowledge, the educators and students meeting was an effective opportunity for developing collaborative work. The interactive meeting supported author1 and students' needs for preparing the digital artwork for a presentation in the city of Rio the Janeiro (Franco, Farias & Lopes, 2010). It brought about the possibility of sharing information visualization knowledge, via covering geography educator's lack of digital literacy skills. Including her interest in knowing how accessible and advanced interactive information visualization technologies can enhance educational activities related to acquiring geography concepts and supporting students' spatial thinking skills development based on information visualization technology (Chen, 2006) used for representing ESB surrounding community's urban life and natural resources as explained in (Franco, Farias & Lopes, 2010) and visualized in figures-1 and 2.

The human to human, and human computer knowledge based interactions exemplified above have been ways, which this IIK-BLF has contributed for developing students and educators' digital literacy skills and competencies beyond their initial education, and can serve a range of purposes, including to: "*update individuals' knowledge of a subject in light of recent advances in the area; update individuals' skills and approaches in light of the development of new teaching techniques and objectives, new circumstances, and new educational research; enable individuals to apply changes made to curricula or other aspects of teaching practice; enable schools to develop and apply new strategies concerning the curriculum and other aspects of teaching practice; exchange information and expertise among teachers and others, e.g. academics and industrialists; or help weaker teachers become more effective*" (OECD, 2011).

3. Related work

There have been several efforts for diffusing information visualization tools, techniques and knowledge and using them on individuals' education and training (Chen, 2006).

Roussou (2004) has carried out long term R&D work, for instance, through the NICE (Narrative-based, Immersive, Constructionist/Collaborative Environments) an interactive virtual learning environment for young children that has served as a test bed for exploring virtual reality (VR) as a learning medium. Her work has integrated psychology, cognitive sciences and learning theories as active learning theory, constructivism and constructionism, focusing on using the sensorial possibilities related to VR possibilities for supporting individuals' learning through interacting with 3D computer generated environments. Roussou et al. (2006) have created and compared interactive immersive and non-immersive VR environments potential for educating. The work has expanded through designing and offering children exploratory learning activities via 3D interfaces. And analysing children' tasks based on Vygotsky's Zone of Proximal Development (ZPD), which concerns the internalisation of social rules. For instance, taking in consideration that an individual using a 3D virtual environment can collaborate and learn with support from a more able peer, "*but is not yet able to complete the task unaided*" (Roussou et al. 2008).

Bricken & Byrne (1992) have developed experimental study using VR for conducting a summer course with k-12 education students. Students' activities have centred on hands-on exploration of new technology. Researchers have created virtual worlds and explored human's sensorial capabilities, which permit step inside to see, hear, touch and modify them. The investigation has evaluated *VR's usefulness and appeal to students ages 10 - 15 years, documenting their behavior and soliciting their opinions as they used VR to construct and explore their own virtual worlds.* As tools individuals have worn a head-mounted, audio-visual display, position and orientation sensors, and tactile interface devices, which allow inhabit actively an inclusive computer-generated environment.

Bricken (1992) has outlined a spatial algebra by mapping the structure of commutative groups onto the structure of space, considering interactions with spatial representations through natural behaviour in an inclusive environment that enforces the transformational invariants of algebra, which the spatial representation affords experiential learning. Experiential algebra permits algebraic proof through direct manipulation and can be readily implemented in virtual reality. The techniques used to create spatial algebra have brought about supporting to explore experiential learning of mathematics in virtual environments.

The Laboratory for Virtual Reality, Psychology, Rehabilitation, and Social Neuroscience at the University of Southern California's Institute for Creative Technologies has engaged in a broad program of R&D applying computer-mediated instruction for learning sciences, taking into account ways how people learn and methods of teaching that facilitate more effective learning experiences (VRCPAT, 2011). "*This is where ICT's learning sciences are making a difference. Through design, guidance, mentoring, and assessment -- we provide education that is both useful and unforgettable*" (ICT Learning Sciences, 2011). The research has also investigated human brain mechanisms that underlie neurocognitive functioning and emotion regulation in persons throughout the life course using as tools a cross-disciplinary environment and an interdisciplinary team integrated by computer scientists, writers, engineers, producers, administrators and artists, including a combination between virtual and augmented reality, psychology and social neuroscience. In addition, ICT's researchers have experienced and reflected that using virtual and augmented reality is an essential component in the evolution of medical and psychological sciences in the digital age. As any technology applied in these areas, both challenges and opportunities have emerged in how virtual and augmented reality are usefully applied and validated. For instance, the Virtual Reality Cognitive Performance Assessment (VRCPAT, 2011) has made "*use of virtual environments to create a battery of neuropsychological measures to assess the ways in which the structure and function of the brain relate to specific psychological processes and evident behaviors: attention-vigilance, effort, abstraction-flexibility, executive functioning, spatial organization, visual-motor processing, processing speed, visual memory, verbal abilities, and verbal memory and learning*" (ICT, 2011).

4. IIK-BLF Strategy and Information Visualization Technologies

As mentioned on this chapter introduction and tacit knowledge sections and exemplified in figures-1 and 2, this IIK-BLF strategy development has used advanced information visualization technologies and concepts (Duralach & Mavor, 2001); (CORDIS Work Program 2010) such as VRML (Nadeu, Moreland & Heck, 1998) and X3D (Brutzman, 2008) for supporting individuals acquiring tacit knowledge and developing cognitive, scientific and digital literacy skills and competencies.

This IIK-BLF has approximated recursively and incrementally individuals from web-based electrical engineering techniques (Pressman, 2006) and information and communication technologies (ICT) through hands-on work approach, which has allowed individuals' direct manipulating (Preece et al., 1994) digital technologies and creating microworlds for developing scientific knowledge as explained in (Bates, 1992); (Papert, 1993).

Hence, this IIK-BLF has also investigated an evolutionary R&D work, which integrates Hypertext Markup Language (HTML5) and X3D (Behr & Jung 2010). Such integration has been designed to allow interoperating diverse open-standard formats and using advanced web-browser capabilities for visualizing, interacting with and creating 3D web-based content without necessity of employing a plug-in (X3DOM, 2011), (Behr et al., 2011).

However, according to our empirical tests, in a computer without or using older consumer graphics card capability as GeForce FX 5200 (Chrome Help, 2011); (X3Dom Platform Notes, 2011), it has not been possible to visualize X3D content embed in HTML5.

On the other hand, having a capable consumer graphics card such as Intel™ GMA 4500M in a computer, the design of the X3DOM integration model and its tools can amplify the ways of using interactive media and electronic environments, computer science, computer graphics, scientific, cultural and digital arts knowledge integration through creating simple and complex applications as in figure-3. This integration has the potential of contributing for solving real world learning problems, for instance, related to enhancing students' math and geometry competences at primary education in third grade level. They have had difficulties for developing math abilities such as adding, subtracting, problem solving and recognizing geometric shapes accordingly a math research in Brazil (G1 Jornal Nacional, 2011).

With the growing accessibility to mobile devices and computers at schools and surrounding community, through using web-based information visualization technologies, as VRML in (Franco et al., 2009) and (X3Dom, 2011), a culture of creating symbolic representation based on scripts and its visualization can and has been diffused (Franco & Lopes, 2011). This kind of culture can support individuals deal with abstraction during simple and complex tasks (Wulfeck & Wetzel-Smith, 2010) through learning activities involving computer programming, describing and visualizing geometric shapes and colors, calculating shapes areas and moving them around the computer screen.

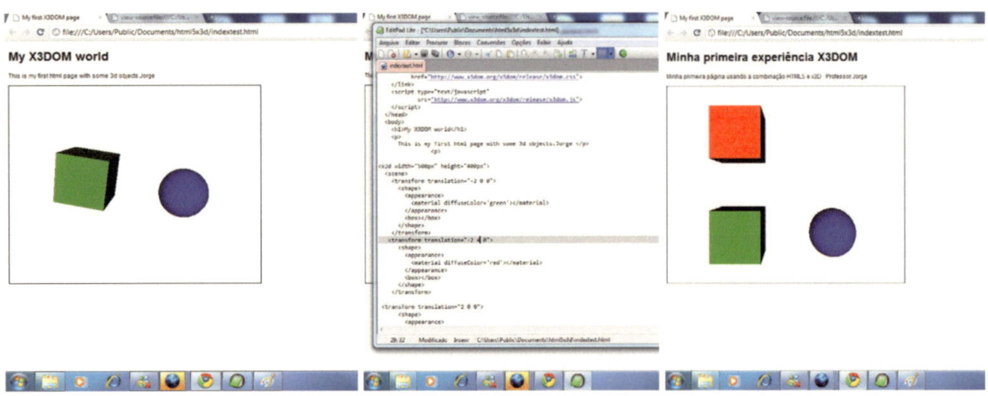

Fig. 3. Demo related to testing evolutionary R&D work, the X3DOM integration model that has been based on HTML5/X3D and supports diverse file formats such as MPG., PNG. JPG. and WAV. HTML5/X3D has been embedded in web browsers capabilities such as in Google Chrome™ and FireFox ™, allowing technology accessibility to all citizens.

These activities can happen through 'learning by doing', across reusing and adapting X3D scripts, in figure-3. So, as in (Bricken, 1992) individuals' interactions with spatial representations onto the structure of space and natural behaviors for carrying out such actions can lead citizens to live experiential learning processes related to *"attention-vigilance, effort, abstraction-flexibility, executive functioning, spatial organization, visual-motor processing, processing speed, visual memory, verbal abilities, and verbal memory and learning"* (ICT, 2011).

Due to their enormous potential for motivating learner and support active education related to exploratory and experiential learning (Osberg, 1997 a, b); (Youngblut, 1998), learning-by-doing (Walczak, Wojciechowski & Cellary, 2006), exploring and applying in practice active learning theory (Roussou, Oliver & Slater, 2008), interactive electronic environments, virtual reality techniques and 2D and 3D web-based formats such as HTML5/VRML/X3D have been objects of education, training and R&D work (Behr et al., 2011); (X3Dom, 2011).

Hence, these technologies can and have been lightweight enable virtual reality solutions for enhancing individuals' cognition, digital literacy competences, learning sciences and entertaining in great scale (Franco, Machado & Lopes, 2011). For instance, through using as media *"web-based I3D (interactive 3D) or emerging 3D TV systems, which may drastically speed up the adoption of VR technology in education. Both the end-users and the client infrastructure are ready for this change"* (Walczak, Wojciechowski & Cellary, 2006).

An example of interactive electronic system that has supported such concept is the integration involving Ginga, the Brazilian DTV system, and the X3D format, which has brought about X3D-GINGA architecture investigated in (Tavares et al., 2007). Another example of evolutionary R&D work using 3D environments by combining web-based standard description languages, such as X3D/VRML and Ginga Digital TV system integration has been carried out in (Souza, Machado & Tavares, 2010). They have proposed a specification that incorporates modules that can enable the implementation, development and execution of 3D applications. Souza, Machado & Tavares's (2010) implementation and comparative tests between a (OpenGL ES API, 2011) in Java and Nested Context Language (NCL), whose main characteristic is the mechanisms for synchronization of multiple media, with X3D have showed advantages in using X3D/VRML as demonstrated in table-1.

Characteristic	Ginga-J (Java) – JSR239	Ginga-NCL (NCL+X3D)
Collision Handling	Implemented by the developer - customizable	Supported in the browser - Predefined
Event Handling	Implemented by the developer - customizable	Supported in the browser - Predefined
Texturing	Implemented by the developer	Supported in the browser - Predefined
Lighting Techniques	Fully Supported	Partially supported
Robust techniques (Ray trace, Fog, Bump Mapping and so on.	Partially or not supported	Partially supported
Time to develop	Three days	One day

Table. 1. It shows a comparison between OpenGL ES API in Java and NCL with X3D based on empirical work developed by (Souza, Machado & Tavares, 2010).

This kind of comparative work has showed that through applying accessible web-based standard languages such as VRML/X3D and a web browser as tools for creating and visualizing information, it is possible developing an inclusive digital literacy, scientific, educational and cultural artwork, because such technologies have become available in great scale on ordinary personal computers and mobile devices as showed in (X3Dom, 2011).

Hence, even ordinary individuals, with low level of technical abilities as well as reading and writing competences can afford to understand how these digital systems work and use them for lifelong learning with autonomy. So, they can apply digital systems as a motivational and sustainable support for enhancing cognitive competences and learning performance.

Step by step, with support of the brain plasticity concept (Sharp et al., 2011) and hands on information visualization technologies, individuals can and have transformed their mental models and engaged in a culture of developing technical knowledge and autonomy for researching, appropriating themselves from digital systems and exploring their learning possibilities (Franco et al., 2009); (Franco & Lopes, 2010); (Franco, Machado & Lopes, 2011).

Influencing these individuals' mental and learning attitudes has been expected to be carried out at k-12 education as in guidelines (UNESCO, 2008); (U.S.DE, 2010) and can bring about citizens'scientific and digital literacy competences enhancements for transforming and creating digital content. For that, we take in consideration the visual culture influence in the knowledge-based society and the competences that have been expected from the workforce (Digital Ecosystems, 2011); (Nachira, 2007). For example, ones be able of doing complex tasks through using advanced technology with fluency and developing abilities for programming computers (Colson, 2007); (Fleming, 2011).

This long-term and recursive IIK-BLF inclusive approach development processes have showed that is feasible to address such society needs since the k-12 education. For instance, through influencing sixth grade level students' learn information visualization techniques for supporting their digital literacy skills. It includes grasping arts and math concepts and using their knowledge and imagination for creating digital content as showed in figure-4.

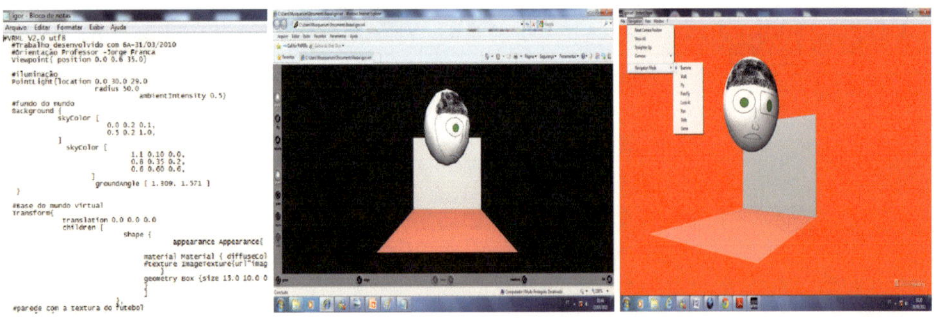

Fig. 4. The two pictures on the left and middle are part of the work carried out with and by sixth grade level students aiming to representing human body in the first semester of 2010. The picture on the right is part of our recent research for learning X3D tools and techniques and it is not implemented at school yet. However, as in the picture on the right, using the InstantReality Player™ can support a more inclusive and evolutionary work based on Extensible Markup Language (XML), virtual and augmented reality and JavaScript technologies (InstantReality, 2011), bringing about approximating individuals from more advanced computer programming skills development (X3Dom, 2011).

Back to ESB School learning and teaching of arts concepts based on information visualization, students from the sixth grade level used paper and pen in the classroom, including computers, virtual reality and web3D technologies inside the computers lab.

Students direct manipulated technologies such as a notepad for programming and debugging VRML code. These learning actions influenced students reading through writing; applying paint software for creating textures; knowing and employing a web-based language VRML; and using 2D and 3D web-browsers such as Internet Explorer™ and Cortona 3D Viewer™, bringing about enhancements on their digital literacy and tacit knowledge.

It was a collaborative work involving ESB School ICT Facilitator and Arts Educator, who participated from a small scale workshop, which the ICT Facilitator conduct for her understanding how advanced information visualization technologies could support students' further learning arts and math concepts initially investigated in the classroom.

During the knowledge-based interactions the educators reflected about the relevance of using such technologies for motivating and teaching students. After that, they used at school the same media and communication tools that entertainment and cultural industry such as movie, video and computer games ones have used to attract and maintain citizens' attention and consuming, for instance, 3D computer games and movies.

Using visual communication tools at school has been a relevant way of expanding a culture of researching and learning that can be linked with storytelling and movies characters, such as the princess Lea in the movie Star Wars. For instance, some physics concepts showed during the mentioned film have inspired information visualization R&D and a holographic system development based on fictional and storytelling culture as well as in the conceptual scientific knowledge applied on the artwork (3-D Teleconference, 2011).

In addition, cognitive sciences research related to brain development and neuroesthetics based on Jean Pierre Changeaux in (Dehaene, 2009, p. 309) has suggested that the culture of observing and creating artwork can support understanding that human brain as the synthesis of multiple evolutions *"harbors a wide selection of mental operations that can explain the complex emotional reactions brought on by a work of art. In neuronal terms a paint is broken down into many parts that are conveyed to numerous brain areas. Each of these regions processes one of the artwork attributes: color, texture, faces, hands, emotional expression. A work of art becomes a master piece when it stimulates multiple distributed processors in a novel, synchronous, and harmonious way"*(Dehaene, 2009, p. 309).

Through influencing hands on desktop virtual reality techniques on individuals' education across writing and reading VRML code and visualizing its symbolic representation, as in the empirical collaborative k-12 education artwork example above, we have addressed Dehaene's investigation about mental operations. Hence, this IIK-BLF development based on direct manipulating numbers through VRML/X3D coding, for instance '**translation 0.0 2.0 15.0**', which is related to Cartesian plan (**X (0.0), Y (2.0)** and **Z(15.0))** and subsequent virtual navigation using mouse/keyboard/other device and web browser interface has supported individuals' approximation from *"mathematical influence on basic and universal competences of the human mind, through structured mental representations of space, time and number that we inherit from our evolutionary past, and that we learn to recombine in novel ways with the help of written and spoken symbols"* (Dehaene, 2009 p. 309).

5. Incremental and spiral information visualization knowledge diffusion

In the course of applying information visualization technologies, this IIK-BLF has supported pedagogy empowerment as practical R&D work (Dede, 1995); (Osberg 1997 a, b) and school surrounding community collective intelligence development related to individuals become aware, understand and use interactive technology on their educational processes (Franco et al., 2008b); (Franco et al, 2009); (Franco, Machado & Lopes, 2011).

Our practical work and reflections have showed that diffusing within recursive, incremental and spiral ways interactive information visualization, media and technologies knowledge and practices can and have been a relevant approach for engaging individuals in a culture of knowledge-based development processes as in (Dede, 1995); (Osberg, 1997).

This research has focused on disseminating advanced information visualization technologies such as web3D and virtual reality and their pedagogical use as showed in sections 2 to 4.

However, as we have carried out work within a primary school, this IIK-BLF has also applied 2D web-based digital technologies such as Hypertext Markup Language (HTML), Scratch™ and blog, broadening the range of possibilities for using human and digital systems integration and interactions for supporting individuals' learning performance enhancements at ESB Primary School and surrounding community in figure-5.

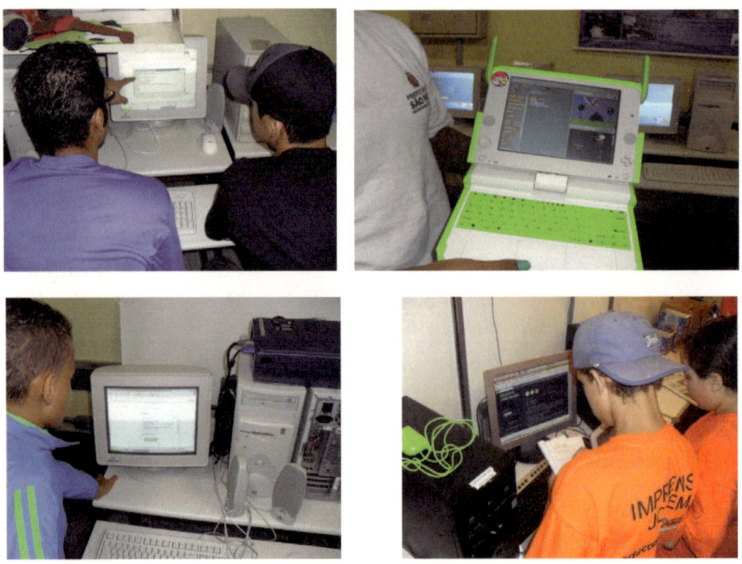

Fig. 5. On the top left an informal collaborative learning work at ESB computers lab addressing student's HTML knowledge; top-right a student showing an example of how to use Scratch™ applying the laptops related to UCA project; bottom-left internal use of blog as learning resource; on the bottom-right using blog at an external event called Brazilian Fair of Science and Engineering 'Feira Brasileira de Ciências e Engenharia' (FEBRACE, 2011).

Through these ways of using interactive media and information visualization technologies we have avoided misusing computer graphics and the mentioned technologies in just one mood as investigated in (Skinner et al., 2010). Hence, step by step, this framework has influenced individuals' cognitive domain and cultural engagement for using information and communication technologies addressing ones' digital literacy, scientific, citizenship and lifelong performance enhancements within multimodal and formative ways as (Dede, 2009).

The information visualization technologies used by children during their formative years can and have influenced their learning strengths and preferences. So, as in Dede's thoughts (2009) *"an increasingly prevalent type of media, immersive interfaces, can aid in designing educational experiences that build on students' digital fluency to promote engagement, learning, and transfer from classroom to real-world settings"*.

This IIK-BLF development has been a real world proof of such concept application. It has showed that learning the mentioned information visualization technologies integrated with educational activities involving k-12 curriculum sciences amplifies the potential of spreading advanced computer graphics principles and web-based technologies and scientific knowledge beyond the classroom environment (Franco et al, 2008, 2009).

Expanding this kind learning activities can and has achieved school surrounding community through individuals' knowledge-based interactions and better use of computers and digital media (Franco and Lopes, 2009, 2010, 2011) as well as supporting ones' lifelong learning attitudes and citizenship actions.

For instance, since 2007, after interactions with ESB ICT facilitator for learning to use (Blender™, 2011) 3D software as in (Franco et al, 2008), through first applying instrumental reading for grasping Blender tutorials, a student has developed further his English language skills. During September 2011, by e-mail, the former student wrote to the ICT Facilitator informing he has done an English language course and has planned to do as graduation course digital design. The former student has gained autonomy for researching further other computer graphics and information visualization possibilities such as creative design through image processing applying software such as GIMP™ that we have used at ESB computers lab. Examples of his digital artwork have been on the web-blog (Garrido, 2011).

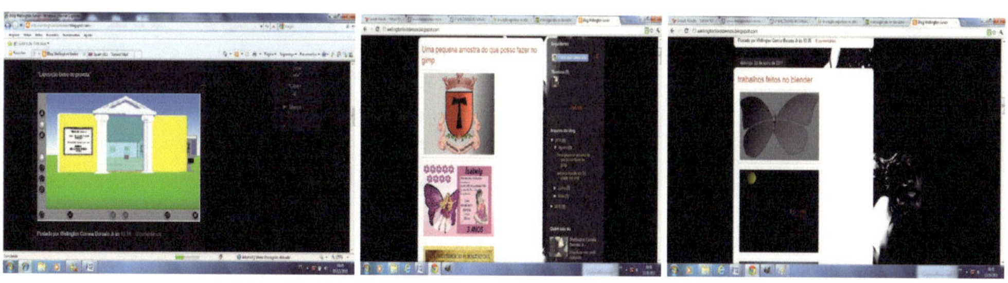

Fig. 6. On the left a web3D-based environment using VRML, which first was developed at ESB Primary School as a virtual museum by a former student, and has been reused at his middle school for presenting a science work related to artificial insemination and sharing computer graphics knowledge with educators and classmates; on the middle his art work with GIMP™; on the right using Blender™ (Borsato, 2011) supporting his lifelong learning as well as scientific knowledge-based learning attitudes.

Another former student has developed his lifelong learning attitudes based on computer graphics using VRML, GIMP™ and Blender™ as educational resources in figure-6. These learning attitudes have brought about his research, reading, writing and communication skills and competences enhanced. It includes practicing his citizenship with conscience through sharing knowledge with other educators and students at the school environment, in which he has done his secondary education course.

5.1 Information visualization knowledge diffusion to educators and ordinary citizens

Although this IIK-BLF development has opened training opportunities to educators from diverse sciences areas (Franco et al. 2008a, b, 2009), including the geography and arts educator in sections 2 and 4, it has remained the problem of educators developing digital literacy skills for applying with fluency and autonomy advanced information visualization technologies (IVT) such as the ones used on this framework, during their teaching actions. Improving individuals' IVT tacit knowledge can and has been influenced formally and informally at school and home with support of standard web-based technologies. However, as in the military filed (O'Connor and Cohn, 2010), there has been a lack of technology specialists for supporting educators' training in large scale for learning how to deal with advanced digital technologies.

So, for instance, it has been relevant during schools district formative meetings as (IISEDJ, 2011), a seminar for enhancing educators' knowledge, which happened in September 23, diffusing ICT knowledge through direct manipulating technology and reflecting with other educators ways of using IVT for supporting citizens' problem solving and inquiring-based learning lifelong (Thirteen, 2004) in figure.7. It includes influencing interdisciplinary socio-technical and digital literacy competences, learning performance and cognition enhancements (Franco et al., 2009); (Franco and Lopes, 2011); (Skinner et al., 2010).

In addition, this IIK-BLF has addressed the concept that "it is very important that knowledge be transmitted to all the members of society. This transmission takes place through structures like schools, families, and training courses" (Thirteen, 2004) as in figure-7.

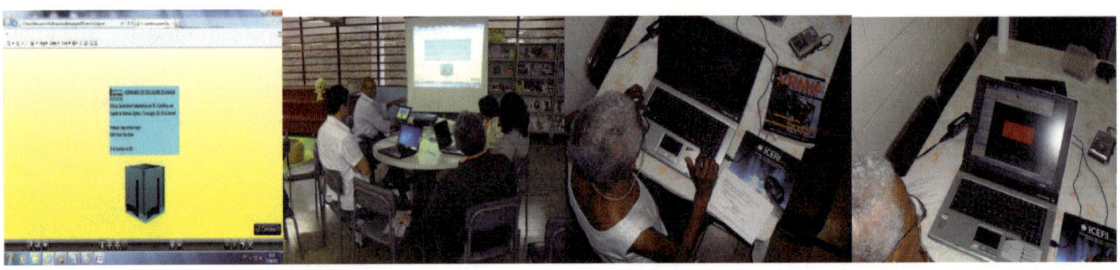

Fig. 7. On the left and middle left part of the information visualization and cultural material based on minimalism art concept used as content support for contextualizing a digital workshop with educators during the (IISEDJ, 2011), in which they direct manipulated VRML files and reflect how to interrelating the bits on the code with k-12 sciences curriculum development; on the middle right and right pictures an adult in the process of developing her digital skills based on informal education and lifelong learning concepts with support of games and simulation technologies (Honey & Hilton, 2011).

6. Reflections and conclusions

Based on the challenges mentioned on this chapter introduction, this IIK-BLF development, strategy and outcomes have highlighted empirical actions we have carried out for integrating technology, human knowledge, educational and sciences paradigms as well as enhancing individuals' learning performance and competences.

This work has showed and reflected about a conceptual and practical educational infrastructure that has been formed. It includes practical and propositional examples of using information visualization technologies attempting to approximate k-12 students and educators as well as ordinary citizens from spiral, incremental and agile programming techniques with support of low cost and free software and web-based engineering approaches (Pressman 2006).

These work strategies have addressed features such as problem solving, inquiring-based learning and exploring scientific models and visualizations with support of the computational thinking concept and its interdisciplinary application with great focus on K-12 education (Wing, 2010). These were demonstrated within our work examples in sections 2, 4 and 5, through applying diverse computer graphics simulations, advanced web-based tools and languages as well as other digital resources for stimulating young students learning sciences as in (Philip, 2007), (Rusk, Resnick & Cooke, 2009).

As has been showed, this IIK-BLF development has influenced early independence of youths' high potential for learning and researching using digital technology and capturing their creative potential. It has fostered youths' leadership and participation in collaborative research projects targeting first-ever and exploratory, multi-disciplinary research (CORDIS Work Program 2010) covering the problem of disseminating to and supporting citizens' access to innovative services and direct manipulate emerging digital technologies (Kaplan, 2010); (Jacobi et al., 2011); (VILNIUS, 2010).

In addition, this IIK-BLF has served as a base for developing a flexible, open technical and pedagogical architecture able to support interdisciplinary and interactive academic and popular evolutionary R&D work (Franco et al., 2009).

It has brought about stakeholders and partners together in order to provide innovation and equitable use of Information and Communication Technology (ICT) in education (Computing in the Core, 2011). For instance, the UCA project at ESB Primary School (Franco et al. 2009) has allowed reaching with effectiveness low achievers and disadvantaged students (Davis, 2008); (ECS, 2011) and increasing the participation of young girls and women in information technology field (Franco and Lopes, 2010 and 2011); (Franco, Machado and Lopes, 2011); (NCWIT, 2011).

Our empirical work has showed that this kind of socio-technical action can be deepened and disseminated in large scale through using emerging technologies such as the integration model HTML5/X3D that have been embedded in recent web browsers developments as in Google Chrome™ and Firefox ™, allowing technology accessibility to all citizens (Behr, J et al., 2009); (Behr and Jung 2010); (X3DOM, 2011).

These kinds of electrical engineering and technical support facilities have influenced carrying out interdisciplinary and interactive learning/teaching practices as in science and technology museums (Ronchi, 2009). Applying interactive media and technologies in museums has increased possibilities of citizens' scientific learning and entertaining experiences going beyond 2D and 3D interfaces enjoyment. At some extent, individuals have experienced *explorative and cognitive trails based on user profiles and the advice of communication experts and cognitive scientists* (Ronchi, 2009).

Interactive technologies, learning and cognitive sciences integration has been used on interdisciplinary scientific research, which has investigated *"from the movement of the ions at the individual neuron level up through learning in the service of complex cognitive functions such as planning"* encompassing *"an interactive, balanced approach that emphasizes connections between neurobiological, cognitive, and computational considerations"* (O'Reilly and Munakata, 2000). Although it is simplified, the above description is referent to neurons acting like detectors and working together synaptic processes related to brain plasticity/neuroplasticity (Brain plasticity, 2011); (Macher, 2004); (Wikipedia neuroplasticity, 2011). The synaptic processes are part of a wired network, in which detectors working together *"can exhibit useful collective properties that provide the building blocks of cognition"* (O'Reilly and Munakata, 2000).

A possibility of improving individuals' learning performance and cognition can be supported by educators' deepen knowledge on the brain plasticity. A current neuroscience research has attracted and integrated researchers from divergent backgrounds such as electrical and computing engineering and chemistry. The investigation has addressed how *"adult brain constantly adapts to different stimuli. This plasticity not only appears on learning and memory, but also as dynamic in information transmission and processing"*. And the research model, which has supported it, is an interdisciplinary *new research model - convergence - which draws on an ongoing merge of life, physical and engineering sciences* (Sharp et al. 2011).

The concepts of brain plasticity and neuronal synaptic have supported the use of information visualization technologies such as VRML and computer programming techniques via text and its symbolic representation such as in section 4.

Applying these techniques has contributed for k-12 individuals and ordinary citizens amplifying their knowledge and competences for dealing with advanced emerging technologies. It includes learning how to work together and integrating their knowledge related to sciences, through collaborative teaching/citizenship actions as the work proposal and practice described in the convergence model (Sharp et al. 2011).

This IIK-BLF development processes have influenced individuals' cognitive enhancements involving fluency building, cognitive, refinement and sense-making processes investigated through the knowledge-learning-instruction (KLI) framework aiming to bridge the science-practice chasm to enhance robust student learning (Koedinger, Corbett & Perfetti, 2010).

Accordingly to psychological assessments related to comparing low-end personal computer based information visualization/simulations with high-end/realistic graphics visualizations *robust learning* can occur in both types of virtual environments (VE). Researchers have showed that what has influenced individuals' better cognitive and learning performance is the quality of tasks they have to accomplish within a VE (Skinner et al., 2010).

For instance, Wulfeck & Wetzel-Smith (2010) have demonstrated that a strategy for enhancing individuals' cognition can be developing visualizations, which make sciences concepts relationships observable. Through developing a relatively simple 3D box model using a web-based script language such as VRML/X3D, individuals can explore concepts related to point, lines, hypotenuse, angles, how calculating the box area, reflecting about attention processes referent to upper and lower cases during the writing and debugging of programming code.

This IIK-BLF has been carried out focusing on "how-to-integrate" information visualization technology and computer literacy skills for enhancing the teaching and learning of sciences (Davis, 2008) with support of adaptive technologies (Digital Ecosystems, 2011).

As exemplified through the empirical work in sections 2, 4 and 5 of this chapter, the mentioned information visualization technologies have supported individuals' learning performance, traditional and digital literacy skills and competences enhancements.

It includes individuals' cultural and cognition development through formal and informal learning activities within a recursive, spiral, incremental and hands on learning strategy (Franco et al., 2009); (Franco & Lopes, 2010 and 2011); (Pressman, 2006); (Ronchi, 2009).

There has been cultural and educational support for developing this IIK-BLF encompassing the visual and digital culture aspects. The visual culture has influenced from pre-historic to 21st century sculptures, paintings, artistic installations and digital art (Colson, 2007); (Graham-Dixon, 2008). And among other applications, emerging information visualization technologies have been used in the state-of-the-art of investigation related to applying games and simulations in education (Honey & Hilton, 2011) and in high risk environments such as military training (O'Connor & Cohn, 2010).

Finally, this IIK-BLF long-term development process with support of computer graphics, virtual reality, other diverse information visualization tools and advanced web-based technologies has brought about diverse individuals benefiting from the learning and teaching actions. It has showed that step by step this kind of inclusive and multilevel educational work has achieved its goals and worth it (Franco et al., 2009); (Franco and Lopes, 2011).

7. Acknowledgement

We thank the individuals that have contributed to this IIK-BLF development, God bless.

8. References

3-D Conference (2011). *3-D Can you see me now?*, 30.09.2011, Retrieved from <http://www.ndep.us/3-D-Teleconference>

Bates, J. (1992). Virtual Reality, Art, and Entertainment, In: *Presence: Teleoperators and Virtual Environments - Premier issue*, Volume 1 Issue 1, ISBN: 1054-7460, USA.

Behr J. & Jung Y. (2010). A Scalable Architecture for the HTML5/X3D BOF Integration Model X3DOM, AR Group, Fraunhofer IGD. In: *SIGGRAPH 2010*, 18.05.2011, Retrieved from <http://www.web3d.org/event/s2010/HTML5-X3D-Integration.pdf >

Behr, J et al. (2009). X3DOM – A DOM-based HTML5/ X3D Integration Model. In: *Web3D Symposium 2009*, 18.05.2011, Retrieved from < http://www.web3d.org/x3d/wiki/images/3/30/X3dom-web3d2009-paper.pdf>

Behr, J et al. (2011). Dynamic and Interactive Aspects of X3DOM. *In: Web3D '11: Proceedings of the 16th International Conference on 3D Web Technology*, Jun 20 - 22, Paris, France, doi>10.1145/2010425.2010440.

Belman, O. (2011). Brave new world. In: *USC Trojan Family Magazine*, 29.09.2011, Retrieved from

<http://tfm.usc.edu/autumn-2011/brave-new-world/>

BEST (2004). What it Takes: Pre-K-12 Design Principles to Broaden Participation in Science, Technology, Engineering and Mathematics. In: *NCWIT is the National Center for Women & Information Technology*, 24.05.2011, Retrieved from <http://www.bestworkforce.org/PDFdocs/BESTPre-K-12Rep_part1_Apr2004.pdf>

Borsato, W. C. (2011). *Blog Wellington Junior*, 12.10.2011, Retrieved from <http://wellingtonlorddemon.blogspot.com/>

Brain Plasticity (2011). Brain Plasticity: What Is It? Learning and Memory. In: *Whashington Faculty*, 25.05.2011, Retrieved from <http://faculty.washington.edu/chudler/plast.html>

Bresciani, S., Tan, M. & Eppler, M. J. (2011). Augmenting communication with visualization: effects on emotional and cognitive response, In: *Proceedings of IADIS International Conference ICT, Society and Human Beings 2011*, Rome, Italy, 20 – 26, July, pp. 11-18.

Bricken, M. & Byrne, C. (1992). *Summer Students in Virtual Reality: A Pilot Study on Educational Applications of VR Technology*. (Report) Seattle: University of Washington, Human Interface Technology Laboratory. 24.09.2011, Retrieved from <http://www.hitl.washington.edu/publications/r-92-1/>

Bricken, W. (1992). Spatial Representation of Elementary Algebra. *In Proceedings of 1992 IEEE Workshop on Visual Languages*, Seattle, Washington, USA, 15-18 Sept, pp. 56-62.

Brutzman, D. (2008). *Computer Graphics Teaching Support using X3D: Extensible 3D Graphics for Web Authors*, 18.05.2011, Retrieved from <http://x3dgraphics.com/examples/X3dForWebAuthors/Chapter01-TechnicalOverview/CGEMS_X3dGraphicsForWebAuthorsModule_Brutzman2008October16.pdf>

BS Contact (2011). *Bitmanagement: interactive web3Dgraphics*, 20.09.2011, Retrieved from <http://www.bitmanagement.com/en/products/interactive-3d-clients/bs-contact>

Camera, B. A. (2011) *Polis legislation aims to boost K-12 computer science education*, 26.09.2011, Retrieved from <http://www.dailycamera.com/boulder-county-schools/ci_18958177 >

Chen, C. (2006). *Information visualization: beyond the horizon*, Springer, ISBN:978-1-84628-340-6, United Kingdom.

Chrome Help (2011). WebGL e gráficos 3D, 03.10.2011, Retrieved from <http://www.google.com/support/chrome/bin/answer.py?hl=pt&answer=1220892>

Colson, R. (2007). *The Fundamentals of Digital Art*, AVA Publishing, ISBN: 978-2-940373-58-1, USA.

Computing in the Core (2011). Issues and Solutions. In: Advocating for K-12 Computer Science Education. 24.05.2011, Retrieved from http://www.computinginthecore.org/issues-solutions

CORDIS Work Programme (2010). Cooperation Theme: information and communication technologies (ICT) EUROPEAN COMMISSION. *In: The Seventh Framework Programme (FP7)*, 22.05.2011, Retrieved from <ftp://ftp.cordis.europa.eu/pub/fp7/docs/wp/cooperation/ict/c-wp-201101_en.pdf>

Cortright, J. (2001). New Growth Theory, Technology and Learning: A Practitioners Guide. In: *Reviews of Economic Development Literature and Practice*, 17.05.2011, Retrieved from

<http://www.eda.gov/ImageCache/EDAPublic/documents/pdfdocs/1g3lr_5f7_5fcortright_2epdf/v1/1g3lr_5f7_5fcortright.pdf>

Crosier, J. et al. (2004). State of the Art and Market Analysis, *VIEW of the Future*, 27.09.2011, Retrieved from <http://www.digital-ecosystems.org/>

Cunningham, S. (2007). *Computer graphics: programming OpenGL for visual communication*, Person Prentice Hall, ISBN:978-013-145254-1, USA.

Davis, N. (2008). Response to ICT competency standards. *In: UNESCO ICT-CST*, 15.05.2011, Retrieved from <http://cst.unesco-ci.org/sites/projects/cst/Lists/Tasks/DispForm.aspx?ID=4&Source=http%3A%2F%2Fcst%2Eunesco-ci%2Eorg%2Fsites%2Fprojects%2Fcst%2Fdefault%2Easpx>

Dede, C. (1995). *Testimony to the U.S. Congress, House of Representatives, Joint Hearing on Educational Technology in the 21st Century*, Committee on Science and Committee on Economic and Educational Opportunities, 11.10.2011, Retrieved from <http://www.virtual.gmu.edu/ss_pdf/congress.pdf>

Dede, C. (2009). *Immersive interfaces for engagement and learning*. Science, 323, 66-69. 07.10.2011, Retrieved from <http://www.sciencemag.org/content/323/5910/66.full#F1>

Dehaene, S. (2009). *Reading in the brain*, Viking, ISBN: 978-0-670-02110-9, USA.

Del Nero, H. S. (1997). *O sítio da mente: pensamento, emoção e vontade no cérebro humano*, 02.10.2011, Retrieved from Collegium Cognitio, Brasil, <http://www.delneroemaciel.med.br/sitio.htm>

Digital Ecosystems (2011). The Information Resource about the European approach on Digital Ecosystems. In: *Directorate General Information Society and Media of the European Commission*, 17.05.2011, Retrieved from <http://www.digital-ecosystems.org/>

Donis, A. D., (2007). *Sintaxe da Linguagem Visual*. Martins Fontes, ISBN: 978-85-336-2382-8, Brasil.

Duralach, I. N. and Mavor, A. S. (Eds.) (1995). *Virtual Reality: Scientific and Technological Challenges*, National Academy Press, ISBN: 0309051355, USA.

ECS - Exploring Computer Science (2011). ECS, *In: ECS*, 19.05.2011, Retrieved from <http://www.exploringcs.org/>

ESRC/ EPSRC (2011). Economic and Social Research Council / Engineering and Physical Sciences Research Council, 03.10.2011, Available from <http://www.esrc.ac.uk/news-and-events/press-releases/17778/new-software-brings-science-to-life-for-young-people.aspx?utm_source=twitterfeed&utm_medium=twitter&utm_campaign=Feed:+ESRCPressReleases+%28ESRC+press+releases+this+month%29>

FEBRACE (2011). Feria Brasileira de Ciências e Engenharia, 03.10.2011, Available from <http://febrace.org.br/>

Fleming, N. (2011). Kinect Project Merges Real and Virtual Worlds, Computing Technology Review, MIT, 03.10.2011, Available from <http://www.technologyreview.com/computing/38731/>

Franco J. F. et al. (2008a). Using Virtual Reality and Web-based Technologies for Improving Individuals' Education. *In: Proceedings of ICEL 2008*, Sydney, Australia, 06.10.2011, Retrieved from <http://services.eng.uts.edu.au/userpages/brucem/public_html/icel2/1/icel/Papers/19_Paper.pdf>

Franco, J. F. & Lopes, R. D. (2008). Developing 3D Virtual Environments Supported by Web-based and Virtual Reality Technology as well as Low Cost Multimedia Files *In: Proceedings of ICEL 2008*, Sydney, Australia, 06.10.2011, Retrieved from <http://services.eng.uts.edu.au/userpages/brucem/public_html/icel2/1/icel/Papers/125_Paper.pdf>

Franco, J. F. & Lopes, R. D. (2009). Three-dimensional digital environments and computer graphics influencing k-12 individuals' digital literacy development and lifelong learning. In: *Proceedings of The 2nd ACM SIGGRAPH Conference and Exhibition in Asia: the pulse of innovation – SIGGRAPH ASIA 2009*, Educators Program, Yokohama, Japan 16-19, December, 2009, ISBN: 9781605588582.

Franco, J. F. & Lopes, R. D. (2010). Interactive Learning Activities Supported by Web-based and virtual Reality Resources In: *Proceedings of IADIS International Conference ICT, Society and Human Beings 2010*, Freiburg, Germany, 26 – 31, July, 2010. pp. 107 -114, ISBN: 978-972-8939-20-5, In: *IADIS MULTI CONFERENCE ON COMPUTER SCIENCE AND INFORMATION SYSTEMS 2010*, IADIS Press, 15.05.2011, Retrieved from <http://www.cs.uu.nl/groups/OI/downloads/Weeghel%20paper.pdf>

Franco, J. F. & Lopes, R. D. (2011). The Energy of Learning and Disseminating Web-based Digital Culture: Bringing about Individuals' Socio Technical Development and a Sustainable Cycle of Collaborative Knowledge Transfer - In: *Paper presented in International Conference for Experiential Learning - ICEL 2011* – The Energy of a Learning Experience, Santiago, Chile, January, 10 – 14, 15.05.2011, Available from <http://www.laptop.org.br/images/conteudo/academico/icel2011learninganddevelopingsociotechinical.pdf>

Franco, J. F. et al. (2009). Enhancing Individuals' Cognition, Intelligence and Sharing Digital/Web-based Knowledge Using Virtual Reality and Information Visualization Techniques and Tools within K-12 Education and its Impact on Democratizing the Society", Chapter XIV, In: MOURLAS, G., TSINANOS, N. and GERMANAKOS, P. (Eds.), *Cognitive and Emotional Processes in Web-based Education: Integrating Human factors and Personalization*, IGI Press, 245 – 315, ISBN: 1605663921, USA. 15.05.2011, Retrieved from <http://m.friendfeed-media.com/2016c9d942abb8b7cdb122301a07d434ba98bfb9>

Franco, J. F., Cruz, S. R. R. & Lopes, R. D. (2006). Computer Graphics, Interactive Technologies and Collaborative Learning Synergy Supporting Individuals' Skills Development. In: *SIGGRAPH 2006, ACM SIGGRAPH 2006 Educators program*, 30 Jul - 03 Aug, Boston, USA.

Franco, J. F., Farias, R. A. & Lopes, R. D. (2010). Using 3D Web-based graphics and information visualization technology for supporting collaborative learning, In: Barros E. A. R. et al. (org) *Anais Cogresso Alice Brasil*, 2010, 28.09.2011, Retrieved from <http://www.alicebrazil.org/fileadmin/Graduacao/EE/Eventos/Alice_Brasil/anais/Alice_2010.pdf>

Franco, J. F., Machado, G. M. C. & Lopes, R. D. (2011). An interactive knowledge based learning framework which integrates web2.0 convergence culture and advanced digital tools at primary education and beyond, In: *Proceedings of IADIS International Conference ICT, Society and Human Beings 2011*, Rome, Italy, 20 - 26, July.

Franco. J. F. et al. (2008b). Empowering an Educational Community Through Using Multimedia Tools in Combination with Mobile Learning actions. *In: Proceeding of IADS International Conference Mobile Learning*, Algarve, Portugal, 11-13 April. pp. 221-226.

Freire, P. (1996). *Pedagogia da autonomia: saberes necessários à prática pedagógica*, Paz e Terra, ISBN: 85-219-0243-3, Brasil.

Fundação Victor Civita (2010). O uso dos computadores e da internet nas escolas públicas de capitais brasileiras, Estudos e Pesquisas Educacionais, 28.09.2011, Retrieved from <http://www.fvc.org.br/pdf/estudo-computador-internet.pdf>

G1 Jornal Nacional (2011). Alunos saem da escola sabendo bem menos do que deveriam, aponta prova, Edição do dia 25/08/2011, 29.09.2011, Retrieved from <http://g1.globo.com/jornal-nacional/noticia/2011/08/mais-da-metade-dos-alunos-sai-da-3-serie-do-fundamental-sem-saber-o-que-deveria-em-matematica-diz-prova.html>

Garrido, M. (2011). Marcio Garrido, 12.10.2011, Retrieved from <http://marciogarrido.deviantart.com/gallery/25421948#/d426rgy>

Ghahan-Dixon, A. (2008). *Art: the definitive visual guide*, Dk, ISBN: 978-1-4053-2243, United Kingdom.

Goode, J. and Chapman, G. (2010). ExploringComputerScience-v3. In: *ECS*, 19.05.2011, Available from <http://exploringcs.org/wp-content/uploads/2010/08/ExploringComputerScience-v3.pdf>

Hernández, F., (2000). *Cultura Visual, Mudança Educativa e Projeto de Trabalho*, Artmed, ISBN: 85-7307-606-2, Brasil.

Honey, M. A. & Hilton, M. (Eds) (2011). Learning Science Through Computer Games and Simulations, National Academic Press, ISBN-13: 978-0-309-18523-3, USA.

Huws, U. (2011). Towards a greater understanding of the changing role of business in society. *In: European Commission CORDIS FTP7*, ISBN 978-92-79-18870-1, EU.

ICT (2011). *Institute for Creative Technology: Virtual Reality Psychology and Social Neuroscience*, 29.09.2011, Retrieved from <http://ict.usc.edu/projects/virtual_reality_psychology_and_social_neuroscience>

ICT Cultural Awareness (2011). *Institute for Creative Technology: Cultural Awareness*, 29.09.2011, Retrieved from <http://ict.usc.edu/impact/cultural_awareness>

ICT Learning Sciences (2011). *Institute for Creative Technology: Learning Sciences*, 29.09.2011, Retrieved from <http://ict.usc.edu/projects/learning_sciences>

IISEDJ (2011). *II SEMINÁRIO DOS EDUCADORES DO JARAGUÁ*, 12.10.2011, Retrieved from <http://educadoresdojaragua.blogspot.com/2011/05/memorando-18052011.html >

Instant Reality (2011). *Instant Reality Framework*, 23.05.2011, Retrieved from <http://www.instantreality.org/>

Jacobi, A. et al. (2011) CIVISTI - Collaborative project on Blue Sky Research on Emerging Issues Affecting European S&T. In: *European Commission Research Area and Innovation,* 23.05.2011, Retrieved from <http://www.civisti.org/files/images/Civisti_Final_Report.pdf>

Kamieth, F. et al. (2010). *Exploring the Potential of Virtual Reality for the Elderly and People with Disabilities,* 07.10.2011, Retrieved from <http://www.intechopen.com/source/pdfs/13659/InTech-Exploring_the_potential_of_virtual_reality_for_the_elderly_and_people_with_disabilities.pdf>

Kaplan, D. et al. (Org.). (2010). INFU_innovations futures...Panel 'The open innovation city'. In: *Innovations Future,* 23.05.2011, Retrieved from <http://www.innovation-futures.org/sites/default/files/INFU_101024%20MiniP%20CityOpenInnov%20FING%20final%20report.pdf>

Karampela, P. et al. (2004). VIEW of the Future: Final Dissemination and Use Plan, Deliverable 6, In: *Information Society Technologies (IST) Programme,* 27.09.2011, Retrieved from <http://www.view.iao.fhg.de/pdf/D9_6.pdf>

Koedinger, K. R.; Corbett, A. T. & Perfetti, C. (2010). The Knowledge-Learning-Instruction (KLI) Framework: Toward Bridging the Science-Practice Chasm to Enhance Robust Student Learning. In: *CMU-HCII-10-102 Human-Computer Interaction Institute School of Computer Science,* Carnegie Mellon University, 18.05.2011, Retrieved from <http://reports-archive.adm.cs.cmu.edu/anon/hcii/CMU-HCII-10-102.pdf>

Lopes, R. D. et al., (org), (2010). *Projeto UCA: Um Computador por aluno; Preparando para a expansão: lições da experiência piloto brasileira na modalidade um para um; vídeos,* 24.09.2011, Retrieved from <http://www.youtube.com/watch?v=ZwQOibphtjc&feature=related>

Macher, J. P. (Org.), (2004). Neuroplasticity. In: *Dialogues in clinical neuroscience, Les Laboratoires Servier,* ISSN - 1294-8322, France, Volume 6, Nº 2, pp. 113-243.

McLoughlin, J., Kaminski, J. & Sodagar, B. (2008). A multi-level approach to the study of the socio-economic impact of ICT at cultural heritage sites, 12.10.2011, Retrieved from <http://public-repository.epoch-net.org/rome/10%20Modelling%20and%20Measuring%20Impact.pdf>

Mervis, J. (2011). Is There a Special Formula for Successful STEM Schools? In: *ScienceInsider,* 19.05.2011, Retrieved from <http://news.sciencemag.org/scienceinsider/2011/05/-is-there-a-special-formula-for-.html>

Mestre, J. (2002). Transfer of Learning: Issues and a Research Agenda (National Science Foundation, Washington, DC. 07.10.2011, Retrieved from <http://www.nsf.gov/pubs/2003/nsf03212/nsf03212.pdf>

Nachira, F. et al. (2007). Digital Business Ecosystems. ISBN 92-79-01817-5 In: *European Commission, in association and with the support of the FP6 projects DBE and OPAALS,* 17.05.2011, Retrieved from <http://www.digital-ecosystems.org/book/2006-4156_PROOF-DCS.pdf>,

Nadeau, D. R.; Moreland, J. L. & Heck, M. M. (1998). Introduction to VRML 97. In: *SIGGRAPH 1998,* 18.05.2011, Retrieved from <http://web2.cc.nctu.edu.tw/~claven/course/VirtualReality/vrml/c18.pdf>

NATE/LSI (2011). The Nucleus of Learning, Work and Entertainment of the Laboratory of Integrated Systems, 21.09.2011 Retrieved from

<http://www.lsi.usp.br/interativos/nate/nate_eng.html>

National Research Council. (2011). *Assessing 21st Century Skills: Summary of a Workshop.* J.A. Koenig, Rapporteur. Committee on the Assessment of 21st Century Skills. Board on Testing and Assessment, Division of Behavioral and Social Sciences and Education. Washington, DC: The National Academies Press. 28.09.2011 Retrieved from <http://www.nap.edu/catalog.php?record_id=13215>

NCWIT (2011). National Center for Women & Information Technology. In: *NCWIT ORG,* 24.05.2011, Retrieved from <http://www.ncwit.org/about.factsheet.html>

NRCC - National Research Council Committee (2011). *Report of a Workshop of Pedagogical Aspects of Computational Thinking,* National Academic Press, 21.09.2011 Retrieved from <http://www.nap.edu/catalog.php?record_id=13170>

O' Connor, P. E. & Cohn, J. V. (Eds.) (2010). *Human Performance Enhancement in High-Risk Environments,* ABC-CLIO, ISBN: 978-0-313-35983-5, USA.

OECD (2010), PISA 2009 Results: Executive Summary, 28.09.2011 Retrieved from <http://www.oecd.org/dataoecd/34/60/46619703.pdf>

OECD (2011). *Building a High-Quality Teaching Profession: Lessons from around the world,* 24.09.2011 Retrieved from <http://asiasociety.org/files/lwtw-teachersummit.pdf>

OECD/PISA in focus2, (2011). *Improving Performance: Leading from the Bottom,* 24.09.2011 Retrieved from <http://www.oecd.org/dataoecd/32/53/47271471.pdf>

OECD/PISA in focus6, (2011). When students repeat grades or are transferred out of school: What does it mean for education systems?, *In: OECD,* 24.09.2011 Retrieved from <http://www.oecd.org/dataoecd/35/58/48363440.pdf >

OpenGL ES API (2011). OpenGL ES, 29.09.2011 Retrieved from <http://www.khronos.org/opengles/>

Osberg, K. (1997a). *A Teacher's Guide to Developing Virtual Environments: VRRV Project Support.* (Technical Report) Seattle: Human Interface Technology Lab, 24.09.2011 Retrieved from <http://www.hitl.washington.edu/publications/r-97-17/>

Osberg, K. (1997b). *Constructivism in practice: The case for meaning-making in the virtual world.* Doctoral dissertation, University of Washington. 24.09.2011 Retrieved from <http://www.hitl.washington.edu/publications/r-97-47/index.html>

Papert, S. (1993). *Mindstorms: Children, computers, and powerful ideas,* Basic Books, ISBN: 978-0-465-04674-4, New York.

Phillip, P. (2007). Computational Thinking: A Problem-Solving Tool for Every Classroom. In: *Center For Computational Thinking,* Carnegie Mellon University, 23.05.2011, Retrieved from <http://www.cs.cmu.edu/~CompThink/resources/ct_pat_phillips.pdf>

PISA (2010). Assessment Framework: Key competencies in reading, mathematics and science 15.05.2011 *In: OECD,* 15.05.2011, Retrieved from <http://www.oecd.org/dataoecd/11/40/44455820.pdf>

Pocsai, Z. et al. (1998). The Common Semantic Model in GENIAL: a critical gateway towards an intelligent access to component libraries and engineering knowledge, Product

Data technology Advisory Group PDTAG-AM, *European Comission, DG III European Conference Product Data Technology Days* 1998. Watford, UK. pp. 47-54.

Potel, M. (2004). A Decade of Applications, In: *IEEE Computer Graphics and Applications*, v.24 n.6, p.14-19, November 2004 , [doi>10.1109/MCG.2004.44], USA.

Preece, J. et al. (1994). *Human-computer interaction*, Addison-Wesley, ISBN:0-201-62769-8, England.

Pressman, R. S. (2006). *Software engineering approach*, sixth edition, McGrawHill, ISBN – 0072853182, USA.

Resnick, Mitchel et al. (2009). Scratching programming for all, *COMMUNICATIONS OF THE ACM*, vol. 52, no. 11, November 2009.

Rogers, Y. Scaife, M. & Rizzo, A. (2005) Interdisciplinarity: an Emergent or Engineered Process? In S. Derry, C.D. Schunn and M.A. Gernsbacher (Eds.) *Interdisciplinary Collaboration: An Emerging Cognitive Science*. ISBN-10: 0805836330, UK, pp. 265 - 286.

Rogers, Y., Brignull, H. & Scaife, M. (2002). Designing Dynamic Interactive Visualisations to Support Collaboration and Cognition. In: *First International Symposium on Collaborative Information Visualization Environments*, IV 2002, London, July 10-12, 2002, IEEE, pp. 39-50.

Romer, P. M. (2007). Economic Growth. In*: The Concise Encyclopedia of Economics*, 17.05.2011, Retrieved from <http://www.stanford.edu/~promer/EconomicGrowth.pdf>

Ronchi, A. M. (2009). *eCulture: Cultural content in the Digital Age*, ISBN-9783540752738, Springer, Germany.

Roussou, M. (2004). Learning by Doing and Learning through Play: an Exploration of Interactivity in Virtual Environments for Children, *ACM Computers in Entertainment (CiE)* 2: 1. Article-1, Singapore, June 3-5.

Roussou, M., Oliver, M. & Slater, M. (2006). The Virtual Playground: an Educational Virtual Reality Environment for Evaluating Interactivity and Conceptual Learning. In: *Journal of Virtual Reality* 10: 3-4, pp. 227-240, 24.09.2011, Retrieved from <http://www.springerlink.com/content/8ptk37170086544h/fulltext.pdf >

Roussou, M., Oliver, M. & Slater, M. (2008). Exploring Activity Theory as a Tool for Evaluating Interactivity and Learning in Virtual Environments for Children, In: *Cognition, Technology & Work 10*: 2., pp. 141-153.

Rueda, R. et al. (2001). *Engaged Reading: A Multilevel Approach to Considering Sociocultural Factors With Diverse Learners*, Center for the Improvement of Early Reading Achievement University of Michigan - Ann Arbor, 12.10.2011, Retrieved from <http://www.ciera.org/library/reports/inquiry-1/1-012/1-012.pdf>

Rusk, N.; Resnick, M. and Cooke, S. (2009). Origins and Guiding Principles of the Computer Clubhouse. In: *Lifelong Kindergarten*, MIT Media Lab, 23.05.2011, Retrieved from <http://web.media.mit.edu/~mres/papers/Clubhouse/clubhouse-origins.pdf>

Saia, R. (2011). 9 hot IT skills for 2012, Computerworld, 02.10.2011, Retrieved from <http://www.computerworld.com/s/article/358381/9_Hot_Skills_for_2012>

Scratch (2011). Scratch program, 03.10.2011, Retrieved from <http://scratch.mit.edu>

Sharp, P. A. et al., (2011). The Third Revolution: The Convergence of the Life Sciences, Physical Sciences and Engineering. In: *MIT*, 24.05.2011, Retrieved from

<http://web.mit.edu/dc/Policy/MIT%20White%20Paper%20on%20Convergence.pdf>

Skinner, A. et al. (2010) Phychological Mesures of Virtual Environment Training. In: O' Connor, P. E. & Cohn, J. V. (Eds.) (2010). *Human Performance Enhancement in High-Risk Environments*, ABC-CLIO, ISBN: 978-0-313-35983-5, USA.

Souza, D. F. L., Machado, L. S. & Tavares, T. A. (2010). Extending Brazilian DTV Middleware to Incorporate 3D Technologies. In: *XII Symposium on Virtual and Augmented Reality*, Natal, RN, Brazil - May, 29.09.2011, Retrieved from < http://de.ufpb.br/~labteve/publi/2010_svr1.pdf>

Tavares, D. C. et al. (2007). *Interactive Virtual Worlds in Brazilian Digital Television*, 29.09.2011, Retrieved from <http://www.ufam-automation.net/idtvec/acceptedpapers/W1_5_tavares.pdf>

Thirteen (2004). *Inquiry-based Learning*, Concept to Classrrom, 29.09.2011, Retrieved from <http://www.thirteen.org/edonline/concept2class/inquiry/>

Tucker, A. (2003). A Model Curriculum for K–12 Computer Science Final Report of the ACM K–12 Task Force Curriculum Committee, ISBN- 59593-596-7, USA.

U.S.DE, Department of Education (2010). *Executive Summary*, 07.10.2011, Retrieved from <http://www.ed.gov/technology/draft-netp-2010/executive-summary>

UNESCO (2008). Policy Framework, In: *ICT COMPETENCY STANDARDS FOR TEACHERS, UNESCO ICT-CST*, 15.05.2011, Retrieved from <http://cst.unesco-ci.org/sites/projects/cst/The%20Standards/ICT-CST-Policy%20Framework.pdf>

VILNIUS (2010). VISION A FUTURE INNOVATION LANDSCAPE 2030 "WIDESPREAD CREATIVITY". In: Innovations Future, 23.05.2011, Retrieved from <http://www.innovation-futures.org/sites/default/files/Vision%20Widespread%20creativity%202030.pdf>

VRCPAT (2010). *Virtual Reality Cognitive Performance Assessment Test*, 29.09.2011, Retrieved from <http://ict.usc.edu/projects/virtual_reality_cognitive_performance_assessment_test_vrcpat/>

Walczak, K., Wojciechowski, R. & Cellary, W. (2006). Dynamic Interactive VR Network Services for Education. In: *VRST '06: Proceedings of the ACM symposium on Virtual reality software and technology*, 1-3, November, Limassol, Cyprus.

Wikipedia Knowledge Spillover (2011). Knowledge Spillover. In: *Wikipedia*, 17.05.2011, 23.05.2011, Retrieved from <http://en.wikipedia.org/wiki/Knowledge_spillover >

Wikipedia Neuroplasticity (2011). Neuroplasticity. In: Wikipedia, 25.05.2011, Retrieved from <http://en.wikipedia.org/wiki/Neuroplasticity>

Wilson, C. et al. (2010). Running On Empty: The Failure to Teach K–12 Computer Science in the Digital Age. In: *ACM – CSTA*, 19.05.2011, Retrieved from <http://www.acm.org/runningonempty/fullreport.pdf>

Wilson, J. (2002). *Virtual and Interactive Environments for Workplaces of the Future*, 26.09.2011, Retrieved from <http://www.ercim.eu/publication/Ercim_News/enw49/wilson.html>

Wing, J. (2010). Computational Thinking: What and Why?. In: *Link Magazine* 23.05.2011, Retrieved from

<http://www.cs.cmu.edu/~CompThink/resources/TheLinkWing.pdf>

Winn, W. (1997). *The Impact of Three-Dimensional Immersive Virtual Environments on Modern Pedagogy*. (Technical Report) Seattle: Human Interface Technology Lab, 24.09.2011, Retrieved from <http://www.hitl.washington.edu/publications/r-97-15/>

X3DOM (2011). X3DOM - experimental open source framework. In: *X3DOM*, 25.05.2011, Retrieved from <http://www.x3dom.org/?page_id=2>

X3Dom Platform Notes (2011). X3Dom Platform Notes, In: *X3DOM*, 29.09.2011, Retrieved from <http://x3dom.org/docs/latest/notes/platforms.html>

Youngblut, C., (1998), Educational Uses of Virtual Reality Technology, Tech. Report IDA Document D-2128, *Institute for Defense Analyses*, Alexandria, Va., 20.09.2011, Retrieved from <http://www.hitl.washington.edu/scivw/youngblut-edvr/D2128.pdf>